DRINK AGAINST DRUNKENNESS:
THE LIFE AND TIMES OF SASHA SOLDATOW

ALSO BY INEZ BARANAY

Turn Left At Venus

7 stories 2 novellas

Ghosts Like Us

Local Time: a memoir of cities, friendships and the writing life

Always Hungry

With The Tiger

sun square moon: writings on yoga and writing

Neem Dreams

Sheila Power: an entertainment

Rascal Rain: a year in Papua New Guinea

The Edge of Bali

Pagan

The Saddest Pleasure

Between Careers

Drink Against Drunkenness

THE LIFE AND TIMES OF SASHA SOLDATOW

Inez Baranay

Published by Local Time Publishing

ISBN 978 0 646 86685 7

First published 2022

© Inez Baranay

Edited by Bruce Sims
Designed by Chris Edwards
Cover photograph courtesy of Pam Brown

Every effort has been made to trace copyright holders and to obtain their permission for the use of copyright material. The publisher apologizes for any errors or omissions and would be grateful if notified of any corrections that should be incorporated in future reprints or editions of this book.

there's a saying in russia — / the past / is unpredictable —
PAM BROWN *click here for what we do*

In all human lives there is a recurring pattern, sometimes difficult to perceive, sometimes on the surface; and the pattern is drawn from within.
AJA SYMONS *The Quest for Corvo*

It is very hard telling from any incident in any one's living what kind of being they have in them. It is very hard to know of any one the being in them from one or two things they have been doing that some one is telling about them...
GERTRUDE STEIN quoted in Janet Malcolm *Two Lives*

Contents

1. **lived and worked and caused trouble** — 13
   By way of a prologue. A conversation where those who knew Sasha talk about him and why he's worth writing about.

2. **being free by acting free** — 17
   Underground and alternative. In Melbourne Sasha had been reading the student and underground newspapers *Tharunka* and its offshoots; once in Sydney he joins its producers.

3. **anarchism and activism** — 27
   The Push, Sydney 1972. Attracted to Sydney's anarchist traditions and this long-time group or sub-culture, Sasha arrives to be part of the new challenge to its sexism and political inaction.

4. **what is this gay community shit** — 39
   What Is This Gay Community Shit? 1983. The well-remembered disruptive pamphlet: Sasha disrupts, charms, argues, reasons. This piece is quoted and discussed right up to the present.

5. **absolutely memorable** — 54
   Student years in Melbourne 1966-69. Mostly recalled by friends from the student theatre world as well as schooldays. Why Sasha is remembered where many are not.

6. **a graveyard of hope** — 66
   Family stories, the migration. Sasha's mother was an immense presence in his life; the fascinating complex story of the Russian immigrant family told in his writings over years, and in recent interviews with his step-brother, step-sister and niece.

7. **condensed into one street** — 93
   Victoria Street Resident Action Group and Green Bans 1973-74. Sasha remembered as a prominent and influential figure in one of the great Sydney stories of corrupt destruction versus united action. And he wrote about life in the squats as no one else did.

8. **news from around the world** — 106
   Scrounge 1973-74. Begun by Sasha and others, more underground publishing, compiling and curating various sources of news, adding their own reporting. Consider the context of news services then and different/limited technology.

9. **all against prisons** — 117
   Bourke Street house; Women Behind Bars 1974-75; Prisoners Action Group; Politics of the Olympics 1980. Sasha remembered by the housemates — survivors with illustrious careers once involved in the radical action groups for prison reform which he always cites as influencing his politics. Their discussions watching the Olympics informs his first book.

10 out for a bop   129
Parties, fun, golden age 1970s. And we know it. So many parties, so much liberation. Even 1975 doesn't stop the discos.

11 agitpoetry   137
Patterns: *the series 1974-76.* Artisanal pamphlets of polemical prose and poetry, written, designed and distributed by Sasha.

12 who do you call at three in the morning?   143
Margaret Fink. Sasha's lifelong friendship with the film producer and socialite, the decades. Sasha also recalled by her three children, who loved him and call him family.

13 who has the most fun?   155
The Only Sensible News 1978. And if not fun then what? Politics through Absurdity. A humorous newsletter with a Dada silliness, which shows up the everyday absurdities we live with.

14 dreadfully romantic   163
Diaries social life men romances friendships 70s, 80s. Sasha often says that his real work and highest value was friendships; he has many kinds.

15 The Bon Mot Gang   177
1970s poetry scene, Pam Brown, Adelaide 1982. Sydney poetry with its factions; Sasha divides the poets, makes lifelong friendships; Adelaide Festival is a high point.

16 if you love me, make me laugh   189
The Larry Years 1977-1983. Idyllic at first, an intense and deep young affair. Larry Strange says, 'He drew my sexuality and my politics out of me'. Horrible fights at the end. The theme of jealousy.

17 time has a fluidity   211
David Marr 1978. The breakup story often told. A much briefer affair during the Larry Years, which was of great importance to both, and would have a sequel.

18 a bellicose wit   220
Poetry + Performance 1980s, Rock-n-Roll Sally. The vibrant poetry scene, readings and performances recalled; poetry scandals; Sasha's unforgettable, brilliant Sally which always stole the show.

19 shadows on the dance floor   236
AIDS and gay publishing 1980s-90s; Cargo *magazine; books by Black Wattle Press.* The changes AIDS makes. Sasha is represented in many new anthologies of gay men's writing, co-edits an issue of *Cargo*.

20 nine poets in the room 1982-1986   247
The SBS Subtitling Unit, the best in the world. The launch of SBS Television and its pioneering Subtitling Unit. Sasha becomes one of its sub-editors, along with many other poets and writers, and members of Sydney's 'ethnic communities'.

21 we believed in something   258
Private — Do Not Open 1987. The first prose collection, the years of preparation, the vicissitudes of its publication, the critical acclaim.

22 the boundary lines of our personalities   268
Bruce Pulsford. Soldatow's long-time partner, who never stopped looking after him. The Bondi parties era. The long relationship that continues even long after it ended.

23 problems are flowers and fade   287
Harry Hooton. The radio program 1988, the book 1990, the biography project unfulfilled. Sasha's work on Hooton examined. How it is treasured by poets today.

24 because I have to   300
Legal action against Australia Council after 16 years of failed grant applications. The literary community divided. It's in the news. The diligent work on the court case. The outcome.

25 famous secular trees   314
Hanoi March and August 1991. Early trips to the Vietnamese city Sasha claims as a favourite place, inspiring some of his best writing.

26 a country of poetry   325
Moscow. To live like a Russian. In Sydney he'd been the Russian poet but here he was a foreigner. The realities of Russian life during the tumultuous demise of the USSR inspires some great writing but begins a kind of personal disintegration.

27 the past is unpredictable   350
Moscow, after the fall. Sasha shatters his hip-bone on Moscow ice. It is treated ineptly. He returns to Sydney in a dreadful state, is slow to recover and begins to alienate many who cared for him.

28 a confusion to you all   358
The Gloves of Mr Menzies. The eccentric historical epic never published. Several extracts were, however. Serious, detailed critical readings by many agents, publishers and fellow writers, but Sasha insists no one understands. Questions of reading.

29 beautifully crafted literary gossip   371
Mayakovksy in Bondi 1993. A brilliant collection of prose pieces. Great launch party, great reviews.

30 always trust the reader   378
Mentoring Tsiolkas. Co-writing *Jump Cuts*. Meeting Christos Tsiolkas galvanises both men; Sasha gets *Loaded* published and co-writes Tsiolkas' next book. Another intense relationship becoming stormy but always acknowledged as transformative.

31 I need my friends to frighten me   397
The friendship becomes destabilised as Tsiolkas gains more attention and Sasha feels overlooked.

32 how can you talk this way?   404
That issue (pedophilia) 1997. Where nearly everyone draws the line in their discussions with him. Soldatow never budges from his position, which is carefully assessed.

33 exchange between cultures   411
Hanoi 1997. New Australian friends. Back in Hanoi, Sasha travels on assignment with photographer Oliver Strewe; and begins a new friendship with musician and writer Jack Ellis.

34 people going past   421
Back in Bondi 1997–99. Old friends are drifting away; new young friends create new parties. Trenchant opinion pieces published. But Sasha will need a new place to live.

35 let me tell you about salad   427
Farm in Casino of all unlikely places 2000. For a while Sasha lives with old friend anthropologist Inge Riebe on her farm, encountering Indigenous Australia, but does not want to stay long.

36 on the verge of being scared   439
Return to Melbourne 2000–02. With nowhere else to go, Sasha goes back to his mother's house, a disaster; then a room at a pub. A bright period is a short-lived project to write a PhD thesis on Hooton.

37 we write for each other   453
Cremorne, Redfern, final years. Jack Ellis gives Soldatow a home for some years, then he moves to a social housing flat. There are high points along with the general decline.

38 memory become a moral category   466
Akhmatova's Requiem 2020. Soldatow's acclaimed translation in a beautiful new limited edition, along with the original text of the scorching poem. A great legacy.

39 'I See'   476
Hospital, funeral, wake, tombola, remembrances: a montage.

Acknowledgments   487
References
   1: works by Sasha Soldatow   490
   2: works by others   494
Index of names   501

Illustrations

	Front cover photograph courtesy of Pam Brown
12	SS from his archives, probably late 1970s–early 1980s
54	SS from his archives, school years; courtesy of Margaret Fink
57	SS from his archives, school years; courtesy of Margaret Fink
67	Unknown relatives (top); and Lily, Sasha's mother, labelled '1942 Vitebsk', from SS archives
68	Sasha's father, passport photo, from SS archives
71	Sasha's stepfather Valentin Valentinavich Sadovchikoff (Val), mother Lily and grandmother Maria Samson (Sasha's Babushka), taken at Daylseford, from SS archives
74	Sasha as a child, photograph courtesy of Margaret Fink
84	Sasha mushrooming (1983), from Super 8 film by Pam Brown (on YouTube)
97	Occupying space with Wendy Bacon, Victoria Street 1973, Getty Images
109	*Scrounge* no.2 masthead, 1973. SS probably designed this; he contributed to the collectively-created content
128	Christmas Eve 1990, SS with Bruce Pulsford and Pam Brown, photograph by Jane Zemiro
131	SS with Inez Baranay, wine and books, from SS archive
134–135	The Marilyn poster advertising a Tin Sheds performance of *The Adventures of Rock-n-Roll Sally* — this has been reproduced often and is the first thing some people remember about SS
157	*The Only Sensible News* no.4, front page, design and some content by SS
165	Polaroid from SS diary, early 1980s
179	Sasha and Pam Brown at the Surry Hills Gay Community Centre, 1982, photograph courtesy of Pam Brown
209	Sasha in doilies as Disco Twit, 1983, photograph by Veronica Ryan
221	SS, Pam Brown and Elizabeth Drake, at the launch of Pam's book *Keep It Quiet* (Sea Cruise Press) in 1988 taken at a women's film group studio in Redfern
227	SS performing at Cabaret Conspiracy, photograph by Maryse Throsby, courtesy of Johnny Allen
229	SS performing *Rock-n-Roll Sally* at the Tin Sheds, photograph by Megan McMurchy

234	*Miss the Opera House Lights*, announcement in the *Sydney Morning Herald*. SS coined the playful title for the show
235	*Miss the Opera House Lights*, programme flyers
244	Gutter Club members Garry Dunne, Laurin McKinnon, Denis Gallagher and SS, photograph by William Yang
245	SS with Peter Blazey, also a member of the Gutter Club
248	SS's *Picasso*, gifted to Megan McMurchy, around 1983
257	SS at North Bondi, 1986, photographer unknown
267	SS self-portrait, from a sequence of self-portraits sent to Nicholas Pounder. Pen and ink, water colour. 1986. Collection, Nicholas Pounder
270	SS picnicking with Bruce Pulsford, photograph from SS archives
275	Sasha's 'Bali Hi' assemblage artwork, gifted to Joanna Savill, courtesy of Joanna
284	SS pen drawing for MN 1990, courtesy Margot Nash
302	SS wearing a string of pearls his own way, photograph courtesy of Margaret Fink
313	SS — no information available
346	SS from his archives
370	SS busy writing a note at Pam Brown's book launch, 1988, photograph courtesy of Pam
373	*Mayakovsky in Bondi*, 1933, front cover with red star designed by SS for BlackWattle Press
426	SS at North Bondi, 1986, photograph by Margot Nash
486	SS headstone, photographed by Jack Ellis. SS wanted this, whatever he meant by 'I See'

1

lived and worked and caused trouble

by way of a prologue

the quality of his presence

'Why should I know about him?' asked Estelle, curiously rather than confrontingly. Her partner John Fink had invited me to dinner in early 2019 to talk about Sasha Soldatow, as part of research for this book. John had been a child when he first knew Sasha, one of his 'gay uncles', a long-time close friend of his mother, Margaret Fink.

Sasha is recalled with much affection and appreciation here, but that is not enough to explain to someone who never knew him why he has become the subject for a book. Estelle had never met Sasha, and was now listening to us talk about him.

Joanna Savill was there too, and her husband Giuliano Dambelli. Joanna told us how vital Sasha had been in her decision to remain in Australia decades ago, how he'd taken her under his wing, introduced her to many new people, and Sasha knew a lot of people. Knowing people was his métier.

How do you show what he was really like, the quality of his presence? Impressions remain while details of their content have faded. There are photos but barely a scrap of audio or video to suggest the way he attracted people and made them laugh and argue, how he really pissed some people off, excited others by his ideas, sparked controversies. Challenge everything you're told was a lesson he often taught.

You'd never forget him if you knew him, we told Estelle; he had an impact on many lives. There was something about the quality of his attention that, I suppose, made people pay more attention to themselves. I'm finding people who remembered him from long-ago contexts in which most other people were forgotten. He made sure of being noticed and his presence was often a joy; people keep telling me how they'd remember laughter as they recalled him.

Eventually many friendships soured, some terminally, some briefly, but people's strongest impressions were usually of the good times, of honesty and laughter.

biography is history

It is not proper to claim I could ever know Sasha's inner life. It's not like writing fiction where the inner life of a character is known by its creator through acts of imagination. What is part of this work, and maybe the point of it, is to give a sense of the times he lived in, how others experienced him. Biography is history, at least as much as it is character study, and the milieus where Sasha lived and wrote and caused trouble were naturally not his alone. Also, he always insisted on historical knowledge in topics he took seriously. Joanna pointed out that Sasha was part of an era, of the post-war babies who became the intellectuals, artists and alternative shapers of underground culture. Certainly not mainstream, we agreed.

Soldatow was a vivid, articulate presence in many of the fringe movements of the 1970s and 80s, notably gay liberation, as well as prison reform, supporting tenants' rights, and opposition to destructive inner-city development — principally by being one of the squatters and activists in the storied battles over Victoria Street in Sydney. He was particularly active in independent publishing, poetry and performance at that time too — who could forget *Rock-n-Roll Sally*? — and he mentored and collaborated with many writers who would become widely known even in mainstream culture. Although his two prose collections went out of print, they were reviewed with excitement and seriousness and are very much worth revisiting in the present. His work on anarchist visionary poet Harry Hooton was deeply respected, and became essential for historians and later poets. I have since discovered how newer poets were grappling with Hooton's work, both dated and perennially interesting.

Sasha Soldatow had many talents: playing the piano, painting, performance, cooking, gardening. But what he most wanted, and most carefully looked out for, was serious recognition of his writing. His career in publishing ranged from early involvement in 'underground' publications in the radical 1960s and 70s, to books with both mainstream and small press publishers, reviews, essays and columns in mainstream periodicals and the gay press, and some distinctive, artisanal publications he designed and distributed himself. To give an account of all this is to survey Australian publishing — its varieties, its changes — over his lifetime.

the litter of his mischief

People remember they liked reading his work, but that it's been too long since they've seen it.

Sasha's body of work is small. But returning to it long after it was first produced, I find some of it quite brilliant and all of it worth consideration. There are six books, many short stories, essays, opinion pieces including regular columns, and the various pamphlets he designed and distributed himself, 'the litter of his mischief' as it's described in the catalogues of rare books dealer, publisher and long-time friend Nicholas Pounder. Pounder in 2020 was producing a limited edition art book featuring Sasha's translation of the heart-wrenching poem *Requiem* by Anna Ahmatova. [chapter 38]

Sasha was brought up in Melbourne reading the greats of Russian literature, and his identity as a Russian, and the turning point of his life in Moscow in 1991–92 as the Soviet Union was collapsing, is a large part of his story.

friendship was his real work

Why then, asked Estelle, did he never 'make it' if he was so talented? No one ever said he was seriously famous, even while he was known directly or by reputation in many disparate circles in Sydney and Melbourne. As for why, hindsight identifies a range of self-defeating strategies.

His work was not like anyone else's, for one thing. Keepers of the mainstream literary world's gates might have looked for, well, something they were more comfortable with. As soon as they knew who Soldatow was, they knew he loved argument and he loved causing disruption.

While Soldatow's published work isn't extensive, it was all well received: lots of acclaim, just enough disparagement. But it was the rejections of his work that he brooded on, with an abiding sense of being overlooked and discriminated against. He caused a major stir in the national literary community when he took legal action against the country's major arts funding body for rejecting his grant applications over sixteen years. It's well remembered that he did that.

He'd always rather have a drink or go to a party rather than stay home alone and work; this was often said.

He regularly stressed that he valued friendship above everything else; that it was his real work. Perhaps it was also one of his talents, to form and maintain a great number of friendships with a wide variety of people. He'd go to every social occasion he could, in gilded halls or squalid squats, as uninhibited among strangers as among his intimates. He was interested in people, what they thought, what they said, how they would reply to his provocations. He befriended poets and lawyers and criminals and artists and people who worked in politics at all levels.

He loved parties, and in some periods gave a lot of good parties himself. His generosity was immense, his hospitality unstinting. His ability to cultivate friendship and acquaintance was unsurpassed.

And then there's the self-destructive side, which became dominant, and ultimately destroyed him. The reasons for this and power of addiction are contentious and defy judgment yet also require some consideration.

And there's also randomness in these things, reputations, types of success.

a kind of mosaic

I sometimes felt bogged down in this work, and had times of being pissed off with my subject — Sasha could be spectacularly unreasonable and self-destructive, and yes, while people always returned to the laughter and honesty and new ideas, it was usually after a story of sad decline.

I've been told some things about biographers' relationship to their subjects — love, hate — but none of it sounded like my experience. I'd spent long enough interviewing people and reading Soldatow's archives (over 40 boxes in the Mitchell Library; he kept everything) to have lost access to my own memories of him.

I kept being encouraged though by friends who thought this biography was a good idea, and told me why. Not only was Sasha one of the most unforgettable, influential, charming, infuriating, brilliant people they remembered, but he is also interesting in terms of the spirit of the times, being at the centre of discourse about being a writer, a modernist, an idiosyncratic artist who was also involved in a collective spirit that manifested in anthologies and identity politics. Those I found to interview often said they'd just been talking about Sasha, and remembered him still.

At that dinner John and Joanna said, as so many others did, that they wondered what Sasha would make of things today? He could be relied upon to steer you to an unsettling reconsideration, an interesting perception. By this point, enough people had been encouraging of this project, saying that Sasha was important to them, that I was thinking of this as a kind of mosaic, with others contributing many of its elements, my own work being as a kind of curator as well as contributor to the whole.

After we talked about things like that, Estelle said it made her want to know about him. It made me want to get back to work on this.

2
being free by acting free

underground and alternative 1972

I am an anarchist. Simply this means that I am against any imposition of authority be it from the State or from elsewhere... I applaud people who break rules because I do so myself. This is a necessary and important activity. [SS 1983 *What Is this Gay Community Shit?*]

thank god for the mercies of persecution

Sasha Soldatow often said that he moved to Sydney attracted to its anarchist tradition.

Sasha was familiar with *Tharunka*, the student newspaper produced at UNSW in Sydney, and its underground offshoots *Thorunka* and *Thor*. Bundles of copies used to be sent, or brought, to Melbourne.

The work of the new editors was both a continuation of that tradition, and something new. The issues they produced were anti censorship anti war anti authoritarian anti hypocrisy anti sexual repression anti racism; they offered explicit stories of sexual experience, reproductions of censored material, accounts of demonstrations in Australia and elsewhere. Melbourne had nothing quite like it in spite of its own radical publishing.

In 1970 *Tharunka* produced a gay-themed issue, calling it *Tharunkamp* on the cover. Sasha Soldatow, still living in Melbourne then, would have noticed this:

'So they won't let homos marry — thank god for the mercies of persecution. Any queer who wants that changed is as nutty as a fruit [della]

So already in 1970, some homosexuals were already arguing against the Gay Liberation line of seeking acceptance. Anti legalisation, anti assimilation, anti respectability.

to be someone else

Soldatow decided he was more of a Sydney person.

It's probably the case with every immigrant from one city to another that to decide on a different life in a different city is to decide to be someone else.

There was a supposed rivalry between Australia's two largest cities then. Melbourne: staid, class-ridden; Sydney: hedonistic, glorying in new money. Melbourne: elegant, European; Sydney: sunny, sexy, to many more cosmopolitan, more gay-friendly. In the early 1970s, the two cities seemed further apart, the road wasn't as fast, it was before cheap flights, and before the internet made communication immediate, and before the internet made its changes to ways in which we think of identity and locality.

The Sasha who in 1972 arrived in Sydney to stay, now identifying himself as a writer, was a confidently out gay man committed to his political values, with a certainty of entering the doors he walked towards.

He was committed to a new world of friendship, fun, outrageousness, disruption, adventure.

Looking for comrades, for arguments.

Maybe for that sense of belonging that people are supposed to want so much.

He knew who his people were: the ones putting out publications like *Thorunka*. And, closely linked to them, the old Sydney Push group.

Here was his natural home.

introduction in place

Wendy Bacon had also grown up in Melbourne. After completing her Arts degree in 1966, she moved to Sydney, where she soon met the Push, and developed her own anarchistic politics. She became one of the editors of the Tharunka papers and would bring copies to Melbourne when she visited.

Trying to verify just how and when the two first met turned out to be tricky, as Soldatow later published this:

> In 1968 I was in Sydney to see the sixth performance of *Hair*. I knew no one in Sydney, but that didn't stop me from going. At the last minute before leaving Melbourne, I was introduced to Wendy Bacon. She was at LaTrobe University selling *Thor*, an underground newspaper. [SS 1996 *Jump Cuts* 50]

But *Thor* didn't exist then and *Hair* only opened in 1969.

Wendy Bacon doesn't remember exactly how they first met but what is clear, by the time he arrived to live in Sydney Sasha had been reading

Tharunka, and he had met Wendy. Sasha, already committed to anarchist politics and Direct Action, soon became Wendy's friend and co-activist.

It's possible that the rest of Sasha's wrongly-dated story is accurate: he says that though she'd known him less than an hour, Wendy told Sasha when he got to Sydney to see a man called Darcy Waters in the room she shared with him above Martin's Bar in Oxford Street, Darlinghurst. Soldatow was casually greeted in the squalid room at the top. He was impressed with the understated, casual acceptance. Perhaps with the squalor also.

Waters, about twenty years older, became a friend of Sasha, something of a mentor as Waters' Push milieu became his own. [more in next chapter]

Martin's Bar, by the way, was known for what tabloids called 'topless barmaids'; Wendy had briefly worked there, in a see-through pink shirt, and hated it. Soldatow doesn't mention whether he looked in at the bar. If you wanted to have a complex conversation about conditions of work for women, though, he'd be in it.

alive with rebellion

For Sasha Soldatow, like for many of our generation, the discovery of the illegality, immorality and atrocity of the American war in Vietnam had shattered the conservative mind-set of our upbringing and culture.

> The Vietnam War brought me to political consciousness when I was sixteen in a way that no books had. Rowdy unpopular demonstrations, quiet sit-ins, all-night vigils and the confrontations, conversations and arguments filled in the rest. I got my political education on the streets of Melbourne. My parents tried forcibly to take me away from all these activities, for behaviour such as this was not the manner in which the aspiring middle class behaved, particular those from a migrant background, but it was too late, I was alive with rebellion and have never looked back. [SS 1996 *Jump Cuts*, 6-7]

Add to the anti-war movement the emergence of the women's movement and gay liberation. Rebellion, especially if you were young, was the flavour of the times.

The best medium of expression and dissemination was paper publication. Best way to unearth your opponents also.

university student newspapers had a lot more impact

People would joke they needed a wheelbarrow to bring home the weekend editions of the daily newspapers: besides separate sections for News and others for more commentary and cultural coverage than we see in print papers in the present, they had additional bulky sections for employment, real estate, business, cars, sport, entertainment. Various paper periodicals were important then: weekly and monthly newspapers and journals had large circulations; they made huge revenues from classified advertisements.

But radical and dissenting politics were more likely to be explored and exposed to a wide audience through the university student newspapers of the time; they were widely distributed outside the campus and often had an impact on the general conversation.

In 1969, Wendy Bacon, then a tutor in Sociology had, along with Val Hodgson and Alan Rees, won the editorship of *Tharunka*, the student newspaper at the University of NSW established in 1953. She calls her 2011 piece about that time 'Being Free by Acting Free'.

> Politically, the ruling conservatives confronted community groups and unions, and movements [of dissent] on campuses and in schools throughout Australia. Such was the situation in which, in late 1969, I joined a group of editors, writers and political activists taking over the University of New South Wales student newspaper *Tharunka*, a paper that had already fought censorship battles in the 1960s. When our money ran out, we launched an underground version called *Thor*, which we sold to students and other eager customers in pubs. Over two years we campaigned for the 'freedom to write, read, think and express without restraint'. [Bacon 2011]

Without restraint, Wendy and the others wrote and published material that otherwise was silenced and censored. Often enough, a tremendous uproar ensued.

massive demonstrations, called moratoriums

It wasn't only the puritanical, hypocritical attitudes to sexuality that were *Tharunka* targets. The sanctity of war remembrances is a huge part of Australian mainstream political culture, perhaps even more so, or less contested, in those days. (Today's controversies over a massive and horrendously expensive expansion of the nation's war memorial in Canberra continues this sorry tradition.) There was a kind of religious piety to it. The RSL [Returned Servicemen's League] was a powerful political lobby. One issue of *Tharunka*, in March 1972, showed the cenotaph with naked bodies draped over it. No regrets: Wendy Bacon says she'd publish that again today, and it would still cause great outrage. [Bacon interview]

When Wendy, Alan and Val became editors of *Tharunka*, it was the era of Australia's involvement in the American war in Vietnam, and the era of massive demonstrations, called moratoriums, against the war. Sasha Soldatow would credit the moratoriums he attended in Melbourne as part of his political formation. Opposition to the war had been building since the early 60s and in 1970 the first of these huge gatherings took place on the streets of Australian cities. *Tharunka* covered them, more than the daily newspapers did. The growth to immensity of the unpopularity of that unjustifiable war was counted as part of the reason the USA and its allies finally withdrew in 1975. In those days, people taking to the streets in tens of thousands actually affected policy.

A lot of the work in *Tharunka* was straight reporting. There were stories on the repression of dissent over Vietnam, and revelations of the atrocities of USA and allied forces.

> If I were to go back and look in *The Sydney Morning Herald* at the time, there'd be none of this. We really even at this stage were filling a gap, publishing hidden news, hidden stories. [Bacon interview]

And there were the detailed accounts of the various court cases over 'obscenity' and the absurdities, inconsistencies and injustices of the courts.

court case going on, an exciting, important case

I was an Arts student at UNSW and was already a keen reader of *Tharunka*. Friends of my shared house in Paddington came around and told us we should be attending the court case, an exciting, important case. We went the next day, Thursday 10 February 1972. My minimalist little diary noted only: 'obscenity trial — Wendy Bacon Darlinghurst'. I would have been certain that note would bring back every detail if I ever wanted it to.

I do recall that the fact you could be tried in court for things you said, whether through voicing them or printing them, seemed absurd, outrageous, and demanding of resistance.

And what you were resisting was resisting you back.

The case was held at the State Law Courts, a Colonial-Grecian style building on Oxford Street right on Taylor Square, across the road from Martin's Bar, an area which would soon be the Out And Proud centre of gay life in Sydney. But this was still 1972 and laws against homosexuality only began to be repealed in 1975. Gay life was still 'underground' then, necessarily rubbing shoulders with a criminal underworld.

the jury was split

Sasha Soldatow, who had been following all this from Melbourne, would enjoy telling people for years ahead about the slogan Wendy Bacon had once worn to court.

Before Bacon's own trial, two of *Tharunka*'s editors, Val Hodgson and Graeme Dunstan, and the printer, were charged in 1970 with publishing an 'obscene' poem, 'cunt is a christian word'. Wendy Bacon, Liz Fell, and others turned up to the court case and gave out copies of the poem, dressed in nuns' habits covered with slogans. Wendy's said 'I have been fucked by god's steel prick'. She was arrested and charged with distributing an obscene publication (the poem) and exhibiting an obscene publication (the habit).

After this, the cover of *Thor* [not dated] printed the image of the Bernini statue of Saint Teresa in a swoon of religious ecstasy that in the gaze of many moderns was regarded as sublimated yet clearly expressed sexual ecstasy. The provocation was not meant simply to annoy, it was meant to create thinking about religion and the strangling embrace of puritanism. Maybe also about how all kinds of ecstasy are related. The nun's costume that Bacon wore to court displayed an incendiary yet theologically defensible slogan. She tells me she wrote about Saint Teresa to argue that for nuns sexuality was expressed in various ways.

A Catholic Brother, doing a PhD, came to court for her appeal, and testified that yes, that was a literal interpretation of the nuns' relationship with god.

> Which was pretty extreme at the time; he was very great to do that; he was quite willing. [Bacon interview]

In 1971, Wendy went before a jury for a single day, and defended herself. The jury was split; some wanted to acquit, some didn't. This is known because in those days anyone could interview the jurors.

George Munster told Wendy about meeting a juror who revealed how much pressure there had been to convict; the court threatened to lock the jurors up for the weekend, and wouldn't answer their questions. The court got their conviction. [Bacon interview]

Wendy was convicted for exhibiting an obscene publication, the costume. She went to prison for a week. Out of that experience, she became part of the group Women Behind Bars: more on that later. [chapter 9]

Her arrest hadn't stopped her continuing anti-censorship activities. By the time she went on trial, Wendy had already been arrested again, with John Cox, selling copies of *Thor* in a Manly pub, charged with distributing an obscene publication.

Their ten-day trial was held in February 1972.

Wendy represented herself, Cox had Civil Liberties lawyer Jimmy Staples. Many people had given evidence, including Push personalities Germaine Greer, George Molnar, Gillian Leahy.

So that was the trial I attended; my housemate and I were there on the last day and had drinks with all the supporters afterwards.

The next day the verdict was handed down. Bacon and Cox were sent to prison for another week, then released on a bond.

I joined the demonstration outside the courthouse, and went on to attend meetings, put up posters, and contribute to future editions of *Tharunka* and its offshoots.

As soon as he arrived in Sydney later that year, Sasha was part of those circles and that's where I met him. His 1973 piece in *Tharunka*, considering how cities and town planning reflect ideology, might be his first published piece. ['and they all lived together in a little crooked house' *Foundation Day Tharunka* 2 August 1973 pp20, 21]

The conviction of February 1972 was overturned in the court of appeal a year later, on 23 February 1973; this led to over 30 other similar outstanding charges being dropped. So ultimately, Wendy says, 'we won'. [NSW Law Report 1973]

really talking

It was probably a *Thor/unka*-related meeting or work group that he and I left together when we walked over to Victoria Park for some live music. After Sasha's death, I wrote about the significance of that day:

> Soon after we first met we sat together one day on a sloping lawn in a park, observing around us a large crowd of largely younger people at an outdoor pop concert, younger even than we were then, and we were young. We were beginning to make our friendship, talking of how we saw society changing. That was nearly 35 years ago. You too would always remember that day. It was the first time we spent time alone together, it was when we began 'really talking'. You asked me what I was thinking about and I told you. Rock'n'roll wasn't sounding revolutionary any more. [Baranay 2006]

There would have been plenty to say about that. What happens to revolutions? What happens to music?

> Conversations with you were exhilarating, everything mattered, everything was connected, everything was politics and sex and art; you had a gift for stimulation, empathy, silliness, challenge — and disruption. Whatever

came after — infuriation, distance, differences, drifting away — to see you again, though as years passed that happened more and more rarely, still was to experience an instant reconnection, to plug into a charge of memories and associations. [Baranay 2006]

I would find that others also describe friendship with Sasha in similar ways.

Tharunka and its underground offshoots

In 2017 an exhibition of *Tharunka*, *Thorunka* and *Thor* was held in Sydney, a week-long event with talks and panels. It came about when an intact collection of the newspapers had been found preserved in an old metal trunk. All of which I'd read at the time; many editions of which I'd helped sell; some of which I'd written for. The editors of those days had favoured stories that defied censorship, official and customary.

I reconnected with Wendy Bacon thanks to this happening. And on my return to Australia later that year I first stayed at the house she shared with her partner Chris Nash, where a few months later she showed me the exhibition copies.

Wendy never stopped being an activist. When I first interviewed her for this book, she was in the forefront of action against the Westconnex, an extravagant, corrupt, destructive main road development squandering public money, and she had been arrested in 2016 in that connection. After years of teaching journalism, she retired in 2015 but continues to do her own independent unpaid investigation, much of it for community groups. During my writing of this book, she's been at the forefront of investigations and activism in several matters of journalism, justice, climate, environment.

The issues we looked through were full of, though not only, stories about sexuality, some of them serious enquiries into its psychological, sociological, historical aspects, in an era where this was uncommon, and some were personal accounts whose candour and explicitness were evidence of a subversive politics, and some were just filth, published in defiance, and many were sexist in the unconscious way of the times, because the radar for sexism had not yet been finely tuned. Also, because the ethos of inclusiveness meant you didn't censor each other.

It was partly the content that mattered, Wendy recalls, but also the belief that by direct action you resisted censorship, you weren't just sitting and arguing but doing.

The issues included, for instance, a first-hand account by a young woman of going to the university doctor to ask for the contraceptive pill; a piece by

Frank Moorhouse about male sexuality and whether ejaculation really was the point of pleasure for men; a piece by Gillian Leahy on the questioning of feminine identity and heterosexuality the Women's Liberation movement had prompted; a rather horrifying frank interview with teenage men about their 'gang bang' activities.

Tharunka and its offshoots also published material that was banned in Australia at the time, like then 'Yippie' Jerry Rubin's *Do It* which was serialised over several issues. Other material was also taken from USA publications like *L.A. Free Press*.

'why not call a fuck a fuck'

Thorunka published an edition in April 1973 containing the text of *The Little Red School Book*, originally written in Danish, an advisory for schoolchildren about various matters including sex. This was given out free at the gates of several schools in Sydney suburbs. The press turned up for that. A reporter asked me, what if parents didn't approve? I said naively, if truthfully, I thought that didn't matter. Interviewed with others on a live-to-air television talk show, Wendy and academic Peter White calmly said, 'Why not call a fuck a fuck?' That was the first time the word fuck had been used on Australian television. There was an uproar. Subsequently, there was imposition of the seven-second delay for live broadcasts.

publishing was a labour-intensive process

By the time Soldatow arrived to join in these productions, he already had experience in print production, and would always have an interest in every stage of it; he taught and assisted many people in the following years in the creation of newsletters and limited-edition publications.

The editors of *Thorunka* and other 'underground' publications worked with what technology they had. They didn't have scanning. The Web didn't exist. The production of these newspapers was in an era where all the headlines were done in Letraset: sheets of typeface. Not many people had access to cameras. Images were cut out from other publications. No one objected.

> For people who produced alternative newspapers, distribution was a problem so they were happy to see things passed on. No one worried about copyright then... [Bacon interview]

Publishing was a labour-intensive process; it was also comradely, sociable. The printers' service for *Thor* publications did not include collation (printers were worried about being caught with banned material; so only small printers were used, and paid in cash); people would pick up the piles of separate pages from the printing press and take them to a house for anyone who could turn up to help to collate them by hand. I remember being part of a group, going round and round a big table picking up the leaves one by one to assemble into the issue. Very time-consuming.

And then it was time to go out to the pubs and sell them. Twenty cents each. No one returned with leftover copies.

3

anarchism and activism

the Sydney Push

I now know a lot of people who can be loosely described as being in power. They were actually always there in the Push pubs when I arrived to live in Sydney in 1972. [SS 1996 *Jump Cuts* 43]

the history of the Sydney tradition

Sasha Soldatow and Wendy Bacon already had friends in common and soon she and other people were expanding Sasha's knowledge of the history of the Sydney tradition of Anarchism that, he would often say, had drawn him to his new city. And the way its history was still being made.

Scottish professor of Philosophy John Anderson came to Australia in 1927 to join Sydney University.

> Anderson was originally a communist but soon came to be very critical of authoritarian notions of socialism and what he called the 'servile State'. You can see why this may have been important in terms of where we were coming from in relation to the rest of the Left in the late 1960s. He became an opponent of authoritarianism. He played quite a distinct role in the public life in Sydney (as far as I know there was nothing similar in Melbourne). [Wendy Bacon email January 2021]

Bacon, looking through her own archives, says that this, from Wikipedia, fits in with her memories of what was said about Anderson:

> Anderson later abandoned authoritarian forms of socialism and became what would today be called a libertarian and pluralist — an opponent of all forms of authoritarianism. Sometimes he described himself as an anarchist but, after the 1930s, he gave up his earlier political utopianism.
>
> In the 1930s, 40s and 50s, Anderson had gathered around him students, academics, outsider acolytes, school of lifers, people starting to make their careers and become the influencers of their day. When Anderson refused

to oppose conscription for the Korean War, and did not campaign against the banning of the communist party, a group had broken away to form the Libertarian Society at Sydney University. That famous sub-culture in Sydney's margins known as the Push had its roots in the Libertarian Society. Some of their views were Andersonian, some not: there is considerable literature on this, and people involved in these issues and personalities debated it endlessly.

The Push apparently cut across classes; that was as much diversity as there was in those days.

Newly rubbing shoulders with these circles, to some extent I educated myself about this history; to a larger extent no doubt Sasha did.

People involved in all of this made up most of Sasha's new social world.

They gathered not only on the university campus but in certain Sydney pubs.

The old Push had new company, younger people started being around, who might or might not have been considered actual members. The old Push had their own ideas and arguments about who were members and who weren't but only they cared.

There were sub-categories, like 'baby Push', to not-quite-recognise newer, younger members and associates. You can find a lot of disagreement about this.

kept on going when it was over

As soon as he arrived in Sydney, Sasha Soldatow was always at the pub and at the demos and meetings and in the thick of things, at the many lunches and dinners and parties and openings that there were a lot more of, then. Many of the people he mixed with were Push. Margaret Fink told me:

> Sasha was instinctively Push, but the Push was well and truly finished by 1972, absolutely. He'd have heard about it in Melbourne. There are people who claim to be Push now, who were hanging round the hotels, who were not intrinsically Push, in my definition. [Margaret Fink interview]

Like modernism, the Push kept on going when it was over, people joined it when it no longer existed, it defined people who might not have claimed to belong to that loosely-knit tribe.

It was in part that 'instinctively Push' aspect that won Margaret Fink's interest, approval and affection and she was to become one of Soldatow's closest longtime friends.

She had been there from the early days, she had lived with the poet Harry Hooton in the 1950s, her close friendship with Germaine Greer started back then, and even after her marriage to Push person (the word 'member' doesn't seem right) and property developer Leon Fink, providing her with a life of wealth and even glamour, she remained an anarchist and a close associate of the Push.

There were several places where she might have first met Sasha. She doesn't remember exactly; she says he sought her out, and she invited him to lunch. That occasion became a story she would tell several times, including, eventually, to Soldatow's obituary writer David Marr.

She told it to me one autumn day in a house I was staying in at Katoomba in 2018.

> I said, I'll meet you at Tony's. Tony's Bon Gout was new and THE place to go for lunch. Anyway I was [out] and I went Christ it's 3 o'clock, I said I'd meet Sasha at Tony's Bon Gout, I'll call in there so I can say I went even if I was three hours late. And he was still there! Hadn't eaten, waiting, sitting the way he does, with his legs crossed, beautiful looking he was then too, and I said sorry and he, no criticism at all, said, that's all right, I had nothing else to do. Instead of storming out. [Margaret Fink interview]

This was the beginning of a long firm friendship that lasted the rest of Soldatow's life. I wouldn't have gone ahead with this book if she hadn't willingly contributed. [more in chapter 12]

women's experiences and points of view

When he moved to Sydney and to the Push, Sasha received a particularly warm welcome from the women.

His good looks did not go unnoticed; he was genuinely interested in women's experiences and points of view; he was remarkably charming and sociable; and his homosexuality was evident and avowed, thus creating an appreciated dynamic in that era where even in these radical circles sexism and heteronormativity were oppressive forces, not yet commonly named. To have a conversation with a straight man meant you were being sized up for sexual availability. Even if in these circles a woman was expected to be well-read and prepared to argue, it seemed mainly for the prestige of her male associates.

Susan Varga says she vividly remembers meeting Sasha.

> I came back from living overseas in Holland just after Whitlam came in [1972]. [Sasha] was a real breath of fresh air, it seemed to me; the old Push had certain mores and ways of being that were quite stale. He came from Melbourne and fell in love with the Push pretty much straight away. He

didn't do a lot of things the Push did do, like go to the races. He did like to talk to women and actually had real conversations with women. He was easy to talk to; even though he was full of ideas there wasn't that same sense of dogmatism. It was such a heterosexual scene it was a relief to have him around. [Varga interview]

Decades later, in the 1990s, Susan Varga's partner Anne Coombs published a book on the Push, called *Sex and Anarchy* where you can read more of its stories, and about its links with power, the academy, criminality, its personalities.

[Soldatow] was becoming very friendly with a number of the older women, particularly Margaret Fink, Judy Smith and their group. They intrigued him, 'They were brash, slightly tough...They could be friendly, but also — like Darcy — they thought you really couldn't call yourself a friend unless you'd known a person for twenty years. It's a very Sydney thing.'

So how did he get to know them so well so fast?

'I'm pushy.' [Coombs 1996, 276]

(I don't know if Sasha was making a pun.)

Sue Howe and Gillian Leahy were among other women who would swiftly become close friends, taken by his wit and spirits and charm. Sue Howe met him in one of the pubs.

Compared to other men he was extremely easy to talk to and his talk was really entertaining... A lot of those men were a lot older. He was so much fun, not like [old Push members] who were no fun at all. Sasha liked women and had a different relationship because of being gay; he would listen, and exchange equally. He had a lot of women friends. [Howe interview]

Gillian Leahy recalls meeting him at a Push party held at a beach house in the early 70s; possibly one that Wendy Bacon and Liz Fell rented at Newport. She was in her 20s then and recalls Sasha coming to sit next to her on the beach, 'this young slim beautiful incredibly attractive man'. [Leahy interview]

She recalls his beauty as apparently androgynous, with a polymorphous-perverse kind of sexuality; a sort of Pan figure, she says. Their friendship lasted to the end of Soldatow's life; Leahy would be one of the executors of his will.

He was prepared to be outrageous, it was so refreshing; even if he'd say things you disagreed with you could have a good argument about it. [Leahy interview]

almost the ONLY out gay person

In my 2006 remembrance, Sasha's always prolific erotic life is recalled as exemplifying gay men's freedom in those early days:

> There were also the days we'd go for a walk and suddenly he'd say, I'll see you back there later and I'd go on back to my flat and he'd return some time after and I had not seen the look that had passed between him and some other man, someone sunbathing on the grass or walking their dog or turning around from talking with friends, just one look is all it took, off he went and had another sex adventure, oh man how I wanted to be a gay man too. Not only for the sex but to be able to notice and read so much in just one look. And yes that kind of sex seemed ideal. It was becoming unceasingly clearer that a gay man had it made in this city like no one else. This was the 70s, our golden age. [Baranay 2006]

Soldatow's sex life was necessarily conducted outside of his Push socialising and activism. Not that he ever hid or apologised for it. Anne Coombs told me that one of the things she always found remarkable about Sasha was that he was almost the only out gay man who became so intimately connected to the Push. (The cartoonist Jenny Coopes was an out gay woman.)

> There was John Cadenzana in the 60s and Richard Brennan, who was bi, but they were subtly denigrated. It shows Sasha's persistence and resilience because, although the older Push crowd would SAY they supported anyone's right to be sexually free in any way they wished, really, they were quite homophobic. And he seemed to just ignore it, and get on with being who he was, which earned people's respect. It might be worth saying a bit more about the oddity of this gay man being so devoted to a milieu that had always been so hetero. [Coombs email July 2020]

It was the anarchist principles, the loyalty of members to each other, the prolific socialising, the acceptance of deviance, non-conformity, even criminality that accounts for Soldatow's devotion. My sense is that the Push men were homophobic but having no good basis for objection would not subject Sasha or others to direct insult. There were other men among them known to be homosexual, to greater or lesser extents in the closet, but it was not generally a subject up for discussion.

Rick Mohr, part of the younger Push cohort (also a Sociology tutor at the time), points to a generational difference. After the 1960s, there came to be more links between the Push and the gay community, he says. To support the publication Thor, a 'fete worse than death' was held in 1972 in Balmain at the premises of the gay organisation Camp Inc.

> Then there's the 78ers. You've seen the list: you're on it, along with several other Push names, including Ross Poole, and the Women Behind Bars mob (though now we're moving well away from hard-core Push). [...] I think the Push lived on into the era I'm talking about here. Maybe it changed in those regards, and I think you could confidently say that even the old, hard-core Push changed: Roelof, Darcy, George (!). [Rick Mohr email July 2020]

But 1978 was several personal and social changes after Soldatow's arrival in 1972, and those changes, to the extent they occurred, owed to the re-education of the old hard core by younger associates; and likely the revelations that assumptions of heterosexuality had to be re-assessed. For example, in 1975 long-time Push member, the film producer Richard Brennan 'came out' very publicly in a long essay he wrote for *Nation Review* [Brennan]. He was already well into his career and considered he was close to dozens of people but very few people till then knew of his homosexual life.

When I met him in 2020 to talk about that, Brennan also said that while he loved the Push in many ways, he also considered one side of this anti-authoritarian group was a covert authoritarianism.

> If you weren't toeing the party line you'd need a talking to. Jim Baker was the Merlin figure. The high priest of Camelot who mentored newcomers and was the chief teller of tales. Darcy was the Galahad figure and one of the principal heroes of the Push; people were spoken of as 'promising young libertarians...' [Brennan interview]

Brennan's friends threw a party for him after his article was published to show their support, and naturally Sasha Soldatow was there.

a practice known as consciousness raising

As Soldatow observed, what took a while to work out for the women who loved liberty was that the men in the Push were as sexist as the rest of the culture, a fact blurred in all those smart arguments and sexual freedoms.

Wendy Bacon and Jenny Coopes both told me that the discovery of the old *Tharunka* issues from over 45 years before had aroused mixed feelings. Among the interest and maybe some pride, it was horrifying to see how sexist some of the material was. Sexism was the water we swam in and we had only started on naming it, being alert to its operations and the call to defy and demolish it.

The ethos of the Push was, women were equal in here in a way they were not outside of here: they were free to argue with the men and to sleep with as many men as they felt like. It seemed a refuge from patriarchy, a word not much used then — a refuge from conformity, from suburban life, from sexual repression; allied to a more arty bohemia.

That was an appeal I understood.

Women were not only free to argue about politics and philosophy and to make sexual advances, they were valued for doing so.

But, really, they began saying, wasn't this freedom for the proof of the difference and free-thinking and anarchist credentials of the men? (Might there have been in the Push culture an undercurrent of bonding through shared sexual partners?) The dominant personalities were men, no less than in the world outside, the surrounding world, the world that was not, after all, outside.

They always talked about ideology but they didn't yet talk about patriarchy; they talked about censorship but didn't yet use the word sexism.

But second-wave feminism was developing, and making clear to the women of and around the Push, many of whom were the ones articulating this clarity — Greer, most famously, and also all the thinking, arguing women at the pubs and parties, demonstrations and seminars — that the *personal was political*, and the truths that that slogan unearthed were profound, radical, and transformative. Soldatow treasured that resonant phrase and would repeat it for years ahead.

first feminist attacks on this ultra masculine form of Leftism

Germaine Greer produced *The Female Eunuch* in 1970, one of the most widely read and influential texts from the new Women's Movement. In her review Fay Weldon said it was as important as *The Origin of Species* or [Freud's] *Civilisation and Its Discontents*. Greer had left Australia by then but remained a close friend of Margaret Fink since their shared youth in Push circles, and stayed with her on her visits to Sydney. One of those visits was in 1972, when Greer appeared at a forum at Sydney University.

Also on the panel were Dennis Altman, Sue Wills and Gillian Leahy; Liz Fell chaired. Altman told me in 2019 that at that forum he announced this was the beginning of gay liberation in Australia.

People didn't notice because they were so excited to have Germaine there. When I look back on it, I realise that there were four of us on the stage, me and three women, and all three women were Push women. [Altman interview]

Not everyone was excited exactly; Leahy's paper, without quite mentioning Greer, argued against Women's Liberation having gurus and leaders.

Later that year, at an anarchist conference that Soldatow attended, Liz Fell and Gillian Leahy delivered a paper on sexism in the Push. Leahy talked about the self-serving mythology about women declared by Push men.

> [They] put this idea around that men were passive creatures preyed upon by women with these sexually voracious appetites, beasts. Now you'd call it gaslighting; in fact the whole free love they espoused suited them very well. [Leahy interview 2020]

As was the case in the counter-culture in general: free love was great in theory but in practice it worked in patriarchal ways.

The New Push, the younger academics, filmmakers and culture workers, some in fields still to be named and recognised, worked in Sociology departments, film production, media, publishing.

Anne Coombs' book discusses the upheavals in the Push's idea of itself. Women gathered in women's-only groups for a practice known as consciousness-raising, and it became clear that sharing our stories revealed an underlying system of oppression. Private experience belonged in public discourse. The discussions brought about a change and perhaps an indication of the blind spots if not outright hypocrisy of the self-styled free-thinkers:

> The illusion of equality between men and women had been one of the biggest illusions of all, and one that Push men only gave up very grudgingly and reluctantly. [Coombs 27]

And Sasha Soldatow was always there, taking careful notice (and maybe being careful to be noticed), and thinking about the affinity of feminist and gay critiques, something he would refer to many times over the years.

> I remember being impressed by the first feminist attacks on this ultra masculine form of Leftism. I was drawn to a feminist analysis long before gay liberation hit the scene. Feminists were confronting the established Left from the outer and in a funny way I felt their attacks contained the substance of my own dissatisfaction. Leftist men used women and hated poofs. An alliance was inevitable. Unfortunately an alliance based solely on being hated cannot be of any lasting value. [SS *What Is This Gay Community Shit?* 1983]

This understanding of his had a lot to do with the special flavour of friendship with Sasha.

the politics of everyday life

Soldatow was already interested in the Situationists, books like Guy Debord's *Society of the Spectacle*, published in 1969, which remains essential in describing the workings of late capitalism. He would have soon found out that Wendy Bacon cites the Situationists in France as a big influence on her as well.

> We were doing Sociology and there was a connection between radical Sociology and some forms of anarchism. There were connections back to DaDa and that you have to see politics not only as hard politics but as everyday life. [Bacon interview].

The politics of everyday life: this became *the* principle of the time. The personal is political: this phrase chimes over and over as the animating insight of the liberation movements: second wave feminism, known at first as Women's Liberation, and Gay Liberation. That's one thing that became well understood, a phrase that would never lose its potency, even as there were factions, offshoots, divergences, new categories emerging that had been barely imagined when this all began.

And there was one striking fact when it came to the politics of everyday life. The immensity, the breadth, the ubiquity of everyday sexism — a term that had barely been coined in 1969, as one analogous to racism, and not yet in wide use — now was being held to the light, exposed, analysed.

Not only that women did not receive equal pay for equal work: for example, in NSW female teachers didn't receive the same pay as males until 1963 and other professions with predominantly female workers continued to earn less than male-dominated ones. But also now facts could be removed from the category trivial and put into the category calling for serious analysis. Who does the washing up at home; why does women's clothing have tiny useless pockets if any at all?

These things have and have not changed.

> The personal is political. This simple phrase, a feminist legacy, had had a grand impact on our lives... There is nothing simple in the challenge of this phrase. It recurs to continually disrupt the safety of our thinking. [SS 1996 *Jump Cuts* 3-4]

a radical course on The Family

Liz Fell, (a significant Push person) was also a university tutor in Sociology and Psychology. She became an important friend to Soldatow around this time. She was already working on her criticisms of psychiatry, criticisms with which Soldatow was in full accord. Fell and Anne Summers gave a radical course on The Family at Sydney University's Philosophy Department in 1973. They invited Soldatow to present some seminars; it was clear they valued his own intellectual studies and points of view.

a refusal to vote

Sasha Soldatow never signed up to the electoral roll.

Voting is compulsory in Australia. The anarchism of the old Push extended to a refusal to vote.

The anarchists' anti-authoritarianism began to come up against new objections from people in overlapping circles of their acquaintance; there was a political crisis in the Australian air. Dennis Altman lived in Sydney for a while in the 1970s.

> I didn't feel comfortable with the heavy-drinking horse-betting pretend-anarchist boys who ran the Push. [...] I have a memory of a couple of them boasting, very proud they didn't vote in 1972 for Whitlam and I thought, you silly fuckers, can't you see how important this is? [Altman interview]

But as the anarchist slogan had it, 'whoever you vote for a politician gets in'. The refusal Sasha and others adhered to had a serious critique at its basis: a refusal to give recognition to existing power structures; a sense that the political systems mean politicians are masters of the rest and to vote means giving up your power. Some old Push people were activist in other ways: being part of a union, like Darcy Waters, who had worked as a wharfie; attending anti-war protests; continually critiquing the workings of power in the political class.

But some people decided to start voting at this era-defining election. Others maintained their refusal to vote, and did so again in 1974 when Whitlam's powerful enemies caused a double dissolution of Parliament, forcing another general election.

In 1972 the Whitlam government, after a stirring campaign — 'It's time!' said the slogans and the song — was elected along with sweeping reforms, including the withdrawal of Australian troops from Vietnam. Anti-discrimination legislation was introduced; an Office for Women's Affairs was created. Some of the Push's drinking companions became femocrats in these new areas of political, legal and bureaucratic reform, and career opportunities for the kind of people who'd been left out until now.

Sasha though maintained his distance from electoral politics, as if this gave him more space to notice the politics of social and intimate moments.

a politics of the Left

While the politics of the Push were avowedly anarchist, often known as libertarian, it was understood that its people had a politics of the Left. And so when critiques of the Left were made, they did not exclude those identifying as anarchist. Idealistic anarchism was based on the certainty that people would cooperate, would help each other.

In the following decades, though, Libertarianism became a credo of the extreme right wing, who wanted no State participation in social arrangements whatsoever because they claimed that a mythical, powerful entity known as The Market would ensure the right outcomes for all human relationships. These days, right-wing libertarianism basically says, if you can't help yourself, you don't deserve to live. The world-wide rise of the extreme right was not visible on the Sydney horizon in 1972.

These days people who were anarchists then now vote (Greens, usually, it seems), and want regulation, even while usually retaining an understanding of politics informed by anarchism. We don't want private enterprise to run everything. Or maybe anything.

freedom, ultimate value and motive [Push-adjacent]

Once you'd been to the demonstrations and the pubs enough times, you were, if not quite Push, at least Push-adjacent.

Even if, like me, you never thought you'd arrived at where you would stay. That, I recall, was something Sasha and I told each other, in our early 20s then, criticising what we would now call the culture of the Push. Once you'd arrived in their orbit, you gathered as much to talk as to drink as to pick up a sex partner, and everyone knew that everyone there basically believed in freedom as a, or the ultimate, value and motive, and the *echt* Push thought there was nowhere worth going from there.

If I hadn't already known I was an anarchist I knew it now, knew I always would be.

But (unlike Sasha) I was also into Tarot cards, Alan Watts, Frank Zappa, the authentic teachings of LSD, Indian clothing — the melange that was becoming known as the counter-culture, especially after Theodor Roszak's defining book in 1969.

In my student years, a scholarship was enough to live on, you were meant to hang out and learn things outside of the classroom, vote in a new government, Gough Whitlam's Labor government. My generation had only ever known a Liberal (that is, conservative) government (in power in Australia from 1949 to 1972). Everything was changing. The effects were tumultuous.

Soon after, I became less interested in the Push, becoming more involved in the world opened up by acting school, and the night life of dancing in the gay discos on Oxford Street, enjoying the drag clubs, a joint in a doorway before you went in, a sniff of amyl someone passed you on the dance floor.

Still, I liked it round the Push for a while and joined in, the fun of arguing at the pubs, going to the parties, starting to read Emma Goldman, joining anti-censorship activities, working on the publications, and to an extent being formed by the articulation of ideas around me there.

Sasha kept close to it for a lot longer, to the end of his life really, loyal to whatever remnants of the Push endured, those scattered yet always connected people.

friendships and close alliances were swiftly formed

The commitment to investigating and reporting stories not included in the mainstream press continued. Friendships and close alliances were swiftly formed. Within a few months of his arrival in Sydney, Sasha was involved in more underground publications, including *Scrounge*. [chapter 8]

By then, in June 1973, Sasha and Wendy had moved into a house in Victoria Street, as part of a radical squatting action. [chapter 7]

4

what is this gay community shit?

'What Is This Gay Community Shit?' 1983

You will be seen as an enemy or a friend — it is as simple as that. [SS 1983 *What Is This Gay Community Shit?*]

the piece of writing that often they mention

At the uncertain commencement of a project, a writer might be heedful of any possible sign, portent, coincidence.

Before the idea of writing this biography was suggested to me, some papers of Sasha Soldatow's, that he'd given me long ago and which I thought long lost, were returned to me.

And soon after, Margaret Fink, who'd been one of Sasha's best friends, gave me a book about biography she'd just read.

And soon after that, my friend the writer Gina Ward visited me at my house-sit when I returned to Australia at the end of 2017 after ten years away with a newly completed novel and about to start a very new life, and she said, I know what you should do next. I didn't know who else could say that to me. She said, you should write a biography of Sasha.

I had never wanted to write anyone's biography, preferring to be obsessed by entirely fictional characters of my own invention. Still, not at once but eventually I began to think, what if, and put the idea to some of the key people in Sasha's life. I wouldn't have gone ahead if they had been opposed to the idea, but they were not opposed. Not that everyone he'd known wanted to talk about him. But many did.

I came across a social media post (I spent very little time on social media) about a new Queer Reading Group forming in Sydney; the reading for the first meeting was to be *What Is This Gay Community Shit?* by Sasha Soldatow.

That pamphlet had been produced in 1983 and while it was controversial then in some marginal communities, it was astonishing to discover its new life. The reading group was formed by a very young man, Benjamin Riley who, I discovered, had written some pieces I had previously noticed in the venerable progressive Australian journal *Overland*; he also was a co-presenter and producer on a new podcast called *Queers*. I got in touch.

At the same time, I was contacting the Mitchell Library at the State Library of NSW where Sasha's papers are held, in what turned out to be over 40 boxes of letters, journals, manuscripts, and drafts of Soldatow's own and others' work. The librarian, Bruce Carter, who dealt with my enquiries, added a personal greeting to his email, for he remembered me from the building we both lived in in the 1980s, and he remembered Sasha and, he noted, he remembered in particular Sasha's pamphlet *What Is This Gay Community Shit?*

As I contacted people who knew Sasha, well or slightly, this is the piece of writing from 1983 that they mention most often.

All the time that's passed means the piece's details are foggy in the mind but people remember it existed, its title, the sense of its provocations, and forceful expression of something they cared to defend or quarrel with.

the focal point of 'gay community'

So what was 'shit', so what was wrong with 'gay community' in the eyes of a gay man who'd been out longer than most, who'd attended the legendary first Sydney Mardi Gras march in 1978 (of course, because Sasha went everywhere), who was active in gay organisations, publications, and parties, what was he saying?

The Mardi Gras's now legendary beginning in 1978 was a march for gay pride and gay identity, defiant and celebratory, held that day in solidarity with the commemoration of the Stonewall riots in New York.

Sydney's parade became a riot when police attacked and arrested, and a resistant and outraged movement was born. That's the story of Mardi Gras in one sentence.

So, originally, Mardi Gras, both by being held and by being attacked, strengthened a sense of community.

By the 1970s *community* had become an enduring buzzword.

A conflation of community defined as a demographic — 'the Australian community', 'the Lexus-owning community' — with the more, or differently, meaningful definition of people with something — belief, identity, cause — held strongly in common, and implying common participation, and most likely a shared understanding of their relationship — that conflation is at the heart of the argument Soldatow makes.

Mardi Gras became the focal point of 'gay community' in Sydney (with effects beyond) as 'community' became the primary category by which representations of same-sex desire were organised. [Hurley 2010]

But what really was 'gay community'?

That's what Sasha was asking. And to read *What Is This Gay Community Shit?* in the present is to revisit the provocative, considered, authoritative, conversational, relaxed tone in which he demanded some fresh thought on the matter.

mercurial and amusing and voluble and chatting

Denis Gallagher and Tim Herbert were members, with Sasha Soldatow, of a gay men's dinner and discussion group of writers called The Gutter Club in the late 1980s [more in chapter 19], and they'd already known each other for years by then. Old friends of mine too, they came to my Sydney flat to talk about Sasha and *What Is This Gay Community Shit?*

Denis recalls Sasha that time in 1983, handing out the pamphlet at a 'homosexual conference', describing a Sasha we recognised:

> He was mercurial and amusing and voluble and chatting to people he probably didn't know, putting on a bit of a show. [Gallagher interview]

A bit of a show: of course. This is one of many instances in which Sasha is remembered from contexts where others have become but part of the blur of others. He was slender, olive-skinned, beautiful or attractive to many, always dressed in a neat clean buttoned shirt, short hair; he added flamboyant glasses with large vivid frames. He exuded confidence, impishness, a certainty of being noticed, and a humorous readiness to provoke an argument. His provocations seemed to give him joy, while arising from a kind of calling, a vocation.

The conference as the first place to hand out his pamphlet was well chosen. It was the audience he wanted to get to, Gallagher says; the people at the conference would have been quite politicised. People like Wotherspoon, Altman, adds Tim Herbert. The writers and thinkers also publicly articulating related questions.

Gallagher took the pamphlet away and says he found it 'a very plausible, very coherent, very intelligent analysis of what was going on'. But not everyone felt that way. It's as if they were proving Soldatow's point, that being gay was not in itself a certainty of like-mindedness. Gallagher found how true that is in gay bars and dances he used to go to; his friends there considered Sasha 'completely verboten' because of what he had said in that pamphlet.

'And I certainly sympathised with his views,' says Gallagher. 'I got to know him better later, and because I was associated with him somehow or other

I wasn't quite acceptable. I won't mention any names.' Herbert says, 'Sasha didn't participate, he didn't go to bars, he wouldn't go to Midnight Shift.

'That's where we were going of course, it was the whole disco era, Oxford Street going crazy...Sasha was sociable...but you wouldn't see him at a gay bar or disco.'

'It was the aesthetics of it, he was the serious intellectual and his tastes were not in that era of music, dance music. He was into classical and jazz, wasn't he?'

'I was too, you were too.'

'But you'd still enjoy Gloria Gaynor.' [Gallagher and Herbert interview]

a means of power and control

Venerable gay historian Gary Wotherspoon said in 2017 that Mardi Gras had become 'fairly tepid, it's a pale imitation of what it once was' but that it still 'does serve a useful purpose...It's important there is some community, a place.'

Today there is still repression and homophobia: blatant, institutional, cultural, unconscious; also we see corporations flying rainbow banners and marriage equality 'Yes!' signs. A lot of popular culture is heteronormative; also there are wise or adorable or complex or unremarkable gay characters on TV shows. There are all those things and more co-existing in our complex world. There are people who love drag, camp, Mardi Gras; there are those who affirm a gay identity without any of that. And what about men who have sex with men and it's not their identity?

So what was 'community?'

In 1983 this was a question Soldatow had been considering for years.

Because you also had to ask, in whose interests was it to speak of *all* gays as *a* community?

The answer, to him, was clear: people who can make money from it. People who can use it as a means of power and control.

a hot ticket for trendies

Since its riotous and politicising beginnings, Mardi Gras became an annual march and party, ever larger, ever more inclusive, and with ever new contentions and conflicts over that inclusion. By the 1990s, the march was no longer an event of outsider celebration and defiance but a family-friendly pageant, and the party, held in massive spaces like the Sydney Showground, with spectacular performances, no longer the place of rare exultant freedom for queers to rage the night away safe among their own but increasingly a hot ticket for trendies, with international stars a main attraction. While to some people it remained what it always was.

The Prime Minister elected in 2013 would disappoint believers in his progressivism when, in thrall to the extreme right wing of his conservative party, he refused to legalise same-sex marriage, which he easily could have, and caused instead an expensive and pain-making plebiscite to be held in November 2017. The success of the Yes vote, and that it was not linked to party affiliations, was a reminder of how apart Australia's politicians generally were from its population.

In 2018 and in the following years, massive corporations — banks, airlines — commissioned floats in the Mardi Gras parade, and politicians including that PM drew attention to their presence there, wanting credit for marriage equality, even while gay and queer workers and customers were far from the visible face of corporations and mainstream politics in daily action.

Soldatow wouldn't be surprised; it's as if he predicted it all.

not only as political but also a 'success'

Already in the early 1980s Mardi Gras was an event that needed to be seen not only as political but also a 'success', as Soldatow points out in his piece:

> Politically the Mardi Gras was to be a celebration of gayness and a celebration of coming out. That was it. Very political. Whako [SS 1983 *What Is This Gay Community Shit?*]

> Oh. I forget. To have a successful Mardi Gras, you need to attract lots of people. The organised Left, being what it is, is more than conscious of needing to create a power base. Lest it be misunderstood, a power base is simply a lot of people who will turn up and do what they're told to do by the organisers and their lackeys the marshalls. It doesn't really matter where these people come from, whether they're politically on side or not. Of course it would be wonderful to be able to attract real western suburbs working-class gays. But, oh heck, if they don't turn up, anyone will do — right-wingers, fascists, christians, sexists, misogynists, exploiters and oppressors — anyone, as long as they're out on the street. Getting people to turn up is, wait for it, also political. Ho hum. [SS 1983 *What Is This Gay Community Shit?*]

Soldatow's insights were not always widely shared or even widely perceived but he went to the heart of the matter, the point and central idea of the piece:

I am surprised that people on the Left forget that capitalism has this fantastic ability to renew itself, to take over radical opposition, defuse it of its political significance and transform it into something that can make money. [SS 1983 *What Is This Gay Community Shit?*]

And this of course suggests anyone who's part of Mardi Gras is, or should be, necessarily opposed to the hegemonic status quo and therefore is of the Left, and that a critique of capitalism is and should be part of their politics.

But of course it isn't like that at all.

a useful text for the first reading

The entire text of *What Is This Gay Community Shit?* can be read online.

Which helped make it a useful text for the first reading of the newly formed Queer Reading Group in 2018.

I met Benjamin Riley at a café, in Redfern, Sydney. The area where, as I didn't know then, I'd move into a flat some months later.

How good to sit outside in the autumn sunshine, the park across the way.

In my decade away from Australia, I had continued to consume journals and radio programs from there to some extent. A new generation had come of age, and embodied the hope maybe the promise that this time, this time... This time the progressive had become normal. In matters of gender, for a start. There were signs.

In Soldatow's youth, in general, people were either straight (aka 'normal') or gay (usually closeted); very few claiming to be bisexual. Since Soldatow's pamphlet, we've seen the rise of queer as a widely-used term, as a category, contested as it might be. Here we have a Queer Reading Group, no further explanation necessary. And we've seen the extent of 'queer' becoming ubiquitous in popular culture as well as in circles that play with theory and/or deviance. Multitudes of gender identities, pronouns, attractions and complications openly flourish.

Differences of emphasis and acceptability will be inevitable. Solidarity and individual tendency might not align.

I discussed things like that with Benjamin Riley, discovering how much he was groking Sasha. Thirty-five years later — he was not yet born when Sasha was writing it — he was finding that pamphlet's arguments compelling, deserving, simpatico. Riley wants disagreement to be aired, tolerated, explored, as well as for like-minded readers to find each other. Not necessarily only to agree with each other. He'd started the Queer Reading Group out of a concern that there wasn't much space in queer circles or political discourse generally for healthy disagreements:

> Either we're screaming at each other or there's this group thing where we all just go, this is the correct politics. [Riley interview]

That first meeting was gratifying in one way, the group being larger than expected, about eighteen people, a mix of ages, most under 30. A mix of genders, hard to tell people's backgrounds, and even one of the '78ers was there.

And it was surprising in another way: Riley had expected a different response to the text; he expected to find 'a bit of an agree fest, that everyone would love it too'. It was a surprise, in a good way, but the reactions were very mixed. [Riley interview]

too quote unquote biased by his politics

Even within the Queer Reading Group, you couldn't assume shared premises.

The over-riding reaction to Soldatow's pamphlet was appreciation of his critiques, particularly about the corporatisation of the gay community and Mardi Gras, *but...*

> But they saw him as too "biased by his politics", his anarchist politics, to be able to present a cohesive [argument].
>
> Or they were alienated by about how up front he was about his politics: he's saying, I'm coming to this from an anarchist politics, which he literally says in the pamphlet, and people were saying ... we want a more quote unquote neutral perspective on this. [Riley interview]

But what could be a neutral perspective?

Even while for sure welcoming disagreement in principle, Riley and I talked about the difficulty of conversations with people who don't share your assumption.

crowd insiders, and acted like it

What Is This Gay Community Shit? is a pamphlet in the style of a series of polemic pamphlets Sasha Soldatow called Patterns, which he wrote, illustrated, and distributed himself in the late 1970s and early 80s. [chapter 11] They contained short prose or poetry and were distributed by him and maybe a few friends by giving them out and passing them on at parties, pubs, dinners, drinks, book launches and gallery openings, the streets, anywhere. That, you could say, was the social media of the day.

There wouldn't usually be anyone else handing out such well-designed pamphlets inside those kinds of crowds. There might be people outside giving out fliers for causes and events, but Sasha and some of his friends were crowd insiders, and acted like it. It meant that usually the guests and audience members would take the pamphlets and read them. Probably on some occasions they could have been seen as a nuisance. That didn't matter. Sasha had something to say and was giving you a chance to see it. He never minded being a nuisance anyway. On the contrary.

What Is This Gay Community Shit? is an A5-size pamphlet — four A4 size leaves folded — with fourteen pages of text. It was published in February 1983 and included a commentary Soldatow had broadcast on the gay community radio station *GayWaves* in 1980.

There are some illustrations, without attribution; they were by the cartoonist Jenny Coopes, who had provided visuals for many of the underground papers Soldatow had been involved with by then, and who worked for a new progressive national newspaper, *The National Times* (1971-1986).

'be realistic, demand the impossible'

Soldatow says that there must be a link between a critique of capitalism and radical gender politics. He affirmed this in *Jump Cuts: an autobiography*, published in 1996, addressing co-author Christos Tsiolkas first and all other readers too. In his view, the emerging 'gay community' was dismantling a whole history of radical political action.

> So-called community aspirations were taking over from the preceding debates of sexual politics, debates that involved both women and men attempting to renegotiate and reinvent the temperament of gender. Simply put, the whole gay community thing was twaddle; it was a matter of emerging gay capitalists smelling the dollars that could be milked from men's cocks... [SS 1996 *Jump Cuts* 198]

Sasha thought that ongoing debate would keep history being written.

His was a position that saw change in laws and culture as necessarily insufficient, for radical politics demanded the constant seeking of an ideal, while along the way there might be rest stops at areas of realism, compromise.

It's an easy slide from compromise into corruption.

Judged by those most adamantly insisting on revolution, compromise necessarily is corruption.

Sasha was always accused of not being realistic.

In a 2018 email to me, Gary Wotherspoon said, 'I remember reading one of Sasha's manifestos, and thought it lacked any sense of *realpolitik*.'

But Sasha held the values of 1968 — the year of social revolution in Western countries. The slogans of Paris May '68 said 'Be realistic, demand the impossible' and 'We are all undesirables!' and 'The liberation of humanity will be total or it will not be' and so on: glorious revolutionary slogans, their expression an end in themselves for some and the way towards broken spirits for others.

For Sasha, to critique, to expose, was an end in itself.

So was disruption.

Attention: Campaign Man with money to spare

One of the inceptions of *What Is This Gay Community Shit?* can be found in a paper Sasha co-wrote with Larry Strange, dated 1978. It's called *Attention: Campaign Man with money to spare*. It was only published in this form: a roneoed five foolscap pages of typescript: three stapled leaves. It would have been given out by hand, the way distribution of independent, small-scale political commentary was done in those days.

'We wrote that to hand out at the National Homosexual Conference in Melbourne,' Larry Strange tells me in mid 2018, recalling the fourth such conference in 1978, over 40 years ago.

Larry Strange's relationship with Soldatow was in a left-behind long ago past when I showed him my copy of *Attention*; it was among the small cache of papers that had uncannily survived the losses and destruction of most of my paper holdings. After years of lost contact, Larry and I had resumed our friendship online a few years earlier, and in late 2017 I had visited him where he lived in Cambodia. Now I was staying in the Blue Mountains when he visited me on a trip back to Australia. Reluctant to revisit those days, without enthusiasm for this biography project, when Larry read this piece over, and another piece or two in this collection, he was struck by its incisive, radical argument, still pertinent and penetrating in today's world of late capitalism's seduction and appropriation of queer issues and identities.

Larry realised his early association with Soldatow had had a profound effect on his life and thinking; the two would have a tempestuous intimate relationship for several years. [chapter 16] 'He drew my politics and my sexuality out of me,' Strange says. Whatever differences and difficulties later arose, he now found that these early polemical essays demonstrate a perception and articulation that were rarely found in responses to the cultural shifts of our time. Rarely still.

At the top of page one of *Attention: Campaign Man with money to spare* a note says:

> My [sic] title comes from an advertisement in The Weekend Australian of March 4–5 1978 for Campaign. It reads: 'Reach the man with money to spare…You'll find him in Campaign, Australian national gay newspaper. Gay people live well because they are able to live for themselves…'

Campaign was launched in 1975, a gay men's magazine, glossy, with full page ads for clothes and liqueurs; these days it might be termed 'aspirational'. As described in the Australian Lesbian and Gay Archives (now Queer Archives):

> The paper's name itself captured this ambiguity, playing on 'camp' as the still widely-used alternative term to 'gay' and 'campaign' in the political sense. In content, it was a mix of news, good-looking men, bar photos and gossip, political manifestos, venue and event listings, polemic, classifieds, advertisements, book and film reviews and celebrity interviews. [https://queerarchives.org.au/posts/history-bites/1975-campaign/]

(As it happened, Soldatow would publish in *Campaign* the following year.)

Attention: Campaign man with money to spare is worth reading in its entirety for its well-structured, conscientiously argued account of the rise of what the authors call the 'homosexual movement' and, as they see it, that movement's lack of sound political analysis and position.

> The movement has never looked at the question of power. So, a simple but crucial problem has never been answered: are homosexuals simply looking for acceptance in the terms of our capitalistic and bourgeois society or, is the struggle more radical, aimed at the restructure of our society? Do we just want a comfortable lifestyle as *Campaign* would have it, or do we have a more profound vision? [SS, Strange 1978]

The piece goes on to examine the idea of oppression in the early days of the gay liberation movement in the 1970s and the way the 'promise of a good time' had drowned out the voices of radical enquiry. It offers an analysis of the appeal of pubs and saunas; and — its most radical, provocative aspect — it dissects the co-option of the movement by capitalism. For after all, it is not oppression but capitalism that emerges as the real enemy and the homosexual movement itself is playing a role as exploiter. Political realities are ignored in, for example, the gossipy thrilled-toned glamour-laden report of a thriving gay scene in South Africa, a Whites-only scene in that country which was then under apartheid, something not mentioned in *Campaign*'s cheery blandishment.

Soldatow and Strange question the character and activities of the Homosexual Conference: 'it reeks of bourgeois values'; the conference organisers are guided by 'their desire for centralism and social respectability', and 'more distressing is the fact that the conference, in its organisation at least, will not look at the meaning of work'; they call for awareness of the exploitation of its own workers.

The piece ends invoking the radical group the Tupemaros [sic] in Uruguay who, burning down a dance hall available only to the very rich, wrote outside it EVERYONE DANCES OR NO ONE DANCES. The piece ends: 'So it should be with us — everybody who works get paid, or no one gets paid.'

radical politics compared with the campaign for acceptance

These days, similar arguments are aired with new relevance in the present era of marriage equality.

There has been a continuing tension between gay/queer as radical politics compared with the campaign for acceptance.

> What we met and worked and marched and wrote and died for was radical transformation. What we settled for was marriage... [Johnson 2018]

Fenton Johnson's *The Future of Queer* was subsequently discussed at the Queer Reading Group, a piece which traces the way the radical visions in early gay liberation movements became movements for acceptance and conformity.

> The assimilationists have won, with State-sanctioned marriage as the very mortar cementing the bricks of the wall of convention that separates us from ourselves, from one another, from all that is unfamiliar, strange, challenging, and thus from learning and growth. The assimilationists have won, with the neocons building their Wonder Bread philosophies upon the ashes of queers who laid their lives on the line in the fight for AIDS visibility and treatment. The assimilationists have won, those men and women whose highest aspiration was to be like everybody else, whose greatest act of imagination was picturing matching Barcaloungers in front of a flatscreen television and matching, custom-designed wedding rings. [Johnson 2018]

It is strange to some of us how acceptance or respectability became the contention and the goal, rather than overthrow, rather than a more radical way of reimagining how things could be.

Of course you have to vote Yes for marriage equality, because equality (also because the vote no campaign was unconscionable); but we don't forget there was a dream once that being non-normative would mean you had to get politicised into a solidarity with the revolution.

Still, as same-sex marriage has become normalised in some cultures, and as we learn how liberating and comforting it has been to many, gay or not, the win for assimilation may become not so easy to regret.

Pretty sure Sasha would not agree.

communication between fellow-poets

In 1983, the responses from Sasha Soldatow's peers must have been gratifying, though in those days it was a great deal slower for communication between fellow-poets to spread.

Ken Bolton, poet and friend, wrote that he'd read *What Is this Gay Community Shit?* the day it arrived. He'd just moved to Adelaide from Sydney where he had seen Sasha for long nights of drinking and talking and laughing with Pam Brown and others of their enchanted circle.

> It's very good: lucid and very well organised & argued, & 'important' [Ken Bolton typed letter to SS not dated]

Ten years after its first distribution, *What Is this Gay Community Shit?* is mentioned in 1993 in a feature piece in the *Sydney Star Observer* (*SSO*).

The *SSO* was at the time the magazine-like newspaper that best combined a range of humour pieces, puff pieces, and selected advertising with some serious reporting, by people and on issues not generally visible in other media. Importantly, as Sydney's main gay newspaper, by then it had made its mark as an important paper in the 1980s AIDS crisis:

> [T]he commercial gay press in Australia was the most effective in the western world in informing a vulnerable community about a major public health epidemic, consistently providing medical information in a non-judgmental way. [Robinson 2011]

The 1993 piece by Campion Decent, discussing gay community, echoed Sasha's pamphlet of a decade earlier, with its title 'What is this community bullshit?' Its argument paid tribute to Soldatow's earlier piece, while taking into account the new factors of queer life post-AIDs, discussing several areas of significant and irreconcilable differences, including the use of the term queer. But this piece ends with a peppy surrender:

> When you find the lesbian and gay communities it is finding people who understand you. And where you can feel relaxed and at home. And you can find people who have things in common with you whether that be political action or whether that be through arts groups or whether it be through being involved in Mardi Gras. [Decent 1993]

his argument would not go forgotten

Soldatow himself made sure his argument would not go forgotten.

In the mid 1990s, the *Sydney Star Observer* published a regular column by Soldatow. In his column in July 1994 he wrote about the continued relevance of his 1983 pamphlet. If you'd never seen a copy of *What Is This Gay Community Shit?*, or had lost yours long ago, this would serve to enlighten or remind you:

> I published this pamphlet myself because it was impossible in the gay press of the time to discuss any of the issues I wanted to raise. In fact, the gay press of the time was part and parcel of the problem.

Another generation later, in 2008, a blog called *slackbastard* reported the story of a particular banner not being allowed at Mardi Gras because it was 'too political' (!). The banner showed a queer Pakistani man who was then incarcerated in a refugee detention centre. After telling the story, the writer referenced Soldatow's pamphlet *What Is This Gay Community Shit?* pointing to the continual usefulness of its argument.

winning respectability or causing a revolution

Similar questions of whether winning respectability or causing a revolution was the goal were debated in what was called the Women's Movement, the 'second wave' feminism that arose in the West in the 1970s. Women gained presence and power in all areas of life and culture, and these included the most conservative and neo-liberal areas. Who wants revolution, who wants reform, who's saying it's gone too far, who's saying there's such a long way to go. The 1980s saw the so-called femocrats emerge from the movement; they held important positions in traditionally masculine environments. Big shoulder pads became conservative fashion. There were so many ways to be feminist. We added an s to the word. Some of us even in hippie clothes still got our legs waxed.

Reforms still had to be called for while reforms had been made; women's rights and gay rights were examples of this.

Gay equality actually became more accepted than women's rights in Australian society, until suddenly it was the early 1980s and AIDS had made its first horrifying, and initially mysterious, appearance. That changed everything.

'the invisibility of liberalism'

Back to the first meeting of the Queer Reading Group in Sydney in March 2018 and their reaction to Soldatow's pamphlet and its interrogation of community. When he thought about it later, Benjamin Riley told me, he realised his reaction to the group's lesser enthusiasm pointed to 'the invisibility of liberalism'. The people in the group were positioning themselves as somehow politically neutral, saying 'corporate gays' might be terrible but the anarchists are equally extreme in the other direction. They were imagining themselves as the sensible centre, who'd have more perspective on the issues.

How often someone will close an argument by saying, 'the truth is in-between'. They are often pleased to say so but this claim makes no sense at all; it's the middle-ground fallacy that says truth is a compromise between opposing views, views at either end of a supposed spectrum.

As Riley remarked, the politics which might be seen as generic liberalism masquerades as not a politics, without acknowledgment of its underlying values; we talked about the invisible bias of the small-L liberal who sees no need to interrogate their own position.

> I was surprised at the extent to which people were just accepting the premise that corporates could be represented in spaces like Mardi Gras; the arguments we had were around their positions in the parade, or which corporates they were, or who do we think is bad or not. [Riley interview]

I can't quite imagine or really know what Sasha would say about all this if he were here but like a lot of people I wish I could. There was something of his spirit in Riley's own thinking. He had asked the reading group whether it was still possible to be radical any more, in the way Sasha was talking of in the pamphlet.

> And one young gay guy said, he'd been advocating being more radical during the marriage postal survey last year; and he said, we should have been blowing up mail boxes and post boxes. I said to him, sure blowing something up, sure that is radical action but it doesn't have a radical politics underlying it. I feel like the actual radical position to take would be, we don't give a shit what the State thinks of our relationships and we do

them our own way. The idea that radicalism is putting a radical aesthetic on top of a conservative politics is so weird to me. [Riley interview]

If you've lived outside of normalising assumptions, you are alert to their existence, their presence. A group brought together because they all identify as queer and all want to discuss readings isn't necessarily all alike in how they see the world they live in.

What I value so much about Sasha's writing: he wears his politics on his sleeve. [Riley interview]

And queer politics, worn on the sleeve or not, should be, in this view, a politics that is radical, that is, one that demands and creates new social organisations and understandings.

One of the most valuable things a queer politics can do is to funnel people into an anti-capitalist politics. At best, being engaged in political movements around sexuality and gender are ways to awaken you to broader structures of oppression. [Riley interview]

But that doesn't always happen.

the legacy of that work

I had met Benjamin to ask him questions, but he put a question to me.

You said Sasha was trying to find forums for these sorts of discussions and this kind of writing. How do you characterise the legacy of that work, not just his, that community talking about these ideas? [Riley interview]

I had no easy or certain reply. To some extent it's going to be answered by whatever this book becomes. But in return I asked, at what point do you sum it up? You never know what the long-term impact is going to be of anybody's life or their work. And when does that long term begin or end?

5

absolutely memorable

student years Melbourne 1967–1971

The city functions not only as the environment in which one lives, but also as the definition of what one is and what one can become. [SS 1973 'They all lived together …']

the cleverest and most cultivated person I had ever met

Alexander Soldatow started a new life at Melbourne University in 1967 at the age of nineteen. There he began making new friends, including a smart and studious girl who would become the historian Judith Brett. I went to her house in Melbourne in 2019, and she led me to a café in nearby Northcote, where she recalled their first year at university over half a century earlier.

Alex Soldatow and Judy Brett lived on the same train line and began to travel home together after meeting in their English Honours tutorial. Judith was still living where she'd grown up in Nunawading, then a 'baby boomer' suburb with market gardens. For her, going to Melbourne Uni was exciting, a move from the suburbs into culture. Sasha then lived in a big house in Camberwell with his grandmother, his mother, and two aunts.

The two of them bonded over their dedication to learning as high achieving students. This in spite of the differences Brett recalls, and all the ways Sasha might have been intimidating.

When I met Sasha, he was a very good pianist, spoke Russian, had read heaps more European literature than I had, was a good artist, knew all about Dada. I was a very dutiful sort of student. I read a lot but I only read what came before me through the school syllabus, I didn't have independent cultural knowledge. Sasha had this huge knowledge and understanding. He was the cleverest person I'd ever met.

He was also much wilder. He was just much more confident, socially confident and knowledgeable than I was. I thought he was fantastic. And he was so beautiful and alive, with an almost febrile energy. And he had these other more way-out friends. [Brett interview]

At times Sasha was with those more way-out friends who evidently appealed to a different side of Sasha from the firmly grounded quest for high achievement in education that Judith represented.

Sasha had quite a lot of difficulty organising himself to get essays in on time. Through university we were close but Sasha would be around me more at exam time and when we needed to do essays. I was steadier... He was really brilliant. And he did have the capacity to be quite disciplined when he knuckled down to work. [Brett interview]

At those times he sought Judith's useful influence.

was never a prefect

Sasha had attended Camberwell High School; it was considered one of the three best state schools at the time, according to his schoolmate, poet and artist Peter Lyssiotis. Elijah Moshinsky and Robert Manne had been students there at the same time (Sasha later would say he had respected Manne at school but snubbed him much later [letter 2004]). Lyssiotis had attended one English class with the slightly older Sasha, who was repeating his matriculation year; it was not unusual to do two years of matric, to repeat the year to get better marks for entrance to the university of one's choice. The school magazine of the time shows that Soldatow was not a form captain or a house captain, was never a prefect, never was in any society such as the Madrigal Society, was not dux of his year, was not in any sports team, did nothing that school magazines noted. Lyssiotis' main recollection is that Sasha, still known as Alex or Alexander, was the first to offer an opinion on the texts they were studying, while other students hung back.

Ric Benson had attended the same school and remembers Alex Soldatow as 'the class clown', funny and naughty and enjoying attention. Though they hadn't been close, Benson remembers him and told me on the phone in 2020 of his memory of a party Sasha held at his family house, with his mother Lily taking part, enjoying herself, even flirting — boys usually wouldn't have their parents at a party. The party stuck in his memory, Benson says, as incredibly strange to him as an 'Australian country boy'. Benson became a conscientious student, but Alex, who was 'brilliant, but with intelligence of a more instinctive kind' had to repeat the final year, and Benson confirms that he is conspicuous by his absence from the school's yearbook. Benson became an educator and with that experience reflects that their school, 'full of very clever hard-working Jewish intelligentsia', which Benson found stimulating, might have turned Soldatow off; it was probably not the right kind of school for Soldatow, who would have been more suited to a school like the present-day Victorian College of the Arts.

Sasha became Sasha

At Melbourne University, Sasha became Sasha. The name on his birth certificate is Alexander Soldatow; outside the home he was called Alexander or Alex. Sasha is commonly a Russian diminutive of the name Alexander.

He began to let his new friends know that he was known as Sasha in the family, or they overheard it in the house — he'd ask friends over even when he still lived in the family home in his first years at Melbourne University, where he enrolled in 1967 to study English, History and Russian.

'We said Sasha is more cool,' say two of his friends from the drama societies he became involved in soon after starting at university.

I met Anne Mitchell and Rosemary Johnson at Anne's house in Melbourne in April 2019. It felt warm and hospitable, and also familiar, with a sense of friendship connections, and a recognition of being women of our generation who've survived this far. The two of them had been friends from childhood and gone to university together; they had met Sasha when they were all involved in Melbourne Youth Theatre in their undergraduate days, now over fifty years ago.

> I don't think you could come across Sasha and not remember him. In the group photo I can name about a third of those people, but Sasha was absolutely memorable... [Mitchell interview]

Anne and Rosemary encouraged him to go by his family's name for him not only because 'Sasha' was 'cute'; also its foreignness appealed. 'It seemed more exotic and Russian to us,' says Mitchell, 'and everyone started calling him Sasha soon after we met him; he grew into that name very fast.'

'He had an exotic quality,' Rosemary Johnson says. They were from 'ordinary Anglo backgrounds'.

Mitchell tells one of several stories of Russian Easter:

Being Russian was unusual, we knew Greeks and Italians but not Russians, so he had the niche of being unusual. He talked about Russian Easter, Russian customs, his identity was in being Russian. He took us to Russian Easter once!

We went to a Russian Orthodox church and we hung about there. Service would be too strong a word; it was more someone was doing various intonings and chantings and everyone was just milling around and talking; it was the first time I'd been in a church where you didn't just shut up and sit down. Then we had this amazing feast back in his family house after the service. All this was totally exotic and exciting.

It was totally a cultural thing and Sasha was proud of it and happy to introduce people to it. He was not religious. He hung his hat on being outrageous and worldly. [Mitchell interview]

Somehow those observances of Russian Easter were seen as part of Sasha's worldliness, rather than an indication of immigrant nostalgia or conservatism. And his pride in his heritage was unusual then, at least among outsiders:

In those days non-Anglos didn't fess up to their cultural backgrounds at all, they tried to fit in and be more Anglo. [Johnson]

He was really proud of being Russian, that was a big deal in his life. [Mitchell] [Johnson and Mitchell interview]

never saw Sasha as husband material

The Women's Liberation movement had not yet taken off and sexism was so much the norm it wasn't named.

Sasha was already an unusual man because of his friendliness to women, with a real interest in their experience and thinking. The expected life for women was drearily conformist, and although de Beauvoir and Friedan had published the texts that 'second wave feminism' made essential, the old ways were resistant.

The people Sasha had connections with at Melbourne Youth Theatre were women by and large weren't they, you and me, Judy Kuring…[Mitchell]

Most of the [prominent] people in Melbourne Youth Theatre were blokes, although the most acclaimed director there was a woman, Lois Ellis. [But even though] there was no female liberation, the women [at MYT] were quite assertive, they weren't shrinking violets. [Johnson]

They were between 18 and 24, the age or stage where you were meant to find a husband.

> You had to find someone to marry you or you had no future really we all knew, so we were [seen as] wasting our time in student theatre really — we never saw Sasha as husband material! [Mitchell]
> We were at university because we had studentships, which meant we had to teach for three years wherever they sent you. [Otherwise] uni would be out of the question for ordinary working-class kids… but if you were a woman who married you only had to teach for one year. [Johnson]
> Another reason to find a husband! [Mitchell]
> Nothing could point to the times more clearly than that. [Johnson]

Sasha was different from the other men they knew. They didn't have a sense of him as sexual being, says Mitchell, 'more a friendly creature, like a sprite'.

> One day I was having a shower at his house… No idea how or why… he was living at home, and he came in, and sat down and talked to me, and I thought my god no man has seen me without my clothes on! He was not interested, had no sense of crossing a boundary, just had something he wanted to talk to me about and was just sitting on the edge of the bath or something, he wasn't constrained by the usual. [Mitchell interview]

the last to go to bed

In those days universities generally did not have Drama Departments. The Melbourne Youth Theatre (MYT) was part of the Secondary Teachers' College. In 1967 they mounted a production of *Measure For Measure*. That's the group photograph Anne had mentioned: of everyone in that.

The production was taken seriously enough to be reviewed in the daily newspapers.

> It was a big success, elaborately staged. Reviewed in the *Herald* and *Sun*. All reviews of MYT were favourable, it was a high standard, they had good directors. [Mitchell]
> It had a buzz on the campus which was funny because Secondary Teachers' College…was regarded as inferior academically to the university but it was the talk of the university campus, it got to be a respectable interesting thing, people wanted to see the productions. [Johnson]
> There were a bunch of us [in the play] meant to be low lives, harlots.

Sasha grew his hair long, put grease through it, it looked disgusting, he threw himself into the role. I never saw him acting in any major role, he just wanted to be part of the culture and fun of it. [Mitchell]

Of course he did! Sasha always went to where the fun was, and made it more fun.

We went away to these rehearsal camps for the weekend. They were a major time in the production, we had a great time, a lot of partying went on, Sasha was right into that, he was one of those up the latest, doing the most outrageous things. [Mitchell]

He was up for anything. [Johnson]

And he'd be the last to go to bed. [Mitchell]

Sasha didn't stay with MYT; he went on to the Melbourne University Student Theatre, where Ray Misson, also part of Anne and Rosemary's friendship group, was directing.

That's where Ray Misson got to know Sasha. Ray was enrolled in a Masters' degree at Melbourne University but spending more time in student theatre. He recalls:

He was younger than the rest of us, very boyish looking, fresh-faced, with dark-rimmed glasses. He seemed confident, good fun, and fitted in well... [Misson email 2.2.2019]

Misson had directed a production of Phaedra, and that was widely praised. Emboldened, he next took on a production of *The Revenger's Tragedy*.

The less said about the production the better: lots of things went wrong, many of which can be sheeted home to my naivety in taking on such a project, and it was not a great success.

I actually can't remember if Sasha played a named role, but if he did, it was fairly minor and he was mostly just one of the members of the court, swelling the numbers. That is when I got to know him well. [Misson email]

Ray reported that Sasha was close with Jane Arms and a man called Daryl. Jane Arms, one of Sasha's new university friends, was one of the 'more way-out friends' Judith Brett mentioned. Twenty years later Arms was an editor freelancing for Penguin Books, working on Sasha's first book. [chapter 21]

The three of them became a strongly identified unit, camping around a fair bit in rehearsals. (I labelled them 'the eccentrinity'.) [Misson email]

When I met Ray in at his elegant apartment in Melbourne in 2019, invited to lunch with him and his partner, he was a retired academic from the Melbourne Graduate School of Education. He had written me an extensive reminiscence of those years.

Ray Misson tells me he thinks the production was a pivotal experience for Sasha, and that Sasha's characteristic disruptions were performed outside the classroom.

> After the *Revengers Tragedy* year [1968] I think [Sasha] did start becoming more Out, and a bit more sort of committed politically, but in a minor way. I certainly know from talking to people who were teaching when I was on staff at the English Department, they would make passing comments about Sasha that suggested he was a good boy in class, didn't make waves, was well behaved… He was becoming the great disruptor in his life outside the class but that doesn't seem to have come into the classroom. [Misson interview]

ironic, shoulder-shrugging reasonableness

Ray Misson wrote his impressions of Sasha's family:

> [During] the time at University, we would quite often drop Sasha home after being at the theatre (particularly if we went to something on at Monash, or somewhere else on that side of town). He was still living with his mother in a big old, rather grand house in Camberwell' […] Sasha treated his mother (and his aunt) with a kind of exasperated dismissiveness, and they treated him in turn with a kind of ironic, shoulder-shrugging reasonableness. I had the impression that it was probably quite a good relationship, and that they were playing out, with some sense of humour, pretty standard child/parent roles in Middle European immigrant families. One didn't feel there was any major tension there. When we went there, his mother or aunt would usually give us some supper, which would often be pelmeni, the little Russian dumplings (a bit like dim sims, but tiny, almost as small as tortellini), served with sour cream. I remember them very fondly. I remember another night, near the Orthodox Easter, when she showed us the painted eggs she had done. [Misson email 2.2.2019]

Sasha would continue the tradition of those painted Easter eggs long after he left home.

As for there being no major tension at home, the opposite is remembered by others.

expeditions that Sasha initiated

There were also expeditions that Sasha initiated, such as that New Year's Eve of 1968/69, when Sasha invited his theatre friends to go with him to Walhalla, the Victorian 'ghost town' that had become something of a tourist attraction, a few hours' drive from the city. Sasha thought an excursion to Walhalla for New Years Eve would be really funny, says Anne Mitchell.

> Sasha knew the people who had bought the Walhalla hospital and were doing it up for a holiday house. And he decided they'd like us to [go there], everything was fine and dandy, and he took about six of us. [Mitchell interview]

But it didn't turn out all that dandy when they all arrived that New Year's Eve.

> The people were obviously gobsmacked, he just turned up with all these people, we got the cold shoulder is how I remember it, we were sent to an outer cottage, it was filthy, hadn't been opened for ages.
> We had to start sweeping and dusting, so we were pissed off [...] [Mitchell interview]

After cleaning up a bit they went to the local pub.

> ...to be very superior and it was [supposed to be] very funny, and we stayed till midnight, none of us drank very much, only the locals. We went back to the hospital to our greasy little cottage and tried to find a hole to sleep. [Mitchell interview]

But not Sasha. His friends in the old hospital were having their own party, and that's where Sasha went.

Ray Misson recalls that night for the insight that Sasha had a social life beyond his university friends and immediate family.

> We went up and had a very pleasant time, some of it spent helping in cleaning things up. We spent New Year's Eve in the Walhalla pub. I have no idea how Sasha knew these people, but I was interested at how socially adept he was at fitting in with them (and with the people in the pub). [Misson email 2.2.2019]

Others who were part of that expedition recall it as less pleasant. As much as the delight and disruption he was usually remembered for, this kind of thing also is remembered about him: he'd readily abandon you to go find a better time.

made her look like an armchair

In 1970, Sasha joined the crew of a production of *Truganini* by Bill Reed, directed by George Whaley, produced by the Melbourne University Actors Studio. Soldatow is listed in the credit for the costumes. Meredith Rogers played a part, a Victorian-era matron, and says he made her 'look like an armchair, very upholstered'. Meredith Rogers and Soldatow became friends, for the rest of his life. She thinks it was probably the search for somewhere he could live more freely that made him move to Sydney a couple of years later — she remembers being devastated when he left. He sometimes stayed with her when he visited Melbourne; once he organised a surprise birthday party for her; sometimes he'd invite his own friends to a dinner party at her place, which she remembers with much appreciation for his stylish, generous hosting, for the way he'd freeze borage flowers into ice to add to a punch, for his favourite old-fashioned chicken recipe. Rogers was in Sydney in the early 80s acting in shows like one on Margaret Preston; Sasha posed for a photograph to make a pastiche of Preston's famous self-portrait. Rogers recalls how well he got on with her children as they grew and how kind he was to her when she needed care.

elaborate high camp make-up

Sasha's zeal for Russian Easter is one of the things remembered from a short-term lover during another university theatre production, where Sasha also turned up, but not to act in it.

I knew Bruce Moore through mutual friends, we'd all had dinner recently when one day in 2018 I met him in the café at the Art Gallery of NSW, to talk about this one time in his past. It was about 1970, Bruce Moore says, and theatre people brought him and Sasha together. Bruce had been persuaded to produce a musical, *Trial By Jury* (Gilbert and Sullivan) for his university college, Queens College, which presented a musical every year.

> Somehow I got dragged in. I had not produced before. So we're heading towards the time when *Trial By Jury* had to be put on and I had done nothing about make-up. [Moore interview]

But he knew Ken Boucher, who said he'd come along and do the make-up, and he said he'd bring Sasha along. Boucher, who much later became the Director of the National Theatre Drama School, had also gone to Camberwell High. He arrived at the dress rehearsal with Sasha, and they created the production's make-up. They applied 'elaborate high camp make-up': blue eyeshadow, round red cheeks, exaggerated lips. This make-up was going to be noticed.

> So I was won over. I can't remember how I met him again and got back to his flat. [In those days] you got to everyone's flat! It must have been within the next six months: my next memory is being at Sasha's place, I think at Parkville, where he had a place of his own. [Moore interview]

It was unusual for a student to have a place of their own, Bruce agrees, but apparently Sasha had this place for a while. They saw each other for about a month.

> From reading later it was the typical pattern: Sasha immediately seems to fall madly in love on the spot. And I'd never quite come across this before. And immediately I got the Russian story: come Easter, we'll be at the Russian Orthodox to experience Russian Easter together. I think it's one of Sasha's standard lines. We never got to it, we didn't last till Easter. [Moore interview]

They had sex a few times, Bruce tells me, and Bruce's impression of Sasha was that he was absolutely confident even 'proud of his performance'.

Their affair 'just sort of fizzled out'.

> Nothing dramatic, he'd have gone and picked somebody else up, simple as that. It wasn't a very significant relationship, one of thousands of very fleeting ones. [Moore interview]

The point of all this is that by this time Sasha was clearly 'out':

> Yes and clearly doing the beats. I wasn't doing the beats. [Moore interview]

And even among people doing musical theatre at the College, no one came out. Because, of course, of the widespread and largely unexamined homophobia of the time, which Bruce Moore knew well.

> If you'd come out as gay at Queens College you'd have been driven out by peer pressure, I saw it happen to two kids who lasted two weeks. You think the 60s is all about liberation, but a male college structure was exceedingly homophobic. When I look back on it, it was appallingly homophobic and most people who turned out to be gay were not known to be gay. [Moore interview]

Sasha's involvement with student theatre continued. In 1971, he directed a play, *Snow Angel*, for Melbourne University's Tin Alley Players, the same year

Bruce Sims directed *The Dumb Waiter*. Sims remained a lifelong friend, and, along with Jane Arms, would be an editor at Penguin working on Sasha's first book; Sims remembers that [chapter 21], but not those earlier plays.

everyone mentions Russian Easter

Everyone I talk to who was part of Soldatow's early life in Melbourne mentions Russian Easter; Sasha always held a party at the time.

Judith Brett remembers an Easter observance held in the early 70s; they all went to the service and then to the party. And Sasha did the cooking himself, Brett told me, and was already a good cook, unusual for young men at the time. By then, Sasha had moved out of the family home, but he continued to observe Russian Easter. And he continued with the observance when he left for Sydney.

an already tempestuous family life

A year after Sasha began university, his mother remarried, an arrangement that brought more strife into an already tempestuous family life.

But it's unlikely many friends at university knew much about that; only a very few had a glimpse.

Judith Brett kept up her friendship with Sasha even though after first year they weren't attending any more classes together.

Like other friends, Judith was invited to Sasha's family home. After his mother remarried, there was a second family home, the country house at Daylesford. Judith remembers going there. She's not certain what they did there; they must have gone for walks around the lake. Her memory came up with the common fuzzy process of delving and sorting, and finding variant versions.

> I went with Sasha and Reinhard, I might have gone just with Sasha, maybe I went twice — once with Sasha and Reinhard and some other friends (Peggy Cook and the painter Rod Withers), and then once just with Sasha, and the mother and the stepfather, that's right. [Brett interview]

Judith remembers Lily, Sasha's mother, quite vividly.

> She was blonde, probably dyed blonde...a big Slavic looking woman, with a broad face. She looked more like the brother [Michael]: he had a broad face, not like Sasha's more delicate features.

He never talked about his father; my sense of it was he adored his grandmother and that his relationship with his mother was difficult. [Brett interview]

And Judith experienced some of that difficulty. Lily didn't want Judith to come, at first, because they were taking a wheelbarrow and she wouldn't fit in the car.

I remember being taken aback by her being so rude. And then [at the house] Sasha and I did the washing up after lunch and she came in and went on about how badly we'd done it and hadn't dried the sink, things that hadn't occurred to me; she was very controlling. Sasha wasn't in my experience someone who had big fights with people — did he? but not yelling — anyway I'd never seen that...I thought she was an unpleasant person. [Brett interview]

Over the years of their friendship, Sasha would often recount his fights with her, and hers with her own mother, his beloved grandmother. Judith asked me what others asked me, does this mother *explain* Sasha, *explain* something about him?

Lily was also considered quite charming by some, as I would continue to discover.

Now we investigate Sasha's family life, his family of origin, in which his mother, Lily, always loomed.

a graveyard of hope

family, migration

After my family arrived in Australia as refugees, officially known as displaced persons as we were called in 1949, I was brought up in Melbourne to be a Russian. Apart from music, Russian was my first language. [SS 1993 *Mayakovsky* 59]

no primal scene, no Rosebud

During my research I hear suggestions that the more I know about Sasha Soldatow's family, the more I'll get insights into who he was, the closer I'll get to understanding, to explaining Sasha. No, I say, you can't *explain* anyone. There is no primal scene, no Rosebud, no psychology theory-of-everything explanation for what makes any of us the way we uniquely are, not even your DNA can predict all of it. (Maybe *not yet*. Even so, DNA gets altered by life events, apparently.)

But this conviction co-exists with the culturally acquired notion that we are all formed by early experience; the thing is, though, that we don't always know exactly which early experience forms exactly which part of us.

So there's a tension between investigating the early life in the family of origin as a way of adding a dimension to the portrait of a person, and a wariness about drawing lines with arrows between events and aspects of personality.

Still, if you get interested in a person, you're likely to ask about their early family life.

their early life was unknowable

Children of migrants especially, it has seemed to me, exhaustively speculated about and analysed their parents. There was such a sense that their early life was unknowable, such a lot that could not be spoken of. That sense that your own life was so very different from your mother's life. Sasha was great to talk with about things like that in the early days of our friendship, at an age where

breaking away from one's origin family mattered so much.

This generation born during the massive post-war migrations was part of the counter-culture generation; Western culture did change radically in the 1960s; there are connections between these things.

More recent writers from refugee families are still saying something like that:

> Connection, in general, can be an impossible goal, but the children of refugees trying to reach a point of understanding with their parents often have to deal with additional forms of disconnect — the loss of language, the weight of guilt, the shame of difference, the pressures of societal discrimination, and memories of incomprehensible trauma. It can be daunting. [Kochai 2019]

history often gives you no choice

When Sasha and I first knew each other, learning the little we told then of our histories — we were both born in countries our parents had not grown up in — we wondered if we might have been at the Bonegilla migrant camp at the same time, he arriving there at over two years old, me at less than one. He was born in Plochingen, Germany in 1947, in the aftermath of the immense disruptions of the Second World War, the greatest displacement of people ever known until the present.

Today it is recognised that being displaced is the central experience of humankind in our time, while in the 1950s — our childhood — rootedness, belongingness, was the 'ideal normal'.

His parents, travelling from Germany on their migration, had first disembarked in Naples, where I was born, and from where my parents emigrated; perhaps he and I had been on the same ship, we once speculated (we weren't). My parents, like his, might have gone to Argentina instead — apparently my Spanish first name is a relic of that expectation; my mother's brother emigrated to USA and I always had the sense of a possible other life lived

elsewhere. I don't know exactly how it came about; the story of my parents' migration from Italy became simply 'Argentina said no more refugees, the next boat went to Australia.'

Sasha talks about that chanciness in *Jump Cuts* (1996). He tells a story about visas. (There were no visas, exactly.)

I sometimes wonder what would have happened if my family's Australian visas had not come through first and I had ended up in Argentina. As DPs, Displaced Persons, in Germany after the war, we were offered three alternatives, and my family predictably chose America first, Argentina second and Australia third. Everyone wanted to go America; after all, they'd won the war. Britain was a mess, there was no point in going there, not that they wanted us. But there was a fourth alternative — to be repatriated to the Soviet Union, as Stalin had negotiated with Roosevelt and Churchill at Yalta, to be sent to certain death — hundreds of thousands died in the Gulags, sent there as criminals because they were termed collaborators, or just summarily shot because they had somehow ended up stuck on the losing side [...] [SS 1996 *Jump Cuts* 120-21]

Soldatow goes on to say it's no wonder that refugees 'from a graveyard of hope, in their new lands of promise, become mysteriously silent.' Many refugee children were not brought up on stories about the family's past. There are many reasons for that silence: not least our parents and grandparents having to put so much psychic energy into the present and future, so much that there's nothing left. The lands of their earlier life, as they knew them, were destroyed. Communications across the continents were restricted, expensive. Also, stories are meant to make a kind of sense of things: what you've landed up in the middle of isn't making sense yet.

And some past experiences were all too literally unspeakable.

To 'explain' your migration, you might say, it's complicated, it's forgotten, it's how things turned out, or you find any reason to stand for all the reasons:

Chris, you say that the stories of migrant generations are fast disappearing. It is no surprise to me [...]; in a foreign land they have no connective language. They feel embarrassed, sometimes even stupid when you draw them out when you push them to the edges while you ask them to explain, and they say, like Reinhard, directly, 'I escaped from East Germany because I had never tasted a pineapple or eaten a banana.' Hass risked being shot in order to satisfy his curiosity. That is one simple explanation of the strength of the human spirit. [SS 1996 *Jump Cuts* 121]

your memories, not recognisable for other people

The literature of migration and displacement is vast now, there are statistics and political analyses, and telling intimate details like this one from a friend who writes about immigrants, refugees and their loss of home:

> I remember one interview with a woman who had lost everything and said it was the small things she missed most — the water kettle of her grandmother, for instance. Heartbreaking.
> I cannot imagine what that must do with your sense of identity, when so much of it only lives on in your memories, not recognisable for other people... [Ingrid Van Der Veken on her book *Wat Overblijft*, email October 2019]

It was this past that influenced Sasha's lifelong passion for history, language and how they intersected.

> The refugees and migrants who arrived at the Bonegilla repatriation camp after the Second World War left one indelible record of their presence. Before them the name of the township was pronounced 'Bone-gilla', the second vowel lost in the laziness of the outback accent. But the eastern and southern European pronunciation has stuck. Bon-a-gilla. [SS 1996 *Jump Cuts* 121–22]

Soldatow claims to remember Bonegilla. So he claims memories from the age of two, remarkable enough.

> My first memories are of Bonegilla, not of Naples, as I would like to imagine […]
> Bonegilla for me is populated only with women. The men have already been placed in factory jobs in Melbourne, my father in Jolimont shovelling sulphur into the furnaces at Dunlop's to make rubber. [SS 1996 *Jump Cuts* 124]

As an adult Soldatow went once to visit Bonegilla. There he found there was little trace of the old migrant hostel and learned its records had been burned in a fire in the 1970s. There is a museum there now, with a Welcome Centre, tours, merchandise.

nowhere near the discussions

Vivien Altman became a friend of Soldatow in the early 1970s, just before he went to live in Sydney.

> My mother was Russian, a Russian Jewess. I always connected with people who had non-Anglo parents because it wasn't that common, those circles were really White, so White. [Vivien Altman interview]

'Those circles' were those of the Left-inclined, artistic and academic worlds where what Vivien said chimed with my experience.

Up until around that time, early 1970s, my early 20s, I didn't think I could ever have a close friendship with anyone who didn't come from... but I don't know what we called it then: non-Anglo, migrant are later terms. 'New Australian' was other people's term, never ours. Those others were just called Australians. In the following decades all that didn't matter so much anymore; like-mindedness or elective affinity was on the basis of shared tastes and values.

And that new language has been created; the migrant experience extensively investigated since.

But for a long time, it simply was not talked about. [More on Soldatow's later discussions about the generational difference in the migrant experience in chapter 30.]

We have talked about the radical politics Soldatow was part of, and came to Sydney to be part of, but consciousness-raising about racism, Anglo-centricism, Anglo-normativity was nowhere near the discussions.

so, his mother?

It was because she too had a Russian mother, says Vivien Altman, that Sasha one day invited her to meet his own mother in the famous Pellegrini's café in Melbourne. The details have faded from memory, but an impression remains:

> I remember her as a very friendly plumpish Russian woman. I probably asked her where she came from, how long she'd been in Australia, did she like living in Melbourne, talked to her about my mother. [Vivien Altman interview]

That friendliness was in contrast to the rude, fault-finding mother Judith Brett had encountered. [previous chapter]

It's usually supposed that if we know about someone's relationship with their mother, we know a lot about them, don't we? So, Sasha's relationship with his mother? He'd talk about her with Sydney friends like Susan Varga:

> He made her sound like a Grand Guignol, like she was a monstrous Russian matriarch…a monstrous woman who dominated him and he had to get away from her and every time he went back she'd try to envelop him. That's what I got all the time. He went down [to Melbourne] quite often, he wasn't totally estranged from her. When he did go down he'd come back with stories of her dominance and her Russianness. I don't think [I visited] but I can see her in my mind's eye. He dined out on her and her awfulness, yet he went and saw her a lot. [Varga interview]

She was awful, but he went to see her a lot, that sums it up. Not that an intense ambivalence in family relationships is uncommon.

And consider this: Soldatow's first book starts with a sentence about his mother:

> What were the faces that my mother would have seen during the war when she was a nurse in a German field hospital? [SS 1987 *Private — Do Not Open* 3]

Later in life Sasha would help Lily write the story of her wartime years, as part of a legal process.

Sasha grew up with his mother Lily, her mother Maria Samson, and Maria's other two daughters, Olga and Sophie. His father died in 1961 when Sasha was thirteen (he says by age twelve in one story); his adolescence, therefore, was spent with his younger brother in a household dominated by women. Sasha was especially fond of his aunt Olga, who was musical, elegant, dramatic.

To that we might attribute his sympathy for and interest in women's experience, evident and notable from his earliest adulthood. (Even while no, not all males brought up around women turn out this way.) No one is only a monster, not all the time. Not even Lily.

something essential which remains reasonably intact

Soldatow wrote a series of personal columns in the gay magazine *Campaign* in the 1990s. In one of them he reflects on the formation of the self, its essential element and its malleable element, and the part his father's death played in what he became; in this telling that event was at the core of his psychological formation.

> In the 25 or so years that I have been involved in issues of social and political change, the accepted wisdom has been that people are capable of change, if not radically, then at least significantly. I now think this is not quite true [...] There is something essential which remains reasonably intact [...]
>
> There are some times we live through though which do change the emphasis of our lives. [...] Curiously it is not the issue of my sexuality that formed my first rupture, the indication that all was not easy in the universe, but the death of my father at the age of thirteen. This not only provoked feelings of permanence vs indeterminacy, but started a quest which I can only describe as a will to know. It is from that period that I can trace one of my strongest emotions — the treason of betrayal. [...] [SS 1996 Undertow column *Campaign*]

It took me a while to make a note of the fact that this column is illustrated by a drawing, or photo-collage (no picture credit, but likely by Soldatow), of a naked man, side on, bent head in hands, seen from below his hairline to mid-thigh where some of the darkest lines create the outline of a flaccid but sizeable penis.

a dim memory, coloured by fantasy and masturbation

The only other writing about Soldatow's father that I found was published a few years earlier as the opening lines of 'Requiem', the first piece in *Mayakovsky in Bondi* (1993), previously published as 'Memento Mori'. These opening lines would be well remembered:

> I am trying to remember what my father's cock looked like. It is a dim memory, coloured by fantasy and masturbation. And an aura of loss. He's dead. Decayed most completely by now. It makes me wonder what I should do with my body when I'm dead. [SS 1993 *Mayakovsky* 3]

Soldatow goes on to muse about the disposal of his own body (burial? burning?), a topic he cared about enough to return to during his life (eventually he would leave firm instructions); then he talks about a friend who picks him up in Melbourne when he comes to visit his dying grandmother, and a couple of pages later returns intermittently to remarks about his father, or his memory; although it is not clear why the memory occurs, it brings into question the tricks of memory:

> As I leave the hospital […] , I am reminded of my father. I see him naked in a bathroom, but it is a green-tiled bathroom in Sydney where he has never stood, never been. He never went to Sydney. So the cock I see, the cock I witness at this edge of memory, is something else. However, I have to note the fact that it is definitely still my father's cock, not someone else's. I have taken it upon myself to reconstruct the shape, the colour, the object, the desire. The place is of no importance. This cock is his and no one else's.
>
> I was never fucked by my father. I tell you this quickly in case temptation brings these thoughts to your mind. I'm also not interested in religion, in the subconscious or the archetype. Nor am I interested in psychoanalysis or shrinks… [SS 1993 *Mayakovsky* 5]

There's a bit more about that, and about sex, and masturbation while writing, then the father again:

> I was never touched up by my father, never raped. Love and respect. No sin. That was dad when he was clothed. Naked, I have made him something else. Something more beautiful, like a soft caress, the touch, in retrospect, of a lover. [SS 1993 *Mayakovsky* 6]

Some paragraphs on his grandmother's funeral follow, then:

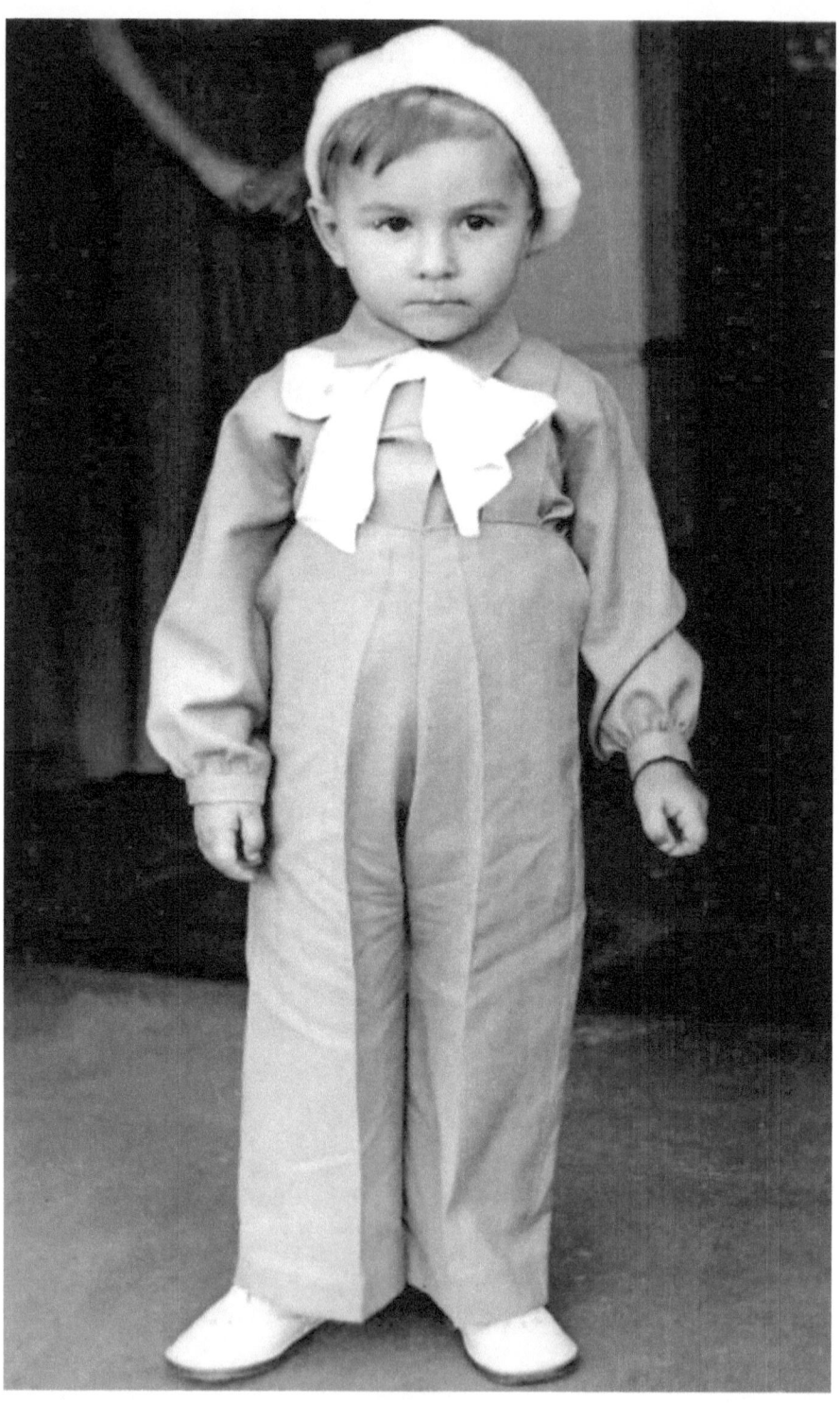

> I am twelve again. My father is shaving. He is naked. Looking at my reflection in the mirror, he speaks to me of science, of mathematics and the universe.
>
> We talk, I look. I can remember nothing of his face, his arms, shoulders, back or legs. That is not surprising since, as I am twelve, he is already dead. [SS 1993 *Mayakovsky* 6]

After more remarks on fantasies and memories, there are a few paragraphs that move into generalities about boys and their cocks:

> Every man I have asked tells of their father' cock in that moment just before puberty. When a cock becomes something to look out for [...]
>
> I have a thesis. Boys remember their father's cocks only when they realise the importance that their own cocks assume as the primary experience and focus of their own changing bodies. [SS 1993 *Mayakovsky* 7]

The rest of the piece constructs its own pathways between more about his grandmother and her funeral, particular friends, friendship, memories and fantasies of sex and kindness.

a family of book-lovers

Soldatow describes his early life and family in *Mayakovsky in Bondi* (1993), speaking of a family of book-lovers, readers:

> I learned [Russian] first on my potty then learned the finer, conversational points on my grandmother's knee, so to speak, learning to read while sitting with her while she read, or by the side of one of my parents as they read book after book. My reading was slower, so my absorption of Dostoyevsky, Gogol and Kuprin is limited to the top left-hand page of the books, not being quick enough to read both sides before the page was turned. [SS 1993 *Mayakovsky* 59]

At the same time he was being brought up in a family whose recent migration was suffused with the sense of a narrow escape from unspeakable atrocity; to convey it he finds an image of a small everyday hideousness that might unforgettably horrify a child.

> They were very lucky, my family, to have escaped the wholesale movement of displaced and vanquished nations after the Second World War. No one called it ethnic cleansing then, but that's what it was, the signatures of the Big Three (all 'free' to do what they wanted) signing away the lives of

millions of toilers. Most of the ones repatriated to the Soviet Union were transported to a quick, very neat and nasty death, worse than a snail in an overnight garden attempting to bubble out the bait it has taken. My family escaped this end, but the living never forget what might have been their fate. [SS 1993 *Mayakovsky* 59]

So much so that his mother was alarmed, he relates, when he brought home from university books by Marx and Engels with his name written inside the cover.

'Why not, they're my books.' I stood my ground. 'We live in Australia,' I said, irrelevantly.

My mother has one of the best collections of classical Russian literature in Australia. Even though she'll lend any book to anyone, even on first meeting, not one tome is signed as belonging to her.

'I have seen people shot for less,' is all she'll say.
[SS 1993 *Mayakovsky* 59]

The brief glimpse of mother here carries a smidgen of admiration for her unstinting lending of books, and a fascination with her life experience implied in the declaration at the end of the passage above.

years of musing on this history, its horror

That earlier piece about his mother, the opening passage in Soldatow's first collection of prose, *Private — Do Not Open* (1987), was published when he was almost 40 years old. He brings to it years of musing on this history, its horror.

What were the faces that my mother would have seen during the war when she was a nurse in a German field hospital? A prisoner and a hated Russian, she was evacuated to help the wounded but mostly the dying. Boys, as she calls them (for remember she is a mother). Boys arriving by the truckload, injured and sick with gangrene and shock. Boy soldiers contorted and twisted by impact of what they had just come through, knowing the immediacy of what had been done to them.

They would come in their endless convoys and she would take them in, knowing there was no more medicine. Knowing they [sic] were critical for help. Knowing they were dying. Knowing that of twenty that arrived in the night, eighteen would be dead in the morning...

And the soldiers would pinch her skin. With their last strength they would remember what they were fighting for. Their instincts tottering, it would still burst through, this need to destroy. It would make valiant forays into the outside which was quickly becoming furry with unconsciousness. But they fought. How they fought. With every last ascent they would return to the cause. For they were men. And they were men at war. And their inhumanity was the rage they lived by. So they told her. 'You dirty Russian pig. You scum, I will kill you. I will wipe you off the face of the earth. I will pull your skin off with my bare hands.' They dug their nails into the woman who was their only contact with a different kind of world. And she, pinched and bruised, she never recounts what went through her mind. She only speaks of how she would see them dead the next morning, and another truckload arriving. She was twenty. [SS 1987 *Private* 3-4]

The first page of his first book (not counting the non-fiction *Olympics*): this was his mother, this was her experience, this is the first thing he wanted the reader to know. Exactly how much of this she told him cannot be known but she told him enough and his imagination demanded to investigate that experience. To imaginatively enter another's experience is to form some sympathy with it.

This was a knowledge that would always have coloured his relationship with her, his understanding of her, the way he tolerated, or endured, her monstrous side.

what have I moved into here!

Sasha's mother remarried in 1968.

Lily married Valentin Valentinavich Sadovchikoff, usually called Val, a widower who was also from the Russian community in Melbourne; they probably met through the Russian Orthodox Church in Collingwood.

The new stepfather meant a new stepbrother, Valek Sadovchikoff. When the families combined Sasha was twenty, his younger brother Michael, known as Misha, was fifteen, Valentin Sadovchikoff's son Valek was thirteen. Valek's sister Olga, ten years older, was already married and living elsewhere. Lily worked in fashion, designing and making clothes. As Sasha's mother owned her house in Camberwell, and seemed fairly well off, Valentin and Valek moved in there. Lily's sisters by then were married and also living elsewhere. Valek recalls it as a rambling mansion, with five bedrooms, and majestic palm trees in front.

I went to see Valek in his music studio in Melbourne in April 2019. While he now runs new businesses, Valek still writes music, still writing with members of his band Informatics which he started in art school — they had a small hit in Germany and Belgium called 'Accidents in Paradise' in the mid 1980s.

I knew music had been a bond between him and Sasha, and I knew him as kind and good-natured through our texts and phone calls and the fond remembrance by Sasha's friends who had met him long ago.

Valek recalls the impression his new brother made.

> Sasha was still living at home. He was really quite unusual especially for a young teenager; he was quite rebellious. I remember he lived in the attic and he painted — one of the huge motifs throughout his life was the eagle, he had a big mural on his ceiling of the attic, it wasn't the Russian eagle, it was more the bird of prey image, so you know, young man, living in an attic with this huge mural he painted, it was like, what have I moved into here! [Valek Sadovchikoff interview]

Valek found his new stepmother difficult, to put it mildly.

> My personal interaction with Lily [made me think] she had this unfortunate kind of frigid insular nature about her, she couldn't handle any emotion. I remember I was studying German, in form four in high school, and she could speak German fluently, and I asked her to help me with my German homework. It took a lot for a fifteen-year-old to come out and say 'thank you a lot and I love you, Mum'. I wanted to create an emotional interaction, and she just froze. And with a child trying to reach out, if the wall comes down it comes down forever, you think there's no access there. That probably influenced me, I never had a positive outlook on relationships.
>
> They [Lily and Val] used to break dishes… [Sadovchikoff interview]

The fact of Lily's experience as a very young woman in the labour camp, though its details were not known, coloured not only Sasha's later writing about her but a more understanding attitude from her new step-daughter, Valek's sister Olga Krasser.

> Who knows what happened to those three young women — those four young women, Babushka [Lily's mother] was very young when she had children — the three sisters and her. The Nazis took them, they had to help Nazis, look after their wounded, who knows what happened to those women, they never talked about it. Each one of their lives screwed up… there must have been some horrible things and the fact they never wanted to talk and the fact it left this terrible thing on their lives — yes, I forgave my mum a lot, I loved her. [Olga Krasser interview]

Olga, Sasha's step-sister, says she got on well with Lily, but she wasn't living with her.

I called her mum cos Lily and I got on well together, nothing like Valek and her. [Krasser interview]

freezing cold in Babushka's house

The day I visited Valek, he had also invited Sasha's niece Natasha Soldatow to be there and she also generously shared her memories. Natasha, though she tries to be understanding, having been told something of the war experience, remembers Lily as forbidding, even cruel.

> [Lily] was my babushka. I think the life she had was quite a hard life. I think she was conditioned to being tough in this world and found it hard to break down her own walls and be loving but she was our grandmother and she did love us.
>
> But my mum's Dutch so I also had an Oma and my Oma was completely the opposite, very warm and affectionate.
>
> I remember as a child always being freezing cold in Babushka's house, the heating was never allowed to be on, because it would cost too much — why would you waste money on heating. And very regimented, you never spoke out of turn, you had to be polite, and polite in Russian, if you got it wrong you'd be scolded. There was certain furniture you weren't allowed to sit on, as a kid, you sit there and be quiet, we're all going to do shots of vodka and get pissed but don't you touch anything.
>
> But they were loving, there was a lot of hugging and kissing and that sort of stuff going on.
>
> I don't have a lot of fond memories of [Lily], she could be loving but at the same time we were all afraid of her. Which is sad, but my auntie Olga, Valek's older sister, explained to me one day the troubles Lily had gone through so I understood where her coldness came from. Just the war. Being a Russian woman in that world wasn't easy. [Natasha Soldatow interview]

Sasha and his brother were brought up with a shocking punitive severity. Natasha feels this childhood created a lot of demons.

> My dad would tell me they often used to get locked in closets, you know, for days, and just awful things, their mother didn't know how to handle them and their grandmother would take over, and they were quite severely punished, I don't know a lot, it wasn't spoken about, but there were a lot of ghosts in the past that neither of them really dealt with. [Natasha Soldatow interview]

Natasha, now a mother herself, makes the compassionate point that Lily became a single mother when her boys were still young; Natasha's father Michael was only nine and Sasha about twelve when their father died of lung cancer. Natasha knew that he had been an athlete:

> He was a 100 metres sprinter. We have an Olympic torch at home. He was an Olympic torchbearer. He was eleven years older than my grandmother but he was a quite popular man because of his athletic activity. [Natasha Soldatow interview]

Could this have anything to do with Sasha agreeing to accept the commission of a book on the Olympics in 1980?

Natasha doesn't know much about her 'real grandfather'.

> When he died I think Babushka was at a loss what to do. She was left on her own with two boys. She still had her mother living with her, so it was these two tough Russian women. [Natasha Soldatow interview]

prayed for thirty years for this death

Sasha was especially fond of his grandmother. Valek tells me he also loved her; she was a very gentle person, he says, very religious. They all called her Maria Adamovna, in the respectful Russian way (where you always call a person by their given name and patronymic).

> She was a character. She would go to church every Sunday morning and then race home to watch World Championship Wrestling at 2pm. This was her second religion. I don't know who she had more faith in, Jesus or Killer Kowalski lol. [Sadovchikoff email November 2019]

Somehow, Maria Adamovna moved out of the household into a small bedsitter in Auburn in late 1969; Valek is not sure whether it was willingly or not.

Soldatow wrote tenderly about her in the opening piece in *Mayakovsky in Bondi*, after the bit about his father's cock and what to do with the dead.

> It is May both here and in Vitebsk. That's where my grandmother was born. My grandmother is now in Box Hill Hospital in intensive care, a catheter in her urethra, a drip in her arm and an oxygen mask over her face. She is dying. It is her time.
>
> She has prepared herself for this. Privately, eight years ago, she told me that she has prayed for thirty years for this death. [SS 1993 *Mayakovsky* 3]

When she died in 1991 Soldatow wrote about that to his friend Sue Howe:

> I didn't really mind gran dying, because I know she had wanted to for so long and I'd said my farewells ages ago. What I did not expect was that now I am treated as the elder male in the family. As you know, Sue, it is a role that I've never wanted, let alone expected. But I behaved with dignity while feeling quite indignant. (By the way, I don't think that the Russian language has a word for dignity, would you believe) [letter to Sue Howe 24.5.1991]

he came out on TV

Sasha seemed to know as soon as it was a possible thought that he was gay, but in those days of silence, invisibility, illegality, criminalisation, widespread ignorance and prejudice, it wasn't a thought you easily enunciate.

He became friends with his new step-sister Olga. I first spoke with her for a long time on the phone in late 2019. She had been 21 or 22, she tells me, when she first met Sasha, when her father Valentin told her he planned to marry again, and took her and Valek to meet the new family.

> There was this big big table; there was Babushka [Maria Adamovna Samson] and mother [Lily] and Michael my other brother — stepbrother; and Valek of course; Sasha was on the far side of the table. He was always studying me, whenever I looked he was looking at me like, what sort of a bird are you? [Krasser interview]

She and Sasha soon became friendly, spending a lot of time debating; Olga also enjoyed 'philosophising'. Olga and her sibling were born in China; Olga was seventeen when they left and says being brought up in the communist regime meant she remained 'a bit communist' and that Sasha was 'that way inclined'; they agreed about a lot of things and had respectful disagreements too. She called him her brother from the start.

And Olga was the first person in the family, she relates, who knew he was gay.

When Olga's daughter was born, in April 1969, Sasha used to come and visit them where they lived in Windsor, often sitting with them until late, after the trains had stopped for the night, and Olga's then husband would drive him home. One night, later that year, driving Sasha home, he was gone a long time.

> And when he came back he said, I've got to tell you something: Sasha was very worried, he wanted to tell you for a long long time that he's gay, he was worried it might ruin the friendship, that you might look at him in a

different light. I said no, no! I rang him immediately and said no, Sasha, I love you, I don't care. [Krasser interview]

I was surprised to learn that Sasha, known for being so defiant and out and proud, had been so hesitant, but that was then.

This response from his new sister must have been heartening, encouraging. But as for coming out to the rest of his family, he chose a typically dramatic way to bring that about.

Valek tells me he had to confirm with his ten-years-older sister Olga that it really happened this way: there was a gay rights demonstration, in those days that meant only a hundred people, in the city square in Melbourne.

At least one television crew was there, and Sasha was interviewed. And thus he came out on TV. Valek thinks this was in 1969, so that would have been later in the year he first told Olga.

He said I'm proud and I'm out. My mother [Lily] didn't see the news clip, and my auntie rang her and said, do you know your son is on TV and you should watch. [Sadovchikoff interview]

The evening televisions news was repeated later at night.

Could Lily not have known? She probably suspected, Valek says. But if it wasn't proclaimed it never had to be acknowledged. And until it was proclaimed, Sasha could still be the one who could do no wrong.

If Sasha had planned his announcement, he did not prepare his mother. It might have been spontaneous, a sudden recognition of the moment he would have known was ahead. Lily had lots of Russian girlfriends, Olga tells me...

And Russians are not renowned for not gossiping! And [one of them] said did you know your son was on TV, and she said very proudly, oh what was he doing? [Krasser interview]

Considering that moment now, Valek says:

So my stepmother found out her son was gay [when he was] on national TV. Which is a great story: if you're going to come out, tell the world. It was quite courageous. [Sadovchikoff interview]

It really was. But his mother wasn't thinking about his bravery or honesty. She was devastated, Olga Krasser says.

Also because it didn't come from him, it came from a girlfriend. For her Sasha was everything everything everything the sunshine the moonlight everything. [Krasser interview]

drama and contention

Valek remembers a scene of drama and contention; for both Lily and his father, coming out meant Sasha was mentally ill. (No wonder he was so against psychiatry.) They were all in Daylesford one day...

> Sasha was very emotional, highly strung, like, leave me alone, like, he couldn't cope with people's challenges about the way he was, he was like, this is me. I remember them running after him. I must have been fifteen. They were saying you're going to go to hell, Lily was grabbing him and saying, this [his homosexuality] is really a sickness.
> So he was confronted by that kind of reaction from her, she really thought that he needed to see a psychologist or psychiatrist or some kind of medical help. So that was reason to move to Sydney in itself. [Sadovchikoff interview]

Valek says his father was also upset, and Lily began to assign blame.

> So Lily started blaming her mother, Sasha's grandma: 'You shouldn't have dressed him in dresses when he was seven or eight, remember when you used to parade him around in a frock.' [Sadovchikoff interview]

As if! we agree, as if people can be explained that way, as if being gay is a cause for blame. Lily also had the 'just a stage' response at hand, Olga recalls.

> She kept saying, 'Olga now it's just a stage, you know young people like to experiment.' Every time Sasha came to the house with a girl, she'd get excited, she would spy on them to see if they would kiss, she was waiting for him to get over [being gay]. [Krasser interview]

I am reminded of what I wrote when Sasha died, in the piece about our friendship:

> In the late 70s I found myself in Melbourne with a research job and Sasha was back down there staying in nearby rural Daylesford, in his family house. I visited; we had a day or two alone and then his mother and an aunt or two and the odd cousin also arrived. They were not to worry about not having enough spare beds, I slept with Sasha in his bed. He told me his mother said to him, how can you sleep next to a woman and not desire her, how can you not love her? He said to her, I do love Inez. We talked about our shared belief in a real love that was separate from desire. Saying that to his mother, repeating it to me, was part of a realisation, a manifestation of our politics as he would say, I would say then politics is morals and that's the kind of thing we liked to talk about. [Baranay 2006]

I am anguished to find I have no direct memory of the mother and the others, only that they arrived.

its resemblance to their former homes

When Lily and Valentin married, they bought the house in Daylesford together.

Sasha treated it as if he owned it or at least was entitled to its occupation.

Daylesford is a spa town about 100 kilometres from Melbourne. It was a centre for Russians and both Lily and Val had been visiting friends and staying there for many years. Valek tells me that Daylesford was attractive to the older generation of Russians because of its resemblance to their former homes — the pine trees, the natural spa waters, picking mushrooms. Sasha loved mushrooms he says.

> Different mushrooms than what westerners eat, ones that look like toadstools. [Sadovchikoff interview]

I had a mushroom story in my piece after Sasha died, telling of the time we met again at the Varuna Writers House in the Blue Mountains (in 1995):

> He went off to meet some friends the next afternoon and came back with some unusual-looking red-coloured mushrooms. All the others at the house were horrified, certain they were toxic, possibly lethal, but Sasha cooked them and he and I ate them, they were delicious. I knew when to trust him. [Baranay 2006]

Several friends would recollect mushrooming with Sasha in later years, at Daylesford or in the Blue Mountains near Sydney. Pam Brown mentioned it in her piece published after his death, *Vale Sasha*:

> When you went mushrooming with Sasha he'd refer to the Fungi species chart before deciding whether to actually pick that mushroom or toadstool — then later, in the kitchen, he'd cook up the rarest and most evil-looking ones and even the utterly sceptical diner survived the meal. [Brown 2006 *Vale*]

Pam put up a video on YouTube of Sasha mushrooming with some friends in 1983. [https:youtu.be/Axs4CY8Xo-Q] (There's no sound.)

Russian school, Russian upbringing, Russian values

Alla Wolf-Tasker (b. 1945) grew up in a similar Russian household in Melbourne; her family and Sasha's family were friends, and, as she told me on the phone, their upbringing was similar. These days Wolf-Tasker is an esteemed restaurateur in Daylesford, and described the household where she grew up in her book about her restaurant, *Lake House* (2006).

> Russians have always been mad about mushrooming and their literature is full of stories about mushrooming parties. [Wolf-Tasker 2006]

Sasha, like Wolf-Tasker, attended Russian school as a child on Saturdays, though he never wrote about it.

> Most Saturdays we travelled all the way to Collingwood so I could attend Russian school. There I learned Russian history, geography and literature as well as the ancient Slavic language still in use for church services. On Sunday the same journey was repeated to attend church. And after the service, in the church hall surrounded by portraits of long-dead Russian aristocrats, we were offered piroshki, blinchaki and extraordinary cakes with black tea in tall glasses. The hall was very much the hub of Russian cultural life in Melbourne. There were concerts, plays and dances. Handkissing was a common form of greeting, sometimes even accompanied with just a small click of the heels. Women wore furs in the winter and smelled of lilac or violets. [Wolf-Tasker 2006]

Sasha's lifelong passion for cooking and providing can be traced to these origins. All of the glorious detail Wolf-Tasker provides, all the food knowledge and culture, was also part of Sasha's life; he would always be known for his hospitality, his cooking, his knowledge of herbs and unusual foods.

> [G]rowing up in a Russian household meant being absorbed in the task of cooking for people [and] setting the table, Some sort of fanfare indicated that whatever had been simmering and issuing delicious smells for hours was about to be served. If guests were coming the best hand-embroidered cloths and rumochki shot glasses were put out. Various salads and zkakuski would already be in the refrigerator in their cut glass dishes [...] The principal days of the Orthodox calendar were always observed. [Wolf-Tasker 2006]

More details on the food preparation are provided. And none of it was to be eaten until after the midnight church service in the early hours of Easter Sunday.

their happy place

One of Soldatow's happier accounts of his early family life centres on large gatherings:

> I think I was lucky, being the eldest child in an extended family circle; grandparents, parents, aunts and uncles, their dates, odd stragglers — there was a party at our house every weekend. People came on Friday night and partied on and sang and danced till Sunday, after which they had to go to work [...] Because there was no formal childcare in those days, I'm talking of the 1950s, and don't forget that my grandmother was much younger then than I am now, I was taken everywhere....
>
> I make a point now, when inviting people over for dinner or a party, to say, bring your kids. [SS 1996 *Jump Cuts* 215–16]

Once his family had a second house in Daylesford there was, besides the food culture, a garden that needed tending. Sasha would always take an interest in a garden. Valek recalls that they spent just about every weekend there toiling away in the garden. Sasha built some of the stone walls there.

When Sasha's brother Michael had children, they too became part of its treasured traditions. Natasha has the fondest memories of going to Daylesford as a child, fond memories of Sasha there, of Easter there every year. It was their happy place.

In the present, the renovated house is available as a dacha for short-term rentals.

Valek: he challenged you

Valek was around fourteen when Sasha moved out of the family house in Camberwell to live in a communal household in Carlton, close to Melbourne University. He invited his stepbrother to visit. Valek says that it was a 'a real eye-opener' for him. Sasha was living with other uni students...

> They had a record player and were playing like 'Bridge Over Troubled Waters' and that kind of stuff, so it was a bit like, wow. He kind of introduced me to intellectual life and politics and stuff. I never really took politics seriously before, I was too young.
>
> I met some of his friends. At that time he was in an environment that allowed him to express his homosexuality. I was definitely a hetero boy but I really appreciated him. [Sadovchikoff interview]

Valek enjoyed his access to this very different household and Sasha's particular effect:

> He had a certain charm, what he'd do was challenge you; he was definitely challenged by society by being gay. He would say things like, why do you think in that way; he'd really challenge you about politics and things. That impressed me, nobody had said things like that to me before, no teacher had said think for yourself, what you read in the papers is not necessarily the truth. [Sadovchikoff interview]

That effect of challenging you, making you question the way you thought and reacted to things, making you think again about your usual ways, was something a lot of people recollect about Sasha.

just the way it was

Sasha's brother Michael married in 1976 and had three children. Natasha, the eldest, was born in 1982. Her father told her many stories of his own childhood with Sasha, like this one:

> When they were boys, there was a staircase going up to their room; he said that every morning we would come down to go to school and Sasha would come running down and punch me in the stomach and Sasha never got into trouble because his mother thought the sun shone out of his arse. And one morning I put my wooden pencil case under my shirt and he punched me and broke his wrist and he, Michael, still got in trouble, for breaking Sasha's wrist!
>
> I remember them telling that story and we were laughing so hard, and they said that sort of sums up our childhood: you know, like Sash could do no wrong and Dad was always in trouble. But there was never animosity between them because of that, that was just the way it was. [Natasha Soldatow interview]

It may be that the adult Sasha people knew later also felt he never could be in the wrong. Sasha was also his grandmother's favourite, says Natasha, but his brother Michael, Natasha's father, never minded. He was always loyal and protective to Sasha.

Natasha grew up knowing from as early as she can remember that she had a gay uncle who lived in Sydney.

When Natasha was a child, she thought of Sasha as 'a bit of an enigma'. Her father would talk to Sasha on the phone — he had a phone in his shed. Their conversation would be half Russian, half English, and the children were allowed to talk with him on the phone.

Natasha was told that her uncle knew he was gay from the moment he was born. And long before he dramatically came out, a lot of other people sort of knew, mostly not in a good way.

> He described Sash to me as always a bit girly, he would do stage productions on the dining room table. My babushka [Lily] was a seamstress and he was always interested in what she was doing while my dad had no interest whatsoever. They'd do boys' stuff then Sasha would get up and sing a cabaret on the table.
>
> Sasha was always described as being the favourite; the women of the family, the aunties, adored him. Dad always said he had that softness about him and that ability to get away with murder. But he also said that his life outside of the family home, at school and that, he would get picked on, they'd get into a lot of fights, the brothers. [Natasha Soldatow interview]

I remarked that Sasha had told a friend that at school he had not been bullied for being gay, he had been bullied for being Russian.

> That's probably just as true, they probably were bullied for being Russian but Dad somehow knew that Sash needed his protection; my dad felt it was his duty to be the more brutish one. My father spent 90% of his childhood defending Sash. [Natasha Soldatow interview]

As for her uncle being gay, as a child Natasha didn't know exactly what that meant.

> Only that he liked men and he didn't like women. My father always said to us don't ever let anyone ever tell you it's a bad thing. He was so proud of his brother, he didn't speak about it a lot but god forbid that anyone should say anything detrimental about Sash and his sexual orientation in front of my dad. [Natasha Soldatow interview]

Natasha was always proud of Michael for that, especially as he was completely different; Natasha tells me the two brothers were polar opposites:

> My dad was stereotypical — what society believes a man should be, a tradesman, wore boots and stubby shorts, loved hunting and fishing, drove

Land Cruisers, drove motorbikes. He was a real man's man and worked in construction. [Natasha Soldatow interview]

There was a lot of disparaging talk about gays in her father's work environment but, she tells me:

I remember on many occasions my dad saying I can call him a faggot but you'd better fucking not. I remember at primary school, kids talking in playgrounds, [disparagingly] 'oh, gay', but I always felt a strong passionate need to stand up, I'd say my uncle's gay so if you've got a problem with that... [Natasha Soldatow interview]

In spite of their great differences she never saw the two brothers argue. Whatever their differences...

...when they were together there was closeness. I saw them come together when they were berating their mother, that was their favourite pastime. [Natasha Soldatow interview]

getting a good education also causing trouble

Her uncle was also important in encouraging Natasha's love of reading. She still has a collection of books that Sasha gave her a few years before he died.

When we were kids Sash would give us funny names relating to books, so one of us would be The Blurb and one of us would be The Spine. And sometimes he would say things to us and we wouldn't understand and he'd say you'd better find out, you'd better look it up. And on the phone he'd say, how's school, are you getting a good education, are you learning. As unruly as Misha and Sash were they always said you have to get a good education. [Natasha Soldatow interview]

And he encouraged not only a good education and a lot of reading, but also advised them in a way adults usually wouldn't:

By the same token, Sash would say, how's school are you learning, yes, are you also causing trouble, yes, good, that's the way it should be, always. [Natasha Soldatow interview]

Both Sasha and her dad, Michael, were themselves troublemakers, Natasha recalls.

> They used to play practical jokes on my babushka right up until a few years before my father died, oh yeah, they were doing horrible things to her. [Natasha Soldatow interview]

Natasha and her siblings loved Sasha greatly, even idolised him, not least for the way he stood up to Lily. At those important Russian Easter celebrations where the whole family gathered, as it approached the children would ask all the time, is Sasha coming, and if he didn't show up they were 'devastated'.

> But we were also very aware Sash doesn't go by any clock or calendar, and if he comes he comes and if he doesn't he doesn't and if he did turn up it was like Santa Claus, like whoa he's here! Cause he was so different, but he was family, and he was funny and he did swear and he told my babushka to fuck off, when she picked on us for having our elbow on the table, she was very strict, and he'd say oh fuck off Lily, and we just used to roar laughing, we thought it was so funny. He'd get away with that. She'd say, oh Sash, and everyone would laugh, she didn't like it by any means but he got away with it. [Natasha Soldatow interview]

women weep but a man has to remain a man

There is an unpublished piece of five pages in Sasha's archives called 'Sister Irony', where he writes about his family.

About his father:

> Women weep but a man has to remain a man. I remember my father's funeral, my unstoppable tears which I cannot recall, only my resonating howling echoing and resonating through the church his open casket and his body which I could not kiss as a final farewell. Sometimes, in the depth of sleepless nights, not in dreams, I regret my failure at his final departure. It is gone. I can truthfully say I remember very little of the event. I was twelve and I knew him only slightly ['Sister Irony' 2nd page; no page numbers]

And about his brother:

> We are not close as brothers. Underneath his male bravado and my publicly open homosexuality, he has a tender, forgiving generous heart, and an unbroken desire for a loving family. ['Sister Irony']

This is a personal, bitter, tell-all-ish piece. It gives the date of first composition as 1985 but it was rewritten in 2003 and 2004, after a stay in Melbourne at Lily's house after the end of her marriage.

in need of a refuge

The end of Lily's marriage to Valentin in 1992 was acrimonious. Lily changed the locks on her house, and Val went to live in Daylesford. There were disputes about property. That was the end of Sasha's access to the Daylesford house, though Lily tried to keep it as well as the family home in Vermont, where they'd moved in 1970.

Near the end of their lives, in 2001, both Michael, his marriage broken, and Sasha, in need of a refuge, returned to live with their mother for a while. Both were drinking heavily, and it ended badly; Lily threw them out. She even called the police to evict them. [chapter 36]

And yet, as if the deep contradictions in some family relationships can only deepen with time, this was around the time that Sasha painstakingly helped his mother fill in a Claim Form from the International Organisation for Migration's German Forced Labour Compensation Programme and helped her write an accompanying statement, an account of her experience of war.

Soldatow kept his parents' old passports, travel documents, photographs. (Australia's *Incoming Passenger Card* then included a tick-the-box question Q 17 'Racial origin (*European, Asiatic, African, Polynesian*)'.)

The effect of seeing and touching the original documents in Sasha's archives, is to find something moving about them, that quality of human making, that aura no reproduction can ever emanate.

after a lifetime of a tempestuous relationship

Lily Samsonova was born in 1924 in Vitebsk in what was then Belarus, USSR, where she was living with her parents and two younger sisters, Olga and Sophie, when Germany declared war on the USSR in 1941.

Lily, for the purposes of establishing her credibility for the claim, describes at length the town; her family had owned substantial property in the area for generations. The vivid descriptions of the German bombing, the fleeing from homes, the digging of trenches are related with the benefit of Sasha's clarity and precision in English. The detailed nine-page statement tells of the loss of their houses, and of the Germans sending Lily, aged seventeen, and her younger sister Olga to do forced labour: laundry, cleaning buildings, domestic work.

> It was hard work, for which we were given some stale putrid gruel and one half of a loaf of stale brown bread a day, when it was available. We took this bread home and shared it with our family, who had hardly any access to food. [Lily Samson Soldatow Sadovchikoff statement]

Horrific scenes are succinctly, vividly recorded. Lily and Olga are sent to work in a hospital. Eventually they were sent to Lithuania, the town then called Vilno, now Vilnius. There they were held in a transit camp. Their new documents gave Vilno as their place of birth (refugees' true past can officially be obliterated). There was another transit camp, where a kind man helped Lily's mother avoid her and her sisters being chosen for the 'entertainment' of German soldiers. Eventually there was the camp in Stuttgart. More forced labour — twelve hours a day, seven days a week. For a while Olga and Lily were separated from their mother and their sister Sophie. The war ended in 1945; somehow the family was united and moved to Plochingen, where Lily married Paul Soldatow and their son Alexander (Sasha) was born on 7 December 1947. Nothing is told here of how they survived until the migration.

In his archives are copies of letters from Sasha to his mother asking her to fill in details of the whole harrowing story. On the last page he writes

> I know this is hard for you, and it isn't really the money you're after — it is your human dignity. LOTS OF LOVE AND KISSES AND TEARS [letter to his mother, no date]

It's already 2001 when these forms and statements are being prepared. By this time Sasha is severely unwell and soon to be finally estranged from Lily, after a lifetime tempestuous relationship, full of difficulty, opposition and pain, yet never renounced. Whatever he thought of her, his mother's story was part of his own story, and all the more so the more he knew of it as he helped her, in the calm prose required here, set out her experiences, her claim to human dignity.

Sasha's brother died just before he did. Lily died a few months after Sasha.

7

condensed into one street

Victoria Street squats

Victoria Street...covers so many areas of human living that it becomes altogether too tempting to look at it as a microcosm — the problems of the world condensed into one street. [SS 1973 'The Victoria Street Experiment']

the scene was set

The story of the Victoria Street Residents Action Group, and the associated Green Bans, is one of Sydney's legendary sagas of greedy, exploitative, even criminal, development, and resistance to it. Longtime residents were joined by unionists, local community organisers, the homeless, activists, academics, and people who joined in at the time and were never seen again.

In June 1973 Sasha Soldatow with Wendy Bacon moved into 115 Victoria Street, one of the terrace houses threatened by developers, to join an occupation by a movement of squatters and activists.

Victoria Street winds through Sydney's Kings Cross, reaching the adjoining area considered a bit more posh, Potts Point; it's situated on a high ridge overlooking the Harbour and city centre. The Cross used to be the heart of bohemian, cosmopolitan, class-diverse Sydney, and Victoria Street contained what was once the best about inner-city populations: a multiplicity of class and origins, housing for low and middle income earners alongside small hotels and various small businesses.

That was then.

It should have been left alone.

But while on the one hand this was a time of Whitlam's radically reformist federal government, the State government was involved in massive development projects often involving destruction of heritage buildings and natural environment, fuelled by fairytales of endless growth.

The scene was set for the virtual destruction of the city under the guise of 'inevitable redevelopment'. [SS 1973 'The Victoria Street Experiment']

Art works and political activism

Soldatow wrote 'The Victoria Street Experiment' for the Contemporary Art Society.

Still new in Sydney, Sasha had been looking for outlets for his writing, for interesting connections. He knew about the Contemporary Art Society (CAS), and the story of its radical place in Australian art history. He sought out Ian Milliss, an editor of *Broadsheet*, the CAS's regular publication. It was a monthly newsletter of 30 to 40 pages, produced by roneo, a cheap printing process in the days before photocopies. It was all text; there was no cheap easy way to reproduce images then.

When I visited Milliss at his Blue Mountains home in May 2018, he told me a bit about the history of the CAS, and its political edge. It was a society for artists plus artists' supporters and had about 300–400 members he said, which was quite a lot for the small art world at the time.

Sasha certainly knew its story, familiar to all in Sydney's art world. In the 1930s, conservative Prime Minister Robert Menzies had inaugurated a short-lived Australian Academy of Art. A lot of artists objected to his attempts to obtain a royal charter and the Contemporary Art Society grew out of their opposition.

A new generation took over the Contemporary Art Society at the end of the 1960s, and Ian Milliss was part of it. Part of the new big loud generation that was refashioning the world at every level.

> We were young, the anti-Vietnam war generation, we pushed it to the Left. So that's where Sasha came in. [Milliss interview]

Sasha was aware that by then Ian Milliss had received a lot of media and social attention for his art works, often large-scale installations, which contained a dimension of political activism. (Some of it was included in a Kaldor Public Art Projects 50th anniversary retrospective in 2019–2020 at the Art Gallery of New South Wales where a lot of this era's work was featured.)

Ian agreed to meet Sasha, asked him a lot of questions, and became convinced Sasha knew what he was talking about. He describes the Sasha he first met the way many others do:

> He was a very charming, very sophisticated, very intelligent, well-read guy, instantly impressive. (The funny thing is nowadays if I meet someone instantly impressive I tend to think they're psychopaths and shy away.) Sasha was just a lovely charming guy, if very bitchy as we all know. He actually knew and understood the innate politics of the art world. [Milliss interview]

Soon after that meeting both Soldatow and Milliss became involved in the Resident Action Group in Victoria Street; and for the CAS Soldatow wrote about life in the squats like no one else.

join the Victoria Street Residents Action Group

Soldatow sums up the inception of the Victoria Street Resident Action Group group:

> The finance companies and private developers bought up the street at highly inflated prices, [...] and began to evict the residents in preparation for demolition. The residents began to object and formed themselves into a Resident Action Group in an attempt to stop the development. [SS 1973 'The Victoria Street Experiment']

Arthur King, long-time Push member, had been living in Victoria Street for some time, and was a leading instigator in the formation of the Resident Action Group. In early 1973, Arthur called the house where Wendy Bacon was living with Susan Varga, Darcy Waters and Lyn Gain and told them about the eviction, and that they were needed to rally around and join the Victoria Street Residents Action Group.

And they did.

nothing got built without the union

The Victoria Street Resident Action Group knew the importance of allies. They found the best possible allies in the NSW Builders' Labourers Federation (BLF).

'Green bans' and 'builders' labourers' became household terms in Sydney during the 1970s, as Meredith and Verity Burgmann point out; in 1998 (new edition 2017) they would publish a book about the union and its stirring actions and legacy, with an extensive account of these days in Victoria Street.

> A remarkable form of environmental activism was initiated by the builders' labourers employed to construct the office-block skyscrapers, shopping precincts and luxury apartments that were rapidly encroaching upon green spaces or replacing older-style commercial and residential buildings in Sydney. The builders' labourers refused to work on projects that were environmentally or socially undesirable. This green bans movement, as it became known, was the first of its type in the world. [Meredith Burgmann and Verity Burgmann]

That refusal to work on projects that were 'environmentally or socially undesirable' extended the union's care over its conditions of employment as far as care over the social and environmental effect of any building project it was involved in.

And nothing got built without the union.

If the BLF declared a ban, the developer of that project faced not being able to go ahead with building it.

The BLF had already saved parts of Sydney — bushland, heritage areas — from destruction.

The BLF declared a ban on demolition in Victoria Street.

Ian Milliss thought the BLF were 'the most effective artists in the world'. [Milliss 2014]

> It is too true to say that without the BLF Green Ban, the RAG [Residents Action Group] would have been fucked. [SS 1973 'The Victoria Street Experiment']

clear and present danger

Arthur King had been threatened by police, apparently cohorts of the developers, then one day in April 1973, soon after the formation of the RAG, Arthur disappeared for nearly three days. It was clear he'd been kidnapped. The horror and mystery of this, the clear message that anyone involved in this resistance was in clear and present danger, shook the residents. Suspicions, rumours, mystery, terror. When King returned, he would not tell anyone what had happened, and moved out of Victoria Street. He had obviously been very severely threatened and was terrified. Long-time friendships and alliances were wounded, destroyed. King spoke to only one close friend about this until 1983, at an inquest into the disappearance and presumed death of another Victoria Street community activist, Juanita Nielsen. Then he finally recounted the terrorising he'd been subjected to. All of that makes a long, even thrilling story that has been the basis for writings, exhibitions, films, podcasts, TV shows.

civil disobedience in the form of squatting

Sasha Soldatow, Wendy Bacon, Ian Milliss and others moved into the houses in Victoria Street that had been emptied by the evictions.

Four hundred people had already been suddenly, brutally evicted, in preparation for the developers to demolish the buildings. People were needed to occupy the buildings to help protect them.

Many of the houses in Victoria Street had been destroyed or badly damaged during the eviction, but some were still habitable.

> We moved in and secured them and got the electricity going and had water and toilets and rigged up kitchens so they were liveable. It was a funny life, it was camping out inside buildings. [Milliss interview]

Wendy Bacon recalls that the rooms there were 'fabulous'.

> The back rooms overlooking Woolloomooloo, we had phones, electricity, plumbing, it was the best place I'd ever lived in! [Bacon interview 2]

The head of the firm of developers, whose plans were to destroy existing housing for a proposed new multi-storey development, was one Frank Theeman. He had an office right there in Victoria Street. Arthur King's kidnapping demonstrated the kind of confederates he had.

> It was really stressful. We were effectively occupying a part of Sydney under constant threat, it was a dangerous place. We had to have street patrols to protect us. The so-called security people on the street all the time were marching round looking as threatening as possible. [Milliss interview]

Anne Coombes' book tells the Victoria Street story in detail and gives an account of the incipient violence on the street, and the realistic fear it caused the residents.

> There were always heavies dropping in and out, bouncers from the Kings Cross joints. Fred Krahe the killer cop, people like this. [Coombes 1996, 286]

It became clear that the developers, their allies being thugs, criminals, and the police, were going to carry out a violent attack.

Some of the activists were saying they should withdraw, it was getting so serious, Arthur King's kidnapping was a terrifying message; they could even get killed. Certainly being arrested was probable, and brought the threat, even presumption, of police violence.

Wendy Bacon recalls the fear she and others had, but they had mostly decided to stay on and face the consequences.

anarchist influence within Green Bans activists

Soon after he became involved in Victoria Street, Sasha Soldatow met Meredith Burgmann when her friends from the BLF brought her to the Residents' Action Group.

Burgmann was finishing her Masters in International Relations at Sydney University, about to start working at Macquarie University and doing her PhD. She had become friendly with BLF office-holders like Jack Mundey, Bob Pringle and Joe Owens through her activity demonstrating against the war in Vietnam and the 1971 Springbok tour (the all-white rugby team from apartheid South Africa; Burgmann's dramatic protest and arrest brought immense media attention to the cause).

Eventually, when she was a member of the NSW Parliament, she launched one of Soldatow's books, *Mayakovsky in Bondi* (1993).

She told me that Sasha was part of the anarchist influence among the Green Bans activists.

Sasha and the others didn't spend all their time at the Victoria Street Squats; they also frequented the pubs where BLF members and anarchists and Lefties drank together — usually the Criterion or the Sussex pubs across from each other in downtown Sussex Street. Serious discussion went on there, says Burgmann, as well as a lot of drinking.

> Sasha was always there, always part of the very, very vibrant intellectual culture that was going on. [Burgmann interview]

I went to see her at her house in Glebe, where she has lived since that time. She told me she had responded to Sasha as so many others did.

> The thing I remember most is how much fun he was, he was always interesting, he always had very definite points of view. He was very pretty, very charming. You'd think, I want to know this guy. [Burgmann interview]

And she particularly valued his unique influence in that milieu:

> Also obviously gay, which was also a reason I wanted him to be a friend,

because the excessive machismo of a lot of the Builders' Labourers I did find off putting — they were lovely guys, very interesting guys, very principled, but very blokey. [Burgmann interview]

because it was a masculine profession

If anyone was going to disturb a very blokey milieu it would be Sasha Soldatow.

Sasha being part of it all was good for the Builders' Labourers. He was probably the first openly gay person a lot of them had met. In 1972, there weren't many people openly gay as Sasha was. [Burgmann interview]

Susan Varga, who also had joined in the squats, remembers Sasha getting on well with the BLs, even though their appearance, demeanour and ethos were seen as that of the typical worker of that type: a kind of hyper-masculinity, which was flavoured with casual homophobia.

The BLs wouldn't ever have had an openly gay bloke close to them before, and Sasha charmed everyone, there was no problem. [Varga interview]

I imagine Soldatow's unrepentant, unapologetic sense of himself, his total lack of bullshit and his humour, his respect for their activism, is why they'd have liked him.

Before the Victoria Street Squats story was over, in 1973 the Builders' Labourers put a ban on Macquarie University when one of its colleges expelled Jeremy Fisher for being gay; this was probably the first industrial action for gay rights in Australia. It didn't come about easily, and Burgmann says Soldatow was an influence.

It was one of the hotly contested bans, and a lot of the rank and file weren't terribly keen on it, a lot of the officials weren't terribly keen on it… They supported all these really radical things — women, Aborigines but the gay ban was hotly contested. And having Sasha there was pretty good, because they all liked him and enjoyed his company… They could have been quite homophobic except they knew Sasha. Poke them and they had actually quite conservative views, on things like drugs… But I think among a lot of the BLs there was a working-class culture going on that a lot of the middle class activists didn't really understand or know how to fit in to. I never heard any criticism of Sasha and he was blatant over the top gay. [Burgmann interview]

Soldatow later wrote about homosexuality and the BLF:

> Don't forget in those early days [1970s] there wouldn't have been more than a dozen publicly out homosexuals in Australia. There were quite harsh laws against homosexuality. There were also very strict codes of heterosexual behaviour among the broad Left. I had a big fight with Bob Pringle of the NSW Builders' Labourers Federation after he said on television that there were no homosexuals in the BLF because it was a masculine profession. A silly thing to say and, to his credit, he later acknowledged this and the BLF did put a ban over an issue of homosexuality. I made a point of wearing a skirt to the next BLF fund-raising in Abraham Mott Hall. It was a dreadful blue denim thing. The wonderful irony is that when the union bought five new cars, all their registration numbers started with the letters GAY. [SS 1996 *Jump Cuts*, 195]

So people like Sasha, and the feminist women who were part of the Action Group and formed casual or more serious relationships with some of the BLs, had their influence on the traditionally masculinist world.

And the influence went the other way too, Burgmann contends, of the Builders' Labours on the generally middle-class-ish anarchists and activists involved in Victoria Street, including Sasha:

> I think the Builders' Labourers was very good for all that bunch, to make them a bit less elitist in their views. [...] We were the original inner-city trendies but having our alliance [with the BLF] they were our liberators really, they were very working-class guys, not much veneer to them; they were intelligent, informed guys but they had views that were a challenge to Sasha. And to me. [Burgmann interview]

The goal of the activists and squatters

The goal of the activists and squatters in Victoria Street was for the developers to say, you win we're leaving, and the State would take over and create public housing.

Victoria Street was adjacent to Kings Cross which stood for a refusal of conformity, conservatism, insularity; the nearby naval base meant visiting sailors partied there; in the general public's mind The Cross was associated with criminality, deviance, foreign influences, and late nights; it was Australia's most unprovincial inner-city life. Post-war European migrants opened cafés and restaurants. There were art galleries in Macleay Street and the adjacent suburbs of Darlinghurst and Paddington, and artists were living all around The Cross alongside working-class and middle-class residents.

All of that was threatened by the developers' plans. At the time there was no heritage or environmental protection legislation.

It was up to the residents, including squatters, to save it.

an experiment in communal living

> Victoria Street…is a unique situation in which various ideas and theories, assumptions and trusts can be tested, modified, kept or rejected. [SS 1973 'The Victoria Street Experiment']

The 'experiment' in Victoria Street was not only in the direct action of occupation, but one of communal living.

The landslide vote for the Whitlam government in 1972 encouraged giddy optimism. Communal living, while not a new idea, was a counter-culture ideal, and a feminist one, in its subversion of the patriarchal nuclear family; this era was a heyday for the creation of various communes, what are now called intentional communities, often where utopian ideals come to die, but not without leaving their fertilised seeds behind.

At the Victoria Street squats, people participated according to their skills and inclinations. A sense of common purpose — defeating the developers, keeping the houses intact — came with a genial tolerance for the multiplicity of the residents: long-term, newly-arrived, short-lived, occasional.

People got along well, Ian Milliss told me.

They were surely inspired to do so by the utter clarity of who their common enemy was.

The Resident Action Group attracted a great deal of media attention.

> Some [people] were more publicly prominent like Wendy… Wendy was publicly well-known, had great charisma, was good in front of a camera. [Milliss interview]

Now considerably larger, with many new members, the Resident Action Group held meetings twice a week, down in the stables. They'd try to plan how Victoria Street could become an ongoing community. Soldatow was always there, very actively participating, among the group of ten to a dozen in the core group who were driving the politics and overall organisation. A range of forceful personalities, Milliss recalls. Sasha always would talk about town planning. On the wall were posters he'd made.

> He did a lot of great stuff, affirmations about what we should think or say about town planning. [Milliss interview]

Wendy Bacon also remembers Sasha's interest in town planning, and how the meticulous side of Sasha's nature — organising materials — as well as his visual creativity — he created charts and posters — became apparent there.

There were plans for community gardens, for childcare. Researching and disseminating information on legal rights for squatters and anyone encountering police was part of the activism of the group. And Soldatow was part of the creation of a Tenants Union at this time, drawing up a charter of tenants' rights.

That work would be seen in both the CAS Broadsheet and the new newsletter *Scrounge* [next chapter]; both published advice on the rights of tenants and how to behave if those rights were violated.

represent the wide spectrum of opinions

Communal living was not all a matter of sweet harmony and easy agreement.

> From the very beginning, legality, a proper mandate and the need for structure posed themselves as central problems. [SS 1973 'The Victoria Street Experiment']

Soldatow was there in the midst of it, observing and participating, arguing and analysing, and eventually writing his percipient, compendious account of early days in the squats.

The Resident Action Group was constantly debating and re-defining its structure. The anarchist influence meant that official positions within the group were abolished.

> This was partly as a result of the recognition that one person did not represent the wide spectre of options held in the group and partly an attack on authoritarianism. [SS 1973 'The Victoria Street Experiment']

He found that people simply making decisions when a decision had to be made was effective, but that people would come into the group wanting the familiarity of hierarchy. There were problems of representation — who would go to meetings with the developer, the architect, the press? There was the problem of the mass media's desire for 'stories', for scoops (rather than simple statements of aims).

And there was, for Soldatow, a problematic point evident to him, and apparently generally discussed in all those passionate debates inside the meetings at the squats and out in the pubs:

> That is the question of creeping moralism and the existence of sexism within the group. [...] [T]he question of restriction is rearing its head. Do

you exclude people without a well-developed radical political conscience? What about people without money — the so-called free loaders? And what about drag queens? One member even wanted to exclude single men because they were there just to fuck women. No one had told her of homosexuality obviously.

This moralism has been the most difficult thing to define, and most difficult thing to fight. [...] [SS 1973 'The Victoria Street Experiment']

Such were the issues of communal living, where people might find their habitual attitudes being confronted, while practical matters — renovating the flats, making them liveable — were urgent.

And one of the most urgent matters was security, because all this time the squats were being increasingly threatened with violence.

dramatic end

The Victoria Street squats eventually came to a dramatic end; that hostile presence in the street carried out its threat.

It wasn't all that easy for the developers; they had to get court orders to demonstrate that the residents weren't there legally. It took them about six months.

> At that stage there were only two legal tenants but the rest of us all behaved as if we were legal tenants, we even paid rent, into a trust fund, to the landlord. ... This all got tested in court. Not everyone was paying rent [laughs] but we'd gone through the motions of playing this legal game. Once they had a court order that basically negated all of that. [Milliss interview]

The squatters and residents foresaw what was coming. The Builders' Labourers had brought scaffolding and erected barricades. Many of the people who were otherwise homeless departed, sensibly, as they could in those days be arrested for vagrancy, threatened by beatings as well as imprisonment. There was terror at the thought of the inevitable arrests. Wendy Bacon remembers the rumours going around: police leave cancelled, all the bouncers at The Cross coming to smash the barricades, with clubs. [Bacon interview 2]

It came on 3 January 1974, early in the morning. Victoria Street was raided, with massive force.

The Resident Action Group had people looking out on the street and when the police cars drew up they knew what was coming. They locked up everything, barricaded themselves in.

We thought they'd be there for hours, but it all happened amazingly quickly. [Bacon interview 2]

It was as violent as their worst fears.

Sure enough come dawn a couple hundred police and thugs started smashing their way in, smashing doors down with axes, and we were arrested, charged with trespass. The cops came in and read the riot act and dragged us out and took us to the police station, they smashed everything, ripped everything out. The cops were there to protect the goons as they went about their work. [Milliss interview]

Film footage from the incident shows the dogged viciousness of the invasion and arrests.

Milliss kept a list of those arrested, about 45 people; the charges were mostly 'Remaining on part of a building without reasonable cause' but also included 'Maliciously damaging property' and (the quaint-sounding) 'Using unseemly words'.

Those arrested included Wendy Bacon, the cartoonist Jenny Coopes, and other Push people including Darcy Waters, Roelof Smilde, Liz Fell, Anne Summers, the philosopher George Molnar, along with several people who gave their occupations as 'student', 'labourer', 'domestic' or 'unemployed'.

Sasha, who had been among those frightened of this coming violence, was not there on the night of the vicious raid, as it happened; he was ill and had retreated to stay at Anne Summers' house.

they can't see it that way

Mick Fowler, a seaman, was one of the vivid characters at Victoria Street, a longtime resident, who had been evicted in his absence. In filmmaker Pat Fiske's great documentary about the BLF, *Rocking the Foundations* (1985, restored 2017), Fowler talks about joining the Resident Action Group. After the raids, he was the only resident remaining, the only 'fly in the ointment' of the developers' plans.

The chasm between the values of the developers on one side and those of the activists of the RAG is exemplified in the footage showing Mick Fowler recounting how Theeman himself, with his bodyguards ('two ex-coppers' says Fowler) came to see him making him offers if he would only move out. Fowler tried to explain his point of view to Theeman:

I said 'Frank, you don't get what it's all about… Don't you understand, I don't want any money. I want to see low and middle income people allowed to live on the street.' I'm trying to get through to the man but he... can't see it that way. [Fiske 1985, 1.00.56]

That 'can't see it that way' experience is well known — finding values and worldview so at variance with your own that there seems no common ground, causing ever deeper or wider polarisation.

green bans lifted, Federal take-over

Eventually, union green bans were lifted as the NSW Builders' Labourers union was taken over by the hostile Federal branch, under the controversial Federal Secretary Norm Gallagher. The first of the NSW BLF's Green Bans to be dismantled was the Green Ban on Victoria Street. It was the beginning of a new era. The Federation was deregistered temporarily in 1974 then permanently in 1986. Trade Unions, in one of the dismal consequences of the neo-liberal era, were made close to being illegal.

Anything they do, they face huge fines; it's appalling. People say why don't they do anything — they just can't, legally just can't. [Milliss Interview]

The destruction of the squats did not destroy the activist spirit, which is still alight. Milliss, Bacon, Varga, Burgmann and others who were part of Victoria Street continue to be involved in activism to the present.

Was it a defeat?

New Matilda, an independent online source of news and analysis, published a concise account of the Green Bans era and its effects on Sydney in 2011:

The lesson that resident activists learnt from the green ban era was that militant direct action worked in the short term but needed to be wedded to the action of sympathetic governments for lasting reform to occur. We also learnt that what might be seen at the time as unacceptable radical action sometimes needs to happen.

After all, the green bans did save the Sydney we love. [*New Matilda*]

Well, they saved a lot of it, and in Victoria Street at least some of the facades of the terrace houses were saved, and remain.

Sasha Soldatow found somewhere else to live, increasingly becoming engaged in writing, design, and publishing. During his time at Victoria Street, with Wendy Bacon, Susan Varga and others he had started a new alternative news publication, *Scrounge*.

news from round the world

Scrounge; old technology

Groups are becoming dangerous to the system not by straight opposition to it, but by the fact that they're ignoring it. [SS 1974 *Scrounge* 13 p15]

a new outlet / the reasons for their emergence

Scrounge provided Sasha with a kind of group activism combining his interests in collective endeavours, expressions of dissent, design, alternative publications and distribution. He wrote no original creative pieces for Scrounge, it wasn't that kind of publication, but he was a principal participant in producing most of the issues. Like squatting in Victoria Street, it was a form of direct action, putting into practice the ideas you wanted to live by. It brought him into the thick of the vibrant small press publishing scene of the time, practising skills he'd use in subsequent self-made productions.

Each issue of *Scrounge* proclaimed its purpose on its banner:

IT IS INTENDED AS AN INFORMATION SERVICE AND A COMMUNICATION LINK FOR POLITICAL AND SOCIAL ACTION GROUPS IN SYDNEY.

Like many alternative publications, *Scrounge* came about when a group of friends talked about what they could do together; and the decision to create this radical newsletter and all the decisions that followed were reached through informal methods of discussion, agreement and initiative. This is the anarchists' way. That's how *Thorunka* had been produced. [chapter 2] Wendy Bacon says that *Scrounge* was also an offshoot of *Tharunka* in the sense of being an outlet to keep reporting grass-roots activities and alternative news in a straightforward and clear way.

It wasn't at the heart of what Sasha wanted to do in terms of writing; but it was something he believed in at the time and he was very much part of. It brought out the more precise, journalistic side of Sasha. [Bacon interview]

That more precise, methodical way of working would also be seen in Soldatow's 1980 book *Olympics* [next chapter], while his idiosyncratic creative writing would soon find an outlet in his Patterns series. [chapter 11]

Scrounge would provide narratives and analyses different from, and often counter to, those in commercial and government-funded media.

And that media had far fewer forms back then. 'In this period print media were almost the only means to communicate with a wider audience,' said Rick Mohr, in a paper delivered at the 2017 *Tharunka* and *Thor* exhibition (chapter 2). Mohr spoke about the context of the 'alternative press' in the 1960s to the early 70s:

> The only exceptions were street posters, graffiti and the 'soap boxes' of the Domain. The radio and TV channels were restricted to the VHF and AM bands that were tied up by commercial licences and the ABC. FM radio didn't start until 1974; UHF television transmission, including community television, began in the 1990s, as did the Internet. [Mohr 2017]

Scrounge appeared at the time of a boom in small press publishing in the 1960s and 1970s. Several small press publishers emerged, many in the field of poetry. Poets would sell their chapbooks and other volumes at poetry readings, where you might find an eager, generous market for other radical and underground publications. Their emergence was due to change, and failure to change:

> The birth of the small publishers is a response to cultural and intellectual developments in Australia in these few years, especially the emergence of many young new writers, and to the failure of the large Australian publishers and overseas publishers in Australia to understand and meet the needs of Australian writers. [Denholm 1979 1]

The advent of offset printing, and a freer approach to layout also account for the boom, adds Denholm. And in the case of Scrounge, the politics of collective action and making information free played their part.

Letraset for headlines

Producing their own newspaper meant the freedom to say and to share whatever you liked. The network of friends and connections that spread out to find new readers, the ways you'd have to find those readers, the ones that would write back, pass it on. The mastering of available technologies. It was exhilarating, wrote Wendy Bacon in 2019; she likens producing underground papers, including *Scrounge*, to blogging in the early days of the Web thirty years later. There was new technology and patient craft.

> Up until then, we had only produced pamphlets on a Gestetner machine. Now we used an electric typewriter, Letraset for headlines, pen and ink drawings and montage. Typos had to be laboriously corrected by cutting out tiny letters and glueing them carefully on top of laid-out sheets that were later photographed to make plates for the presses. We paid cash to a small offset printery. [Bacon interview 2]

Scrounge began without any funds, during the time of squatting in Victoria Street, and so beginning with the simplest and cheapest of methods: Gestetner reproduction, the simplest of images, hand collation.

changes in style and means of production

The developments in cheap printing technology are reflected in the style and appearance of Scrounge throughout its 16 issues in 1973-74.

In earlier editions of *Scrounge* it's clear that cheap printing technology was used. The creators didn't have much money — it was the Gestetner and basic images.

Later, the appearance of *Scrounge* became more sophisticated, while individual copies were still marked as costing 20 cents. *Scrounge* Number 13, dated Friday 19 April 1974, added three colours to the front and back pages.

Data security, even through simple duplication, wasn't great back then either: on that issue's front page under CONTENTS this plaintive note was added:

> SCROUNGE HAS UNFORTUNATELY LOST ITS SUBSCRIPTION BOOK. SUBSCRIBERS PLEASE CONTACT US

For the first time, an all-illustration front cover was used for *Scrounge* Number 14, Friday 3 May, 1974.

The next issue, May 31–June 14 1974, has no issue number on its cover. The front page is all illustration: a picture of an industrial scene with large banner reading WYONG. Inside, a four-page piece, including more pictures, covered a building dispute in Wyong, a town in NSW, where the BLF played a significant part.

Increasingly art-directed, and with more pages, *Scrounge*'s last issue, no 16, August 1974, has a great graphic of a red bicycle on front cover.

These later changes reflect the involvement of Tomato Press as designers and printers.

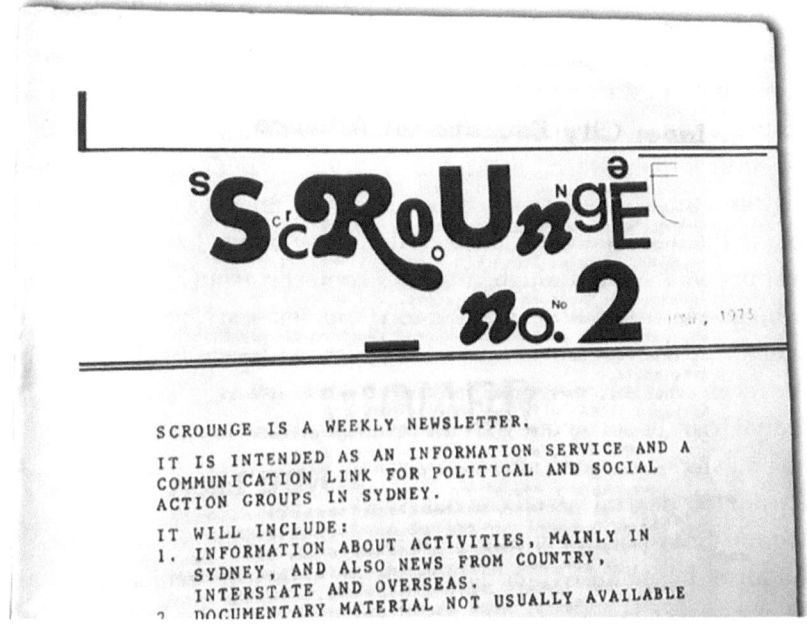

a total lack of business sense

Sasha Soldatow would also print many of his later, self-designed pamphlets at Tomato Press. [chapter 11]

Tomato Press was created in 1972 in Melbourne by Pat Woolley; she moved to Glebe (in Sydney's inner west) in 1973. It provided a venue for alternative publishing.

> The early work of Tomato Press consisted mainly of leaflets, business cards, stationery and occasional books, which were produced at a cheap rate with a total lack of business sense, party through the concern of the founders for the needs of their customers. [...] [It is] mainly important for the role it has played in the printing of small publications and little magazines. [Denholm 1979, 45-6, see also Whitton 1975]

Many names follow, creators of the numerous small press publications of the time. That 'total lack of business sense' of the press was, quite likely, shared by many of its customers, certainly by *Scrounge* — a business sense just didn't go with these endeavours; and probably others, like *Scrounge*, not only had no expectation of profit but might not have been able to exist without the support of its contributors, whose work was voluntary, plus maybe occasional patrons.

tried to call but couldn't get through

Over and over, collecting material for this book, I am reminded how different that era was, our early youth. The ways there were to think about communication, about finding, sharing and creating like-mindedness.

Of course, there wasn't any internet. There weren't mobile phones, for a long time there weren't even answering machines. Fax machines would appear in the 1980s. People mailed cards and notes and letters saying, 'Tried to call but couldn't get through. X tried to contact you but hasn't got through. Can you give my new phone number to Y. Your letter of November addressed to [place A] just reached me now in January at [place B]. Please confirm you've received this by ringing Lorraine on ####.' It was as if we lived in a pre-industrial time. People wrote a lot more letters. In a letter to Sasha, David Hay wrote, ' ... somewhat alarming that you can't read my writing, so here's the typewriter for the while that I can bear the loud clunking of it all.'

We must have been a lot more used to deciphering handwriting; I now find a lot of the hand-written letters in the Soldatow archives elicit an *oh no*. (Before everyone was typing, was hand-writing easier to read? You can glance at lines of typescript, even a page, and get the gist; could you ever with handwriting?) My friends and I tended to keep a few new postage stamps on hand and have a drawer full of postcards and cut-out images pasted on cards, and good notepaper, and we'd send them often in the mail to people we'd just had dinner with, to thank them, or to remind them of something, or to invite them somewhere. This practice lasted until at least the 1990s; eventually everyone succumbed to email and texts.

Strange to realise that these days people can have long intimate relationships and never have seen each other's handwriting.

When someone went overseas they almost never telephoned; it cost far too much.

There were a lot more parties.

No one would think to ask a drunken driver to surrender the wheel.

contributors also changed

There were changes too in the names cited as producing each issue of *Scrounge*. Wendy Bacon is the only person named as a contributor on all the issues. Sasha Soldatow participated in most of them, up to issue 14; only two issues more followed. The first issue also names Darcy Waters, Susan Varga and me. Neither Susan nor I can dredge up any memories of creating *Scrounge*, and neither of us appears again after the first few. (I went to live in the country, that then meant remote from all this.)

Other contributors to various issues were:

Rebecca Meier, Chris Sharp, Teresa Brennan, Liz Fell, Jenny Coopes, Jane Arms, Graham Pitts, Dave Morrisey, Gill Leahy, Brian Morrison, Dave Morrissey, Dennis del Favero, Jennie and Rennie Tomato (sometimes called the Two Tomato Technical Terrifics).

Most of these people had been involved in producing *Tharunka* or in the Victoria Street Action Group or both.

in today's terms 'curated'

Scrounge in today's terms 'curated' a selection of news — it was an aggregator of sorts. *Scrounge* provided a service for those who wanted more news than what they usually saw, and for those who might not have realised what gaps there were in available media.

There was nothing methodical in the curation of pieces for the various issues of *Scrounge*. It was not easy in those days to find news other than that reported in the main newspapers and on broadcast media. Pieces would have been chosen according to their availability and the decisions of whatever collective was putting out a particular issue.

Items range from a few lines to a few pages.

Here are just a few of the headlines or subjects of items in *Scrounge*, in pieces ranging from a single paragraph to several pages:

> Childcare. Homosexuality Bill. Abortion. Around the courts. The Rocks. Blacktown Boys High. BLF love in. Inner City Educational Alliance. Womens Studies. Marijuana Action Group. Tabloid Story (notable that the first print run of this free insert of short stories was 50,000). Blacktown Drop-In. Alternative Omega Inquiry. Censorship. Abortion — Canberra conference. Leichhardt Council. Redfern Blacks (about the unjust and vicious arrest of 'blacks' and the increasing brutality of police. Note that this was the acceptable terminology of the time for Indigenous people. This story continued over several issues). Progressive schools. Strike for women's courses at Sydney University. Squatters action groups. Darlinghurst Rd development. Film co-op in Sydney. Coming event (Tariq Ali to speak). Judicial Progress. Clitorectomy. Self-examination technique (of so-called 'cunts': actually vagina + cervix). Liberated POL? (the new glossy women's magazine tried to censor an article on infections by Wendy Bacon). Cox case: Charged with being in building without reasonable cause (an account of this case over 7 pages). Behaviour research (behaviourists).

Elsie Women's Refuge (the recent set-up of the refuge. details from a research project on hostels for destitute women). No lesbian teachers (that was when Penny Short lost her Teachers Education scholarship because she 'had not kept her homosexuality quiet'). News behind the Media (several items covered with notable dryness, no comment). Bathurst Riots: the other side of the wall (a dense three pages of three columns of text, including further (horrifying) statements about the brutality at Bathurst collected by the Prisoners Action Group). Victoria St Court Cases. 'time gentlemen' [sic] (a group of women had been refused service in a pub in Carlton on previous visits, went back to demonstrate, it got violent, arrests were made). Victoria St Court Cases (more convictions 'charged with being on [sic] a building without reasonable cause'). Woolloomooloo Action Plan (a description of plan on display ends with the comment 'it seems likely that any of the residents' 'further ideas' will only be taken into account if they conform to pre-determined economic usage').

whether or not to vote

One of the longer pieces revisits the issue of whether or not to vote, interviewing anarchists whose traditional resistance to voting might have been unsettled at this time. Some had voted who usually didn't; some never would. Further discussion followed on the election and voting. There was talk of this being a particularly important election; in 1974 the hostile elements of the Australian Parliament had forced a double dissolution. As it turned out, Gough Whitlam was re-elected again after his 1972 victory; he would last another year until the Dismissal. Then even more anarchists beginning to vote couldn't save the Whitlam government.

occasionally we will publish a viewpoint or an interpretation

Individual pieces not taken from other sources, those covering local issues, rarely had a byline and many would have been written together, in a group session, the outcome being that everyone present was the author of the piece produced.

But nobody was going to make you keep to any template or house style, not even to conform to the 'only the facts' ethos of reportage. In issue no. 3&4 June–July 1973 (a single volume) *Scrounge* declared

> While *Scrounge* is principally concerned with reportage, occasionally we will publish a viewpoint or an interpretation.

So reports or humour pieces with bylines found a home in *Scrounge*.

Scrounge no 12 (March 1974) included the item 'Unseemly Standards', a report on the arrest of Anne Summers for using the word fuck in public. That was then!

> The basis of her defence is it is not an unseemly word. ... The magistrate found the offence proved.
>
> Anne was fined $10 in default 48 hours hard labour. She has appealed.

Scrounge permitted itself a comment (conscientiously labelling it as such), opining that the putative 'offence' of 'unseemly words' is based on a fiction:

> Comment. Since there is no such thing as a community standard, and consequently no way of establishing what the 'standard' is, so long as the notion is accepted in the courts [...] whatever the evidence on actual attitudes, a magistrate will simply pluck it out of the air when they want to convict. W.B.

In the same issue, *Scrounge* inserted a 4 page pamphlet produced by the Prisoners Action Group. It was headlined: BATHURST RIOTS MADDISON LIES AGAIN A TRANSCRIPT FROM A TAPE DELIVERED TO THE PRISONERS' ACTION GROUP BY A CRIM JUST RELEASED FROM PARRAMATTA JAIL WHO WAS IN BATHURST DURING THE RIOTS.

Those riots, in reaction to inhumane conditions in the jail, were subject to violent reprisals from prison staff; this and other unrest eventually led to a royal commission and some reform. From that time, Sasha Soldatow archived a lot of material on prisons and calls for reform, and he was involved in some of the prison reform activism of the time [next chapter], which he would always cite as a great influence on his life.

Soldatow also added a Comment to a piece of three pages of three-column text, 'Bankstown interview', an interview with William de Maria, a social worker appointed as the 'Social Planner' in Bankstown, an outer suburb of Sydney. Soldatow's Comment is a pointed analysis of what has been revealed in the interview, including the uses of language that made radical thought sound like the language of power. Soldatow opines that community organisation is repressive.

> I call [de Maria's] technique Community Therapy. It aims to reproduce the power function of the family, but on a more sophisticated and much wider basis by controlling 'deviant' groups. But then, the rule of power must prevail. [SS 1974 Bankstown interview 15]

news from outside Australia/*Scrounge* found its sources

A regular section was called FOREIGN FRAGMENTS or FARAWAY FRIENDS, with news from outside Australia, including that favourite, oft-repeated (including by Sasha) story of the radical group in Uruguay, the Tupamaros, who burned down a dance hall for rich people leaving behind only the slogan *Everyone dances or no one dances.*

(One might recall Emma Goldman's defence of the value of dancing and pleasure for the revolutionary. [Shulman])

A longer than usual piece was an account of a documentary film on the Tupamaros. (The chances of anyone reading this being able to see the film were vanishingly slight. Who even imagined video on demand, streaming, torrents?)

The sources were largely other newsletters and journals. Wendy Bacon and others had already begun to exchange their own counter-culture publications with other ones in London and the US, which were posted, with stamps, via a postal service. If anyone they knew travelled overseas, they'd bring back any interesting publications.

A few overseas newspapers, magazines and journals were sold in a very few newsagents, such as the one at Kings Cross.

No one cared about copyright. Alternative publications would have been part of the ethos of 'share freely'.

Other Foreign Fragment/Faraway Friends headlines pointed to brief items on:

Community Action in NZ; Zimbabwe; May Day in Europe; Russian Pop Pirates; Squatters in Milan; New Evidence (Sacco and Vanzetti); Prison struggles in Italy; Spanish strike; London squatters; strike in France; Vermeer painting 'kidnapped' in England; the ills of pharmaceutical drugs; Women (in Libya, in Egypt); Press censorship in Israel; Three Marias (three women and publisher on trial in Lisbon for publishing 'pornographic' book); France (strikes); India (strikes); Turkey (bombing Kurds); Israel (arrests).

Similar items were headlined as being from Portugal; Dublin; England; USA.

sold copies to other friends

It is one of the appalling black holes I come to in my memory that although I was involved in the first few issues I have no memory of this, and none is prompted by looking though the collection of issues. My only memory is of somehow being the one to go on a radio talk show hosted by Anne Deveson, and being stupidly shy and failing to ensure I knew what I wanted to say and saying it. 'And where can people *scrounge* a copy from?' she smilingly asked. What did I say? Did I give a post office box address where you might send a postal note for a subscription? Tell them which pub to turn up to, to catch one of us selling it?

There was other media coverage of *Scrounge*; small as the publication was, it was mentioned in both mainstream and alternative papers.

An advertisement for *Scrounge* in *Tharunka* produced in August 1973 says it's available at the UNSW newsagency and the Third World Bookshop. And there actually were a few subscribers. But more usually *Scrounge* was distributed as all such things were distributed then, the way *Thorunka* and *Thor* were once they were 'underground' and no longer university-based and -funded publications: the people who created *Scrounge*, and their friends and associates, sold copies to other friends, and to people in pubs and other gatherings, and solicited subscriptions. The ever-sociable Sasha would have enjoyed selling copies — an opportunity to meet people, to interact, to be that memorably voluble, charming person. Covering your costs would be a nice knock-on effect if it happened. From this time on, soon after the last issue of *Scrounge*, this is the way Sasha Soldatow would distribute his Patterns pamphlets and *The Only Sensible News*; some one-off polemics, and later *What Is This Gay Community Shit?*

the sky over the port

> Don't ring cos it costs a FORTUNE [SS letter to Christos Tsiolkas from Hanoi 1.5.1997]

The telephone had a rotary dial; you didn't like phone numbers with a lot of 9s or 0s; if you had long fingernails you used a pencil. You couldn't walk with the phone further than the length of the cable connecting it to the wall plug. Getting an extension cable was amazing, you could carry the phone into the next room. Cordless receivers? Much later. A call outside your own zone was cheaper after 7pm, cheaper again later, cheaper on Sundays. On a long distance call someone would say, this call must be costing you a fortune. You could dial the operator, speak to a human, and reverse the charges. You'd have these really long talks on the phone with friends who lived in the same city. People'd be always ringing you up just to talk a while. You might pick up a ringing phone and say, X residence Y speaking (politely, or with an edge). People had signals, like, let it ring two times then hang up, I'll know it's you and come and get you. There weren't that many intercoms on apartment buildings either; people would leave hand-written notes for their visitors on their building's locked door: 'there's a phone box on the corner'. So you could tell them to come down the stairs and let you in. You had to have the coins. An operator's voice might say, if you wish to speak longer insert more coins. Later, there were phone cards for public phones. You could ring a free number to find out the time; a steady voice would say 'at the third stroke it will be ...'. If you wanted someone you just met to call you, you could say 'I'm in the book'. If you felt angry or insulted during a call you could slam the receiver down. Radio National closed down at one a.m and they'd play the national anthem.

> I called just now — out. Get a machine. [Margaret Fink postcard to SS 23.10.1989]

Soon after I got my first answering machine — it used a cassette tape to record on — in the early 1980s I ran into a friend who said, 'I've been trying to phone you but there was no answer.' 'Why didn't you leave a message?' I said. The look on his face told me he had lied about trying to phone me and didn't know I'd got a machine. People were only just starting to get them, amid the usual objections to a new technology. People, even in business, would refuse to leave a message — a voice mail as we'd say now — because they 'hated machines'.

When you answered a ringing phone you could not know who was calling. If you called someone and got a busy signal they could never know you had tried to call.

The TV would shut down at midnight and you'd get the test pattern, or the colour of the sky over the port. Australia got colour TV in 1975. You'd have to walk across the room over to the set to change channels for years ahead; remote controls were only ubiquitous later and that changed TV content.

I've been reminded of these things by threads I've come across online. That sentence would have made no sense back then.

all against prisons

Bourke Street house; Women Behind Bars; Olympics

The exciting thing about working together was the structurelessness, and I have only felt this working closely with women. [SS 1996 *Jump Cuts* 27]

his lifestyle as a poet

Sasha continued to make his new life in Sydney, expanding his network of friends. He found some who shared a spirit of playful performance, a gift for spontaneous and theatrical games.

One was Virginia Bell, known among friends for her unsurpassed droll wit. When I went to talk with her in 2018 about Those Days she had been a High Court Judge since 2009.

When she met Sasha Soldatow in about 1973 or 4 she was a law student, sharing a house with actor Pete Bensley in Edward Street, Chippendale, and Sasha was spending a lot of time with Sue Howe who lived next door. The neighbours were becoming acquainted.

Bell and Bensley had somewhere picked up a little white wooden sign which read enigmatically 'Tuesday and Thursdays between 2 and 4 By Appointment Only'. They stuck that on the front gate. One day, Barry Prothero, who would have been going to visit Sue, knocked on the front door. They hadn't met before. Bell describes him now as a wonderfully funny fellow.

> He was very formal and I was very formal. Pete and I booked him in for a few days' time, a Tuesday or Thursday, and we spent a lot of time turning the house around, creating the front room as an office, getting one of the girls from across the road to come and be our secretary, we had charts on the wall, and Barry came in, and we had this hilarious Python-esque afternoon. We didn't say what we were and he didn't enquire. I think on all sides it was viewed a very successful afternoon. [Bell interview]

Virginia Bell had planned on studying law from an early age, 13 or 14; she'd been a good debater at school. But she might have taken up an equally illustrious career in acting; she even has an item in IMDb:

Bell also had the alter-ego Ginger de Winter, the self-appointed president of the mythical NSW Barrel Girls Association; appearing as a regular guest on the 1980s nostalgia program The Golden Years Of Television. [https://www.imdb.com/name/nm10651238/bio?ref_=nm_ov_bio_sm]

After that hilarious afternoon, Barry Prothero (1945–1996), a gay activist, came to their house again, this time bringing Sasha who struck Bell then as 'just implausibly handsome, gorgeous looking'.

As Bell's household became more friendly with Sue, Sasha would also call around. Besides her law studies, Bell had a couple of jobs as well, which might be why she sounds a bit caustic looking back on Soldatow's expectations at the time, expectations that never were realistic for someone without independent means.

> He had already started doing *Patterns*, so he'd come with *Patterns*, he had no money and we had no money but he'd expect us to subsidise his lifestyle as a poet. [Bell interview]

She might not have been caustic about it at the time. There was more laughing in those days. And next thing, they were all living together.

When Bell moved out of the Chippendale house, both Sue Howe and Sasha Soldatow moved with her, and Jenny Coopes, into a house in Bourke Street in another inner-city area, Surry Hills.

none of that 'democracy' shit

Besides a devotion to amusement, the household shared political passions. Virginia Bell was one of the members of Women Behind Bars. Soldatow writes about WBB as 'a loose friendship network' he belonged to in the 1970s:

> There was a core group of about forty people, mostly women, but five or six men as well. We were all against prisons. [SS 1996 *Jump Cuts* 27]

When Wendy Bacon was convicted for 'distributing an obscene publication' in 1971, she was jailed at Mulawa Women's Prison for eight days. It was long enough for her to comprehend the extent of unfairness and cruelty experienced by imprisoned women and on her release, along with clearing up the remaining obscenity charges and continuing to defy censorship, she co-founded the group Women Behind Bars with Liz Fell and others.

Women Behind Bars was a small but effective group of prison activists campaigning in NSW in the 1970s and early 80s. They used both conventional and unconventional methods to draw attention to their campaigns, including graffiti, posters, pamphlets, occupations, demonstrations and all-night vigils. They were even prepared to be arrested and go to prison to meet their constituency. A number of their campaigns were incredibly successful, resulting in the release of people from prison and changes to the law. [Hindsight]

Soldatow's experience in anti-war and gay rights protests, of threats and actual brutality by police at Victoria Street, and his work on *Scrounge*, already indicated he'd be disposed to solidarity with groups against prisons.

In *Jump Cuts*, and elsewhere, Soldatow cites his association with the Women Behind Bars group, and how impressed and influenced he was by the way decisions and actions were carried out, the efficiency of working together without structure, saying he felt this only when working with women:

Because we were in total agreement as to our causes, we didn't need to hold meetings or have huge discussion groups about tactics, or pass motions and vote; none of that 'democracy' shit. We formed and reformed into small action teams that basically determined what they were going to do by themselves. The end point was our consensus as to what we wanted to achieve. [SS 1996 *Jump Cuts* 37]

the brutality and injustice of prison life

Ian Milliss was one of the other men associated with Women Behind Bars (WBB), and an associated group, the Prisoners Action Group (PAG), which similarly supported men prisoners.

I'm not sure you would have had to be particularly motivated or well-placed to have at least some awareness of how dreadful, and how much under official sanction, police practices were then; it was common knowledge: cops were corrupt, cops were brutal; any cop who didn't start out that way didn't last or was forced into conformity.

It was also a time of conditions of horrendous brutality generally in NSW prisons, largely unknown to the larger population. It is well remembered by people who had to think about it:

You had prisoners who were viewed as intractable where they were subjected to what was called the reception biff and that was a fully officially sanctioned procedure where on the arrival of a 'tract prisoner', as they called them, they would have to run the gauntlet of guards beating them with batons and administering really savage beatings so that people suffered permanent injuries as a result of that.

And when they exercised, if you were a tract prisoner at Grafton [Prison] you weren't allowed to raise your eyes, to look up as you walked in the exercise yard. The treatment of prisoners was appalling. [Bell interview]

And as your common sense will tell you, none of this worked to transform the imprisoned into model citizens. People who'd never been violent became violent in prison.

All of this was revealed when the Royal Commission into New South Wales Prisons, also known as the Nagle Royal Commission, was established in 1976.

Virginia Bell and her comrades in the Women Behind Bars group were concerned particularly with the rights of women prisoners and through counsel were making representations to the Royal Commission.

So I followed it closely and I'm sure Sash did too. [Bell interview]

As we've seen [previous chapter] *Scrounge* devoted space to news about prisons, including the four pages devoted to the Bathurst Prison Riots in Issue 12 1974. From that time, Soldatow archived a lot of material on prisons and calls for reform. The Commission's report was handed down in 1978 and the government responded to it at once, setting up the Corrective Services Commission (1979–81), appointing Tony Vinson, a social worker from UNSW, as Commissioner.

And this made quite a difference, to an extent that might not have been predicted:

That was a remarkable change in style from the top. I remember as a solicitor going to meet clients in Grafton, after the change and after Vinson was Commissioner, and it is amazing how a change at the top can affect the culture. Some police officers who were notorious for their deeds in the bad old days were still working at Grafton when it was no longer handling prisoners who were intractable and I found it confronting to meet people I had known were associated with administering these appalling beatings to [prisoners], and were now behaving perfectly reasonably. You just see institutionally the importance of moral leadership from the top. It was quite confronting, interesting, surprising. [Bell interview]

Women Behind Bars was part of a lot of activism at the time, says Virginia

Bell, and two things were driving it. One was the concern about the conditions of prison and the appalling conduct revealed at the Nagle Royal Commission; it was officially sanctioned, that's what shocked people. And the other was, this was a time when police were inclined to verbal people and there were terrible scandals associated with the police. [Bell interview]

Verballing was the fabrication by police of damaging confessions by suspects, and the technique was widespread. A police officer's word was taken to have more value than that of anyone who'd been arrested or detained. It was widely known that police could make up anything they cared to and it would be admissible and privileged evidence. Years later when Bell came to be counsel assisting the Wood Royal Commission [1995-7] into the police there were still problems but none like those when she'd been a young solicitor. [Bell interview]

Ian Milliss recalls that the Corrective Services Commission was deliberately undermined by the Public Services Association, which was the prison warders union. Eventually Vinson was forced out, after endless newspaper stories about prisoners' escapes.

> The screws used to just let people escape to create bad publicity. Vinson was pushed out so the single worst prison warder of all was made head. [Milliss interview]

Wikipedia: The Government backed the union in the dispute, and Vinson retired to academia. The tenure of his replacement, Vern Dalton, was memorable for a corruption scandal that saw the Minister for Corrections, Rex Jackson, sentenced to ten years' jail for corruption. https://en.wikipedia.org/wiki/Corrective_Services_New_South_Wales#Post-Nagle_Royal_Commission_(1978%E2%80%932009)

essential to act for freedom and justice

Activists like Sasha Soldatow were not inclined to respect lawfulness, under the circumstances. Whether it was publishing censored materials, demonstrating against injustice and corruption, occupying condemned houses to save them, exposing prison conditions, or agitating for prisoners' rights, it was essential to act for freedom and justice even if — especially if! — that could mean acting outside of legal constraints. When there was so much to despise in the way the law was carried out — 'justice is just arse' was one slogan splashed in publications and on walls — when so many laws were ridiculous, unreasonable, unjustifiable, if you indulged in activities you knew were good but were against the law (reading banned books, smoking cannabis, homosexuality), then you might be inclined to see all prisoners as victims.

Soldatow like others in the movement was inclined to sympathy for prisoners, any or all of whom were likely to be treated worse than anyone ever should be.

In 1978 notorious criminal Ray Denning became the only man to escape Grafton Jail. Sasha Soldatow was one of a group of people who through their activism got to know Denning, assisting him to hide and survive.

A 1979 piece by Denning, a poem of several pages in short lines, is among Soldatow's papers. Soldatow read it out on the new radio program *GayWaves*.

> *GayWaves* was Sydney's first regularly broadcast gay and lesbian radio program and was considered groundbreaking when it went to air in November 1979, a month after 2SER started broadcasting and a time when male homosexual behaviour was still criminalised in seven out of eight States and territories. The independence of community radio allowed those voices that were often absent from the mainstream media to be heard regularly for the first time. [Arneil]

One of the people involved in setting up *GayWaves* was poet Amanda Stewart who was also, with Sasha, Pam Brown and others, one of the people involved in poetry readings in the 70s and 80s [chapter 18]; later, in 1988, Stewart produced Soldatow's ABC radio program on Harry Hooton. [chapter 23] Not many people had radio skills back then; Amanda Stewart was one of the students from UTS in those early days who were crucial to the station and to its radical charter.

> Some of us had been involved in helping put together the broadcasting licence application for 2SER FM in the preceding year or so and, from memory, it was put into the station's founding documents that the station had to facilitate a free gay programme, women's programme, a current affairs and also a writers' programme, requirements which hopefully still stand to this day. I remember at one point one station manager tried to change this but was unsuccessful. [Amanda Stewart email 2.9.2019]

Although Denning's poem has no gay content, being a précis of the events of his life, *GayWaves*' inclusion of it was a concession that as long as homosexuality was illegal, gay culture should be in solidarity with other outlaws. Soldatow annotates his copy of the poem 'broadcast in Gay Waves which was a battle I won to deal with issues not only to do with homosexuality — i.e. a support of prisoners during (I can't remember) a screws strike?'

why anyone does the things they do

Ray Denning was recaptured in 1980. In Grafton Jail he wrote his *Prison Diaries*, which was published in 1982 and revealed his and others' experience of verballing and violent abuses.

Soldatow kept up his connection to Denning, and would continue to write to him while Denning was imprisoned.

> Hope you're as well as can be.
> Sorry about the silence.
> The short meeting made us friends — prison is a harsh place to communicate in.
> If I don't see you in person soon, I'll write.
> Much love and solidarity.
> If you need anything — tell me, okay?
> [SS carbon of hand-written letter 1.10.1982]

Denning once more escaped in 1988, and after the next recapture became an informer and thereby one of the most despised men in the prison system, most emphatically by other prisoners who had a deep contempt for informers. [See also Reasonable Grounds 2011]

Writing about a three-months writer's residency he held at Long Bay Jail in 1990, where he was not granted access to his 'old friend' Denning in the special protection unit, Soldatow says

> Ray had turned dog, prison slang for someone who's become an informer. Who knows why anyone does the things they do? After most of his life in jail, Ray probably just wanted out. He got it — dead of a heroin overdose in Glebe. Self-administered was the coroner's decision. Yet there are puzzling questions. He shot up in a pub, walked home opened the front door with his key and went inside. This is no simple OD. A hot shot? We'll never know. [SS 1996 *Jump Cuts* 78]

we Brauned Sasha's letters

Jenny Coopes had provided many cartoons and illustrations for *Tharunka* and *Thor*. When she moved into the Bourke Street house in 1975, she was already contributing to several newspapers, at the time the only woman cartoonist in Australian newspapers, and would begin working for the *National Times* in 1977. She would provide illustrations for Soldatow's 1980 *Olympics* book, and later for Sasha's *What Is This Gay Community Shit?* Coopes met me for coffee in Darlinghurst in 2018 to try to dig up some memories. (Curiously enough, she was now formally studying art at the National Art School.)

She remembers that Sasha moved a piano into the Bourke Street house, which turned out to be not a simple matter, and led to some fresh artistic improvisation, when the removalists got the piano half way in...

> ...then started shoving in the front door and knocked the door off. The front door. Luckily we got the piano fixed but we didn't have a front door. So we got a piece of canvas and did a very good replica of a door that hung there till we got someone in — there was nothing to steal apart from a piano and who'd want it? Sasha used to play a bit, he'd delude himself that he was musical. [Coopes interview]

Coopes is possibly a bit snide here — though they had good times in that house, Sasha eventually exasperated and even alienated his housemates. If there's one thing people who know music and knew Sasha usually agree on, he really was musical.

Virginia Bell also recollected the incident of the piano and the door, and other Sasha-related vexations:

> Pete Bensley came and painted a door on canvas. And it's surprising you can have a canvas front door and no one does come in.
>
> It was in the Bourke Street house that we Brauned Sasha's letters in exasperation with him. [Bell interview]

She didn't say they *burned* them.

> No, we Braun-ed them. None of us had much in the way of money. Sash was insistent on getting good quality things. He was in a phase of believing it was good to have carrot juice or some shit like that, so he went off and bought a Braun, an electric juicer, and for us at that time it was a costly ridiculous thing to buy. And he was behind in the rent. So that just sort of drove us crazy. And then he must have been away and [there were] letters from someone with whom he was corresponding, he always was very conscious of keeping things, he always had a sense that someone would be writing a book about him, so we knew these letters would be important to him because it was some equally full of himself bloke who was living in New York and thought he would be a writer. So we took the letters and put them through the Braun. [Laughs] I remember that quite vividly. I think we stuffed the Braun and we lost the letters. Sasha was pretty good, he understood. He was out to provoke but he didn't really mind being [provoked]. [Bell interview]

Another memory from the Bourke Street days has to do with Russian Easter — Sasha for a long time after leaving his family environment in Melbourne continued to invite friends to join him in this observance. On this occasion it almost turned into a disaster. It was Russian Easter and Sasha cooked up a storm, an enormous feast, and then took them all to the Russian cathedral, probably for the midnight service. The others got back home before Sasha, to discover that Bell's dog Katy had eaten a lot of the food that had all been carefully laid out.

> So we got a curtain, which may well have been the old door. The table and all had been set and we didn't want him to see it. So we hung something, and we got some vodka, and set out the few little things that were left.
>
> Sash came home with someone, and we plied him with vodka before we let him see. He was very forgiving about that. [Bell interview]

dedicated to all those people in jail

One amusement shared by the household was watching the 1976 Montreal Olympics on television. Sasha might have initiated this pursuit; it would turn out to provide invaluable material.

> We'd put the scores on the wall. Sash was obsessed with the Olympics, so that was the start of him actually writing a serious book about it. It was all a big joke. We had a bank of televisions, one on top of the other and they were constantly on the Montreal Olympics. [Bell interview]

Watching TV was not commonly what People Like Us did in those days, or so I'd thought. It seemed hilarious, or maybe just strikingly eccentric, when I used to go round there, the way the household observed the practice of television watching. (Popular culture was not yet an academic study.) They were familiar with commercials, soaps, and television celebrities, then once they began it was just the Olympics on all the time. And this household would not have been passive viewers, oh no, everything was an invitation to comment, to enquire or mock or applaud or oppose.

At the same time they were also always concerned with questions of justice and their activism on its behalf.

And so Sasha's dedication in his book on the Olympics does not allow you to forget the incarcerated:

> This book is dedicated to all those people in jail
> who spend their time running fifteen

> to thirty kilometres a day in their cells,
> who exercise their bodies, train their muscles and
> prepare themselves for the moment when they can escape:
> the only worthwhile and ideologically sound form of sport.

Soldatow's *Politics of the Olympics* was published in 1980.

The Acknowledgments page begins with thanks to his housemates, saying the stimulus for the book came from discussions while watching the Olympic Games on television with Virginia Bell, Jenny Coopes, Sue Howe, Larry Strange. (It was while Sasha lived at Bourke Street that he met Larry Strange [chapter 16]) Coopes also provided cover and interior illustrations.

In the biographical note, Soldatow says that he had attended the 1956 Olympics (they were held in Melbourne; he would have been eight years old) and that his father 'was one of the 3000 athletes who carried the Olympic flame from Athens to Berlin in 1936' — a historically-charged moment with the Nazis newly in power. Less known: 1936 was the first time the Games was televised, however minimally then. Soldatow's claim to a longtime awareness of the Games brings to it his study of history and his education in politics. And his alertness to cultural mythologising.

> What is this 'spirit of the Olympics' that refuses to die, haunting the next four years as it has done since 1896? 'We have only the strength of a great ideal,' said Brundage [president of the International Olympic Committee]. But what is this *ideal*, from where does it derive its strength, and is it the movement's true foundation, the anchor which holds it firm?
>
> If it is, it is a flimsy base. For the ideal is beginning to reveal itself as a hopeless jumble of cliches. [SS 1980 *Politics of the Olympics*]

Soldatow's book is a deconstruction of all the usually uncontested myths about the Olympics, especially more so then — their origins, their traditions, their peace-making, the flame — and the insupportable claim that sports should have nothing to do with politics. Soldatow's well-researched work is convincing, based on the irrefutable declaration that '...politics, rather than being an unfortunate intrusion, has always been an integral part of the Olympic Games'. Discussions of those politics, key events, people and controversies are explored in a vigorous, clear voice, both conversational and authoritative.

Curiously, the book didn't seem to mean much to him in later years, in spite of the mania shared with his housemates for watching the 1976 Montreal Olympics in the Bourke Street house, or the amount of work evidently undertaken to produce it. When the Olympic Games were scheduled to take place in Sydney in 2000, people were saying it would be a great time to republish this book but Sasha seemed to have zero interest in this. He added its title to his biographies; it was counted among his book publications; otherwise he barely mentioned it.

In 1982, *Politics of the Olympics* was remaindered. It's a hard book to find these days, but well worth revisiting.

it had helped to form him

Women Behind Bars not only played a role in the Nagle Royal Commission; it ran a number of successful campaigns to release women who had killed violent husbands, whose defence of provocation or self-defence had not been seriously considered. Cases like those of Violet Roberts, who had killed her husband after many years of severe abuse by him, made a lot of people consider the extent of domestic abuse, and how biased the law could be in the way 'self-defence' was understood. Soldatow kept newspaper cuttings and other materials related to this in folders labeled 'biographical material'. His involvement in the prisoners' action groups might have been marginal to some of the principal activists, but he would always declare it had helped to form him.

day leave from the jail

Sasha's interest in prisons made him an eager candidate for a program run by an old friend, the artist Loma Bridge, who worked as an educator at Long Bay prison, and managed to place other writers and artists there. Sasha turned up for his Residency there most days for three months in mid 1990.

Although not allowed to see his 'old friend' Ray Denning, he met and befriended other prisoners.

On Christmas Eve in 1990 Sasha was at a party at the house Pam Brown shared with her partner Jane Zemiro in Camperdown; it went on 'until all hours' and Sasha and his partner Bruce [see photograph, following page] stayed the night in the spare room. Bruce was going to his family the next day; Sasha staying on for the Christmas Day lunch. He hadn't mentioned until now that he'd invited someone else.

At around 3 a.m. Pam, Jane and Sasha were cleaning up in the kitchen and Sasha told them he'd invited a prisoner from Long Bay Jail to Christmas lunch with them and Jane's daughter.

They were a bit shocked, Pam told me: what kind of person could this prisoner be, a thief, a murderer, someone disruptive, violent, what?

Turned out he was a lovely young Italian man who played the piano really well.

He was on day leave from the jail.

Jane was cooking risotto for lunch & the jailbird was very sweet & sentimental about his Italian mother & he also played Jane's piano for us several times during the day. [Brown email 28.8.2020]

10

out for a bop

parties, fun, our golden age 1970s

I was going to tell you about how I once went to 21 parties in 20 days, but it's all a bit of a haze. [SS 1992 *Outrage*]

a lot of parties with Sasha

In those days, you'd expect to go to at least one party every weekend, often more than one in a night. I went to a lot of parties with Sasha, some that other people remember more than I do. One of my few memories from the earliest times with Sasha is of a party.

It was the early 70s, soon after we first met. I have the feeling we were already well known to each other. I was in a small group, maybe we all came in one car. In those days you considered yourself invited to a party if you ran into people who knew where it was on. A large house, lots of people, not all people we all knew.

We noticed a girl — 20s, I guess, like we were — dancing, alone, dancing really well, with a quirky, confident style, dressed, as I think of it now, in a more Melbourne way, stylish in a self-made only-me street way.

Sasha said, hold this, pulling out his wallet and keys and whatever else might have been heavy in his pocket and dropped it in someone's lap, mine it must have been, as he skipped to the dance floor to bop along right in front of her, and they faced each other, two really good dancers dancing. And that was Sasha, confident, talented, and what's that something else where he assumes the right. He went to dance, you could hold his stuff. He didn't need for there to be more people dancing before he'd get up. He was very watchable.

He was also very watchable at the poetry readings. Later in the 70s, Sasha began performing at readings around town, and his readings were the most theatrical of all the poets. Some people had moved to Sydney especially for its vibrant poetry scene. [more in chapter 15] There were a lot of readings, held in pubs or at large houses — notably one by the Harbour at Balmain, with a large amphitheatre-like lawn between the house and the water's edge. Things could get raucous, the poets were known for it. On one occasion Sasha took off all his clothes and read to everyone in nonchalant nakedness.

smashes bottles on the road after a party

The parties after the pub or a reading were often at those big houses people could rent cheaply then, where the music might get louder than the talking, where you drank some more after coming from drinking, where people might be passing round joints out in the yard.

I might not have known, but there didn't seem to be all that much other social drug use in those days; there were pills, I did not know who took what pills, speed, 'mandrax'; a sense that some people must have been into pharmaceuticals but not in a party way but then again, that story Sasha often told, about smashing bottles on the road.

'To think I've become the kind of girl who smashes bottles on the road after a party,' Sasha would remember me saying after another party; he would repeat this, it was in his repertoire of faithful remembrances, part of the myth we make of each other. He was repeating it the last time I saw him, in the early 2000s.

As Sasha tells it in the Memoir section of the *Rock-n-Roll Sally* edition published in 1990, the party was the night after he posed for photographer Brett Hilder in 1977, posing naked on red sheets in the famous Marilyn Monroe calendar pose; this picture would go on the posters for the show, and be resurrected for display over the years. (In 2020, the poster was featured on a panel, one of eight, in an exhibition called 'Yesterday's Heroes' as part of that year's Mardi Gras festival in Sydney.)

> That night Inez and I went to Steve J. Spears party in Surry Hills where the contents of many medicine cabinets had been tossed into the punch. The day ended much later sitting in the gutter throwing many empty bottles across the road. Inez said, 'To think I've become ...' [SS 1990 'Memoir' *Rock-n-Roll Sally*]

Darlinghurst, not Surry Hills, I thought, and just that house's medicine cabinet — which, it was understood, would include a stash of uppers and downers and various things with side effects — but 'many medicine cabinets' fits the hyperbolic mood. In my mind the scene is of us affecting something affectless in our stupid petty vandalism but he says crying and crying was easy then so it might have been like this:

I can't remember if we were crying with laughter or laughing to stop from crying. 'We've become all kinds of person since then,' says Inez. [SS 1990 'Memoir' *Rock-n-Roll Sally*]

things started getting separated

Another party story we'd remember from that era was the night we drove from one end of Sydney to the other — well, from inner east to inner west — and couldn't get into the parties we turned up for.

> One night Inez and I go to Vanities for a bop. 'Sorry' says the guy on the door. 'Can't go in. [...] We don't let heterosexual couples in.'
> My friend protests. Pointing to me she exclaims: 'But he's a poof!'
> I nod in agreement.
> 'That's what they all say' retorts the guy coolly.
> [SS 1978 *Anarchist Honi Soit*]

The story continues with the two of us going over to Balmain but at the party there the woman at the door refuses him entry because it was for women only. The story ends

> 'It's not fair', she finally said. 'But then, what is.'

Research for this book does not so much agitate memory as create material to displace it.

It was a story about how things started getting separated, Women's Spaces and Gay Men's Spaces.

And of course the exclusionary policies did have a point and purpose at the time but that didn't stop them from being exclusionary and absurd and so to be mocked. Why did you have to be only one or the other?

It was a story about how Sasha and I were forced to see over and over again that while there was sometimes an alliance between women and gay men, there was also a division. This was a long time before Fluidity, Intersectionality and other developments.

a golden age side to our life

'Here we are in Sydney, and over there, just over the Pacific, is the West Coast. [...]

I'm with a friend who says:

'It's true, you know. It's like LA. The streets smell of sex.' [SS 1978 Anarchist Honi Soit]

We'd go out for a bop — apparently that's what we called it — quite often and usually got in where we wanted to. We bopped at parties and 'dances' held in suburban town halls, sometimes to raise money, for example for the Womens Refuge.

There is this myth of the 1970s as a kind of 'golden age' for those who lived in Sydney, young and healthy and hedonistic, and I know there are many reasonable demurrals and debunks but there was a golden age side to our life and not only looking back, we said we were in one at the time.

Especially gay men.

And people who loved gay men.

And as the 1970s moved along with new young adults arriving at the good times, the goldenness got shinier.

There's nothing like the intensity of that time of life, to be in your twenties or thereabouts. In the 1970s Sydney felt like the best city to be in — sure: you kind of wanted to be in New York (it seemed to be The Source of everything currently interesting at the time) but in Sydney the nights were warm and you were never far from the streets where there was always something open very late — we had all-night restaurants and bars and nightclubs in Kings Cross; never far from the glittering Harbour, or from beaches that reached across the Pacific — a bond, a distance — to the country providing inspiration for most of our popular culture, counter-culture and radical politics, just as the political overclass was strengthening its alliance with the USA (Australia was pretending to be less of a British colony).

It was an era of newness and renewal, as Labor Party leader Gough Whitlam's popularity rose. The slogan and campaign promise 'It's Time!' was sung by a televised chorus of famous folk and he was voted in as Prime Minister in 1972; sweeping reforms were carried out and everything was going to get better forever.

It was in effect still the 1960s, a time of nearly full employment, when you could drop out for a while and then get a job when you wanted one. Live comfortably on part-time work. The end of military conscription, the introduction of free education, free medicare, these were just some of the changes brought in by the Whitlam era.

Not an era, though, after all, but a short-lived sense that parliamentary politics had arrived at enlightenment and openness and would never leave. After 1975 (the Dismissal) there was still for a while the righteous sense that reformist government would be returned, only better; there'd be liberation movements for anarchists and law reform for anarcho-syndicalists.

keep on dancing

It turned out it was never going to be that way.

The Dismissal in 1975 caused disillusionment and anger in some, a confirmation of their realism in others; it coloured the sense of the post-Whitlam era as one where you had better not lose your distrust of power.

So what to do about it? Keep on dancing.

I was convinced the moment it was a possible idea that those of us going to the nightclubs were also being political.

Historians are arguing for serious consideration of the liberating dimensions of nightclubs:

> Wotherspoon and other historians have argued that gay-libber activists were aware at the time of the limited appeal their consciousness-raising meetings had in comparison with the physical and erotic liberation thousands of gay men expressed on Friday and Saturday nights and identities they fashioned in bed, at beats, and on the dance floors of gay clubs and bars. [Robinson 2014]

Also the physical and erotic liberation of the few women who also loved to dance at gay clubs and bars, which welcomed them then.

It was the most fun being political could ever be.

The adventures o

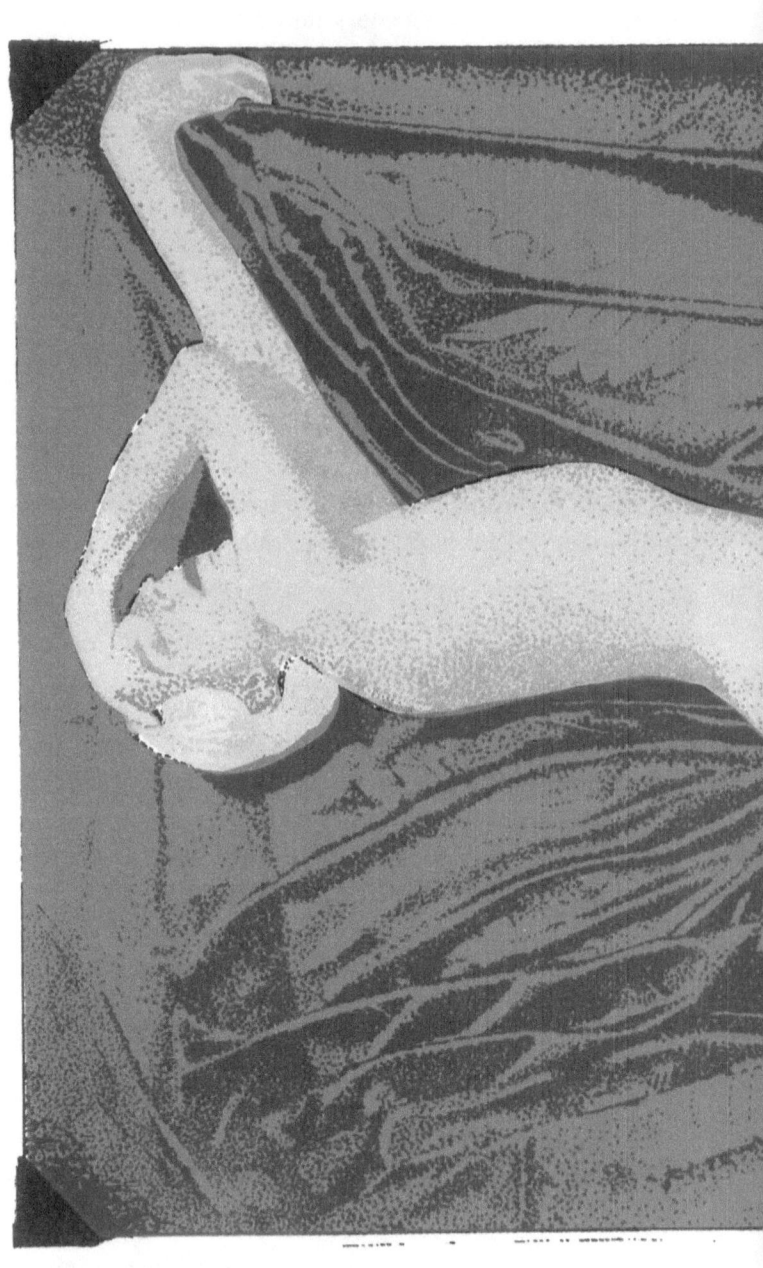

Sheds, 9-30p.m.

Rock-n-Roll Sally

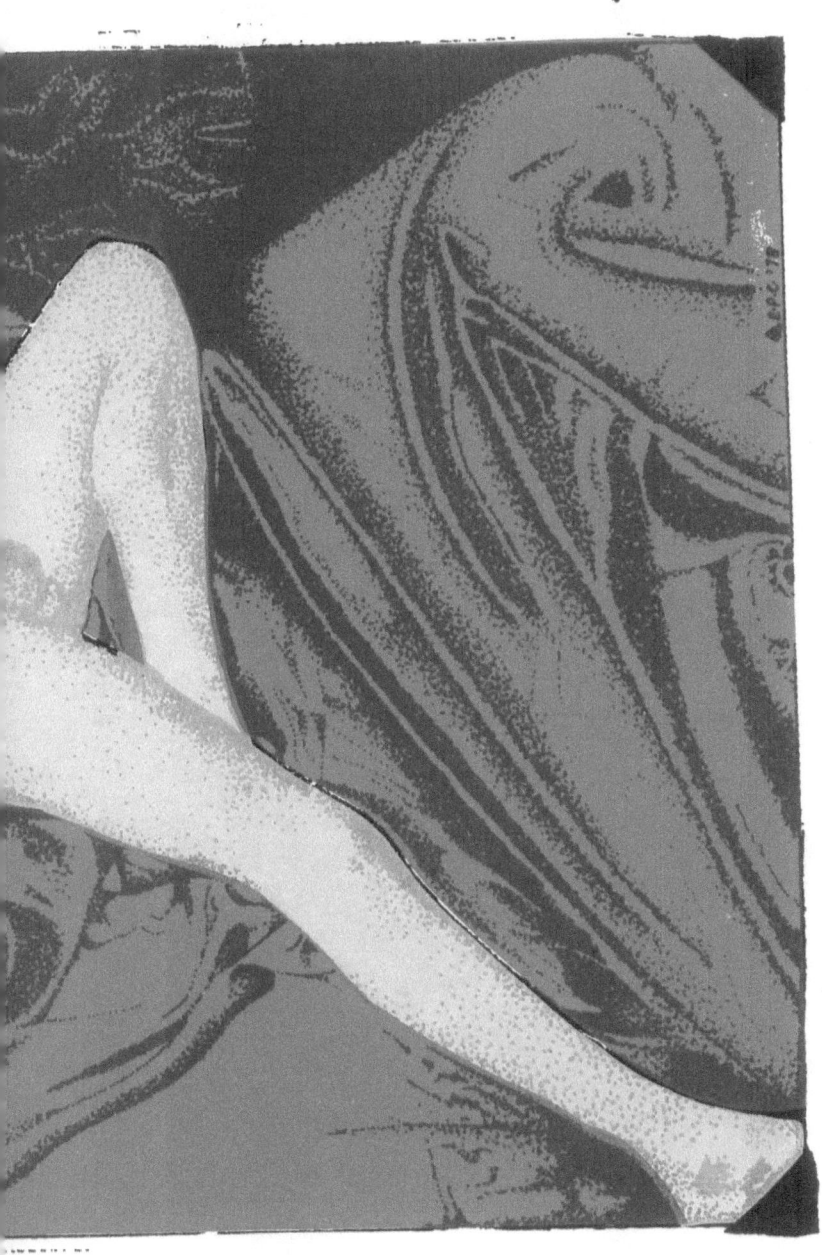

Tues 17th January

Sasha wasn't into the disco and bar scene

Sasha wasn't into the disco and bar scene, Denis Gallagher and Tim Herbert said when I talked to them about *What Is This Gay Community Shit?* which came out in 1983. [chapter 4]

No, he wasn't among the friends I'd usually go with and run into in the discos and drag clubs. Sometimes he'd go, though; doesn't seem like he went straight to the dance floor; he was alertly deconstructing his perceptions:

> We walk into Patches this guy and I. It's dark with disco music blaring and beating away.
>
> The room is full of guys smoking, drinking, watching, waiting. Moustaches are in this season: never trust a man with a moustache.
>
> The place feels slightly edgy and old-fashioned.
>
> 'This feels like where the 1960s love generation finished' I say to David.
>
> Just then the disc jockey changes the record. It's a disco version of Macarthur Park. We look at each other with I-know-what-you-mean type of respect. Boy, have we lived through it. [SS 1978 *Anarchist Honi Soit*]

I remember we'd amuse each other by naming bits of music they should make disco versions of.

As the 1970s burned out and the next decade with its new darkness loomed, Sasha's theatre of pleasure increasingly involved the politics and practice of underground publishing and poetry.

11
agitpoetry

Patterns 1974–1976

Or didn't you know/That I sit in my room-house/Disturbed for days on end [SS 1974 *Patterns no. one*]

total control

The activism of underground writing and publishing in some ways continued with *Patterns*, but it was not intended as *Scrounge* had been to provide information, and in this case, Soldatow produced the series himself. He had total control over its design, contents and initial distribution.

Patterns contained imaginative, personal writings of a kind no existing publications had space for.

Patterns took the form of pamphlets. The word pamphlet might suggest something you toss in the bin after the demonstration or concert or monument where you acquired it, or it might be something to leave around at home until it was no more through natural causes.

But these are printed on thick good-quality paper; these are pamphlets meant for keeping.

The six publications in this series provide a sample of Soldatow's early writing, its range and boldness, and of his design sense; several of the texts would be included in later book publication.

If you stay with this chapter, I'll tell you more about the contents and some details of each one.

credit to Tomato Press

Sasha Soldatow's *Patterns* series of pamphlets gives credit, from issue number two, to Tomato Press for the printing. (Number one has no credits.)

As noted in chapter 8, Tomato Press was a significant enterprise in that era of independent printing, often called 'underground' printing for its definite apartness from what would be called mainstream media, and for its willingness to produce materials that defied conventions of reporting, writing or illustrating, and materials that were otherwise censored by authority, convention or timidity.

And the press had an ethos that Soldatow and others appreciated:

> Perhaps the most important aspect of Tomato Press is people. This is not to say that printing takes second place, but that the commercial aspect of the business has always been subject to the needs and involvement of its customers. This is the essential difference between Tomato and the average small-case printing concern. [Whitton 24]

your reality and existence are denied

The first pamphlet in the *Patterns* series is dated 3 June 1974. It was called *patterns no. one*, indicating the intention of a series; its all-caps title AGITPOETRY a reference to Mayakovsky's 'agit poems'. Printed on both sides of a single sheet of blue paper, it is folded to make four pages, the title page plus three pages covered in text, set out like a poem with broken lines.

It starts:

> Tonight I heard Phyllis Chesler who wrote *Women & Madness* [...] on the radio.

Soldatow goes on to say he found Chesler's 1972 book, a feminist classic, 'difficult to read', quoting a couple of troubling passages about male homosexuals and male homosexuality, one of them including

> ...I must suggest that male homosexuality in patriarchal society, is a basic and extreme expression of phallus worship, misogyny, and the colonisation of certain female and/or 'feminine' functions [Chesler quoted in SS *Patterns no. one*]

Soldatow goes on to say that he could not finish reading a book

> That ridiculed my living
> That hated me so much
> For things attributed to me.

The poem is a confession or revelation of the disturbed feelings sparked by the radio interview.

> I couldn't listen any longer.
> My feelings fought my senses

And my feelings won.

Soldatow goes on to write of the anguish he experiences in some social situations (where you might expect like-mindedness and understanding) and when trying to write out of that; using words like conflict, pain, desperation, stress, conveying a sense of how hard it is to write when your reality and existence are denied or wrongly characterised, leaving no achievements to show.

Instead I write:
Feminists can be poofter-bashers too.

The piece concludes with the bitter remark

Every time I fall in love with a guy
I perform a travesty on what is called
A relationship.

Patterns no. one would be included in Soldatow's first book, the prose collection *Private — Do Not Open* (1987), set out in paragraphs of prose rather than the broken lines.

quite different territory

The title of *patterns no. two* is 'For Lou Reed without permission'; it's dated September 1974.

Patterns no. two is printed on yellow paper, of a larger size, folded to make four pages: a title page, the poem on the third page, and the second page and back cover with pen-and-ink illustrations, highly stylised heads, by Soldatow.

In very small print, above the credit to Tomato Press, a line reads

Patterns is an irregular publication. Subscription, $1 for five issues.

One dollar bought you five coffees at Sweethearts café then.

Not only the pamphlet's design but its text goes into quite different territory from *pattern no. one*; it starts:

He wanted to be anointed. He wanted to be sainted.
He wanted to have it good, both ways.
He wanted to lie down in green pastures,
Be trodden on by hobnail pricks as hard as bricks.
He wanted to lick the man who pushed him to the brink.

Reed's influence can be found in some of the rhythms, some of the punk imagery of damaged people, in half-quoted lines:

> 'Who is to feel (wham) what I feel.
> Through the something-or-other-of hate.
> Is it too late to get it straight?'

I remember two Lou Reed concerts, the second one revealing an amazing physical transformation, after Reed's *Transformer* album (1972) mentioned in Soldatow's poem. I took acid for that one; Sasha didn't; he wanted to soberly analyse the performance afterwards but my tripping little crew laughed at the possibility and went back to a house to play music loudly the rest of the night.

The concert ticket (showing Tuesday 13 August but not the year; it was 1974), and Soldatow's idiosyncratic review of it, was published in his *Rock-n-Roll Sally* (Blackwattle Press 1990) ending with the odd words:

> A stunning performance. Except he pitches his products into disturbing areas. He just denies that everything's okay. That life's got no problems. He denies that everything's okay. [SS 'Inverse Reverse and Perverse Lou Reed in Concert' in 1977 *Rock-n-roll Sally*]

The volume contains the suite of poems Soldatow had often performed by then, which owed a great deal to Reed in tone and tropes. Also the name Sally. First performed in 1976, there were several more of Soldatow's electrifying performances of *Rock-n-Roll Sally* into the 80s: more on that later. [chapter 18]

playful perversions

Patterns no. three is printed on pale grey paper, again one sheet folded; its date appears as 6.1.74 and the difference this time is signalled on the title page:

Poetr. Mark Young
Illustr. Sasha Soldatow

The front cover includes besides the series title and credits another stylised head illustration, and the whole back cover is Soldatow's drawing of a man behind a horned animal, with a suggestion of sexual congress.

The two inside pages bear the title 'A Season in Hell' and Young's exuberant poem, not only its title but its content being homage to, emulation of, Rimbaud, and playful perversions.

The poem, which later appeared in the anthology *Big Smoke: New Zealand Poems, 1960–1975* (Young 2000), can be found online.

intensely personal and somewhat tortured

Patterns no. four and *no. five* have a similar design to one: back to the smaller size paper, and containing text only.

Patterns no. four, on pale yellow paper, its title inside 'VIRGINIA WOOLF for Brian', is dated November 1974.

Though set out in paragraphs, many forward slash marks indicate possible line breaks. The poetic prose is impressionistic, its tone intimate and wounded; it's about writing itself, its practice entwined with an experience of an indistinct, disappointing 'you':

> I started rhyming. But my cadences could not stand up under pressure of grammar fractured. They broke. I hated most your friends [sic]. They were black holes of the n-th dimension — you slide easily into their spaces. And we were never parallel.
>
> You had me as a vacation. [...]
>
> My important actions were meaningless to your presence.

The title of *patterns no. five*, is WITHDRAWAL. It's the same size, on buff paper, containing dense paragraphs of prose divided into sections (i) to (iii), and is dated March 1975.

Like *patterns no. one* it appears in the 'Writing It Down' chapter in *Private — Do Not Open* [pp75-78], with small alterations. The tone is intensely personal and somewhat tortured.

Part (i) contains lines which seem to be about the very process of producing this work:

> A search for something that would give me no desire or dread. I worked on it, called it my soliloquy, wrote it quickly, sped with the machine that was typing my thoughts, translating my expressions.

The piece records dream states, dream images, mysterious disembodied voices translating uneasy experience of places potent with presence, attempts to express the ineffable, and concludes with an italicised paragraph that starts and ends thus:

> Death is the natural extension of everything: the end-point at which you are barred away: the finish. But death is so vast. Can we not condense this vastness into an activity [...]
>
> All doomed. All destined to die away from one another. Everyone pushed into closing away.

That final paragraph is eliminated in *Private — Do Not Open* and the piece ends:

When I awoke I felt as if I knew something. [p78]

What it was that he now knew, he does not say.

tender affection

Patterns no. six is on yellow paper; a single leaf folded to four pages; its front says only 'patterns number six sasha soldatow', its back only the credit to Tomato Press. Inside, the left page is covered with an ink drawing of a man's head, and the right with a poem in 24 short lines; its title is 'specifically for dave'; at the end the date written 'Feb '76'. The lines are addressed in an intimate tone to a man to whom the narrating voice (Sasha's) expresses tender affection, a recognition of his heterosexuality, an admission of desire, and the last lines:

I am as afraid
Of your sex
As you are of mine.

An undated card from a friend, Suzi Roux, who had recently moved away from Sydney, compliments Sasha on his *patterns* series, especially number six which:

shows your compassion and love

and she ends:

miss your sense of fun and delight in life

12

who do you ring at three in the morning?

Margaret Fink

My friend Margaret shocked me one day, years ago, by saying, 'Friends are there to be used.' It worried me, this gesture which appeared on the surface to be clothed by indifference. But then, who do you ring at three o'clock in the morning when you need someone, the police? [SS 1996 *Jump Cuts* 31]

how much she missed Sasha

After that first lunch date, and Sasha's uncomplaining wait at the restaurant, which Margaret Fink never forgot, their friendship flourished.

Margaret is one of a small number of people who I needed to agree to this biography project before I'd go ahead. Whenever I spoke to her after that she would express her love and respect for Soldatow — what an extraordinary person, what a remarkable person, how special he was, how, even if others didn't see it, everything he did had a serious purpose.

Several people, as I began to research this book, mentioned how often Margaret had just been talking about Sasha, how much she missed Sasha.

the importance and value of Hooton

Margaret called Sasha 'instinctively Push' [chapter 3] and she was considered by others as part of the original Sydney Push. As a young woman Margaret had lived with the poet Harry Hooton, who she always said was the love of her life, and a genius. She told journalist Nikki Barrowclough that she and Hooton, while they had friends from the Push, never defined themselves as Push, although others did. They led a 'very minimalist life' owning little. Hooton did occasional menial work; she taught art and sewed clothes for friends.

> It was the most felicitous life. I've never been happier. Harry had so much grace. The artist's way is the only way of living because you are not restricted by convention or finance. [quoted in Barrowclough 2004]

Many years later she introduced Sasha Soldatow to Hooton's work and Soldatow soon formed the ambition to write Hooton's biography.

Hooton became a lifelong obsession. Soldatow continued occasionally to work on, and never give up the idea of, writing a biography of Hooton. He would publish a selection of Hooton's poems in 1990. [chapter 23] It includes a scholarly introduction that Margaret says is Soldatow's best work.

Their concordance over the importance and value of Hooton was one instance of the large degree of like-mindedness the two found in each other.

personal notes, cards, cuttings and invitations

After Hooton's death Margaret married Leon Fink, a wealthy property developer. They later divorced but remained friends. She was living with their three children in a glamorous house in Woollahra at the time she formed her friendship with Sasha.

Evidence of their closeness is in the many personal notes, cards, cuttings and invitations Margaret sent to Sasha over the years and decades in her distinctive, elegant handwriting.

Soldatow in turn sent quirky notes to Fink throughout his life, offerings of unusual words (sphairistic), odd facts (identical twins don't have identical fingerprints), notable quotations, an opinion of a writer or film.

He also kept many cuttings of stories and profiles about Fink: she was a frequent subject of many colour magazines, from the kind of gossip magazines you'd find at the supermarket checkout to the more toney supplements in the broadsheet newspapers, as well as glossy publications of fashion and culture.

In the 1970s, Margaret Fink was becoming a well-known producer of independent films, always insisting she was a creative producer, closely involved in script development and casting and art direction and the director's work. Someone else's work was to be the line producer, dealing with the nitty gritty of schedules, daily logistics, budgets. Fink made her name with the screen adaptation (1979) of Miles Franklin's 1901 novel *My Brilliant Career*, which proved her ability to identify and cultivate talent; the film launched the famous careers of director Gillian Armstrong and actors Judy Davis and Sam Neill.

Travelling on producer business she'd write to Sasha from London, confiding professional and personal moments; often she'd say, 'only you would appreciate', 'only you would understand'.

Sasha became a trusted confidant in all matters, and his passion for archiving meant he was relied on to carefully file Fink's important documents. In his papers is a faded telegram:

RING ME IMMEDIATELY. SERIOUS. LOVE MARGARET 12 NOV 1990

Sasha made a photocopy, and annotated it in ink: 'She wanted to know where her divorce papers were […] '

In turn he counted on her to understand all his states of mind, as he told a friend in a letter:

> […] I truly feel that life is so much rubbish. It's an awful feeling and no one that I have to tell here. Maybe only Margaret. [letter to 'Brophy' 14.4.91]

choices and judgments with confidence

Soldatow and Fink evidently delighted each other, appreciating each other's wit and candour and taste. Margaret often talked about 'taste', a quality she possessed, one that guided choices and judgments with confidence in its unerring rightness.

The two of them mirrored their generous natures, their adherence to anarchist values, their highly developed aesthetic sense and sense of style, their knowledge of art, music and literature, their certain judgments, their interest in the new and the young, their sociability and enjoyment of mutual acquaintances. They both loved to entertain, to invite guests who had not met each other before.

Soldatow began staying at Fink's Wallaroy Road mansion (the spacious house was usually referred to as a mansion) soon after they met in the early 70s. Margaret's children were small then, and Sasha was invited to their birthday parties, her two sons' bar mitzvahs and her daughter's bat mitzvah. Many of these invitations were personally written, uniquely hand-drawn. Sasha kept many of the artistically hand-lettered notes and drawings from the children, like this from the youngest, Ben:

> Dear Sasha, thank you for the thank-you note you gave to me about the thank-you note I gave you about the great gift you gave me, Ben

a perfect sense of being with a family without presumption or intrusiveness

Sasha was part of the Fink children's lives, and they recall him with love and appreciation.

Hannah (born 1963), now an art historian, and author of a great biography of artist Bronwyn Oliver, expressed the love Sasha ignited in them in precise, tender words:

> Agh. Inez I don't know what I can say except I loved Sasha, me and my brothers loved him, he had a perfect sense of being with a family without presumption or intrusiveness. This might sound like nothing but being able to do that, being that, is so rare, so exquisite. All I can say is that for us to say that we loved him, quite absolutely, is no small thing. This is an extremely select pantheon. He is one of perhaps one other person that I would say, he was family. [Hannah Fink text message 28.7.2019]

Sasha was very important shaping how I see things

The older son, John (b. 1966), now a restaurateur, invited me to dinner one night to talk about Sasha, with his partner Estelle and our mutual friends Joanna Savill and Giuliano Dambelli — that's when those of us who knew Sasha had to tell Estelle why he was worth writing about. [page one]

Like his sister, John said Sasha was part of the family, and part of his 'atheist, anarchist upbringing'.

> He was a constant presence. It was great.
>
> I grew up with what I call all these gay uncles — Steve MacLean, Sasha, the actor Arthur Dignam would front up now and then, Bill [Harding] of course, John Paramor, William Yang. I can't remember a time him not being there. He'd stay for a while then he'd have an argument with Mum and disappear then eventually he'd come back. But he was always at the parties. [John Fink interview]

From the time John was a small child, Sasha would be at the house, and John would go down to the basement, where photographer William Yang kept a darkroom, and find Sasha's papers, reading there things he did not quite understand but felt to be powerful:

> I remember reading some stuff Sasha had written, and I was eight or ten, not old enough to know anything, and my child brain going, this guy is

really full on, what's this guy talking about, he's blowing my brain, steam coming out my ears, imagine. [John Fink interview]

Those 'gay uncles' provided friendship and care.

I was wagging school. In those troubled years, people like Sasha and Bill and John and Steve McLean, they were people I leaned on. I'd wag school and I'd go to Bill and John's apartment [at Bondi Beach], I kept my surfboard there and I'd go surfing then go put my school uniform back on and go back home. [John Fink interview]

More than those not-quite-understood writings, he says Sasha was very important in shaping how he sees things; it was Sasha's way of being in the world that John remembers:

I love to offend people just for the sake of it, and Estelle hates it. Anything to do with political correctness. It's not about what I believe, I like to get a rise out of people, so they can go, I find that offensive, and I go, *why*, and I learned that from Sasha. [John Fink interview]

We talked about the current cultural climate, all the care over correct forms of address and expression, the necessity and the censoriousness, and wondered, as others also told me they wondered, what Sasha would make of it all — it'd certainly be something worth listening to.

He has the mind that would bring you that fresh perspective and you'd go wow, yeah. [John Fink interview]

John also remembers an act of generosity, characteristic of Sasha in spite of his not seeming to have much money.

I remember I was pretty strung out one time, and I went round to his place, in Bondi, and I said, can you give me some money, I've got to get some heroin, I'm really feeling yuck. And he said all right, here you go; and he pulled out a book, he knew what book it was, and page 165, and there was $150 and he just gave it to me. A godsend at that time. He was never judgmental about all that, never any moralising from him, like you know you're going to kill yourself or bla bla bla. I'm sure other people would think it was irresponsible. It could have been the last money he had. I never paid him the money back. [John Fink interview]

After we talked that night, John sent me text messages with more thoughts about Sasha.

> There is not a day goes by I don't think about Sasha. What would he say in this or that situation. [...] Sasha is with me still. I hear him every day. I miss him [...]. Sasha was one of the people who made the world make sense, even though nothing about his world made sense — to him or anyone else most times. And he was an anarchist, so pretty much anything he came up with quite obviously didn't fit into the matrix of daily life in the construct of whatever this society was throwing up at the time [...] but somehow Sasha's world view made more sense than any prevailing wind of opinion at the time. Sasha didn't fit into a box, and he never made one. He also never slept in one. But a lot of people who think like him do end up in a box on the street — muttering incohérents [sic] from the gutter. Sasha was never in a box while alive, but he is in one now — and I guess as the tombstone says 'I See'. [text from John Fink 25.6.19]

obligation free, cheeky and fun uncle

I spoke with Margaret's younger son the musician Ben Fink (born 1969) in early 2020. Ben says that Sasha was more like part of the extended family than a visitor, one with his own role.

> He was just there, a permanent impermanent presence at Wollaroy Road. [He was] a de facto, obligation free, cheeky and fun uncle. He could say the naughty things. In our household Sasha was the resident anarchist keeping the flame alive if it got too normal suburban. If he wasn't staying with us, he was at every dinner party or event, and he was always a happy character at those parties. [Ben Fink phone interview]

Ben recalls a framed photograph, hung over the back stairs at Wallaroy Road, of Sasha posing under a Le Corbusier quotation: 'The first proof of existence is to occupy space.' As a child, Ben found that photograph compelling and would often contemplate it. The enigmatic, generative declaration by the great architect was for him enmeshed with a sense of Sasha:

> It was like Sasha was [both] there in my life and he was under this quote. The whole thing was mindblowingly deep for me, I'd sit on the stairs and look and wow. [Ben Fink phone interview]

Many artists, activists, personalities came through that house, Ben says, but Sasha was the closest to the Fink children.

> He was always slightly mysterious: what did he do and where did he do it?

The bright coloured glasses were a wonderful trademark. [Ben Fink phone interview]

Ben also remembers the hepatitis, having to get that 'traumatic' needle, his first injection. 'But I never held it against him.' [Ben Fink phone interview]

hepatitis

Soldatow was diagnosed with hepatitis in May 1977. His liver never quite recovered. Margaret says she was cross that it meant the three children 'had to have horse needles'.

Bill Harding remembers Sasha would tell anyone who asked how he got hepatitis that it was 'from licking bums' (he also says that in *Jump Cuts*). There was no google to ask if this were possible.

Soldatow was put into quarantine in the Fink house for a while, then he moved back to Melbourne to recuperate, to his mother's house.

claims to authenticity; love of luxury

There is a testy tone in one of the exchanges in *Jump Cuts*. The co-authors have been in disagreement, and their difference turns into a kind of taunting about claims to authenticity:

> Yes, I love luxury. Can you say the same of yourself? You do, you know, but the fantasies you hold of yourself are unobtainable — you ain't no prole, you ain't no peasant. Proles and peasants don't live like you do. In this world, they live a life of misery. [SS 1996 *Jump Cuts* 248]

Soldatow came to become acquainted with his love of luxury, if he had not before, by staying with Margaret.

While he sometimes fetched up in derelict surrounds, he also basked in above-average comforts and aesthetically crafted surroundings, while feeling something like guilty for it. For many of his friends this complexity was evident in his long close friendship with Fink.

Margaret was also considered to be a 'socialite', that is, a member of Society with a capital S, which means rich people who enjoy Art and Culture, who attend balls and exclusive openings and parties for celebrities; yet Margaret also was always a bohemian at heart, always an anarchist, as well as a woman of exacting and independent taste. Fink was a generous host, in those days in that beautiful mansion in the wealthy suburb Woollahra in eastern Sydney.

She tells me not to make too much of the 'wealth' of her life then; it was superficial luxury, she says, and other things count more.

> In my terms, I lived in luxury at Wylde street [Potts Point] with Harry [Hooton]. The noblest luxury is in the world of ideas, which was a crucial part of my life with Harry and of my times with Sash. Sash was courageously intellectual and quintessentially anti-bourgeois. [Margaret Fink email 21.12.19]

She and Soldatow loved in each other the equal ardency for anarchist values and refined aesthetic appreciations.

Margaret Fink's house, her wine, her catering staff were employed at times for the pleasure of artists who might have found these pleasures rare — while in some cases it was what they were running away from, in the sense that wealth in some contexts was seen as inextricable from conservative values.

Soldatow admired his friend's values, and unpredictable utterances, as in this story:

> She had her bag snatched one night while walking from a restaurant in Circular Quay, torn from her shoulder. She had all her bank and credit cards in it, her driver's licence, cash, her make-up, moisturisers, photos and a cheque for $25,000. She's a film producer.
>
> She rang me about two in the morning quite upset — you do lose a part of your personality when objects of direct use are taken — and we practised bag snatching up and down her hall. That cheered her up. Finally I said, 'don't worry, Margie, you can always cancel the credit cards and the cheque, and I bet you the bag will be found,' which it was, minus the cash, which is all they wanted.
>
> 'I don't care about the money,' she replied. 'It was a really good bag and you can't get that colour lipstick anymore.' [SS 1996 *Jump Cuts* 31]

entitled to material support by others

Margaret's wealth, especially compared to the restricted means and frequent or constant economic struggles of the poets, artists, actors, layabouts and others of slender means among many of Sasha's other friends, was a problem for some of them.

Still, Margaret's spirit, humour, generosity, and bohemian ethics endeared her to people who were otherwise resistant.

For example, when Margaret planned her trip to Hanoi in 1992 she took Pam Brown to lunch to ask for advice about that city. Writing to Sasha, Brown said she'd enjoyed being with her, she'd told stories...

> ...and so now I understand your friendship — although I don't regret shouting at you! I just wish she weren't so rich — she doesn't think she is — but frankly, she is!! [Pam Brown letter to SS 9,10.1991]

poverty and boredom are his two greatest fears

Soldatow from early days struggled with the lack of financial reward known to many artists, plus the lack — which might have been inherent or wilful — of an ability to 'manage money wisely', not unknown to many; and in addition he apparently had an extraordinary sense that he was entitled to material support by others, a sense that it was fine for other people to give you money, to pay for things, from a drink at a bar to everything you might need. Soldatow's penchant for asking others to fund his various projects apparently began early: Bruce Sims told me a friend reminded him of when Sasha had stayed with them in East Melbourne, probably around the mid 70s, and he had a scheme where all his friends would give him ten dollars or so on a continuing basis to support his artistic endeavours. [email 28.2.19] There were later schemes; in an unpublished 'Biography and Statement' in 1979:

> Poverty and boredom are his two greatest fears. He is at present extremely anxious about his poverty and would like it known that small donations would be more than appreciated: his postal address is Box 972 Potts Point NSW 2011.

Wendy Bacon, talking about this with me in 2018, said that Sasha's sense of what we might call entitlement was 'like Darcy' — that is, Darcy Waters, the long-time layabout and gambling addict and Push associate, whose youthful days of employment on the wharves were long over before most people knew him; he shamelessly cadged from everyone. In 1988, in Waters' last years, Sasha and Gillian Leahy created a fund for his rent and expenses, rigorously hitting on everyone they knew to contribute. Remembering this, Susan Varga suggested that Sasha might have done this seeing his own future.

> That was one reason I supported him as much as I could towards the end of his life. Because I remembered so clearly what he'd done for Darcy, making sure Darcy got a bit more money. It was sheer kindness. So when Sasha was down on his luck I could support him though I didn't do enough. [Susan Varga interview]

It should never be forgotten that Soldatow's sense of entitlement was inextricable from an essential generosity. Bruce Sims remembers when, in the early 70s, he fled Melbourne after a complicated marriage breakup:

> ...Sasha took me into a squat in either Paddington or Chippendale and sort of looked after me. I still can't smell oranges without going back to that time. I think that they were virtually all we ate. You mention how moralistic he could be: I remember him saying you should never pass a beggar without giving them everything in your pocket, and he often did, even if it was all he had. [Bruce Sims email 7.4.20]

The generosity and a crazy extravagance went together. Speaking of a shared house in the 1970s:

> Sometimes he'd drive Sue Howe crazy, he wouldn't pay his rent but when he got his dole money he'd go and buy a lobster. [Larry Strange interview]

As we've seen [chapter 9] Sasha bought a Braun juicer while not paying his rent in the next house he lived in. He filed several reminders of money owed and never repaid:

> I am upset that you have made no attempt to pay any rent unless I ring and beg for it nor have you paid any of the $900 back rent you owe me... I did pay rent for you all the time I was in the States not earning anything... [Anne Summers letter 4.7.1978]

A foolscap-size double-sided single-space typescript, apparently one of Soldatow's hand-distributed publications, undated but certainly 1970s, is called *My life and hard times as an artist and poet in Sydney, the city of sin, where there is hardly sufficient compassion to enable a true creator to survive in the manner to which they expect to be accustomed, or, How I worshiped an ideal that led me to fall on unfashionable times: a true horror story*.

In a hyperbolic tone, both sending himself up and actually pleading for people to give him money he wrote:

> PART TWO: needs of the soul.
> Poets and mystics have yearned to know the secret of the soul. They have searched for it in the humble violet, the showy daffodil, they have trudged mountains, chanted hymns, fasted for weeks, abstained from sexual intercourse. SOME HAVE EVEN DIED. But all to no avail. The secret has eluded them. Now for THE FIRST TIME IN HISTORY the TRUE NEED OF THE SOUL CAN BE REVEALED:

MONEY. [SS My life and hard times etc n.d.]

He wasn't only joking. Payment for an artist's work typically was slight and intermittent.

Another of Sasha's schemes to raise some cash in the 70s is found in Nicholas Pounder's catalogue, an undated item:

> One of approximately thirty copies run off one afternoon. A squib that was personalised and offered as a receipt for the ten dollar cost of admission to a performance by Sasha Soldatow. A collaboration with Virginia Bell, it is signed 'The Artist Your [sic] Supporting, Sasha Soldatow'. F/cap [335 x 205] [2] pages duplicated typescript on one sheet. A few short tears and some creasing. Unused.

tested the limits of her hospitality

Sasha stayed at Margaret Fink's house on and off during the 1970s. It certainly made his otherwise poverty bearable, beauty, luxury, the stream of film people and theatre people who came to dinners and parties, the old Push friends, the friends in politics and art.

But he tested the limits of her hospitality and tolerance, on at least one occasion too far. Margaret tells of coming down to the kitchen one morning and seeing a perfect stranger sitting there, rather offhand. She thought maybe Leon had called in a workman or something. But ...

> ...it was Sasha's fuck. And I said to Sasha, no way, you do your fucks somewhere else. And he — so fabulous he was so shocking [laughs] — he said, I will fuck who I like wherever I like. I said, not here, and booted him out. So he lost his free board then. But he came back, because you tend to forgive so I forgave him, but that was unconscionable. [Margaret Fink interview]

And yet recalled with that fondness, the tribute of her humour. The limits of Fink's hospitality were experienced by Sasha and some friends at least one other time. Megan McMurchy remembered that we and some other friends were thrown out at the end of a lunch party, along with Sasha, but anyone who remembers that can't be clear on just how it came about — Larry Strange recalls being blamed for stealing a painting which someone else had hidden in a closet — but of course before long all were reconciled.

creative disruptions

Once back in Sydney after recovering sufficiently from hepatitis, Sasha often returned to Margaret Fink's house, inviting his friends over as well — that's probably how I came to know her. He was the most frequent guest, and was often relied on to help with preparations for dinners and other parties, into the next decades as well, when Fink moved from Woollahra to Darlinghurst.

Nicholas Pounder — dealer in rare books and publisher, invited to many dinners and parties — was also a repeat guest at Fink's house and later at Sasha's flat.

> Margaret more than anyone else enjoyed the creative disruptions of someone like Sasha. He was always there as a spontaneous or exciting element, always quick with the interjection or witticism. We used to take our children to dinner parties and they'd always ask whether Sasha would be going. Because he was so naughty. [Nicholas Pounder interview]

It wasn't only the children who enjoyed this aspect of Sasha.

13

who has the most fun

The Only Sensible News 1978

Truly, if I didn't turn life upside down, make it absurd (which it is), what point is there in living? [SS letter to 'Olb' 6.10.2005]

In 1978, from the family home in Daylesford, Sasha, in a long letter to me [chapter 16] said he'd been talking about 'putting out a little mag again. Only small and roneoed but regular of things we want to say' and asked me to think about it. The first *The Only Sensible News* (*TOSN*) appeared later that year.

It was small, it was roneoed, and apparently the things we wanted to say were... what would I call them now?

TOSN wasn't an artistic creation, as *Patterns* had been; it was nothing like *Scrounge*, based on factual, 'objective' reportage; quite to the contrary, *TOSN* was a naive-design, fact-free zone, meant only to amuse.

fun, after all, was a great value

When I first took a look at copies of *The Only Sensible News* for this project, I began to roll my eyes and shake my head and wonder how we thought this stuff was so funny.

When I talked to Sue Howe about this in 2018, she also wondered if it wasn't all somewhat embarrassing now. But we did have a lot of fun, we also said. And fun, after all, was a great value, allied to freedom and fairness and didn't it seem that the people who promoted war and censorship and authority didn't know what fun was? Fun was our guiding value.

> Dear Patti Smith Who do you think has the most fun in all the world? And if not fun then what? ['Ferrol Redd's New York Letters' *TOSN* Bumper Third Issue, nd]

Remember how Virginia Bell had met Sue and Sasha: that performance game [chapter 9]; it was how you lived then, some probably still do, deciding on a domestic challenge for the amusement of its participants at the time and the rest of us when we heard about it. I recall a dinner party challenge Sue and

Sasha held where each person had to make a dinner where all the food had to be a single colour, blue one time.

LITTLE KNOWN FACTS ABOUT DRINKING

1. Old Russian saying: If you drink you die. If you don't drink you die. Better to drink and die.

[...]

4. The Persians, when they had to make a decision, got drunk and decided. If on the next morning, when they were sober, they still remember and liked the decision they did it. Alternatively, they made up their minds when sober, then got drunk. If they liked the decision when drunk, they did it. If they didn't they repeated the process. [*TOSN* Number 2, 9.6.1978]

stealing material from other publications

It must have been fun with Sasha, putting out *The Only Sensible News*, but, Sue says, she now thinks it was probably a waste of time and she doesn't like to dwell on it. 'I should probably have been doing a PhD,' she says.

But again, think of the times. Of all those faraway publications that were not available, all the technology not yet invented.

We were stealing material from other publications, ones that most of our readers were unlikely to see. Different ones, though, than *Scrounge* utilised. I was a fan of Andy Warhol's *Interview* magazine, which published very long interviews which seemed to barely be edited: asides, repetitions, stumbles, digressions were included. For *TOSN* we stole stuff from *Interview*.

I faintly recall writing the first section of the first issue with Sasha, 'Feminism and Clothing', a little satire on making ethical choices about what to wear. Or maybe I only think I recall it because in the small hard-cover Diary 1978, Sasha wrote on Sunday 1 January (though that probably wasn't the date)

OSN writing at Inez's flat. Feminism and Clothing. Inez. Sue. Larry.

classic insurrectionary irreverence, black comic mischief

In his catalogue, rare books dealer and publisher Nicholas Pounder describes this issue of *TOSN*:

Sasha tickles and ridicules the po faced yearning for collective consistency. [...] The first side of this number is headed 'Feminism & Clothing', and the second 'No God No Master No Fuck'. Classic insurrectionary irreverence, black comic mischief...what a relief.

The editorial credo probably was something like, if it made us laugh, it went in.

Humour was found not in the intentions of a piece so much as in the way a piece is read, or life is observed, the utterances of people made funny by the way we repeated or read them.

There was nothing like it around, *The Only Sensible News*. We'd never have used a word like hip or wanted it used and I'm not sure now that's the word, but it might have been 1978 hip. Or no, probably something more marginal.

... as submitted to Women's Weekly
the First Sensible Questionnaire on ...
ARE YOU AN ANARCHIST OR A SPARTACIST?

1. How do you spell Spartacist?
    - Spartacist
    - Sparticist
    - Spartanist
    - Spartacyst

2. How do you spell Anarchist?
    - Anarchist
    - A narchist
    - Anarcist
    - Antichrist
    - Ananarchist

3. Are 'ladies fingers'
    - (a) sexist
    - (b) delicious

4. What have these three things got in common
    - (a) holes in your aura
    - (b) critique
    - (c) vitamin C

5. When confronted by people you don't agree with is your first desire
    - (a) throw a bomb
    - (b) throw a person out of the meeting
    - (c) throw up
    - (d) go home in tears

6. What is different about these three persons
    - (a) Rosa Luxemburg
    - (b) Winston Churchill
    - (c) Alexander Berkman

7. Distinguish between the following
    - a motion
    - e motion

8. What came first the chicken or the egg?
    IT JUST SHOWS YOU, DOESN'T IT

The Only Sensible News Bumper Third Issue

Apparently for Sasha and his friends calling people 'serious' was to belittle them, I was told, when Steve Corbett remembers meeting them around that time. (chapter 16)

Maybe serious meant something like rule-bound, pious, humourless, but whatever it was it was clear to us.

When I first went to Europe as an adult in 1979, I heard people who impressed me belittle or rather dismiss other people by saying 'they are not serious', and I was never the same. I meant to be serious now (a sense of purpose? knowing things mattered? being more educated?).

Well, in the days of *The Only Sensible News* to be unserious was the defiant point.

what is achieved

In 1980 a new magazine called *Magazine* was launched, a broadsheet-sized newspaper-like format with a cover price of $1. There was only ever one issue, published and edited by Peter Crayford, with additional editors listed. Certainly influenced by *Interview*, *Magazine*'s black-and-white pages offer mostly interviews. One page has photographs of people at an opening of Peter Kingston's work at the Hogarth Gallery; their names are not divulged; maybe you're meant to recognise them. The interview subjects include composer Cameron Allen, filmmaker Albie Thoms, exuberant fashion duo Jenny Kee and Linda Jackson, the gallery director Clive Evatt, retired politician Don Dunstan (*Magazine* promised a second part in which 'Dunstan expresses his views on Marxism, Socialism and political ideals'). An interview with Sasha Soldatow about *The Only Sensible News* is slyly titled 'I'm a metasexual'.

> *Magazine*: What is achieved by publishing the Only Sensible News?
> *Sasha Soldatow*: it's a way of preventing boredom. Our editorial meetings are to basically get a few flagons, buy up the cigarettes, get a tiny little bit to eat and switch the vision on and start laughing and joking and things. Our first drafts are usually covered with wine stains — red ones — red wine is a meal in itself like 'twisties'. ['I'm a metasexual' *Magazine* Vol. 1 no 1 1980.5]

Twisties was — still is, google says — a packaged snack product, and Sasha calling it a meal would have been a funny brattish defiance of classist or foodie attitudes to food. (One issue of *TOSN* provided cocktail recipes including one mixing tequila with salad dressing.)

It's a safe bet that Sasha knew the people putting out *Magazine*, and probably everyone mentioned in it. It seems that the editors liked *TOSN*, and that while *TOSN* mightn't have had a wide distribution, people who were meant to read *Magazine* would be into it. *Magazine* also included 'The Three Stages of Fun', part of the issue of *TOSN* dated 8 December 1979

As for *Magazine*, there was only ever the one issue. Apparently they had a launch party at a posh theatre in Adelaide and someone spilled a lot of drink into the very precious piano there, and paying for that put an end to any more production.

you were meant to be funny

To glory in the idea of *fun* was our hedonism, our anarchism; it was to laugh in the face of the earnestness, sometimes piousness, sometimes disapproval, expressed by many of our peers and comrades — even while we might have held similar views on a lot of things — and certainly to laugh in the face of anyone who'd consider our ideas, our humour, our way of life deserving of censure.

The way we thought we were funny. The way you were meant to be funny all the time, to always strive for amusement. It was funny if you just said something true about someone in a tone of letting people know you noticed these things.

I suppose it was something like that combination of sincerity and mockery that is known as camp. And so it became funny to make everydayness the subject of our attention: current fashion, banal remarks, unexamined truisms, popularity.

At best the humour we shared was seeing/experiencing as bizarre what was not usually meant to be.

Maybe its degenerate side was to fall into a habit of unconsidered mockery.

This is a time when popular culture was rarely considered a subject of serious attention. That fact has something to do with these publications. I now suppose that then there was a tinge of an implied 'we, producing *The Only Sensible News*, consider ourselves well-educated, well-read, well-connected, thinking people and still we see a point in silliness and this kind of marginal reflection on the world'.

Also 'send money' at the end of each issue would have been Sasha. He always asked people to send money. (He was 'not good with money' — and he archived the notes from people reminding him he hadn't paid the rent or returned loans.)

Each issue of *TOSN* claims to be produced by 'DRINK AGAINST DRUNKEDNESS' or more usually 'Drink Against Drunkenness'.

And something changed.

When I read the issues again they struck me as truly amusing.

You can be the judge of that; scans are on the Sasha Soldatow website.

'gay sensibility' informed the humour and tone

I wonder now about the extent to which 'gay sensibility' informed the humour and tone of *TOSN*. The fact that Sydney's — indeed, Australia's — cultural life, its arts, owed an immense amount to the queerness of the majority of its practitioners, its creators, its influencers, was evident and something people were starting to write about.

When I was a schoolgirl and queer people referred to themselves as camp I began to recognise my attraction to their world, and find reflections of that in an account by Rebecca Solnit in her memoir of her discovery of the better company of homosexual men:

> [Gay men] knew words could be festive, recreational, medicinal, that banter and flirtation and extravagance, that humor and wryness and anecdotes of the absurd were pleasures worth pursuing. They knew that talk wasn't, as many straight men seemed to assume, just transactional, a way to dump or extract information or instructions. It could be play, riffing on ideas and tones; it could give encouragement and affection, and it could invite people to be themselves and to know themselves in order to be known. [...] [Solnit 130]

other uses of 'only sensible'

In 1978 the Sydney University student newspaper, *Honi Soit*, published an 'anarchist edition'. Its front page says No Date but an inside footer says 21/9/78. The words 'only sensible' are inserted before the regular *Honi Soit* banner in its antique-looking font. The design and other features are taken from *The Only Sensible News*. The 28 broadsheet pages include densely printed articles on anarchism, on prison reform, on the novels of Ursula Le Guin. A two page spread contains Soldatow's 'Notes from a Gay Album'.

In the mid 1990s Soldatow wrote a regular column, 'Wild Card', for the free gay newspaper *Sydney Star Observer*. He called his piece on 15 December 1994 'Ho Ho Hmm: The Only Sensible Awards for this year'. 'The Only Sensible' had become Sasha's kind of trademark phrase by now.

the only sensible ticket collection

Sometime in the '70s Sasha began collecting tickets — all kinds of tickets: theatre tickets, bus tickets, tram tickets, raffle tickets, cinema tickets, and labels off jars and packets. It's something often remembered about him.

Like others of his friends, I began to save for him any ticket that passed through my hands, especially when I began to travel and saved for Sasha train tickets and tram tickets and museum entrance tickets in Italy and elsewhere. I never stopped thinking of Sasha when I'd notice various tickets, even to the present — he made me consider them, how they were designed, the choices made, as objects worthy of at least a moment's contemplation beyond their obvious fleeting utility.

Meredith Rogers, theatre director, actor and academic, and a lifelong friend of Sasha's starting from his university days in Melbourne, found a filing card sent to her on which Sasha had typed:

> Sasha Soldatow: Remember that box of tickets from the Ewing show — they turned up at the National Gallery and when I turned up to retrieve them — saying loudly at the Information Desk: 'Ive come to collect some of my work which is being held illegally here, who do I talk to' — well, they offered me $400 which I took and ran before they could change their mind. [n.d. typed on filing card]

The National Gallery did not buy anywhere near all of the ticket collection in 1998. Soldatow left the rest of the only sensible ticket collection with Nicholas Pounder in a Globite suitcase and a small metal filing drawer. Next to Pounder's shop of second-hand and rare books, in Lesley McKay's bookshop, there was a young woman working, Samantha Sinnayah, and she also collected tickets and other ephemera. With Sasha's blessing, Pounder handed over the collection to her. While working for what was then the Historical Houses Trust a few years later, Sinnayah exhibited the ticket collection at the Sydney Mint. She still has it, merged with her own collection, rehoused in a special cabinet; 'a real curator would keep it in the smelly old suitcase and the rusty filing drawer' she told me, but she has carefully placed it in museum quality display envelopes.

14

dreadfully romantic

diaries romances friendships 70s 80s

You were right to call me dreadfully romantic and of course I am. That's me... People are the most important things in my life — I devote most of my time and energy to them. That's why I can't work — it takes up too much of my time. I've often said, half seriously, that relationships is my profession. (You are meant to laugh). [SS letter to Robbie McGregor 29.11.1978]

declarations of love

Sasha loved to be in love. His archive of letters — he kept carbon copies of the ones he wrote — is rich with declarations of love to many men and he usually decided he was in love very soon after meeting them.

He told his love openly and often. He became obsessive about those he fell in love with. He could be jealous and possessive even while insisting on complete freedom for himself to have sex and close relationships with other people.

There were endless sexual adventures. Not all of them were fun — if you're going to experiment, to be open, you'll have some bad experiences too; if you're lucky they'll sound funny when you tell them:

> After taking a valium or two, he lay naked on the bed begging rape me, rape me. I said I wasn't any good at rape, at which he screamed — stand over in the corner till you get an erection — and passed out. [SS diary 13.10.1984]

Who takes valium for sex, is only one thing one can wonder about this account. All else it says on that diary page is:

> The fateful Tim afternoon lunch.
> 4.30 in the morning go home

A friend, Margaret Fink, who was also keen on going to parties, and hosted quite a few herself, says that Soldatow's unfaltering pursuits were at the expense of his writing:

He was too interested in fucking. He wanted romance, he fell in love all the time. What is over sexed — I don't know. He was a faller in love-er, you know that. [Margaret Fink interview]

Fink says that's why she wasn't interested in Sasha's writing besides his work on Hooton.

his middle name was 'Party Fun'

Soldatow acquired printed diaries every year from the 1970s. These diaries are studded with names and phone numbers and appointments — drinks, lunch, meeting, dinner, party, ring, see; names, often more than one, often several, in one day. 1970s, 1980s, 1990s diaries. Occasionally a ticket (from a bus or a theatre) is inserted, or a label or a photograph. There are occasional quotations, whether from texts or overheard lines; words from songs; occasional jottings of ideas; occasional cuttings of a news story, or a picture (e.g. a beautiful modern chair); the rare diary-like note:

> He thinks nothing of taking a trip to some remote island in New Guinea, shooting their flying foxes and 'wild pigs' and giving them sugar and tobacco in return. Person I met at Joanna's. [diary 9.1.1983]

Probably Sasha thought he would always easily remember anything he had to, wanted to, with these diaries as a reminder. For someone so certain of a future biographer, he rarely recorded his funniest jokes, wittiest lines, the most salacious gossip passed on. He rarely wrote in details; he did not use these diaries for confiding or examining his inner life or secret self, or maybe he thought he did. They're a record of his social life. Sasha began telling people his middle name was 'Party Fun'. He'd go to any event where people gathered.

many affectionate letters

Some of the friends from Melbourne University student days mentioned Sasha's friend Reinhard Hassert — 'art gallery director' in Soldatow's index to his letters. Judith Brett said she had gone to Daylesford with Sasha and Reinhard.

In Soldatow's archives, there are many affectionate letters from Reinhard to Sasha, dated 1972, written before Soldatow moved to Sydney. Hassert often says he misses 'Sashka', tells of art and music, and often mentions someone called Eddy who sends his love. The letters continue from Bali, Java and Thailand later in 1972.

There is only one letter from Soldatow, hand-written in red ink, and it is marked in pencil 'not sent'.

Monday 30 April 1973
Reinhard, I don't see the purpose of continuing this charade of involvement any further. It just hurts both you and me. And it's not worth all the tension and time to keep the memories.

What Soldatow did send to Hassert can't be found; he hadn't begun keeping carbon copies of his own letters.

Also in the voluminous collection of Soldatow's personal correspondence, there is a cache of hand-written letters: for once the handwriting, clear and elegant, is easy and pleasurable to read; somehow you can tell a good fountain pen was used on the blue letter paper. These are from Eddy Batache, who writes in tones of affection and concern of his travels in Paris with Reinhard, telling of museums, of artworks, speaking as if one art connoisseur to another.

So, that would be the same Reinhard.

Batache even writes about selling a painting of Sasha's in Paris, with an advance payment of $100. I thought, Sasha always drew and painted as well — and maybe as much — as he wrote: who could know then which directions he would take: it was possible then that the painting might have turned out to be an early work of someone who later became more productive and well-known in visual art than for his writing.

I found a video of a talk by Eddy Batache at the Art Gallery of NSW in 2012, where he tells fascinatingly of life in Paris, where he and his partner Reinhard had lived for a long time, developing a strong friendship with their neighbour Francis Bacon which lasted seventeen years until he died. By the time of this talk Eddy and Reinhard had a fifty-year relationship.

I was put in touch with Batache, who wrote back to me very graciously. As usual, Sasha had made a great impression:

> [...] Sasha struck me as a very intelligent and sensitive boy. He was able to talk brilliantly on subjects of all kinds and I thought him very entertaining. He definitely had multiple talents and I loved the drawings he did every now and then. [Eddy Batache email 17.10.2018]

Batache was on his way to Paris to work on his thesis when he met Soldatow; by the time he returned in 1974, Sasha and Reinhard had stopped seeing each other. Reinhard now did not wish to speak about Sasha, who had met him through Dennis Altman and they 'were quite close for a while'.

> As far as I know their relationship did not finish in a pleasant way, as related in the Hass Story, which Reinhard did not appreciate at all. [Batache email 17.10.2018]

After I sent him an early draft of this chapter, Batache revealed that, as for that art work by Sasha, in fact he had not sold it but only pretended he had 'because it gave me the opportunity to help him financially and to encourage him in what I felt was a talent for draughtsmanship'.

He told me that during the brief period of their relationship Reinhard was grateful to Sasha for introducing him to authors such as Anais Nin or Virginia Woolf. They were both interested in aspects of European culture and there was none of that bitchiness which appears later.

Hassert preferred to keep fond memories of the time they spent together in Daylesford and would rather forget what occurred later. Apparently when he wished to end their sexual relationship, Sasha took it badly, expressed his disappointment violently.

But Sasha would create his own interpretation of their estrangement.

they face up to their differences

I recalled that 'Hass Story' was in the collection *Private — Do Not Open*, published in 1987. [chapter 21] It is the second chapter in *PDNO* [p17ff], divided into sections with titles, one of which is also 'Hass story'.

The first subsection 'Early morning, Daylesford' has the narrator 'dreaming thoughts and feeling out patterns in my living', recording his inner state along with sensory impressions of a night in the country, and then a memory of 'Hass' in this place ten years earlier, a lover who is about to leave:

> He is cultivating a delicate love tor the East. He will leave in two days time for Indonesia and Cambodia. In Bali he will search for bronzes and carved wooden deers. In Cheng Mai he will unearth heads of stone deities from antique dealers while I stay on here. It has been decided. [p20]

The narrator — everything points to an autobiographical story — tells more of their love affair and how it continues while he stays behind, observing nature in the bush, foraging for fungi, making fires, worrying, contemplating. And cultivating his accusations, in which personal and geo-political perceptions are entwined.

> Later, I become aware that his purpose in going overseas is to collect the exquisite accomplishments of dead generations.
> Later, I will accuse him of cultural imperialism when it slowly dawns on me that art treasures have become available from Cambodia because of the presence of the American Army there and in Vietnam. I will recognise the significance of corruption and international politics to the industry that supplies decoration for the elegant rich. [pp21-22]

In the next section, the narrator visits Hass and they face up to their differences. Hass has a pungent point to make; it's not refuted:

> '... Your radical friends, they like their comforts just as much even though they pretend not to.' [p24]

The apartment is full of ancient treasures, 'polished artefacts', but while our narrator is knowledgable about what they are he sees them through a haze of disapproval and harsh judgment. Clearly this relationship is over. He leaves; the next two sections dwell on emotions and memories this break-up gives rise to, the awareness of the surroundings, and of a familiar illness taking hold, that makes him recall childhood, and, in the chapter's last few pages, a scene that seems to be part memory and a lot fantasy, of being a child having sex with a strange man; there is no clue as to what that has to do with what has just gone before, unless it is this:

> Something happens when you discover that sex involves other people. [p29]

messily overlapping relationships

Dennis Altman dedicated his celebrated, timely book *Homosexual: oppression and liberation* (1971) to Reinhard Hassert.

I had not remembered this when I went to interview Altman in Melbourne in 2019.

And if indeed it was Altman who had introduced Hassert to Soldatow, as Eddy Batache said, Altman did not mention that then. I had to ask him about that later; in his politely sufficient reply Altman said,

> I had a relationship with Reinhard for a few years in the early 1970s; after we broke up he may have had one with Sasha. Throughout this period he lived with Eddy [email 5.7.2019]

Having already learned of Hassert's reluctance to speak about Soldatow and their past relationship, I was in turn reluctant to probe further.

What for? Enough to note that relationships can be overlapping, sometimes messily, and especially it seems as part of those times, part of our youth. Maybe anyone's time, and not only in youth. I face the unpleasant fact that although I embarked on this project knowing that Sasha wanted (even expected!) a biography to be written, not all the other people in his life did. No life is lived in isolation, least of all Sasha's. Not everyone is keen on being included in the accounts of lives they are in. Most people who knew Sasha were happy enough to talk about him. Most people don't like being written about, I hear a writer say on a podcast, even if it's done in a loving way.

I ponder the relationship of biography to gossip.

Sasha delighted in gossip and being blatant about it; partly this was to defy the malevolent meaning given to the word (that was then), which had its origins in female expertise. He defied notions of propriety, confidentiality and the like, though reportedly would say the only stipulation for passing on gossip was that 'it had to be true'.

divergent branches of gay liberation

When I went to see Dennis Altman in his house in Melbourne, he had unearthed an old diary, which divulged the date of his meeting with Sasha. It was 23 March 1972. Altman had come from Sydney to speak at an early gay liberation forum at Melbourne University. Of course Sasha went to that. Although the date had been forgotten Altman remembered that he'd been put up at a motel and Sasha spent the night there.

> I remember this because he coughed, he had a bad cough. So, very little sleep. [Dennis Altman interview]

Altman describes Sasha as 'very intense and quite exotic'. Consulting the diary entries agitates memory only up to a point: points of focus and blurry bits.

> He was already working in the media department at Melbourne Uni — it would have been a small amateurish outfit in those days before universities had big PR departments. Next day I had lunch with Sasha and Sue but I don't know who Sue would be. Someone in Melbourne. Then on the 25th I was obviously still with Sasha because I went with him to a picnic but I don't know what the picnic was. Then I went back to Sydney the next day. And a couple of months later he moved to Sydney and we sort of fell out. [Dennis Altman interview]

Altman says that the three-day affair was the total of his involvement with Sasha, until a drink in a pub with him and Christos Tsiolkas in the late 1990s.

The connection with Altman was more important to Soldatow. Anne Mitchell, his friend from university theatre days, who had moved to Sydney in 1970 for three years with her then husband Ray Misson, told me that they used to have Sasha over for dinner and he once said he would be bringing Dennis Altman with him, which excited them: Dennis was already becoming famous as a spokesperson and theorist of gay liberation and its politics. But Sasha turned up without him.

no happy reunion

As it happened, by 2019, when I met her, Mitchell was by then a colleague and friend of Altman's, and introduced me to him (we had mutual friends and I'd seen him at various events).

Altman says that after their short fling, there was no happy reunion when Sasha came to Sydney.

> I was involved in ending a relationship and starting another relationship. I think Sasha thought there was more to our two-night stand than I thought there was. So when he came to Sydney and I was clearly not enthralled [...] I certainly didn't need a third person to complicate my life. [Dennis Altman interview]

Altman and Soldatow represented, to some, two leaders of divergent branches of Gay Liberation: Altman's liberal, more pragmatic reformism versus the uncompromisingly anarchic spirit in the analysis of *What Is This Gay Community Shit?*

Soldatow's philosophy of liberation seems perhaps the more romantic one — more idealistic, and with more emotional attachment.

If he had wanted, even expected, more closeness at one time, Soldatow had to reconsider what his relationship to Altman might have been, what his expectations had been.

And that might have been the reason for Soldatow's ungenerosity in his published assessments of Altman's work. Soldatow occasionally wrote reviews for *The Sydney Morning Herald* and there he reviewed one of Altman's books.

> ... and it was quite nasty and I remember writing to Susan Wyndham [then editor of the book review section] saying I don't think you should have let this person review me, and a few years later she let him review another book of mine.
>
> And it was, well you can't do anything about it, that's how it works, there wasn't anything sinister, it was a fuck up by Susan. So I don't have much to tell you about Sasha. [Dennis Altman interview]

Dennis Altman's sister Vivien, who talked with me about her friendship with Sasha in Melbourne and later in Sydney, was affectionate and appreciative in her remembrances, but also talked about a side of him that could be 'destructive and hurtful'; one example was in the way Soldatow treated her brother's work.

> It's good to be critical, it's important, but there was a nastiness. [Vivien Altman interview]

Dennis Altman was a lecturer at Sydney University until 1980. He told me that he'd run into Sasha occasionally and it was unpleasant. Naturally there were mutual connections.

> Do you know Bill Harding? Maggie Fink and I fought over Bill. I have this memory of the Sydney Film Festival, and I remember Maggie looking at me saying, don't you dare, he's mine. And I think Sasha was part of that world a bit, right? [Dennis Altman interview]

'a sexual friendship'

Bill Harding has been a friend of mine since I met him at a party at Margaret Fink's in the late 1970s. I remember that Sasha had already excitedly told me about meeting Bill.

Harding had made his name as a television writer in the mid 1960s when he was still at school and sending in scripts to the comedy sketch show *The Mavis Brampston Show*. In the mid 1970s he was writing for, among other things, the popular satirical talk show series T*he Norman Gunston Show*, the parodic interviewer character played by actor Garry McDonald. It was in that connection that he met Soldatow. Angus & Robertson were publishing the scripts.

> Something like *Norman Gunston Finest Moments*. Richard Walsh was the editor. I had to go into A&R, Cremorne or somewhere, to see the layout or something, and Richard Walsh was there, and Sasha. And I think it was just the three of us, one Saturday morning. We did lock eyes, and I think Sasha was somebody who liked falling in love. Also, it was not just sexual romantic, he'd make the move to meet someone intellectually. I remember asking him to a big party where John [Paramor] and Sonia [Hofmann] and I lived, Northbridge, and I remember leaving the party, my party, with Sasha, who lived in Bourke St. And that's the first time we had sex. [Harding interview]

They kept on seeing each other (not exclusively of course; they were both of inclusive tendency).

Bill and Sasha for a while had what Bill calls 'a sexual friendship'.

> I think I'm being fair to say I never fell in love with Sasha. He was lovely and amazing. To some extent he fell in love with me but he fell in love with a lot of people in a way I don't fall in love with a lot of people.
>
> I remember *The Only Sensible News*; that kind of writing. I remember what it looked like, those typed roneoed pages. He was on the artistic end of anarchist, the artistry of anarchy kind of thing. [Harding interview]

When he and Margaret Fink fell in love, Bill began staying at the house in Wallaroy Road, where Sasha sometimes stayed. They both remained close to Margaret, in different ways, with Bill becoming a constant escort, companion and lover, and meanwhile Sasha and Margaret's friendship continued.

Sasha and I at the time were avid readers of the published diaries of USA composer Ned Rorem, who probably inspired a lot of new diaries. Sasha gave Rorem's diaries to Bill, who took them to read in Greece in 1975 and was thus inspired, but the diary-keeping didn't last long.

Soldatow writes about Rorem, by the way, in one of his Wild Card columns in the SSO in 1994, in an erudite musing on music and sexuality, saying he first picked up Rorem's *Paris Diaries* (1966) in a second-hand bookshop in 1974.

Commenting on that in a phone talk in 2020, Ian Milliss reflected on those diaries and their influence:

> Those diaries are notoriously appalling. Entertaining in a ghastly way. I think they inspired some of Sasha's worst behaviour. They're funny but Ned Rorem was so narcissistic and exploitative of those around him and careless of involuntarily outing people. I think in a way it helped loosen Sasha up [...] I think in a weird way it gave him an idea how far he could go. And not in a good way. [Milliss phone 24.7.2020]

an affair that could not last

Sasha kept copies of his letters; some of them reveal affairs saturated with romantic agony; hand-written and typed missives agonise over every nuance of attraction and attention. In 1986 during an intense eighteen-day affair, his lover declared it was the best sex ever; it was an affair that could not last, because they lived in different cities, and because, probably, Sasha demanded total attention.

> I don't want our sex interrupted for your angst about editors. [SS letter 1986]

Sex and relationships were a kind of arena of the self for Soldatow. Limerence, obsession, pursuit, these things seemed to fuel his life-force, both driving and impeding his drive to write. Maybe like the addictions that came to light later. He is exercised over his feelings and their meaning:

> [...] Listen, I don't even know if I really love you. I am more than sure when I am with you that I do, but you can't spend 18 days sleeping with someone without some degree of intimacy so I use the word love as a shorthand. What else can you call that feeling that makes you go off into daydreams and relaxed fantasies all through the day, thinking of this lovely man who nuzzles up to you and you respond and nuzzle back. Of course I love you. [...] Oh sure, everything eventually can be confused with expectation, as if we're all cautiously dawdling on one road whose ultimate goal is the jaws of TOTAL COMMITTMENT [sic]. Well, that's socially constructed fantasy which we all hold singly. [...] [SS letter 13.4.1986]

a terrible romantic drunk

The drinking and the falling in love were related, in some kind of co-dependency. Pam Brown recalls the time they were neighbours in Newtown.

> In Ferndale Street, we used to say, if you do more of that it'll fall off; he used to fuck a lot of people. [Brown interview]

And this was in a time when we were all young and there seemed no serious impediments to anyone's sexual adventuring.

> He had all these unattainable lovers who were probably straight young men; he'd fall for them and try to entice them to his bed.
>
> I remember sitting in Petersham one morning; he rang up and he was crying and he said, can you bring a flagon over, so-and-so doesn't want me. He'd met some guy two days before who had a girlfriend and a child and he thought they were going to be lovers. He was sitting on his own in my old house, 3 Ferndale, which he'd rented after I'd moved, so I dutifully bought a flagon and went over to cheer him up. And when I think about that, he was an impossible romantic, with that guy it was never going to happen, but it was another excuse to drink a flagon. He was also a terrible romantic drunk. [Brown interview]

outrageous exchange of conversation, then move on

The writer and editor Mark Macleod recalls an affair of about eighteen months in the early 1980s. He met Soldatow at one of the Harold Park pub literary readings. The initial approach was not exactly seductive:

> I was standing up at the bar when I suddenly heard a voice behind my shoulder say, 'I suppose a fuck's out of the question.' I said, 'Well, it is now.' [Macleod email 9.11.2020]

Macleod knew Soldatow by reputation, more as a kind of celebrity activist than as a writer.

> And to be honest, I suppose being a parent and newly divorced and a tentatively 'out' gay man, I was flattered by the attention of one of the gay scene's icons. We chatted for the rest of that evening and the following week he asked me to go over to his flat in North Bondi for lunch and a walk.
>
> I found him interesting, well read. He knew some friends and business acquaintances of mine. Sasha was not comfortable with silence

so the conversation kept flowing. He was an irrepressible gossip and an entertainer. All that was appealing.

He was kind to my children, being a big kid himself, and amused them with his popular culture collection — pencils, souvenirs, erasers. [Macleod email]

In the social arena, though, their differences became apparent.

Sasha early on liked to show me off to his circle of friends, at least as much as he was showing off his circle of friends to me. I didn't have the same appetite for social networking. [Macleod email]

Macleod says that while the intense social life was at first interesting, he tired of the drive to go to not just one party on a Saturday night, but a second and a third. If Macleod was enjoying chatting to someone he'd think, why move on. Sasha though always liked to move on.

I eventually came to see that he felt an obligation to 'work the room'. Yes he did know everyone. And he would spark off some outrageous exchange of conversation, but then move on before things became too deep. And he would make bitchy judgments of people who were supposedly friends, or formerly friends, behind their backs. [Macleod email]

And Soldatow made harsh judgments of his lover's friends. For example, the novelist Thea Astley was one of Macleod's closest friends, and Sasha 'pestered' Mark to take him to visit her on the south coast. Macleod now says it was foolish to do so; a mistake he didn't repeat.

Thea had a huge sprawling house inland from Nowra, which she described as 'Katingal' (the women's prison) and when we arrived she showed him to a room at one end of the house and me to a room at the absolute other end of the house, where I always stayed when I visited. Instead of Sasha understanding that she had known me in my married life, and probably felt uncomfortable with gay relationships for various reasons, Sasha took this as a deliberate insult to him.

He needled her for the whole weekend. Thea's often outrageous conversation and occasionally outrageous actions were a front for her quite conservative upbringing and views. Sasha didn't see this, and challenged or dismissed every single thing she said. They hated one another instantly. [Macleod email]

Inevitably, the relationship changed. It might be one of the classic plots of relationship stories: the difference that attracted Soldatow seemed to become intolerable.

> His affection for me was real I believe, and the sexual side of the relationship was kind and pleasing. But he became increasingly judgmental of me. He said to me one day, 'You know, being gay saved you. Otherwise you would have been a very ordinary suburban boy.' More sympathetically he said to me one day, 'We went to the barricades, but if gay men of your generation try to do that, you'll self-destruct. You'll need to be active in other ways.' [Macleod email]

Macleod says now it was 'surprisingly kind' of Soldatow to say there was no point in going to the barricades; people like him had benefited from the risks taken by Soldatow's generation. But there was no kindness in Soldatow's insistence on his own correct outlook, and that brought things to a bitter close.

> The night we broke up, I had picked Sasha up in the car, and instead of being grateful, he went on and on about my religious beliefs, belittling me, making it quite clear that if I were really evolved, I would be an atheist like him. I asked him repeatedly to stop. I reminded him that I never criticised him for not sharing my outlook on life, and he wouldn't stop, so I pulled over and told him to get out. It was raining. I had pulled over on Parramatta Road in Glebe. He said 'You're not serious' and I told him I was deadly serious and wanted him out.
>
> That was the last I saw of Sasha for some time. It had become what we would call now an emotionally abusive relationship. [Macleod email]

mischief for its own sake

Soldatow's provocations occasionally were simply vicious. He liked mischief enough to make it for its own sake. One friend recalled going to roll a joint at a party, when Soldatow suddenly snatched the bag of weed away and wouldn't give it back. (Sasha smoked cigarettes only.) In this case the guy got the better of him by snatching Soldatow's glasses off his face and holding his foot over them on the floor. Silly moments like that; the word 'childish' repeatedly comes up when people talk about Soldatow. Sometimes he seemed to like upsetting people for no good reason.

One group of friends would remember the occasion of The Slap.

Bill Harding was sharing a flat with Priscilla Yates in the early 1990s. Sasha Soldatow, John Paramor and another woman friend or two as well as Priscilla were also still there after a sociable lunch. The talk turned, as it often would, to various matters to do with sex, and Soldatow kept insisting that Paramor had told him that he, John, said that 'I like cocks and I don't like cunts. Or something like that.'

John, speaking to me in 2018, said he had no memory of ever saying that but Soldatow kept insisting he had. Priscilla was showing her photograph albums, including a set of photos from her and John Paramor's very young days, before John's life as a gay man, when they had been a couple for three years, pictured at nightclubs and restaurants together. Appalled that Sasha in effect was insulting Priscilla with his insistence, John slapped him.

> With the back of my hand. It was hard but not really hard, he wasn't going to get knocked out, it was a stinging little slap. And he jumped up and said, that hurt, and I said, it was meant to. And we had a short exchange, it was only two or three sentences each, and he said, you're a real bastard. And the whole thing got out of hand and he left and caught the lift down. [Paramor interview]

Then Priscilla told them that she'd had a drink with Bruce Pulsford and Sasha only a few nights before and she'd told them about her long-ago affair with John, and this showed John that Sasha had come to the lunch with the intention of making this kind of mischief. Still, John told me, he liked Sasha. 'I thought he was charming and delightful and mischievous, we never got along easily but I certainly appreciated him... His sweet side came out more fully in the last couple of years of his life.'

15

The Bon Mot Gang

1970s poetry; Pam Brown; Adelaide 1982

You cannot be a poet without politics. [SS 1990 Introduction]

contribution to anti-censorship action

The underground printing scene at the time made available radical and non-conformist poetry, manifestos, posters and fliers, T-shirts.

Tomato Press was important in this scene. Begun in 1972 by Pat Woolley in Melbourne, when she moved to Sydney the press was housed in a building on Glebe Point Road. Soldatow took his *Patterns* series to be printed there. That's probably where he met Pam Brown, who, with Paul Lester, had their screen printing business, Cocabola's Screen Printing, out the front. Pam for a while went by Pamela Cocabola Brown; Tomato Press also published some of her work.

However radical its products, still it existed within the same old repressive society with strict censorship, and laughable decisions — restrictions in fact — about what you could read and see made by people you couldn't respect. *Tharunka* and its offshoot *Thor* had been challenging censorship by printing banned material, and these battles against censorship inspired others.

Pam Brown was involved in a similar project, in 1972, and Sasha also participated. Martin Fabinyi had invited Pam and others to create a 'porn book', as a contribution from artists to anti-censorship action.

So people would come upstairs and fuck [while being photographed]... Sasha was one, who fucked and had photos [taken of that], participants weren't named but you could tell who they were if you looked at [the photos]. Rienie [of Tomato Press] printed it, that guy was a very good printer. [Brown interview]

Brendon Stretch took a lot of the photos and Fabinyi edited the book. They called it *X* and gave it a silver paper cover inside a plastic bag. It was distributed through Gould's anarchist bookshop, or, like a pamphlet, was given out at parties. They weren't printing in sophisticated ways. Involvement in the means of production, the technology, was part of the ethics of underground creation. The publication was made using the technique of 'tone dropout', Pam explains: half tone dots eliminated by overexposure in the camera work increasing contrast. They hand-painted over the photographs. It was a good production, she says. It does look beautiful — Pam still has a copy she showed me — the photographed bodies somehow made semi-abstract, thus disturbing the possibility of drawing a line between pornography and art. She reiterates that it was an anti-censorship action and an art thing.

> No one was named — we probably didn't mind being arrested but had other things to do. [Brown interview]

friendship and collaboration

Pam Brown was Sasha's muse, Denis Gallagher told me. Pam rejects this appellation: 'I was always Sasha's friend & accomplice, never a "muse".' Pam was just beginning to make her name as a poet when they met, and Sasha's respect for her work and her insights never wavered.

> I have always described [Pam Brown] as the most important poet writing anywhere in the English language. Which she is. [SS email to George Zisopoulos 29.10.2001]

Pam Brown was to form one of the closest and most significant friendships and artistic collaborations with Soldatow.

Pam was another who I needed to agree to this project. She came to visit one winter day when I was house-sitting in the Blue Mountains, so that I could record her talking about Sasha. I'd known her since those early days; known how much the two of them shared love of making music and poetry, some exclusive wavelength, and they'd be drinking and singing and uttering wisdoms and witticisms and keeping it all up when others had succumbed to tiredness or new-found reasons to get up early.

> Sasha loved women. He loved men too, very much in a different way. He had great friendships with women. There was love between us. There was no sort of sexual thing at all so you could be completely free as a woman with him, because his [sexual] focus was blokes. Maybe it was growing up with the babushka and the aunties.... If you were a fool he would shut you up... [Brown interview]

poet-led production of magazines, pamphlets and books

Pam Brown was involved in the vibrant poetry scene in 1970s Sydney. It wasn't only writing and performing but publishing; it was a flourishing milieu that saw all the known and unknown names of Australian poetry at the time producing imprints. A golden age of small presses, independent publishing.

> The city was central to the circulation and cross-germination of poetic experimentation in Australia
>
> It would be contentious to few to cite Sydney as central to a poetic boom in the 1970s. It was a movement of experimentation and poet-led production of magazines, pamphlets and books in which you [Pam] took part with a number of once Sydney-based associates and friends. These are some of Australia's most important poets: [Wakeling and Brown 2012]

Illustrious names follow; Pam Brown was among them, as poet, anthologist and editor.

In his Introduction to her 1990 book, Soldatow points out that Pam was a staunch supporter of small presses in Australia; all nine of her books had been published this way.

> Partly it is a way of maintaining control over her own product, and partly it is a hangover from the do-it-yourself philosophy of the 1960s. And it is also an important political statement. [SS 1990 Introduction]

> everyone grabbed it, who could resist?

Soldatow, while a champion of and practitioner in small presses, did also attempt inclusion in the more establishment well-funded journals.

In a 1980 essay critically examining the boom in indie publishing at the time, and the vexed ongoing question of the funding of small press enterprises, writer and publisher Michael Wilding discusses the uneasy relationship that would result from some of its practitioners' acceptance of government funding:

> The great boom in small press and little magazine publishing was not a result of Australia Council funding. Both the boom and the funding were consequences of the energies of the previous years, the anti-war movement, the release of energies pent-up under 23 years of Liberal-Country Party coalition rule, the bourgeois prosperity following on from the mineral boom. But the coincidence of the boom and the funding resulted in an inter-relationship. The funding was there, why not grab it; everyone grabbed it, who could resist? The new activities, the new energy became dependent on the government funding. Few people tried to set up a base independent of government grants, PiO was one of the few writers to make the case that Ferlinghetti always made in the USA, that to depend on government or institutional handouts is to put yourself at the mercy of governments and institutions. One day the funding stops and then where are you? In 1980, the shortsighted dependence on grants, the failure to establish any secure base for future political change, resulted in the collapse of the Australian small press movement. [Wilding 1980]

a re-analysis of the function of deviancy

In 1976 Sasha submitted a proposal to the editor of *Meanjin*, Australia's most prestigious literary magazine at the time. (Frank Moorhouse used to joke its Aboriginal name translated as 'rejected by the New Yorker'.)

> PROPOSAL: A critique of the gay movement and to some extent the women's movement based on a re-analysis of the function of deviancy in an advanced capitalist society. This is the starting point from which to show why it is that an advanced post-industrial society such as our own cannot collapse simply through the result of the contradictions inherent in its structure. Put simply, capitalism needs the opposition generated by the contradictions, for its own regeneration.

It would be the first piece of writing from the gay movement that would connect homosexuality back to a wider social environment (much the same as the women's movement did with feminism, but not, interestingly enough, with lesbianism, though they tried). [SS letter to Jim Davidson, not dated]

Soldatow thus was implicitly challenging the (generally accepted in intellectual circles) Marxist idea of capitalism, as a historical stage, being so full of contradictions that these must lead to its collapse. Which would lead to socialism. Soldatow, to the contrary, wanted to investigate or develop his idea that capitalism actually thrived on its contradictions. Half a century later, as we see that late capitalism (thriving so far) has created unprecedented, growing inequality and the devastation of the natural world, his idea does not seem so very outrageous

However bold and intellectually innovative Soldatow's proposal might seem for 1976, it was not up the alley of the prestigious journal. Then editor Jim Davidson shared his genuine interest in the proposal, engaging with Soldatow's argument in his letter, but he rejected it, in as friendly a manner as possible, as not suitable for this particular publication,

So I find the idea interesting. But Meanjin is not, I'm afraid, the place for it. (Arena probably would be.) And I say that with regrettable certainty, since six weeks ago I had to fly to Sydney and persuade the Literature Board that M is a literary magazine! So — quite apart from the controversy such a piece would engender — it would be seen by too many people as lying outside the magazine's rightful ambience. For that reason I cannot consider it. An article on the Homosexual Vision of E.M. Forster, yes; but that's about where I'm obliged to draw the line.

However next time you're down we might discuss other projects which could be relatively more easily accommodated.

All good wishes for 1977. [letter to SS 29.12.1976]

Only the second editor of the journal since the 'legendary' Clem Christesen [Sullivan 2010], Davidson made his mark by publishing new writers like John Tranter and Frank Moorhouse, but a lot of his work was lobbying for funds to keep Meanjin in print. And he who pays the piper...

continued to think about the ideas in his proposal

There is no evidence that Sasha submitted his proposal to *Arena*, another Melbourne-based culture journal, or anywhere else, or that he wrote the piece he proposed to *Meanjin*.

There didn't seem to be an audience for it, not one big enough, anyway, or powerful enough; there wasn't enough enthusiasm for his proposed work; and there was always a lot going on, things that did have an audience.

Soldatow continued, though, to think about the ideas in his proposal, and a year later, with his new lover and intellectual comrade Larry Strange, he would elaborate on them in the paper *Attention: Campaign Man with money to spare.* [chapter 2]

another poet was needed

After the production of *X*, Pam moved to Melbourne for a while, returning to Sydney in 1974. She joined Clitoris Band in 1975, travelling and performing in ACT, Victoria and Queensland. In 1977 after the demise of Clitoris Band she and a group of like-minded women formed the Lean Sisters Theatre Group and then the Sydney Womens Writers Group in '78; she was involved in Women's Liberation and with Micky Allan in the local arts scene. She was pre-occupied with feminism, but did see Sasha around, and thought of him when another poet was needed for a reading.

> I did put him forward as my substitute for a Tin Sheds reading that John Forbes & Ken Bolton were hosting at the Tin Sheds in 1977 because I couldn't do it — but they didn't invite him (I thought that might have been unthinking homophobia on the part of J Forbes). [Brown email November 2019]

John Forbes (1950–1998) had started publishing and giving readings in the 1970s. While it was possibly homophobia, as Pam Brown suggests, that at first made him exclude Soldatow (who certainly thought so), Soldatow came to respect his work and in 2001 wrote in a letter lengthy recollections of Forbes, another poet's poet, saying:

> Forbes will grow in stature as a poet in time — he unfortunately died at the height of his powers… [email to George Zisopoulos 29.10.2001]

He was right, just as he was right about Pam Brown, often cited as an inspiration and mentor by younger poets these days. In 2021 Zenobia Frost says:

> wherever there is a picture of the queen in a hall in Australia, replace it with a portrait of Pam. [Durbin 2021]

so many things you could say about Sasha

Brown wrote about Soldatow after he died, posting on her blog:

> There are so many things you could say about Sasha. [...] I loved him for his inventiveness, his wit and his daring lack of concern for limits. He believed in an anarchic philosophy that could set people free, he certainly wanted that and acted that way, boundlessly. [2006]

She shared his anarchist spirit, love of modern poetry, and involvement in underground publishing.

> It was fun and a bit risky to get around with Sasha. I have a strong moral streak that compels me to loathe hypocrisy, calumny and, well, in general, smooth explaining. But I'd credit Sasha with showing me how to laugh at peoples' foibles and jealousies rather than judging them and also how to laugh at life's absurdities.
> He was forgiving and generous.
> He liked to get drunk and play powerful music that nobody could resist. Especially at two in the morning.
> He could also be a terrible nuisance — like an ant in your warm and comfortable armpit.
> He liked to rock the boat. He lived in harm's way.
> He was an original kind of troublemaker.
> I know that in the years of our friendship, that Sasha was sometimes 'too much' for his friends and 'too much' for me too but I have not one, not even a smidgin of regret.

a Boys Own poetry world

The poetry scene in Sydney in the 70s attracted people like Laurie Duggan, who moved up from Melbourne when one of his 'good poetry friends' John Scott had reported 'it was pretty good up there'.

> [It was] a Boys Own poetry world, everyone trying to write the Big Poem that explained everything. I was as guilty. Adamson, Tranter. [Duggan interview]

On the one hand Duggan discovered that world of poetry machismo. But getting to know poets like Pam Brown and Ken Bolton provided his 'escape from the big boys'. In that context he met Sasha Soldatow. When he first came across Sasha, he thought he was 'a nut case, a weird guy'.

I didn't take him seriously as a writer, thought him just a bit crazy, but the more I heard him do things including reading, I thought, he's actually good at what he does [...] and by the time I saw him at Gung Ho poetry readings [which became the Harold Park readings] I was on board and... I did take him seriously. I just came from a fairly kind of boring ordinary background, suburbia basically, so I needed my eyes open to certain things. [Duggan interview]

So often Soldatow played a part in others' learning to see things in some way new to them.

no great measure of public recognition

In 1979 Soldatow wrote a 'biography and statement'; it's not clear whether he had a particular publication in mind or if it was practice for when he'd be implored to supply one. It starts:

For the past ten years Sasha has been writing, drawing, publishing, performing and yelling, but has achieved no great measure of public recognition as yet.

No great measure. What has he published by now? The six pamphlets in the *Patterns* series, and *What Is This Gay Community Shit?* A short story in an anthology. Some reviews and essays in newspapers and magazines. Some of his drawings illustrated his self-produced publications; some went to friends. He first performed *The Adventures of Rock-n-Roll Sally* in 1978 (its text was published in book form in 1990). He read at readings, performed in counter-culture venues. More stories in anthologies and his books would begin to appear in the '80s.

Sasha was aware of himself as multi-faceted, active, doing work of notable value. And the doing in itself was never enough.

As yet. He always kept a close eye on his reputation, in the literary world and its sphere of influence. It was one of his obsessions.

Soldatow's aggrieved sense of being under-valued, ignored, his sense of outsiderness was part of him from early on; it was a source, it seems, of both resentment and incitement.

An example of Soldatow's expression of this resentment is found in a three-page typed letter to Sydney poet Nigel Roberts.

Apparently someone called Eric Beech [sic, really Beach] had said he didn't like Soldatow's work and this 'Eric Beech' had the power to invite writers to the USA and Soldatow says it's the only way he'll get overseas. 'Beech' had only seen one performance of Soldatow's, who had read first when no one else would. Soldatow points out to Roberts the work he does; he memorises, he performs; he does 'hard work'. Responding to what supposedly has been said about his work, he says:

> What they're really talking about is what they think of ME and my sexuality. And then the things that I write about. [SS letter to Nigel Roberts 23.11.1978 typescript (carbon) 3pp]

Soldatow outlines some of his rejections and requests. He had been requested to read then told stuff was unsuitable; he'd been told don't wear drag, and more. And yet:

> I can hold an audience, and most poets can't. [letter to Nigel Roberts]

Soldatow mentions the rejection of his work for publication by publisher Michael Wilding, whose criticism was that the work was 'not saleable produce' and then, Soldatow claims, runs around looking for gay writing; Wilding had told the writer Vicki Viidikas that he couldn't understand Sasha Soldatow's work:

> Of course he couldn't. Cos it's all new and something that hasn't been done or even tried before. [...] I'm a bit sick of the fact that I have to strive to be twice as good as everyone else to get any recognition. And then, even that's not good enough. [letter to Nigel Roberts]

Michael Wilding, also an author and academic, was an acquaintance from the Push so when he set up Wild & Woolley publishers with Pat Woolley (of Tomato Press) in 1974, it would have seemed to Sasha that they would be likely publishers for him. Yet, although they existed in the world of outside-the-mainstream collectivist-consciousness, and although Wilding's rollicking memoir of the press relishes its counter-culture-ish ethos, the hand-written note of rejection to Soldatow cites commercial considerations as the reason for turning down his manuscript.

Nigel Roberts does not remember getting this letter, and points out that Eric Beach would never have claimed he had the power to invite writers to the States, and that he and other poets enjoyed and appreciated Sasha. [email 2.11.21] Soldatow usually conscientiously wrote 'not sent' on unsent letters he kept in his archive, and this is a carbon copy; still, maybe he didn't send it, but he wanted it read.

the living I had to do

Nigel Roberts wrote an affectionately observant poem about Sasha in 2019, published by Nicholas Pounder in a limited art edition 2020. In part it reads:

> but I came out
> as a writer / journalist / gay activist
>
> because
> I had a thing
>
> about the living
> I was allowed
>
> & the living
> I had to do.

Sasha said, don't run

After the infamous — or, now, legendary — night of the police attack on the first Mardi Gras parade and party in June 1978, Sasha reconnected with Pam Brown at the subsequent meetings and demonstrations. She recalls getting to know Sasha better and respecting a kind of savvy he had, at one of the demonstrations. The demonstrators were trapped along the fence of the Darlinghurst Courthouse. There were a lot of them, it was a large demonstration. They were surrounded when the police came towards them on horseback, and other police arrived too.

> Now they'd call it 'kettling' but they didn't have that expression then. I was standing with Sasha at the time, police on horses came towards us and people started running. I was going to run and Sasha said, don't run. And I thought, he's right, if you run they'll catch you, they'll beat you with their truncheons, they'll arrest you, and I stayed with him; I thought, oh good, a radical who knows what to do! So that was an important moment. [...] Sasha was the one who saved us from being beaten and arrested by sticking to the fence instead of running into the melee. [Brown interview]

the greatest festival on earth ever

Even while he raged about the perceived lack of understanding and appreciation of his work, Sasha did however have his comrades, supporters, admirers, and fellow-travellers in writing, hedonism and anarchism. Pam Brown, one of the most constant, loyal, and like-minded tells me about one of the best periods in the early days of her friendship with Sasha, at the legendary 1982 Adelaide Arts Festival.

By then Pam had moved to Adelaide with her then partner Micky Allan. She stayed in touch with Sasha, sending occasional postcards.

She had a job at the Experimental Art Foundation, and was working for the inaugural Artists Week in 1982, at the festival directed by Jim Sharman, which, she says 'was the greatest festival on earth ever.'

No way Sasha would have missed that. He wrote to Pam from Sydney, and said, we're going to form a gang.

> And that was the Bon Mot Gang. So I busily screen-printed these beaut T-shirts at work, that said Bon Mot Gang, we had no idea what we'd do but we had some T- shirts and we'd be a gang. [Brown interview]

When Sasha came to Adelaide, he stayed at Mary Christie's house. Christie recalls the shared house at Westbury Street, close to the Festival venues, as a hive of activity.

> There was a constant flow of people in and out of the house which meant there were groups of people drinking, talking and laughing in the garden a lot of the time....We did a lot of walking in and out of town, front garden to the back garden, over to the park, over the road to the pub to drink, talk and play pool. Lots of walking, talking, laughing, shouting, laughing, intense conversations about books, music, gossip and life. [Mary Christie text 29.7.2020]

In this perfect habitat Sasha met saxophonist Craig Tidswell, called Crab or Crabby by his friends, fell in love with him, admired his music, and began a long-term friendship. At the time, Tidswell had a band called Speedboat, reportedly brilliant.

Fun was even more fun when it had a serious purpose. The Bon Mot Gang found its purpose. Being who they were, the gang's idea of fun included a strident response, an objection, a demonstration, of a kind, against acts of repression.

The writers invited to the Festival's Writers Week were taken to a dinner up in the hills. And Craig's band Speedboat was engaged to play at the dinner.

But they didn't play for long; after two numbers Writers' Week chairman Andrew Taylor cancelled the performance, reportedly saying everyone hated it, or that no one could hear themselves converse. While the audience argued someone pulled the plug out of the sound equipment, and reportedly on purpose the sound engineer retaliated by making sure the microphone screeched during Taylor's announcement.

'"Art rock" crushed by writers' wrath' was the artful headline in the newspaper report.

The Bon Mot Gang heard all about it and declared it had been an act of censorship, that Taylor had taken objection to the content; after all, the band's songs were political, besides being, perhaps, musically challenging to some. Action was called for. Taylor was having a book launch at Writers' Week. The artist Ken Searle was there too, and has a vivid recall:

> It turned into chaos because when Andrew Taylor got up everyone yelled 'Bon Mot to you Andrew Taylor'. And Speedboat got up on the stage and started playing and everyone was throwing stuff around and John Forbes was yelling stuff, putting Taylor down as a poet and Laurie Duggan was yelling stuff... That was Sasha's contribution to Writers Week. [Wheatley and Searle interview]

It was front page in the *Adelaide Advertiser*. There was always an event that was a scandal at Writers Week, says Pam Brown, and that week, it was them. A thoroughly satisfying Writers Week then — a gang devoted to fun, old and new friends and crushes, reason for a demonstration and causing a front-page-worthy scandal.

After the Bon Mot days, Pam returned to Sydney and soon after moved into Ferndale Street, Newtown, three doors up from Sasha.

16

If you love me make me laugh

the Larry years 1977–1983

I get sex and affection, friendship and politics, lust and power, being generous and rude all mixed up. I always have and always will. In my mid-twenties, this led to the churning pain of a broken heart, sometimes causing it myself by smashing glass and throwing eggs and wine and cigarette butts across a lover's bed till there was nothing left but to leave. [SS 1996 *Jump Cuts* 230]

a very good recollection of meeting Sasha

When he met Sasha Soldatow in March 1977, Larry Strange had returned only two days earlier from a period of several months in India, mostly in Delhi and Calcutta, as part of his work towards his Master of Indian Studies at Melbourne University.

On 26 March 1977 Strange wrote in his diary:

Sydney. Meet Sasha.

That's all it says on that page.

It's one of those kinds of diaries. Cryptic. I once kept diaries like that too, fully believing that a word or phrase would bring back the memory of the event entirely. Such faith in memory when you're young, when you think you'll always be able to remember everything you want to.

And it's a diary not meant for anyone else to read. But Larry kept it. And eventually, after our talk in 2018 about the paper he co-wrote with Sasha in 1978, Larry let me see the diary along with some other papers, including letters between him and Sasha; we'd agree on the grounds of usage later.

I saw Larry again on another of his visits to Australia in September 2019. It turned out that he had a very good recollection of meeting Sasha, which began a relationship that would last seven years.

At the time Larry was involved with a woman called Helen, a lawyer who had also been involved in Women Behind Bars. She took Larry to meet some good friends of hers who were living in a house in Bourke Street Surry Hills:

Virginia Bell, Jenny Coopes and Sasha Soldatow.

> I was very intimidated because I was new to this racy gay lesbian mixed political scene, so I was very quiet, but Sasha told me later he was doing a serious checkout which I was probably not aware of. [Strange interview]

They all had coffee together and agreed they'd all go to the Tin Sheds that night for the 'feminist pool party' which featured a performance piece that would remain a vivid memory:

> There was a big above-ground pool, a metre and half deep, and the highlight was when a beautiful recording came on of Virginia Woolf reading *The Waves* and a woman, Chris Sharpe, came on in a taupe skirt and cardigan and she just quietly walked up to the pool and put two big stones in her pocket and sank into the pool! To me it was so shockingly irreverent, it was hilarious, it brought the house down. [Strange interview]

And it was a taste of what that scene was like at that time. Sasha made a point of sitting with Larry, who began to feel his interest, and probably Helen did too. They all went on to a party, with people Larry would eventually know well. After the party they went back to the Bourke Street house, had another drink.

Virginia and Jenny went to bed and there was just Helen and Sasha and Larry.

> Helen was lying on the floor and seemed to be asleep — whether she was lying doggo I don't know. We kept on drinking a bit and Sasha said, well I'm going to bed now and I just want to tell you that if you were interested in sleeping with a man tonight there'll be one upstairs available very soon. And I was completely unnerved by this and incredibly excited, something had clicked and I said okay and Helen stormed out and I had a night of incredible passion with Sasha. [Strange interview]

Strange went to see Helen the next morning and said he was sorry.

> She said you should leave, and that's the last time I ever saw Helen. [Strange interview]

Helen died in a car accident the following year. Meanwhile, Larry was staying with his long-time friend Jude Baker.

> And Jude just opened the door and said, oh Larry. It was so shocking. She knew all the people involved. And I said, I can't explain it, it's shocking, I've

hurt Helen, it was incredibly exciting, and I'm going back to Melbourne tomorrow. [Strange interview]

And he did. And now he reflects on what that incident says about Sasha.

Both his single-mindedness about it and his lack of concern for Helen. [Strange interview]

And the effect Sasha had on him remained. Larry says now, 'He drew my sexuality and my politics out of me.'

the anticipation of the next meeting

Larry and Sasha planned to meet again. Back in Melbourne Larry kept busy, with his Bengali studies, his friends, readings, films, his involvement in a production of *Macbeth* at La Trobe (worst *Macbeth* ever, he says) and some new sexual involvements.

But Sasha is there in the anticipation of the next meeting; the mutual interest had not waned.

letter from Sasha, coming last week May. [Strange diary 29.4.1977]

But that meeting took a bit longer than expected, as in the meantime Sasha contracted hepatitis. Sasha was staying with his friend and frequent host Margaret Fink, and after the quarantine period she made him leave. [chapter 12] That illness took Sasha back to his mother's house in the suburb of Vermont in Melbourne.

Phone call from Sasha, confined at Vermont with infectious hepatitis [...]. S too weak to talk for long [diary 1.6.1977]

The first of June: Sasha might only just have arrived at his mother's house, and wasted no time before phoning Larry, who noted a couple of long talks about 'the Helen situation'. About a week later, they could finally see each other again.

Talk to Sasha, much better. Will meet him in city in few days time. [diary 15.6.1977]

On 18 June, Larry's diary notes that he was at an all-night session to take down the set of a previous production and build the Macbeth set. And then...

Still later very welcome visit from Sasha on the way home from his first outing since hepatitis set in. [diary 18.6.1977]

A few days later, Sasha arrived at Larry's for a longer stay.

a glimpse into a family life unlike any

Larry tells me about going with Sasha to pick up some books from the family home in Vermont, where he had a glimpse into a family life unlike any he'd known.

> We go to this bourgeois leafy suburb to this impeccably kept brick veneer home with tasteful decor and we're walking through the house to go to the room where his books were and we passed the master bedroom and I said, Sasha what is that. There were axe marks. In the master bedroom door. And he said, oh that was Val [his stepfather]. Lily of course was in the rag trade and kept very long [working] hours and Val loved his stereophonic music and even at Daylesford used to blast out over the lake very inappropriately. And one night he's got his music on very loud… modern loud music, not the balalaika, rock I think.
>
> And she comes out and complains, goes back to bed, it doesn't get quieter, she comes out a second time, the third time she pulls out all the wire connections and takes them to the bedroom and locks the door. Val goes to the shed, gets the axe, and uses the axe on the door until she opens the door. This is in suburban Vermont. I saw the axe marks and Sasha told me the story his mother told him. [Strange interview]

Coming from such a different background, all of this, as for the friends in Sydney with such unlike homelives, was 'as exciting as it was scary'.

They understood from the start that their families were different. Larry, like other people Sasha would befriend, was entranced by Sasha's exoticism, by the Russianicity of him.

Again one must remember those times. That very Anglo Australia. You barely ever saw a non-Anglo person in public life.

No one talked about multiculturalism.

A book on the 1970s in Australia published in 2019 barely mentions multiculturalism. It says:

> [The Seventies] was the decade in which Australians began to accept the reality that their country was no longer just 'White', and adopted multiculturalism. [Arrow 5]

It is telling that in that sentence 'Australians' can only refer to White (i.e. Anglo) Australians, who as ever consider their experience as universal or central; the Indigenous and migrant were long familiar with 'the reality'.

Larry tells me about first meeting Sasha's grandmother. Sasha's mother, Lily, asked Larry about himself, about his family. Sasha's grandmother was actively present, paying attention, silently nursing her cognac. When Larry said his parents had divorced, grandmother made her only utterance: 'Oh, life is so hard.'

Larry tells that story doing the accent as well as he can, conveying in that utterance and its diction its pessimism and sympathetic resignation, a long melancholy tradition of separation, failure, disaster. The way he remembers that, 40 years later, the way that memory got replayed, was an indication of how the specific otherness of Sasha's family struck him, stayed with him.

As it had with those other friends of Sasha's youth in Melbourne.

Lily took Larry mushrooming, getting him alone to implore him to explain to her 'why is he like this?' — gay, temperamental, contrary. As if there could be an answer.

sinks into grim depression

This might have been the first time, but soon Larry would see that side of Sasha where his mood plummeted to a dark depth:

> Eve. Set out with S to see Uranium Salon at Pram — bitterly cold. S sinks into grim depression — we come home. [Strange diary 13.7.1977]

A happier time was just ahead.

I also consulted Soldatow's equally cryptic 1977 diary for July.

In early July he was having trouble accepting Larry's lover N but the acceptance seems easier for a while once they have a threesome.

In those days, or at that age, or in some circles, it was an unremarkable way to resolve a situation, or take advantage of one. N was part of both their lives for a while.

There'd be other threesomes, not an issue. (I recall the envy women like me had for what seemed like the uncomplicated, mutually respectful, prolific sex lives of gay men then.)

in Daylesford a kind of idyll

In July 1977 Soldatow invited Larry to the family country home in Daylesford. Their trip began the day after the grim mood. They travelled there by train; both of them in their diaries noted the snow along the tracks for much of the trip.

This period in Daylesford seemed to be a kind of idyll. The two were excited by each other and the time being alone together in Daylesford seems like a dream of a young love affair.

They explored what they had in common, a love of books, of literature, of modernism. Their aesthetic and political sensibilities harmonised. They excited each other in all ways, in that period of youth hungry to know everything, feeling that it was possible. 'It was formative, it opened horizons in me,' Larry says now.

Soldatow's diary recorded how he enjoyed showing Larry around the place he loved, gathering pine cones for the fire, taking up knitting when he couldn't find wool gloves in the shops.

Although it was cold and wet in Daylesford, the two of them were happy there, until family arrived to ruin it. Well, ruined it for Sasha apparently.

> Mum and Gran arrived and ruined the plans made for the weekend. And the dog + cat. I could feel myself getting tense. Started to be aggressive. Their mania for putting things away — even when you know they will be in constant use. So went to the shops. Then for water — but no pumps working! So all drove to Hepburn for some of the last spa. Came home and I erupted. That I wasn't there for amusement, last couple of months no joke for me — want to be left alone but as soon as I get away I'm again tether to someone else expectations = Control. Anyway. Evening proceeds calm, do cards. New series (#3) 'Russian Bam' 13 cards. [SS diary 1977]

Larry doesn't mention this in his diary; his says nothing on that and the following date but 'Daylesford'.

The days are full of reading — Larry read de Beauvoir, Orwell, Brecht, Hunter S. Thompson — walks into town, pine cone fires, visits from friends, drives in the country, card games. Sasha works on a card collection, on a project he calls 'Picasso Coloring-in book', and knitting a right-hand woollen glove for Larry.

Soldatow was also doing some writing in this period, and found in Strange one of the best things a writer's friend can be, someone willing to give a critical reading, in this case a gratifying one.

> Larry later reads through some of Iron Kisses which convinces him that I should write a sustained piece. He repeats that all of my prose writings seem to be like extracts from long novels. [SS diary 22.7.1977]

On his return to Melbourne, Strange found he was missing Soldatow, even among friends, and soon returned for another couple of days in Daylesford.

> Get up at 7.30 full of enthusiasm for getting back to D'ford. Leave N in bed –>Spenser st. Old parlour car style trains, alone in compartment. Sleep in

sun. Arrive midday, regular taxidriver to S's. He is quiet but not annoyed at all, glad to see me. I am relieved and relax, able to realise how good it is to be back with him. [Strange diary 7.8.1977]

Larry was willing to continue discussing Sasha's work with him, plans for publishing; he suggested edits, and they planned to work seriously on the material again in Melbourne.

On 9 August Larry returned to Melbourne alone, leaving 'reluctantly' (Diary) though he records a busy life in Melbourne — meetings with friends and academic advisors, going to see films, pub bands. And he was continuing to sleep with N.

plenty to talk about

Along with their affinities, their differences included the fact that Larry was immersed in his Indian studies — not an area of concern for Sasha, though he took some interest in the critique of British colonialism this entailed.

But they had plenty to talk about: the books they had both read, the books one of them had read, the books they meant to read, friends in common, friends of one becoming friends of both, tastes formed by similar films, introducing each other to music, films, ideas.

Sasha gave Larry *The Complete Plays of Mayakovsky*. He inscribed it 'for a wayward youth/from his insensitive friend/ 17 July 1979'. Larry gave Sasha a book of Bertolt Brecht's poetry, a gift which could not have been better chosen:

feel suddenly as if I've found a mentor in BB [SS diary 11.7.1977]

Brecht would continue to be a touchstone for Soldatow's writing and performance. Lines from Brecht are the Epilogue to his 1993 book *Mayakovsky in Bondi*.

leave everything I own and everything due to me

Among Soldatow's papers is this evidence of a jokey seriousness in this affair:

I Larry Strange being of sound mind in the event of death leave everything I own and everything due to me from whatever source to my dearest friend Sasha Soldatow. [hand-written piece of paper 9.8.1977]

Another hand-written note from Strange among Soldatow's 1977 papers explicitly expresses happy anticipation of a sexual reunion, but also:

Miss you very much some of the time at least a bit all of the time — certainly not just the sexual thing, more the talk, communion sort of feeling. But still won't belabour the point. [Undated]

jealousy is the curse that cursed Sasha

Later that same year (1977), Sasha was in Sydney and Larry, in Melbourne, was busy with friends and studies, and seeing another man as well. Sasha was depressed and jealous, and tells Larry about his feelings at length in a letter. He's been crying a lot, making scenes while drunk, while knowing he's being unreasonable. Twenty years later he recalled:

> In my twenties and thirties, there were periods when jealousy ruled my life. I can strongly remember the imbalance the emotion provoked. They are not pleasant memories. ['Undertow with SS' *Campaign* January 1997]

Jealousy is the curse that cursed Sasha. Especially in circles holding his kind of politics, jealousy was simply not to be entertained, it was to be banished or denied, because nobody owned anybody, sexual exclusivity came too close to owning somebody, freedom was everyone's shared ideal. Sasha knows he shouldn't care so much about Larry seeing Tony, a friend of both of them.

> I am feeling strong unmotivated jealousy, about one or two small matters but across the board, toward everything and everyone I care about. [...] And then the thing of Tony and you. Well I love you both strongly and my reaction is of course that my best friends should all be close friends which is perfect. But there's this awful nag. [...]
>
> Oh my dearest one. I do love you so much and I know it is returned strongly and all those commitment things are there.
>
> Actually you and Tony both being such sensuality [sic] makes me feel I am missing out something horrible and that's what I think it is all about. [...] I feel like this and I feel like that and nothing nothing nothing is going my way and its [sic] frustrating and depressing and I'm jealous of all those friends of mine who are having a good time while I'm miserable. I want to be with you all. I feel like I am following you all around tugging at your experiences saying me too again me too. [letter to Larry Strange 21.11.77]

Sasha's life was full of these cycles, Strange says now: depression and highs.

The letter adds that also Soldatow has been reading 'a wealth of good things'. 'Have at least ten things to introduce you to.'

After some weeks in Brisbane and Sydney, Strange returned to his home in Melbourne, for a happy reunion.

> 11.30 am arrive Spenser St. Home to find evidence of Sasha strewn around room. Slept for couple of hours. Annie rang — told her I didn't want to see anyone but S. Finally arrives early eve and all is little short of wonderful. [Strange diary 7.9.1977]

At the best times, it really was, says Larry now.

day was full of hedonistic pleasures

Once Sasha was back in Sydney, while Larry returned to conversations, parties, walks and so on with other friends and lovers, he noted several times that he was missing Sasha, and recorded phone calls, cards received, reports on the improved health.

> Talk to Sasha over phone. He's much better, on naturopathic diet, playing Chopin. Seeing only Margaret and Bill [diary 28.9.1977]

In October Larry joined Sasha in Sydney. A typical day was full of hedonistic pleasures with a close group of friends:

> Sydney. Up at midday. Leave Bill's walk through Rocks with S and into city for 'best cappuccino in the world'. [...] Night. Meet Bill and John Paramour [sic], eat at Circular Quay. Then to Rocks. Get drunk on martinis. Session with B & S then all exhausted. Sleep. [diary 26.10.1977]

More days of seeing friends; apparently I had just arrived back from Bali when I joined them. And we all gathered to watch the John Berger TV programs, the *Ways of Seeing* series. Larry notes more reading of Berger, whose influence took hold on us all.

It's a golden time, and these brief records arouse wisps of fond memories of places that no longer exist: a café in The Cross, a Greek restaurant in the city, and fun like this:

> Dance at Petersham Town hall with Stiletto — everyone there. [Strange diary 28.10.1977]

Two days later Soldatow returned to Melbourne, staying until 11 December. With Strange, he saw friends together, went to Judy Brett's wedding. Sasha also worked on a submission he planned to offer to Penguin 'on radical perspective on Australia Arts'.

> **radical perspective can be found in an essay**

A great example of his own radical perspective can be found in an essay Soldatow wrote at the time, after seeing a photography exhibition in the State's art gallery. It's called 'OLD NEGRO, HE HOES, PICKS COTTON, AND IS FULL OF GOOD HUMOUR' SAYS WHO?'

The title is in caps. Four typed foolscap pages contain the essay by Soldatow, subtitled: 'Thoughts about the National Gallery of Victoria's exhibition of photographs, titled "Farm Security Administration".' It's dated December 1977.

At first I found no record of any attempt to publish this anywhere else, or of the extent, or way, it was distributed. It seemed a piece whose forceful, crafted argument craved readers. At first, it was roneoed and handed out in the usual way.

But the piece was also published in *Arts Melbourne: A Journal of Australian and 20th Century Art* in 1978.

One of its editors, a long-time friend of Soldatow's, Meredith Rogers, published an essay in 2008 — 'Arts Melbourne and the End of the Seventies: the ideology of the collective versus collective ideologies' — in the publication *When You Think About Art*, a history of the George Paton Gallery (1971-2008). Set up in 1976, funded by a grant, the *Arts Melbourne* journal was edited by a collective. Of course it was:

> The collective was the preferred and seemingly natural organisational model for alternative cultural and political groups in the 70s. [Rogers 2008]

The publication might have been doomed to a short life but the fourth and last issue did include Sasha Soldatow's essay.

The 1978 journal had published an edited version, and as a postscript Soldatow wrote:

> I distributed the leaflets for about an hour before being stopped. As I attempted to find out why I could not continue I was assaulted by a senior member of the curatorial staff. I was then asked to leave. Police were called to remove me at which point I left without resistance. ['Old Negro' in *Arts Melbourne*]

Soldatow's 'leaflet' is a work offering a response few gallery visitors would have expressed, especially at the time, when a widespread awareness of a viewer's 'gaze' was not a standard of criticism; it is evidence of the diligence he was applying to his thinking, to his responses to art and the context in which it is displayed and viewed.

Soldatow records his disquiet at the disturbing images, from the 1930s, so at variance to 'this neat clean air-conditioned building'. He sought further information; some printed material reported the pictures' dimensions but little more.

> [...] I wanted an explanation of what the US Government thought they were doing, employing people to take photographs of starving, sometimes sick, homeless and helpless people. ['Old Negro' in Arts Melbourne]

He goes on to consider the position of the photographer, often with his 'small, unobtrusive' camera 'that allowed him to capture his subjects unaware'. Soldatow investigates the other work of a couple of these photographers, often in the service of, for example, a casino and a penitentiary.

And he goes on to elucidate a historical understanding of the effect of the 1929 crash, especially on tenant farmers.

Some of the photographers were aware of the contradictions under which they worked. Walker Evans was one; with James Agee he produced a book *Let Us Now Praise Famous Men*. Soldatow approvingly quotes Agee, who excoriated the 'parading the nakedness, disadvantage and humiliation [...] for money and for a reputation...'.

> He says it all more clearly when he writes: 'ABOVE ALL ELSE: IN GOD'S NAME DON'T THINK OF IT AS ART.' ['Old Negro' in Arts Melbourne]

friends, parties, readings, films

Later in December Larry joins Sasha in Sydney for the holiday period, staying with him chez Margaret Fink, making notes on friends, parties, readings, films on TV.

And the visit culminates in a great New Year's Eve:

> NY's Eve. Wait at Inez's for Jeune. Party on beach at Rose Bay — fireworks over harbour etc. Repulsive advertising crowd incl John Singleton. Rest of night dancing to good rock n roll band at Tin Sheds. [Strange diary 31.12.1977]

Everyone should have this much fun at some time in their lives.

creative energy to burn

While Sasha and Larry were together in Daylesford, Sasha wrote me a long letter, about the bucolic pleasures of the place, Larry, family drama, book troubles, recognition troubles, and creative energy to burn. (He often wrote to people about the pine cone fires he enjoyed there.)

> Well my dearest Inez I just had to escape to the country. And what an escape. Hot all day, perfect weather, then slightly coolish in the evening, a fire, more out of aesthetic considerations than heat. Larry and I have been here for a full day and already I've packed so much in. We're sort of living off the land, but not in the uk way that the dirts do. No. Yesterday we had the zuccinis [sic] from the garden down the bottom. Actually only one as it was abt [sic] a foot long. And today it's been a steady picking of blackberries with cream and chewing a bit of dill and a bit of wild sorrel and trying out the apples off the tree, and the plums and looking at the pears waiting to ripen. And I went around and snipped and cut and collected the pine cones while L read and lazed out in the sun. And now a glass of red while listening to the possums chewing away on the apples. One reason for coming up here was to write out some of the '1968 Monash Labor Club Spectacular' cos the pram factory has advertised for three new playwrights for which they've got two thousand each. [letter dated Feb 77 but it is 78]

Back in Melbourne he had been occupied with the latest family drama, and taking a firm position on the others' behaviours:

> But also needing to get away from Melb. Gran has been in hospital with an indefinable something which was thought to be cancer of the womb but it isn't. But she is still in hospital so I will stay in melb til she's out which will prob be middle of next week. [letter]

His gran would not die until 1991.

Meanwhile, Soldatow had also performed his *Rock-n-Roll Sally* poems, this time to an audience different from the one at Sydney's Tin Sheds in January.

> What else. Did another perf of Sally at the Pram Factory on Sunday. It went off quite well. Different from Sydney cause there was not the understanding of what I was doing to anything like the same degree there. Took at least three numbers before the audience realised it was funny. There was some shock — like a sonic boom. And I changed a lot of the presentation. It was a lot more low key, less tambourine, more connecting bits that I made up on the moment. Actually there was a marked initial

reaction to the costume. Melbourne isn't Sydney even though Sydney isn't all that hot. Well I still found it hard to feel the audience. But here it was a more obvious feeling that they didn't know what I was giving. [letter dated Feb 77 but it is 78]

Once back in Sydney, writing to Larry, Soldatow reported on the first production of the new Paris Theatre in Sydney, a reasonable if unsparing analysis of how bad that play was, and how badly behaved he and his cohorts were at the after party. Bad behaviour was a kind of point of honour, of self-satisfied amusement anyway.

I caused a bit of a stir with my publication handed out in the foyer called 'The Cameron Allen Love Sheet' — they tell me that Patrick White loved it. [letter to Larry Strange 6.7.1978]

That was a comic-but-serious poem about Soldatow's crush on musician and composer Allen, who reportedly said only that he was both flattered and embarrassed.

In the February letter to me from Daylesford, Soldatow goes on to mention several other friends he's seen, including Jane Arms. He'd had a tempestuous friendship with Jane Arms since their student theatre years; now she was a freelance editor for Penguin and they are already disagreeing about his proposed book, which wouldn't come out until 1987. [chapter 21] He is cross about the delays on submitting his manuscript, on decisions she changed her mind about. The slow progress of the book certainly wasn't going to be enough to satisfy the cravings to write and publish.

And as a way to do that with full control and immediate distribution, what could be better than a little magazine?

I was taking to Larry yesterday and again this morning about putting out a little mag again. Only small and roneoed but regular of things we want to say so think of it again will you. Cos quite truly I don't see that the Pram or Penguin are all that good prospects for me and I need to do something. [letter dated Feb 77 but it is 78]

We'd start creating *The Only Sensible News* later that year. [chapter 13]

Not only that Jane Arms at Penguin wasn't being as amenable as he wanted, the Pram Factory theatre group was another source of disappointment.

I feel out on a limb, but this time feel the forces of trendy Left conservatives closing around excluding my work. Interestingly there, the Pram performance had to be okayed by their collective and it went through as a Party. I felt so cheated. Felt like saying look when you perform is it work or play. In many ways the Pram is finished unless they can get some new ideas quick. They are looking for new actors to join them but they've only advertised in the Equity newsletter that really exploded me. I had to say to them — where did you come from, professional theatre? Or were you just a nobody who wanted to play around with some new things. Really I am discovering new sources of anarchism in me every day.

Well they're my gripes. No use sending me yours cos I'll be back probably before I can get them. See you soon, Love, Sasha. [letter dated Feb 77 but it is 78]

the Marx play at the Pram

In May 1978 I was in Melbourne again (a research job).

I was also recruited to join Sasha, Larry and others in a performance at The Pram.

The Pram Factory was a legendary alternative theatre run by a collective, many of whom Sasha was closely associated with. That month The Pram invited people to offer productions and somehow with Sasha, Larry and other friends, we put on a play there, a play about Karl Marx. One night only.

Marx Play with Inez. Larry. Ingrid. Kathy & Paul on the tape recorder. Perf. [diary 6.5.1978]

No one recorded anything then and my memory fails except that I wore a big old suit of Larry's to play the part of Marx but apparently it was fabulous. I met Pam Brown there.

make me laugh

During 1978, the affair was often carried on by mail, cards and letters, unstinting in loving and honesty and gossip.

On 4 July 78, Soldatow sent Strange a telegram that said only

If you love me make me laugh.

Larry still finds this amusing.

Remember telegrams? Young people often don't know what they were. You went to the post office and filled in a form, or you could telephone. You paid by the word, so you made it snappy. A telegram signalled urgency. A slip of yellow paper arrived with a knock at the door outside of normal mail delivery, the recipient probably feeling dizzy with alarm or hopefulness at the sight.

Anyway, that was one of Soldatow's lines that could be re-used and was. About fifteen years later Christos Tsiolkas said:

> At least twenty-three times you have said to me, 'If you love me make me laugh.' [SS 1996 *Jump Cuts* 254]

To my astonishment, I find in May 2020 that in a 2005 letter Soldatow said

> As my friend, Inez, a writer, said to me one day, when in the dumps — 'If you love me, make me larf.' [letter to Howard Smith 2005]

With no memory of this I make no claim to being the originator of this invaluable directive. It's his. Though then a faint memory stirred of me suggesting the line as he was hesitating at the Post Office desk over what to write in his telegram to Larry. It's clear by now that few memories can be verified.

their politics is action

A year after the first trip to Daylesford, in August 1978, Soldatow and Strange co-wrote *Attention: Campaign Man with money to spare.* [chapter 2]

Thoughts about the politics of gay life continued to occupy Soldatow; the following month he produced his piece 'Snaps from a Gay Album' in *Anarchist Honi Soit.*

> Stories that have to do with a process which many homosexuals ignore — that the path from oppression to liberation has got stuck at exploitation. That what happens is this: as one set of values is replaced by another, someone else becomes a deviant in another person's eyes. And nothing much happens except that power is transferred from one set of hands to another. ['Snaps from a Gay Album' *Anarchist Honi Soit* September 78]

A series of anecdotes follows; but the piece is more than a series of small narratives, it ends with a contemplation of their implication:

> There are two differences in practice.
> There are those who fundamentally accept the way the system functions. They argue, pass motions, draft resolutions., put questions and demands to those in authority. They respond to the power of the State with respect and use the methods of our corrupt parliamentary democracy. Their weapon is words.

> There are those whose knowledge comes from the street. Their politics is action. They comprehend the meaning of power since they are witness to its injustice. They align themselves with life as it is lived: that is where their struggle starts. ['Snaps from a Gay Album' Anarchist Honi Soit September 1978]

And those of course were Sasha's people: their politics is action.

a new dynamic to the relationship

The following year brought a new dynamic to the relationship with Larry Strange.

The two spent more time apart; in 1979, Strange was travelling; he went to India, Paris, Japan — always sending cards and letters to Soldatow, who always wrote back.

> I miss you more than I ever thought possible. Please catch the next plane home. However, since I know you won't, I get close feelings about you by wearing your clothes and sleeping in your sheets. Can you bring me back a few pairs of those floppy black pants? Hey! I honestly cannot bear how strong I miss you and want you here. Will write longer letter. Give Jude my love. [letter to Larry Strange, Friday 2.2.1979 hand-written on pink paper]

The next periods of the relationship would be increasingly marked by tempestuous outbursts and passionate reconciliations.

In an undated letter, hand-written in red ink on lined foolscap, Soldatow sets out his resentments, including not having been asked along to someone's place where a lot of other people, including Larry, were going.

> I know it seems a trifling thing to you, and that you do not take these resentments of mine seriously. But I do. [...] I would like to have come, not doing anything as I am, but no one asked me. It's not nice you know, knowing that your supposed friends are out having a bit of a good social time (which we all like) and that you are left by yourself.
>
> [...] I am terribly low. I kind of need my friends at the moment. But I feel to an extent abandoned by them. [letter to Larry Strange nd]

In 1983, Larry Strange is in Paris again, with his friend Jude, and loving all that is splendid in that city, but making time to write seven pages to tell Sasha of the many things he's enjoying. Strange also writes of the arrangements for when he returns to Sydney, saying 'would like to stay with you a couple weeks'.

Soldatow's reply could not have been nice to receive. The letter begins:

> Well you. This is not going to be a pleasant letter and its [sic] a very difficult one to write. [letter to Larry Strange 20.1.1983 typed on green paper, carbon nb SS kept carbon]

Recriminations follow. Reasonableness has no place here. Even though they both wanted the break from each other, Soldatow insults Strange for his letters about his trip, saying it sounded like a travel piece not something written for him alone, he said it was glib.

> You left out tons. [...] Why do you leave out all the important things? I mean, you were writing to me. Not to National Geographic. Posterity? It's like the letter you wrote me from India going down some river. I don't care about that letter either. But I do care about the one you burnt. It was important. Yes I am keeping a copy of this. Only in the most casual way for posterity. In the back of my mind I have a little half hope that sometime it might prove useful to some poofters to see what happens and what happened. Yes I have that sort of historical sense. But it isn't academic. I crave that information from the past. I crave it because there is so little. You know yesterday MT said to me that she'd found one of the Patterns at the press, the one on Dave, and she loved it. She'd never seen a poem written from one man to another. Okay, trite. But it matters. [letter to Larry Strange 20.1.1983]

It's a long letter; it goes on about the possibility of Strange moving into a house just down the road and Soldatow not being able to bear that.

> I am resentful. My house becomes a tomb. I hear you visiting other houses in the street. This does not have to be real — imagination is enough. And the shopping and going to the station and walking up the street. Mister, I am too old to stand in front of known windows at three in the morning waiting to watch the lights go off imagining who is there. [...] [letter to Larry Strange 20.1.1983]

Larry replied:

> I hated your letter. [...] I thought I had written you a good letter. I thought it was in itself an expression of affection, caring, communication. I tried to make it witty and interesting. I wrote it to you with enthusiasm and had it flung back as if it were some particularly tasteless insult I should be ashamed of. Do you prefer a letter like this? [letter to SS 7.2.1983]

Strange explains methodically about the house plans, about the guy he's seeing. It ends:

Yes I suppose I still love you too [letter to SS 7. 2. 1983]

fights their friends were witness to

The relationship continued to be on again, off again, and increasingly marked by jealousy, by bitter, even vitriolic, fights their friends were witness to.

A woman who was close to them both at the time, and we are friendly still, didn't want to talk to me about those times. It was a horrible time for her, and she doesn't care to recollect it.

A work colleague of Strange during those times who saw a lot of this acrimonious side also doesn't want to talk about those days either; they said Sasha spread a vicious and false rumour about them for no good reason back then.

Vivian Altman worked at the Workers Health Centre in 1979, where Larry Strange was working, everyone in an open area without privacy, and remembers a lot of yelling on the phone, Larry upset with Sasha.

Larry suggested I speak to his longtime friend Stephen Corbett. I met Stephen at a Sydney University café in 2019. After Larry first met Sasha, Corbett for a while lived in the same apartment block where Sasha often stayed, and met the group of friends that included Virginia Bell, Jenny Coopes, Sue Howe:

They were the most amazing people I had ever met — I thought they were fantastic. [Corbett interview]

Corbett helped Larry get a job at the Workers Health Centre, which was the start of a career that led to Larry's law studies and beyond (as I write this, Larry has lived mostly in Cambodia for several years, working at high levels in law and policy; Corbett has become one of the State's leading epidemiologists).

Larry moved into the house where Stephen was living with his then partner, so the pair also saw a lot of Sasha. And they saw a lot of the conflicts, the fights that went on with the two of them, which could get very nasty, even violent.

One time Sasha came down with a ripped shirt and he'd written on it 'fun, 19 May 1980'. [Corbett interview]

Ripping each other's clothes wasn't the worst thing, there are stories from others about things thrown about, furniture overturned, rooms spray-painted with black graffiti.

This was the time we were both seeing other people but of course there was always a double standard with Sasha. I was seeing an actor called Robbie McGregor, who now is happily heterosexual and has a partner. Sasha adored him. Robbie thought he was trouble. He came to stay with me in Jude Baker's house, where Sasha actually had a lot of his stuff with me…I came home one day, Jude had this lovely quite grand two-storey house in Annandale, I got home and thought what's that funny smell. [Sasha] had spray-painted three rooms of the house with black enamel, like graffiti, vilifying me… he was angry and jealous, Robbie was staying there. [Strange interview]

Larry reflects that they never had a clear agreement in this relationship, and maybe that was the issue. (What kind of clear agreement would Sasha have observed anyway, one might wonder.)

So I just calmly moved all of his things outside into the rain and said [on the phone], you'd better come and get them. [Strange interview]

A period of estrangement followed.

The house of course had to be repainted before Jude's return — black enamel is not easy to paint over! [Strange email 23.10.21]

Soldatow wrote his own version twenty years later, in his piece about jealousy.

> […] Breakdown, sob, smash, smash, run away.
> In moments like this, there is something very therapeutic about breaking things — you have to come back and clean up. Or, when you spray paint the inside of his house, you end up paying for the repainting and his drycleaning. (I still can't forgive him for this. Moving someone in who was only passing through for a week, all the time fucking him, not me. I smashed up big that night, when I found out. Books, paintings, precious objects, his grandmother's 19th century ivory painted fan.) ['Undertow' in Campaign January 1997]

Larry Strange clarifies that the spray-painting incident in 1979 (where Sasha's jealousy was misplaced) was one of two major scenes of violence, the other being in 1983, when Sasha flew into a rage at not being invited to something, at being excluded, blaming Larry:

> He raged and raged then become violent, throwing books and desk things on the floor, smashing paintings off the walls (and cutting his foot on

the broken glass) and smashing my grandmother's antique ivory fan ... (Later remorsefully he said he would have it restored by the well-known antiquarian Ann Schofield in Paddington who he knew — I never saw it again! Wonder who has it.) It then peaked when he tipped the wardrobe over onto me in bed. I had to stop it. So I grabbed him, still bleeding, and pinned him down on the bed by his shoulders until the spasms of rage stopped.

Next morning he calmly made a cup of tea for [my guest] who was of course alarmed and exhausted by what she had heard then went off to his subtitling job at SBS. That afternoon he rang and in a meek voice said 'Hi Laz, it's me. Can I still come to the party?! ...And I agreed. And so it went on until late that year when I think we had both exhausted each other and it was over. Hard to understand now. [Larry Strange email 23.10.21]

A feature of Sasha's jealousy was that it was aroused if his partner had other lovers while he insisted on his own freedom to do as he pleased.

There didn't seem to be this degree of ferocity in subsequent relationships.

Sasha was loveable, he was totally loveable

Of course it wasn't always like that; Sasha's attractive side was undeniable. He charmed people, and he taught them useful things, practical skills. And that's what Stephen Corbett mostly talked about.

> And Sasha was loveable, he was totally loveable. One of the things he said to me that makes me laugh in retrospect, he said, my job is human relationships...For a time I'd have to say he was my closest male friend. [Corbett interview]

Stephen tells me about Sasha helping him through a difficult emotional situation with a mix of sensitivity and toughness; and he remembers Sasha's stories about his earliest years: his parents in forced labour camps, the migration from Germany, the refugee years, growing up pampered by several Russian women, his precocious piano-playing. He remembers his outrageous statements and his hilarious, twistedly topical and inventive performances:

> At one stage there was a feminist trend to show doilies as art, [as] a feminist art form, so Sasha started doing these paper-cut doilies and dressing up in them...One night we had a party and his character was The Disco Twit — he dressed up, he had a moustache. [Corbett interview]

Doilies were the kind of fussy, antiquated, feminine bits of domestic ornament whose reclamation by feminists might have seemed absurd, and might have been considered ironic.

Corbett later sent the photos. Sasha in red tights, long socks and sports shoes, had fashioned some crudely forged paper doilies as ludicrous appliqués to his top, and wore a paper hat cut with patterns, and silly paper eyebrows fasted to his spectacles' frame. He had affixed a small moustache to his upper lip (moustaches were in fashion for the 'clone' version of gay appearance).

I wonder if only good-looking people have so much fun looking ridiculous.

Corbett also talked for a while about making the newsletter at the Workers Health Centre and how much Sasha taught him about typography and how to set up a newsletter.

> Sasha taught me to lay things out, his sense of typography and composition, that's what he was so good at, his drawings, his stylistic stuff, beautiful, his pencils, his attention…That's the important thing to say — drawing was important, getting the look of the page, I felt it was a real European sensibility, he loved the German Expressionists, and some of his work looked like the Expressionists. He loved Walter Benjamin, he loved that European intellectual stuff. [Corbett interview]

One of many times the attribute of 'European' is applied to Sasha by himself or others.

Next comes the story of another significant relationship of those years, one that was conducted at the same time.

17
time has a fluidity

David Marr 1978

Time has a fluidity that only hurt emotions can bring into focus. And even then, one can never be sure of the accuracy of one or other of these disparate perceptions. [SS 1993 *Mayakovsky* 27]

a life-shaking experience

David Marr wrote Soldatow's obituary in the *The Sydney Morning Herald* in 2006.

> To fall in with Sasha at this time was a life-shaking experience. He marched and drank under the banner of Liberty. Behind him he trailed the notion that he was a spirit from another place [...] He had things to teach and he was not to be contradicted. The deal he offered was this: place yourself in my hands, and I will set you free. [David Marr 'a spirit from another place' *SMH* 8.9.2006]

The alert reader might suppose that Marr was one of those who 'fell in' with Sasha. They met during, and contributed to, a formative time for both of them.

I would have first met David Marr around the same time. I went to see Marr at his house in August 2018; I had last been there in the mid 1980s to interview him about writing biography for a bookshop magazine I edited; he was then working on the biography of Patrick White and had just signed the publishing contract. It turned out to be one of the most widely-acclaimed literary biographies; Marr never wrote another biography while becoming increasingly prominent in several media for his journalism and commentary. He always expressed himself forcefully, with a fluent eloquence, articulating progressive, if not radical, positions. He had been thinking about what I'd be about to ask him.

I can't remember when Sash and I met. My wife and I separated in late 1976, she went off to Italy for a long time and I set about the business of being a poofter and it was difficult and I was saved in a hundred different ways by meeting Jenny Coopes, who was an artist at *The National Times*, and the women of the Glebe commune. [Marr interview]

Those were the women who around that time began to live in a sprawling old complex of apartments that Roelof Smilde bought for himself and friends to live in, which became known as the Glebe commune. Marr remembers women like Coopes and Virginia Bell — who, earlier, Sasha had shared the Bourke Street house with [chapter 9] — and Jeune Pritchard, also a friend of Sasha.

In those days it was a pool of wonderful bright free funny and fundamentally serious women, serious about the law, serious about art, serious about changing how we felt about sexuality, serious but with lots and lots of laughter and that's where I met Sash. So that was forty years ago, roughly. [Marr interview, next quotes the same unless noted]

They began an affair that was important to both of them.

[The relationship was] one that was kind of shattering and profoundly unsettling and in many ways good for me, that sounds awful, good for me, but it was quite something in my life.

But there was a secret Marr only learned later.

It was only about eight or nine years ago maybe ten years ago I discovered that while Sasha and I were having our fling, which was a serious business for me and I thought a serious business for him, he was living with Larry. He was living with Larry! That was all happening behind Larry's back. All this stuff about freedom, and doing what you must, and not being bourgeois is terribly important, all of which I took very seriously in him, was just fucking behind Larry's back. I had no idea, absolutely no idea.

A secret where there was meant to be openness and honesty.

There he was lecturing me about decency and freedom, and true values which are not bourgeois values, while betraying Larry.

Larry Strange confirmed that while Sasha freely told him that he'd be going off to see David, making Larry uncomfortable in shared social situations, he only learned recently that David didn't know about him.

I now think of Sasha insisting that his 'historical sense' insisted on intimate tellings: 'it might prove useful to some poofters to see what happens and what happened.' [letter to Larry Strange 20.1.1983]

Back in their time together, Marr was exploring his ethical and erotic horizons. He says Sasha took him on as a sort of mission, and that was what he wanted at the time.

> I believed if I was going to be a poofter — and I *was* going to be a poofter — then it was very important that I shake off bourgeois values and arrive at a more properly based set of principles by which to live etcetera. So he was going to instruct me in this while having quite a lot of sex. And oh it was so long ago that I've got to be really careful about thinking back to that time because to some extent I enjoyed it, at times enjoyed it profoundly, and it was important and I can still see quite a lot of it. I can see what he looked like, I can remember what he felt like, I can remember something about the sex that we had. I thought it was pretty good though I was to learn further down the track it wasn't all that great and I'm sure that was much more my fault than his as he was pretty adept and I wasn't.

But then I just was writing my first book.

And as many a writer might agree, a writer's book in progress is the most important emotional and intellectual relationship in their life at the time.

Marr, far from alone in this, was profoundly affected by the 1975 dismissal of the reformist Whitlam government, an event still mired in secrecy and contention. The Chief Justice had advised the then Governor-General how to bring this about. Marr has spoken of this many times:

> 'The most important political event of my life was the sacking of the Whitlam Government in 1975,' says David Marr. 'It taught me how ruthless, how daring, how unscrupulous the conservatives in this country can be in their pursuit of power. It's been a guiding light for my entire career.' [Wilson 2015]

In 2020 the so-called 'Palace Letters' were released and 'confirm the worst fears of those who viewed Governor-General Sir John Kerr's sacking of the Whitlam government as a constitutional coup.' [Wallace 2020] 1975 must have been the start of Marr's pitiless scrutiny of the political class and of its alliances with repressive forces of fundamentalist religion and ruthless capitalism.

The book he was working on then became essential in a study of Australian politics at the time, but Soldatow had nothing to do with that at all.

> I was writing a book [*Barwick*, 1980] about the Chief Justice of the nation, to tear him down because of what he'd done in 1975, and I was determined to do it in an absolutely professional and appropriate way. I had a big task on my hands, and I don't think [Sasha] gave a shit, because it wasn't poetic enough or something, it wasn't enough about the soul. It's now looking back. But I've just started to think he was trivial. You know, I was very fond of him, I hugely enjoyed his company, he was such fun, so enlivening by being so unexpected, and by knowing things that were out of my ken, and that was always a great claim of his of course for attention and love, that he knew things. And he did. Then we had the big bust up. [Marr interview]

a question of principles

The story of the precipitating event of their emotional break-up became one of Sasha's defining stories; he told it often.

At issue was a question of principles, about which both felt strongly and sincerely, but not in the same way. Marr recalls a night in his car. Sasha had said they needed to talk and they drove for a while.

> Then finally and I can't tell you what it was all about but part of it was my utterly bourgeois and incomprehensible behaviour in speaking to the police about the burglaries that had happened in my street. And it ended in fisticuffs.
>
> It ended with him beating his fists, not particularly hard, it was exasperation, trying to make me see, you just didn't deal with the police. Well, my friends had all been robbed and I'd seen the robber and I felt I could help them. [Marr interview]

Sasha told his version of the story then and in the future. It was one of a solid repertoire, told in several places, in conversation and in publications.

David had 'called the police' is how Sasha put it, and Sasha's undying principle was that you never ever called the police, not for anything ever. Old Push values.

'Attack' in *Private — Do Not Open* (1987) is a piece less than a page long in a chapter called Quick Exchanges. Previously it appeared in 'Scenes from a Gay Album' in *Anarchist Honi Soit* 1978. Soldatow/the narrator tells a story about himself and an unnamed man. It starts:

> I've known him for just under two months. He's nice. I like him and we get on well together. We go out together a lot, sleep together. I think I understand him, and I'm getting quite involved.

> He comes round one night to my new flat for dinner. We chatter on, drink, gossip. It's pleasant with him being there and me cooking. Relaxed. A new friend. [SS 1987 *Private* 103]

Then the new friend tells him something that makes him drop his cooking. In Sasha's version, he had 'called the cops'. The evening is not pleasant any more. The new friend doesn't stay that night.

> I spend three days worrying about my new friend. I write him a long letter pointing out why one never calls the cops. [SS 1987 *Private* 103]

This where Marr found out for himself what he wrote forty years later in the obituary:

> He had things to teach and he was not to be contradicted.
> [Marr 2006 'Spirit']

It seemed not to be a practice of Soldatow's to try and see things from another point of view. Soldatow's version became solidified: in the famous way of memory, once told, the memory of an incident becomes the memory of the last telling and the initial incident no longer can be directly remembered.

David Marr had been at home working, there was a knock at the door, and at the door was a strange man.

> And he said something, like, is Cecily here, it was the old trick of burglars, if someone was home you asked for a fake name. I didn't think any more of it. But when my neighbours, who I was fond of, came home they knocked on the door and said, did you see anyone on the street today, because our house has been completely turned over, and a couple of other houses on the street have been completely turned over. And I said yes, and I went to the police station and they showed me piles of photographs and I couldn't identify anyone and didn't identify anybody.
>
> But that was too much for Sash. And he was passionately passionately disbelieving that I could have done such a thing. It wasn't why but how could it have even crossed my mind to have done it. [Marr interview]

This was a mismatch not so much of principle but of something else, some aspect of character; an aspect that eventually caused problems with many of Soldatow's friends, an aspect that included an immovable certainty in his own position on things.

> We didn't break up because of my insistence on the right to speak to the police under certain circumstances, but I just didn't find the passionate

rage at all congenial, I thought it was crackers. And I do not much go for crackers people, because in my experience, and it only became true of Sash a long long time later, that the mad and drunks and crackers people deserve our pity and our care and our help but they are boring. And I thought in the end of Sasha, it was simply boring. And I think that was the end, the night in the car was the end, I can't remember exactly now. Anyway, all that time he had Larry to go back to it seems. [Marr interview]

The end but not the last time it was the end.

Here he, I'm pointing to *Mayakovsky in Bondi*, he describes the ending as a disaster and it was, it was really unhappy. [Marr interview]

That's where Soldatow wrote another version of that first break-up after he and Marr had their second fling in Moscow in 1991.

We were lovers many years ago.
Fifteen, to be precise.
Both of us gullible for companionship.
Lovers too soon, so it ended badly. […]
We parted enemies and friends.
That is the truth.
[SS 1993 *Mayakovsky* 27]

police were the enemy

It's true that in those days [1977-8] the overwhelming fact about the police was the kind of brutality, corruption, and mendaciousness that was common then, revealed in the Nagle Royal Commission (1978) that Virginia Bell described [chapter 9], and the brutality of police at demonstrations that Pam Brown mentioned, telling of how she formed a friendship with Sasha [chapter 15] and what she experienced in the Victoria Street squats. [chapter 7]

To what extent was Sasha's horror shared, at the thought that a friend might voluntarily talk to the police? It was part of the credo of anarchist and radical circles: police were the enemy, you never helped them, you thwarted them when you could. Those values were behind the sheltering of escaped criminals like Ray Denning. [chapter 9]

a friendly tone established again

Soldatow continued to send letters to Marr that year, bitter and accusatory; one was a letter of recrimination about not being invited to a party by Marr. Soldatow kept carbons, carefully filed in labelled folders.

> I'm enjoying this letter; enjoying being pleasantly nasty [letter to David Marr 25.9.1978]

Ten years later, a friendly tone between them had been established again.
With a network of friends in common, friendliness in spite of that resonant moment of disagreement is a good option.

A few years later, there would be a reunion full of romance and drama in Moscow.

later perceptions of Sasha

Marr's research for the obituary included his own reconsideration of the past, and his later perceptions of Sasha, which my visit had returned him to.

> Sash never doubted he was fascinating, never. Whatever he doubted about his life, his friends, whatever, he never doubted that what he was doing was compellingly interesting. For somebody somewhere at some time. And I've been thinking about that the last couple of days and one of the things is, he lived by charm, he lived by fascinating people, for a good part of his life, and he was very good at it, very good at it. So there was lots of evidence available to him that he was charming, so that looking after him and feeding him and fucking him and drinking with him and things was worthwhile for others. Because I honestly don't think he ever saw himself as a sponger which is what he was, I don't think he thought of himself as that, he saw himself as giving good value, great value, and Margaret Fink in here [Marr's 2006 notes] told me when I was doing research for his obit that she looked after him financially for 25 years.
> So Sash knew he was fascinating and was good company.
> [Marr interview]

And plenty of people confirmed that sense of himself.
Even if, as Marr posits, Sasha had huge literary ambitions and they were not fulfilled.

> Every step, every fragment, [is] catalogued and saved, he was waiting for you, Inez, he was waiting for you. A collection of papers like that [Soldatow's in the Mitchell Library] speaks from the grave. He always always wanted to be taken seriously. It was such an interesting, perpetually interesting — not really a contradiction but — he was so funny, he was so witty and sharp and most of the time light — but he wanted to be taken seriously. He wanted applause and laughter and he wanted people to think he was gorgeous and he was charming and in his early life he was beautiful and sexy and all of that and all of that was his strength but he wanted to be taken seriously and he had a Russian notion of what serious was.
>
> It involved suffering. Sacrifice. Throwing yourself on the winds of chance. It involved disappointment. Injustice. Cruelty — victim of cruelty not inflicting cruelty. It involved being misunderstood, overlooked. All of that tremendously Russian and he certainly achieved a lot of that. [Marr interview]

Marr had a theory about what kind of experience forms the character of someone like Sasha:

> But the one thing we must never forget is the overwhelming damage done to someone applauded at the age of six for playing the piano in the Collingwood Town Hall or wherever it was! I've had this theory that people never truly recover from that. The six-year-old, the eight-year-old who is a sensation, they never truly recover. [Marr interview]

I could find no evidence of this early public piano playing, but certainly Sasha was a gifted player from an early age.

Constant applause, treated as one who can do no wrong: if (to any extent) childhood forms a person, Sasha (to some extent) was formed by such treatment, as we've seen. [chapter 6]

bonfires of drama notion of intimacy

After the time in Moscow [chapter 26], some friendship was maintained for a while, and in October 1991 Marr wrote a long letter from Sydney. He would go on to give, as requested, his critical reading of a manuscript Soldatow had sent him [chapter 28], but before he opened up the package carried from Moscow, he wrote some pages of a personal letter, with painstaking care to express honestly, without haste, his then analysis of the effect on his life of their time together.

...I've been thinking how much my life has been shaped by our time together fifteen or so years ago and your bonfires of drama notion of intimacy, commitment, love. I withdrew then exhausted, embarrassed, baffled, unsatisfied. That was my first truly intimate contact with a man and I thought for years — still suspect — that it always has to be like that. The fear I've always had of losing myself in other people was stronger by the time I broke with you, has always been strong. I thought you were asking me to show my love by disappearing into your idea of myself, to throw myself into a drama that was about me but not my own. But, Sash, drama bores me as a way of life — then & now. [...] [hand-written letter to SS 27.10.1991]

The generous allotment of time and thought, in the letter of many pages, hand-written during a retreat from city life in an isolated country house, is a testament to how much an experience of care and closeness with Soldatow could not completely be destroyed.

18

a bellicose wit

Rock n Roll Sally; 1980s poetry scene

Performance was something that we all did at that time. Many of them were impromptu, like the ones Susan Howe and I did at Mrs Meier's Easter and Xmas parties for us waifs and strays. There was often a lot of nudity. Sometimes these performances got a public showing. [...] There is no record of these events mainly because they were done for the heck of it. [SS 1990 'Memoir' *Rock-n-roll Sally*]

a golden time of your neighbours being your friends

After the days of the Bon Mot Gang at the Adelaide Festival in early 1982, Sasha told Pam Brown that a house was available three doors along from the one he was sharing with Sue Howe in Newtown.

Brown didn't have a job yet then but had received a small inheritance when her mum died so she could pay the rental bond. Jenny Coopes and Jeune Pritchard were her next-door neighbours. Ferndale Street was great, she says. They were living close to each other, in a golden time of your neighbours being your friends, and you made music and performances together.

> Sasha also helped spend almost my entire little inheritance. I got a small grant from Ozco [Australia Council]; you used to have to give an itemised budget [in your acquittal] in those days, and I included 'one pair of jeans for Sasha Soldatow'. We just bought grog, and lived, and I used to pay for a lot. [Brown interview]

Whoever had money paid, that was the ethos, at least if you hadn't been brought up rich.

Sasha Soldatow and Pam Brown found and tended in each other their creative spark, more of a blaze really, and all in a spirit one might call anarchic: pure play, with rules you made up as you went along and broke as soon as you felt like it. They used to compose together; Sasha parked his piano at Pam's; Pam played her guitar and sang. They made little movies. One was called *The Limited Theatre of Thunder*. Two short clips with Soldatow are on YouTube.

There's very little video from those days, and very little audio. Imagine that. And not so very many pics.

> So we spent a lot of time making up songs, he was writing, I was writing, he'd edit, he'd always want you to edit, you've probably done that with Sasha, endless editing with Sasha. [Brown interview]

he was always right

Pam was becoming good friends with Elizabeth Drake, and Pam listened as she and Sasha shared a lot of music knowledge.

> [Elizabeth] was a concert pianist, Sasha was a pianist too, not as advanced as Elizabeth, but it didn't matter. So I learned a lot about opera. I'd never listened to opera, he knew everyone. [Brown interview]

He actually did know.

One day they were driving to a party in Brown's little Fiat and they had the radio on, listening to John Cargher's ABC Radio Saturday afternoon show, *Singers of Renown*. The music was still going when they arrived, but they couldn't get out of the car …

> Because Sasha had to guess who was singing and what year, and he had to check whether he was right and of course he was and then we could get out and go to the party.
>
> He really did love opera and knew a lot about it. He was so dramatic himself. [Brown interview]

Elizabeth Drake remembers that they listened to contemporary music also — *Stimmung* by Stockhausen — and Sasha knew a lot about that as well.

The surprising thing to learn was that Elizabeth Drake didn't know Sasha played the piano, let alone that he was generally considered to do it very well. He might have refrained from playing in her presence; she was already a highly-regarded musician and composer of deep and wide experience. But he did know a lot about pianists, Drake recalls; they'd listen to piano music together and pick who was playing.

> Sasha was always right, and I was good at that too; we'd go, definitely not English could be Russian, so we'd suss through. When I think about that he must have listened to a lot of pianists. [Drake interview]

They had both grown up in Melbourne, Drake a few years older, but she didn't know him from her piano student circles; there were two main schools, she relates, the one she went to, and so Sasha must have gone to the other one, the Spivakovsky school, founded by another immigrant, and that seems likely. (Or perhaps he only had private lessons.) The school does not have records of the students from that time. Soldatow did keep some of his certificates from the Australian Music Examinations Board of Music for pianoforte: 1960, passed 4th grade; 1962, passed with credit 5th grade; 1963 passed with credit 6th grade.

any excuse for a party

When Pam moved out of Newtown to share a house with Elizabeth Drake in Petersham, Sasha moved out of Sue Howe's and took over Pam's lease at 3 Ferndale Street.

Sasha somehow obtained a front-loading washing machine — he bought it, Pam Brown tells me — and you could watch the clothes go round. He held a party for the washing machine. He placed chairs in front of it, facing it. Any excuse for a party. I remember that party.

> He'd put a pot plant on top and he'd be, 'come and see', and the plant would shake to the vibrations. Like a big kid with his washing machine. But everyone was a bit poor, so, a washing machine. I didn't have one. [Brown interview with Amanda]

Sasha actually knew about washing machines too, Elizabeth Drake tells me; he told her which one she should buy (a Hoovermatic) and she had it for years. It was just one other thing he had learnt with his habit of curiosity and desire to know. He was interested in everything, Drake says. There was the time they drove down to Coalcliff to visit Ken Bolton:

> Sasha knew all the trees and all the herbs and all the birds and everything, all the names. I remember driving into the country and being amazed at all the knowledge that came pouring out about all these different things we were going past. [Drake interview]

dedicated, contemporary performance-art centre

Amanda Stewart, who had helped start the radio program *GayWaves*, came to the party for the washing machine; she and Pam had met by then.

Soon they were all performing at readings together and doing performances at the Performance Space. The Performance Space, in Surry Hills, had been a derelict building that a man called Mike Mullins squatted in, in the early 80s...

> ... and set about turning it into a space for 'critical dialogue in the research and development of contemporary arts in Australia'.
>
> So came about the idea of a dedicated, contemporary performance-art centre for Sydney. The Greek landlord didn't seem to mind too much, either, for the idea was soon incorporated legally into a charter and a statement of artistic intent.
>
> [...] In March 1983, an inaugural season of contemporary performance, visual art, multimedia works and forums was launched on to the public — and Sydney's idiosyncratic Performance Space was born. Mullins was its first director. [Bennie 2004]

At the Performance Space in 1983 or 4 Elizabeth Drake played 'Care Nome' from Verdi's *Rigoletto*, and Sasha did his 'Percy Grainger and the Whips'. Pam Brown remembers she took some photos of him wearing only underpants because he was being Percy Grainger. Those photos, alas, were not found.

Sasha performed his Grainger piece also at the Sydney Gay Centre in 1988.

combination of musical virtuosity and sexual non-conformity

Elizabeth Drake isn't certain where she first met Sasha. The performance crowd would hang out at Exiles Bookshop (in Taylor Square) after shows and it might have been there.

Sasha invited Elizabeth to play at a salon concert at Margaret Fink's house; Drake remembers playing Chopin's Ballade in G minor there. Subsequently, Drake accompanied Soldatow on his Percy Grainger piece.

Drake already had a history with Percy Grainger.

She had told Soldatow about the time she had performed at the Percy Grainger Museum in Melbourne in 1967, in front of Grainger's widow, who then stayed overnight in the place, to commune with him. Elizabeth herself didn't think Grainger was there, though says the place felt ghostlike, with all the theremins Grainger used to play. (Grainger often composed for this electronic instrument.) She didn't see the Museum's collection of whips — you have to apply for access — but thinks Sasha must have at some point. Those whips were the basis for an art work Sasha made and gave to her.

> It's got needles through it and it's on a green piece of paper, a bit bigger than an A4. They were threaded needles, provocative, visceral, effective, a homage to Percy Grainger. That's the kind of thing he'd like to do; he'd pick up on something that you shared, and he'd create things and make things and give you things, very generous. [Drake interview]

Sasha gave away his drawings and paintings freely; many people testify to Soldatow's artistic talent but for him it was like playing the piano, he knew he did it well but it was a kind of sideline.

Percy Grainger (1882–1961) had been a popular composer and concert pianist in his day — a 'megastar' says the Grainger Museum website — and probably best known for sampling British folk tunes. The rather twee sound of his best known work *Country Gardens* does not make intuitive the knowledge of his extensive accomplishments and interests, which, besides musical composition, performance, and the invention of new instruments, included a long-time bondage and discipline practice in his private life.

This combination of musical virtuosity and sexual non-conformity made him a certain object of interest for Soldatow, who drew a connection; in a letter that he said included some slides — which cannot be found — he says

> They're from a performance I do titled 'Percy Grainger's Theory of Music based on Moaning' in which I trace the similarities (confluence) between Grainger's sexuality (whipping) and his interest in 'free music', a precursor to electronic music. [letter to Ken and Louise, 7.11.1985]

Laurie Duggan sent me this extract from his old diaries, a snap of a poetry event in 1985 where among other notables Sasha performed:

> [...] Friday night, primed up at the pub, then went across to Newtown for the first of the Gung Ho readings [these metamorphosed into the Harold Park Hotel readings]. Read second, after Joanne Burns & went o.k. (read

'Blue Hills 14', 'Pastoral Poems' & 9 of the short 'Dogs' pieces). After me were Sasha Soldatow (taking his clothes off, putting them on again and tearing his shirt accompanied by doctored slides in a piece about Percy Grainger), then a break, then Carol Christie (the co-organiser), Amanda Stewart & Pam Brown. [Laurie Duggan diary 18.8.1985]

In November 1989 Sasha Soldatow published 'Percy Grainger's Theory of Music based on groaning: an opera in twelve scenes for two characters played by one performer who cannot sing' in *Cargo* magazine no.7. [next chapter]

It's curious that Soldatow never made more of his work on Grainger; there were only very few performances and that single published piece.

Cabaret Conspiracy

I spoke with Elizabeth Drake and Jan Cornall at Jan's home in Newtown in early 2020. Jan hadn't known Sasha as well — must have seen him around the film scene she thinks; she's a talented and widely experienced performer herself, a writer, an entrepreneurial workshop leader, so it was surprising that she said she experienced Sasha as a very critical person, and was 'scared to death' of him:

> He could cut you dead with a comment... I thought he was so intelligent and intellectual I was intimidated and I felt he could with one word about a show or a film he had seen he could demolish, but brilliantly demolish [it] in a sentence or a phrase, so sadly I was always a bit too terrified of him. [Cornall interview]

Jan and Elizabeth had recently been the highlight of a concert with a revival of their show *Failing in Love Again*, first performed in Melbourne in the 1970s then in Sydney as part of *Cabaret Conspiracy*, and resurrected to audience enthusiasm as part of the *Sedition* arts festival in Sydney in late 2019, a celebration of public art and protest of the 1970s.

The concert was promoted using an old photograph of Sasha performing at *Conspiracy*. It was produced by John Allen, who's been a tireless producer of a range of counter-cultural events — music festivals, concerts, talks — since the late 1960s, (the Nimbin Festival in 1973, 'Australia's Woodstock', is always mentioned). *Cabaret Conspiracy* was started in 1978 by Johnny Allen and Fifi L'Amour (1954–2012); its home was Garibaldi's Coffee Shop in Darlinghurst, an anarchist coffee shop above a motor garage in Riley Street. *Cabaret Conspiracy* ran as an open mic event, an open stage. I met Johnny Allen in a longtime favourite Kings Cross café to talk about it. He told me there were about 300 performers in just its first year.

> It was compeered by two wonderful drag queens who poured shit on the performers so the worse the act was the more the audience would enjoy it because they'd play up. [Allen interview]

Allen says that they did the best cabarets in Australia at the time. Real cabaret, with its roots in Weimar Germany, and in Paris, where it was by artists for artists. Half of *Cabaret Conspiracy*'s audience was other artists. Allen says that for him one of the main purposes of art is to create a sense of community. Also, mischief.

> I see the job a of cabaret — indeed all art — is to stir things up, make trouble. Sadly now cabaret has come to mean torch singers, an anaesthetised version of what cabaret really was. [Allen interview]

True to the counter-culture ethos, *Conspiracy* was never supposed to become commercial. Various people wanted to put them on TV, he says, but he always thought that'd be the end of it.

> Whatever authenticity and whatever value it had was in being underground and being subversive and as soon as any of that [TV] happened it was going to lose that quality. [Allen interview]

The cabaret moved to a venue in Oxford Street and became the Palms cabaret. But while it was still at Garibaldi's, Sasha Soldatow turned up, and performed from his *Adventures of Rock-n-Roll Sally*. Allen remembers it as very witty, funny, dark in places.

The cabaret remained underground and true to itself, he says.

> Being authentic to your roots is one thing that has not changed, there is a huge difference between art and cabaret and theatre that is authentic to its roots and that which is not. To me. And I think Sasha would have agreed. [Allen interview]

He might have preferred to argue!

> He would have argued doubtless! We used to enjoy arguing. What didn't we argue about!? Sex and politics and art. He was a lovely and generous man. Soon after I first met him I got very sick — I got a case of hepatitis — and he became a bit my guardian angel, came and cheered me up, he brought along his fruit juicer, which he had called Eva, because it was a Braun. So he brought along Eva. [Allen interview]

Maybe the same Braun his Bourke Street housemates had exasperatedly 'Braun-ed' his letters in a few years earlier. Sasha's friendship with Allen is warmly remembered.

> We'd go to the movies together and have long chats, just enjoyed one another's company. His friendship circle and mine overlapped a little bit but was also quite different. [...] I remember him talking about one acquaintance whom I shall not name and they had sessions which consisted in listing and naming everyone they'd slept with, a bit competitive. And there was a bit of commonality, people who turned up on both lists! And to me that was very Sasha. [Allen interview]

Allen says he was never good at documenting but *Cabaret Conspiracy* was well documented thanks to a wonderful photographer called Maryse Throsby, who'd unobtrusively take pictures at the Sunday night shows then drop off 10 or a dozen of them a few days later, without having been asked and wanting no recompense.

She took the wonderful photo of a young Sasha Soldatow that illustrated the postcard size flyer distributed for the 2019 *Sedition* event. He's bare-legged, dressed in a short sleeved shirt incongruously formalised with a bowtie, dark glasses, a tambourine in one hand, a microphone on a stand in front of him. That had been Sasha performing at *Cabaret Conspiracy*.

what our artistic influences do

When Larry Strange gave Sasha Soldatow a book on Bertolt Brecht, Sasha wrote that he had found a mentor. Most likely he was already familiar with Brecht's lyrics, notably sung by Lotte Lenya. Everyone knew 'Mac the Knife' but fewer knew Brecht's intent for theatre to be part of the revolution.

And then Sasha found another inspiration in Lou Reed. [also discussed in chapter 11] Lou Reed would begin performing Brecht songs in 1985.

In the early 1970s I used to hang out at a student share-house in Glebe where they'd acquire imported LPs, and it was there I first listened to the Velvet Underground and soon acquired my own copy of the LP with the Andy Warhol banana on its cover. I made a few people listen to the Velvets, not all of them were thankful at all.

But Sasha shared my passion, and it was shared with one of his 1970s partners, Brian, with whom I'd socially bond over Reed's 1973 album *Berlin*, one of those records that made you feel you would never be the same again. Also made some people rip the needle off the record.

Reed inspired Soldatow's suite of poems *The Adventures of Rock-n-Roll Sally*; he would go on and perform it at various venues.

The 1990 published edition of Sally lists its 'Performance History', with twenty events in the years 1976 to 1983, mostly in Sydney and Melbourne, and also Wollongong and Adelaide.

It also includes the 'Publication History'; it cites the 1974 *patterns no. two*; publication of three of the poems in *Dodo Two* in 1976 and an edition of twenty copies in 1977. The 1990 edition was published by BlackWattle. [more on BlackWattle in chapter 19]

> *Lou Reed* oh not to be whistled or studied or hummed or remembered at nights when the eye is alone but to skewer and ravage and savage and split with the grace of a diamond and bellicose wit to stun and to stagger with words of such stone that those who do hear cannot again return home [Reed 1972, 1990]

Something about Lou Reed gave Soldatow a kind of permission, freed him up — this is what our artistic influences do, they seem to make us see what we had meant to do all along but would not necessarily otherwise have known.

naked on red sheets

For the poster for a performance of *The Adventures of Rock- n-Roll Sally* Soldatow posed naked on red sheets in homage or pastiche of the famous Marilyn Monroe calendar. The poster is remembered as much as the performances and is reproduced on the back cover of the 1990 edition.

> Brett [Hilder, the photographer] had a mattress in his studio and found a large silk sheet. Drunk by now, I asked him whether he took photos like the character in *Blow Up*, saying, 'Give it to me, give it to me,' as he snapped away. He said he didn't as I stripped. I lay down on the sheet and took up the Marilyn pose. Brett started photographing, saying as he

did, 'Arch your back a bit more, arch it, that's right, push, push your leg.' Marilyn was much more athletic than I was. And I didn't have the radio on. From the photo Chips Mackinolty and I produced a poster at The Tin Sheds. [SS 1990 'Memoir' *Rock-n-Roll Sally*]

There was a rumour that Sasha had included this picture with a grant application, reported by some as meant to be evidence of work done and by some as a nude pic meant to provoke; or even, some speculated, improve the assessment.

referencing drag, but at a slant

Sasha was a compelling performer. People keep mentioning this. In the piece I wrote when Sasha died in 2006 and I was travelling in Europe:

> Among my photos there's one of your electrifying performance, your short hair bleached platinum, you wearing only tiny denim shorts, one arm raised high. You were thin and young and beautiful. You could really dance. You were dazzling. [*Really Talking*]

Not only fun to see but generative of thoughts and insights. Poets Amanda Stewart and Pam Brown appreciatively recall Sasha's *Sally*.

Amanda: In a way I'm sad that he didn't continue with his performance stuff, it was really excellent. And I love that he turned drag on its head.

He was informed by feminism and a really rigorous political and ethical analysis so here he was purposefully messing drag up, at a time that it was quite divided in the gay scene between political gays and commercial gays. And also the commercialisation thing was seeking its way in and he did that pamphlet *What Is This Gay Community Shit* and that was crucial.

He used to wear tiny little shorts and platform shoes. That's Sally. There were heaps of drag shows, all through the 60s, 70s there was drag, but it was not very political, so with Sally he was referencing drag, but at a slant.

Pam: It was a bit of a critique, because he modelled that poster with him as Marilyn Monroe — that's brilliant — it's the same pose so he did critique it but also — it sounds a bit Keatsian — but a work of beauty; it all looked pretty wonderful because he was very good visually.

Stewart: And he would have wanted to look good.

Brown: Of course! [Much laughter] He probably stole someone's clothing. [Brown, Stewart interview]

Made me remember there was that the time he stole my underpants. I don't know what performance it was for and I don't remember why I wasn't going to it.

> One time he took every one of my underpants, and I had some really nice ones, silk and lace and not cheap either, to do a performance, he put them all on and took them off one by one and threw them at the audience and never got them back and never said sorry. Times like that you weren't meant to care about property, you were a lesser person if you did. [Baranay 2006 Really Talking]

recollections of those vivid, energetic days

I spoke with Amanda Stewart and Pam Brown together one afternoon at Amanda's house in Surry Hills. Amanda served tea and cake and the two of them seemed to enjoy the recollections of those vivid, energetic days of poetry and performance in the 1980s.

Amanda said she cherished the memory of performing with Pam and Sasha at Jura Books at La Peña Centre in Newtown. Downstairs was a shop and upstairs the large space with the stage:

Amanda: They were amazing events, there was a huge range of people. A lot of refugees from South America — from Chile and Argentina, El Salvador, maybe Bolivia. You had great age difference too. There were old Spanish anarchists there as well. And a lot of kids running around.

Pam: Because a lot of Chileans were anarchists, so, that connection. Sasha and I used to go to Jura Books meetings, we identified, I still do, as anarchist. We used to go to meetings and we knew, he's dead now, Peter McGregor, who was the loveliest anarchist of all time, devoted to hedonism and good works, very good guy, so I think it was Peter who used to invite people to read, so that they [Jura Books] could pay the rent; you'd get Frank Moorhouse, I remember him because I was dubious about his anarchism, but I'm sure he is, he's definitely a hedonist so that qualifies; they had music ...

Amanda: I loved those nights. Pam and I would be reading poetry basically; we'd do a ten or fifteen minute set.

Then there was the wonderful Fabian [Fabian Lo Schiavo], Porca Madonna. He was brilliant.

Pam: The Sisters of Perpetual Indulgence, didn't he intro it, give us a blessing, he was the Pope, he had an automated blessing hand. [Brown, Stewart interview]

Inspired by the San Francisco activist performance group, The Sisters of Perpetual Indulgence performed the kind of drag that made no attempt to hide the masculine features of its wearer, the kind of camp that had married punk to glamour, street/guerrilla performance to religious imagery. The Sisters turned up at demonstrations, parties, openings, and events such as these readings at La Peña. They signified a new, activist aspect of messing with gender stereotypes, one in which the start of the plague years had made their mark.

Drag no longer meant fantasies of sequinned glamour, ruffles, shiny fabrics, 'female impersonators', an ultra femininity as it had when I hung out at drag clubs in the late 70s, once part of some friends' video recording of a Drag Queen Ball. [see it on Vimeo] The defiance extended by the Sisters of Perpetual Indulgence was exhilarating. (They were surely influenced by the punk drag group Sylvia and the Synthetics from early 1970s.)

And then of course we had Sasha who did his Rock-n-Roll Sally which was absolutely brilliant. And at the end of the night we'd have a bluegrass band. [Brown, Stewart interview] 'festival averse to verse' 1983

Another performance by Sasha Soldatow caused the dramatic derailing of the poetry readings in Hyde Park in 1983; this became part of Sydney's poetry scene legend.

Hyde Park is in the city's central area and includes a 1930s fountain whose sculptures based on classical Greek mythology are a testament to the city's colonial roots. Poetry readings took place in a range of venues in those years. The editor and publisher Tom Thompson had been holding the Red Press poetry events at the Ned Kelly Bar. With the poet Rae Desmond Jones, Thompson set up the 1983 reading as a so-called Umbrella event to that year's Sydney Festival. [Thompson email 26.4.2020]

They decided to hold it in Hyde Park, on the Elizabeth Street side. The poets were ready to read; besides Rae Desmond Jones there was Pam Brown, Larry Buttrose, Joanne Burns. Somehow, a troop of boy scouts was doing something right alongside.

> And Sasha read a poofy poem — can't remember which one. We were amplified and the scoutmaster heard it and decided to take offence. He was obviously a closet homosexual what'd'y reckon! So he complained to the security that there were these homosexuals. [...] I don't know if homosexuality was legal yet. [It wasn't, not till 1984.] Of course there's homophobia everywhere. So the security moved us. It was in the paper. [Brown interview]

The heading of *The Sydney Morning Herald*'s item was 'Festival averse to verse'. The piece concludes:

> Mr Sasha Soldatow said last night: 'I am a homosexual person. There is nothing offensive in what I have written or done. I feel that I wrote things about love and beauty.' [Isabel Lukas *SMH* 24.1.1983]

However, Sasha annotated that quotation on the cutting pasted into his diary. 'Not me. Rae D.J. said this.' [diary 24.1.1983]

Poet and critic Michael Sharkey attended the event and includes a detailed report in his book *The Poetic Eye: Occasional Writings 1982–2012*:

> Sasha, louche and gangly, neon-blue-rimmed sunglasses a-glint, and cigarette dangling from a lip declared '[...] First, a tape-recording of a poem with piano accompaniment. It's a poofter tape about two men fucking.' Stun, shock and amazement all round. [Sharkey 63]

Sharkey writes about Soldatow's work and reputation at respectful length if with severe reservations. After describing the shambles following this reading, until the whole thing was forced to a close, Sharkey takes a position:

> Poetry hasn't advanced much when boring shock tactics are employed. [Sharkey 63]

Who was really shocked though? Much later, Humphrey McQueen recalls:

> [The] poets failed to shock the matrons in the Writers tent. The more the poets said Fuck the more the matrons said Superb! [letter to me 24.8.2020]

such unsophisticated behaviour by organisers

Frank Moorhouse published a long letter of admonishment in *The Sydney Morning Herald* writing as the President of the Australian Society of Authors; it ended:

> And I hope that all sponsors of art events will always make it clear they will not condone such unsophisticated behaviour by organisers using their names and their money. [Moorhouse letter *SMH* 29.1.1983]

Note the appeal to sophistication — a variant of the word is used three times in this letter, unsophisticated being the ultimate rebuke. Australia was used to being considered from abroad as a place of yokels and yobbos, inimical to art and poetry and lacking the kinds of taste and discrimination that sophistication implies. I remember how people at theatre or music performances would gush, this could be anywhere, this could be seen in New York, as if there were no higher accolade. This wasn't a place where *only here!* could be said with pride. Bad enough that a poetry reading was stopped because of a scout master; possibly worse was that this coloured the city unsophisticated.

But the good news, Tom Thompson tells me, was that after this he secured the Sydney Town Hall for the Sydney Festival, to direct the first four 'Sydney Writer's Weeks', 1984–1988, always free events then. Thompson and his partner Elizabeth Butel paid the performing writers $100 each to be on the weekend panels, quite good money in those days. Later Writers Week became the much larger and commercial Sydney Writers' Festival, most of its events expensively ticketed.

Soldatow's long-lasting pamphlet *What Is This Gay Community Shit?* was first circulated in February of 1983, the same month as the disrupted poetry reading.

By this time, Sasha's reputation as provocative, disruptive, disputatious had built firm foundations.

Miss the Opera House Lights 1984

Sasha performed with Amanda Stewart and Pam Brown in other contexts besides the readings at La Pena. They were part of a collective who created a 'crazy performance' that they took to Adelaide for Writers' Week in 1984. Sasha did *Sally* at that. He always upstaged them, Amanda said.

Later, Pam sent me the recording, digitised from a cassette tape. There are no photographs; not many were taken in those days, and there were no camera phones of course.

> **Miss The Opera House Lights**, which may be meant to be the title of a beauty queen, or an instruction to a pilot, or an expression of homesickness, but which certainly involves various Sydney poets reading their works with bits of film, is at the Sydney Trade Union Club from 8 pm tonight only.

The group won a small grant from the Australia Council to cover their trip to the Adelaide Festival in 1984, after Literature Board Director Tom Shapcott attended the performance held at the Trade Union Club in Surry Hills. They called the show *Miss the Opera House Lights*. That was Sasha's idea. Brown appreciates the phrasing, the kind of thing he'd do: it wasn't *we* miss the...

Part of the show was a Super-8 film. This was a film Pam made of the TV screening of Tommy Leonetti singing 'My City of Sydney' that used to close one of the TV channels' broadcasts every night in the 80s; 'I miss the opera house lights' is a line from the song. They screened the little movie in the performances.

a unique audience was presumed

The poems Soldatow read in *Miss the Opera House Lights* were from his *Sally* sequence. To listen to this recording, especially if you've heard other versions of the show, is to appreciate how his delivery was never solidified by repetition or a decision to do it a certain way — as with the best performers, each time was different, another version was being tested, a unique audience was presumed or found.

The spontaneity was in the version; the content was emphatically crafted.

In this version, Soldatow is putting on an American-ish accent. It's very rhyme-y, even to reminding you a bit of rap; you might also think of cabaret, of something Brechtian, with that very rapid delivery, musical, actor-ish,

dynamic, emphatically reciting not talking, way more than the usual poet reading. While many poets aimed to show something like a true, authentic self, Soldatow always performed in a theatrical persona.

In the poem 'Where does love go?' Soldatow starts in faux old and tired voice, emphasises the rhythms of the piece, speeds it up to the end.

It's the voice you hear when you see the poems on the page now; I can't imagine how they can be read now if you've never heard them.

You have to listen to them. Other people who witnessed the performances say that too.

No wonder the others preferred not to go on after him.

no one else notices that

Soldatow valued his friendship with Pam Brown; he admired her and frequently quoted things she said to him. He'd tell people how, on her return from Paris (Pam, a long-time francophile, in 1992 actually won a trip to France for two from a competition in a newspaper she fished out of a bin!) Pam talked about the poverty that she'd noticed in Paris, and he'd say, no one else notices that in Paris.

Meanwhile, Soldatow continued to make grant applications, carefully counting his rejections. And he continued to have trouble paying the rent, as if he'd be blessed by Oscar Wilde's deviant dictum that if you took care of life's luxuries the necessities would take care of themselves. As several people have noted, Sasha would buy a whole smoked salmon, a whole ham, a Braun juicer, and of course alcohol, while he didn't pay rent he had been meant to pay, or repay money given as a loan.

Sasha wasn't earning from writing, but in time he heard about an okay-sounding job — a job using his writing and editing skills.

19

shadows on the dance floor

AIDS and gay publishing 1980s

It was 1989. I went to a doctor about difficulty breathing. [...] She took blood, asked me if I wanted a test for HIV. Ten minutes later I regretted it. [SS 1996 *Jump Cuts* 185]

suddenly knew a lot of new things

In later years we'd try to remember when we had first heard about it. We all suddenly knew a lot of new things. *As if Overnight.* That was one of the great titles from Gary Dunne's books (1990), one from this new literature about these new things. (It's online.)

The disease hit like a plague formerly only known from shadowy if hideous medieval and biblical imagery, entwined with ideas about curses and the wrath of some one god or the inescapable infections in *Death in Venice*, especially inescapable for romantic lingerers. For a while they hadn't even found the HIV virus (not until 1983) so there were ideas slamming around about where the illness came from and how it was transmitted. The battiest were unaffected by evidence and retained by the kind of people who think god created fossil records to make people realise those too had been formed within the Creationist period. There was the 'Patient Zero' story; there were unconscionable delays in recognition and research support; there were arguments about the implications for gay life and for promiscuity; there were only rare reminders that people other than gay men in the first world were victims of the disease; there were proposed vetoes on using the word victim.

It was a while before the medications were available, it was another while before the medications were good.

Whatever else the 1980s was, it was also the decade of, another Gary Dunne phrase 'shadows on the dance floor' — the title of his 1992 book. Shadows as in ghosts. As in fears. As in places to hide.

We began to be aware of who was missing, who always used to be around, and why.

There was the time when to get infected meant virulent illness and a soon and ghastly death. So many people we all knew got sick and died. Among them were many of the most talented, brilliant, necessary people in Sydney, where Sasha and his friends lived; among them were people fiercely loved and so movingly memorialised in the massive AIDS Quilts projects; all were people who should have had more life ahead of them.

If you think of the early 80s onwards it's to realise AIDS was always in the background: it was part of the fury and urgency of a lot of music, a lot of poetry. Writings like Dunne's and others in the Gutter Club. Anthropologist Eric Michaels' *Unbecoming: An Aids Diary* was published in 1990: a fiercely intellectual and honest account of the last five years of his life. AIDS influenced the outrage and outrageousness of the new style of punk drag, as Pam and Amanda talked about when recollecting the Jura Books /La Pena days with Sasha. [chapter 18]

I remember Sasha once looking with worry at some marks on his arm, and saying something about karposi's sarcoma maybe looking like that. It was no such thing, and he escaped being infected. 'I think I'm lucky,' he said in *Jump Cuts* [185] He never went back to the doctor in 1989 for his results and only learned of his negative status years later. Deciding not to know was a choice some would make.

I suppose the anxiety was strongest in the first days of knowing about AIDS and lessened as safe sex practices became de rigueur. Lessened more, we've heard, among sexually active people who now feel threatened by no more than a regimen of pills.

For Sasha's generation, the advent of this plague meant considerations of sexual manners and mores needed to be considered all over again. It was a shattering of the dream of endless liberation. For the following generation, it meant the age of youthful exploration of sex and sexuality was undertaken under this shadow. Christos Tsiolkas, in the same section of *Jump Cuts*, says he first got tested in 1984, and was relieved to know he was negative. But everyone's thinking about the world was changing:

> Suddenly we were using words like responsibility, protection, safety. Straight words. [SS/Tsiolkas 1996 *Jump Cuts* 186,188]

(Those early days were inevitably remembered in 2020 when another virus, which came to be called covid-19, spread throughout the world. See for example Gessen.)

The advent of AIDS created a massive shift in the culture, beginning on what was seen as culture's fringes.

There was the disease, there was the response to the disease. The campaigns undertaken in Australia, particular its gay centre Sydney, for getting tested, knowing the facts of the matter, practising safe sex and in general being sensible were exemplary. The Hawke Labor government funded programs, and even more important, there was the work of activist groups and gay newspapers in educating their community, the media and the wider world, and providing health and support services. 'Dance proud fuck safe' was one of the popular slogans: 'pride' would be a necessary affirmation until all stigma had been eliminated. [Bateman]

an accelerating cultural lift-off

And part of the response, as queer people increasingly insisted their voices be heard, was a brilliant new lot of publications.

1983, when Soldatow published his *What Is This Gay Community Shit?*, was also the year when the Gay Writers Collective launched *Edge City On Two Different Plans*, the first collection of gay and lesbian writing published in Australia.

The title is taken from a poem 'Gay Liberation' by Lee Cataldi; in part it goes:

> it's a sad trip to discover
> love can be a bummer
> drowning or drifting
> nowhere to go
> sometimes an accident
> and sometimes
> edge city on two different plans

Soldatow's contribution to *Edge City* was a story called 'Intimacy'; it was later included in his short prose collection *Private — Do Not Open* [1987; 95-99]. The story shows two old friends at lunch, Paul and Judy; the initial awkwardness revealed to be about a third friend, Alan, who Paul had had an affair with and Judy, she announces, is now engaged to; a bitter taunting ensues and Paul leaves early.

In his Foreword to *Edge City*, Dennis Altman provides an overview of gay writing in Australia at the time:

> When we speak of a lesbian/gay writing of the sort referred to in *Edge City*, we are referring to a sense that one is part of a community of lesbians and/or gay men, a community which has only come into being in our lifetimes.

In the time of the AIDS crisis, there was arguably reason — *pace* Soldatow's

'Community Shit' pamphlet — to see all gay men as a 'community': a community of those seen by the world outside as primarily members of the at-risk demographic. The kind and extent of the risks were debatable but a certain sense of living in a world where they're a hot topic was not.

And in that community, gay men's writing was emerging, with new voices formed by the new times, and now new connections between them.

Denis Gallagher also published a story in *Edge City*. He says the volume reinforced confidence in the idea of a gay literary culture, as well as familiarising Australian gay writers themselves with one another. [email 23.2.2020]

From 1983 to 1985 Gallagher was the editor of *Oxford Weekender News*, and subsequently, *Oxford Lifestyle*, both free fortnightly news magazines distributed to the many gay venues around Darlinghurst, Paddington and Kings Cross. They were financed by advertising revenue received mainly from a wide range of gay businesses large and small along The Golden Mile, as Oxford Street had become known, and far beyond. This put him in a privileged position, Gallagher says, to observe and participate in 'an accelerating cultural lift-off' in those years; he came to know many of the artists, writers, photographers and performers who were involved in the Mardi Gras Festival with its art exhibitions, theatre productions, sports events, forums; the Festival grew along with the size and success of the Mardi Gras Parade. The advent of the plague had given it new grim purposefulness, and reason for its emphasis on community.

While *Edge City* has only passing mentions of AIDS — it was early days — Gallagher would create an anthology that was a response to the crisis.

the elemental implications of the title

In June 1986, Sasha Soldatow received a form letter from Denis Gallagher who was soliciting contributions for *Love and Death*, the anthology of prose and poetry he would edit and produce.

> The elemental implications of the title should give you a sound idea of its themes(s), although I should add that my original notion in this regard was prompted by the phenomenon of AIDS and its effects on desire. [...] [Denis Gallagher letter to SS with 'Dear Sasha' in handwriting 30.6.1986]

Although Gallagher allowed contributors to interpret the title as they chose to, Michael Hurley's indispensable *Guide to Gay and Lesbian Writing in Australia* says *Love and Death* might be the first anthology of AIDS writing in the world.

All profits from the reading and anthology sales would be donated to the Bobby Goldsmith Foundation, a registered charity established to give support to AIDS sufferers. All eighteen of the contributors supported this donation.

Denis Gallagher recalls the launch, the date, the place, the people, the performers. It was a Mardi Gras Festival event in February 1987, at the Harold Park Hotel, then *the* place for readings and launches in Sydney. It was packed for the launch, not only to hear the contributors but to add donations to the cause; probably the biggest gay literary event ever in Sydney.

They raised over $1000 on the night.

a 'golden era' for gay print publishing

Dennis Altman was well-placed to compare this particular literary culture in Australia to those elsewhere, saying that in Australia, compared to the US, in spite of a commercial gay scene and a gay press, the development of enough of a gay community to support its writers has been much slower. He supposed this was due to the small scale of Australia, and the fact that so many potential lesbian and gay writers remained closeted. [Altman 1983]

That swiftly changed. A recent historical study affirms that the last decades of the twentieth century were a 'golden era' for gay print publishing in Australia; an era of dramatic change. (Calder 2015)

'practising dying'

Soldatow's 'Practising Dying', the first story in *Love and Death*, was republished in his *Private — Do Not Open*, as part of a longer piece of the same name. It's a reflection on friendships alongside an account of a conversation with a somewhat garrulous, philosophical taxi driver taking the narrator to a party.

> 'In life all chances are the one before the end. Whereabouts in Kings Cross? ... You can be dead at thirty,' says the driver. 'You can spend your whole life waiting for true romantic death and yet be dead all that time.' The taxi pauses at the lights.
>
> [...]
>
> 'At a hundred I'll want to live forever and know everyone,' you say. [SS 1987 *Private* 7]

AIDS is not mentioned; possibly the fact of its ambience makes the narrator's ambition particularly poignant.

gay books for gay people

In July 1987 Soldatow received a letter from Laurin McKinnon, who introduced himself, and asked for a submission for a new magazine. It sounded as if he hadn't met him before — 'Dear Mr Soldatow' — but he would soon be addressing him as Sasha.

On the back of McKinnon's letter, Soldatow wrote 'Justice Plus sent'.

The new magazine was *Cargo*; the new publishing house was BlackWattle.

Cargo had a print run of 500 copies for its fourteen issues. When McKinnon began to publish books as well, the print run was increased to 5000. BlackWattle soon was supplying over 100 bookshops in Australia, as reported in *Campaign* where McKinnon was asked why he had established the press. McKinnon replied, 'I wanted to help claim our own ground, create our own image [...] I just wanted to publish gay books for gay people.' [Johnston 1993]

Soldatow was to form a strong relationship with McKinnon, BlackWattle and *Cargo* magazine. BlackWattle would publish two of Soldatow's books and several anthologies in which his writing appeared; it was run by a collective which became part of his circle of acquaintance and social activity.

Soldatow published short pieces in several issues of *Cargo* and he and Pam Brown co-edited an issue. Alternate issues of *Cargo* featured gay men's writing (McKinnon editing) and lesbian writing (edited by *Cargo* co-founder, the poet Jill Jones). The Brown/Soldatow issue was inclusive. *Cargo* published fourteen issues between 1987–1993.

'Justice Plus' was published in *Cargo* number one. Not a story exactly: a series of eccentric observations about death and dying, connected only by the writer's idiosyncratic train of thought.

> [...] Laugh with my wrong-doing friends (for it is thought we have no shame) and survive this living time, a time which can never, like some films, be 'medieval', no matter how much we stretch this term in our imagination (already the topic is absurd, but let that pass). No matter how much we get to know about the imaginative people who have not lived here (for we live here, you understand) and who are now dead, (who drowned, or shot themselves, or cut their throat, their hair, or cooked breakfast, ate porridge, mowed the lawn, or simply just awoke, opened their eyes and phoned someone, during a thunderstorm, killed by lightning, lucky.)
>
> [...]
>
> My fear of death dissolved (though I still fear it) when I accepted that Bertold Brecht and Anna Magnani both faced death and died. [from 'Justice Plus' in *Cargo* number one]

The relationship with BlackWattle continued. On 10 October 1988 Soldatow sent *Cargo* a submission, an extract of his novel in progress, called *The Gloves of Mr Menzies*, which, he says is 'to be published by Picador in July 1989'. Laurin McKinnon replies 'love it … will be in Cargo 5 … what's a legong?' The story was published as 'untitled'. [see chapter 28]

Sasha Soldatow's 'Percy Grainger's Theory of Music based on groaning: an opera in twelve scenes for two characters played by one performer who cannot sing' was in *Cargo* 7, November 1989. [discussed in previous chapter]

On 31 October 1989, Laurin McKinnon wrote on BlackWattle letterhead to the Literature Board of the Australia Council, in support of an application for a writing grant from Sasha Soldatow. It was one letter among many solicited by Soldatow that year in the saga of his continuing lack of success in winning a writing grant. [more in chapter 24]

we were put here on earth to be naughty

Cargo 8-9, a double issue, 1990 was called *Writings from lesbian & gay male perspectives*. The editorial by guest editors Pam Brown and Sasha Soldatow in layout and tone was — of course — in quite another style from the sober, more conventional tone of previous issues:

> […] We read all your submissions. Thanks. The range, as they say with chooks, was truly extraordinary: coming out, confessional poems, unhappiness […], yearning for a fuck (almost Christian!) and all wot leads to S&M which should hurt but doesn't/ it was all too metaphoric. LIKE— who does eat shit? (ring this number …)
>
> Not that either of us believes in censorship, but 'where do you draw the line?'
>
> This is a question we can't answer, but we went hell for leather rejecting:
>
> (a) Soooo serious …sssszzzz .. zz.
>
> (b) 'I had an orgasm and went back for more and when I was really fucked out I wrote this poem. I'd welcome any criticism.'
>
> (c) 'Please put thy pseudonym, my real name is …'
>
> (d) Visits from the goddess who left this old shell.
>
> (e) Spicy, tamarind, real good island fucks.
>
> (f) My libber blubber lept me.
>
> (g) Camp tails from an Oxford Street stool.
>
> We print what was left over.
>
> We were put here on earth to be naughty. [SS and Brown editorial *Cargo* 8-9. 1990]

The issue includes 'The revelation' by Sasha Soldatow (50-52) subtitled 'South Australia, 1942.' It features the character Amelita from *Gloves of Mr Menzies*, pregnant and newly religious, musing by the seashore.

A piece from Soldatow was also included in *Cargo* no 14 January 1993: 'Aha oe feii?' (32-34). A footnote explains the title is from a Gauguin painting, interpreted as *What are you jealous?* (The painting is housed in Moscow according to Wikipedia.)

This piece is included, with some changes, in *Mayakovsky in Bondi* (1993) (25-27) but without the Gauguin-esque title, in the chapter 'Critical Mass' about his time in Moscow, the piece beginning

They were in Moscow.
There was a revolution ... [25]

[discussed in chapter 26]

we should call ourselves The Gutter Club

Besides *Cargo* BlackWattle published its Contemporary Australian Gay Fiction series. Four books were launched together, books by Soldatow, and his fellow Gutter Club members Gary Dunne, Ian McNeill and Denis Gallagher. Tim Herbert's *Angel Tails* and others were also published in the series which continued until 1998.

Soldatow's slim volume was *Rock-n-Roll Sally*. The others were Gary Dunne's *As If Overnight*, Ian McNeill's *TV Tricks and other poems* and Denis Gallagher's *These Tattoos: a personal miscellany*. The celebrated photographer William Yang took a photo of the four authors sitting side by side in a bed, to publicise the books. That picture, Gallagher says now, 'ended up with a life of its own': it was often reproduced, including in Yang's exhibitions, and his book (1997) and short film (2014) *Friends of Dorothy*.

Gallagher kept a diary, recording several meetings of the Gutter Club, including its founding on 6 April 1988 after a night out, beginning with dinner at a Thai restaurant in Taylor Square ...

Carried on to Midnight Shift, danced. At some stage an uneasy consensus that we should call ourselves The Gutter Club and have further dinner parties.

Besides Denis, Gary, Tim and Sasha, other members (there was no formal membership) and invited guests included Tassio Sclavenitis (office manager, *Sydney Star Observer*), Richard Turner (journalist and filmmaker), Laurin

McKinnon, Mark Try (an editor of *Campaign*), Ian MacNeill, John Fowler (South Sydney Councillor), Kerry Bashford, Paul Knobel and Peter Blazey. Dennis Altman was one of the guests invited to the irregular dinners, where he shared more of his USA experience.

Gallagher noted at times 'Sasha particularly amusing'. Some more Diary extracts for a whiff of the times and Sasha's notable appearances:

> Ian MacNeill makes debut appearance at the Club, seemed suitably engaged. Sash wants to call his next novel, The Foreskin of Jesus. Dinner comprised pizzas. [diary 24.1.1989]

> Last Monday night The Gutter Club met for drinks at The Oxford and then dinner at an Indian restaurant in Oxford St Paddington. Present — Laurin, Tim, Peter Blazey, Sasha, Gary Dunne, Mark Try, Tassio and I. Peter and Sasha seated beside one another and opposite me. Sasha put on a good performance, mainly for Peter's benefit it seemed. Peter wasn't drinking, said very little, but compensated by pulling faces. He did describe a conversation with Vicki Viidikas in which she threatened suicide unless she got a grant. Surprised he'd be speaking to her at all after she burgled his house a year ago. Mark Try is the new editor of Campaign now Tim is going overseas. Gary D presented me with manuscript of his upcoming book with BlackWattle for comment. Publication of Sasha's The Gloves of

Mr Menzies has been postponed until later in year. He is about to depart for Wagga as writer-in-residence after recently returning from there on a two-day stint with Joanne Burns and others. He took along a collection of material to show the kids, remarking to me they didn't know what to make of 'Woof' [an anonymous, scurrilous, satirical pamphlet by me centred on Oxford St denizens] [diary 21.9.1989]

I brought out a box of books to give away. Sasha set upon the unwanted remains, shouting 'Oh, how I love books' as each one fell victim to his prankish inscriptions eg in Tallulah Bakhead's autobiography — 'Please read this. Callas'; and, in 'The Miracle of the Rose', 'poof!' [diary 17.12.1989]

'Memento Mori' in *Travelling on Love*

BlackWattle's first big success was the collection *Travelling on Love in a Time of Uncertainty* edited by Gary Dunne (1991), which had been turned down by all mainstream publishers. It included Soldatow's story 'Memento Mori'.

The story, renamed 'Requiem', would be the first piece in Soldatow's *Mayakovsky in Bondi* 1993. Its first sentence would be remembered more than the rest of the book: 'I am trying to remember what my father's cock looked like.' It wanders poetically, with its own internal logic, among memories of sex and masturbation, friendship and family. It might at first appear chaotic, unstructured, but the unifying voice and the sense of consideration in its phrasing holds that impression in tension.

William Yang sent a letter to tell Soldatow how much he enjoyed this story, saying, 'I thought it was outrageous and exciting and unpredictable and finally moving.' [letter to SS 3.10.1991]

David Marr cited this story as Soldatow's writing at its best, sadly in contrast to the novel manuscript he was reading. [chapter 28]

revisiting many of these publications in the present

Revisiting many of these publications in the present is to be struck anew with the sense of brilliance and freshness of these writings, as much today as in the days they were produced. There is a sense of something unleashed, a freedom to use language as you know it, to tell the stories you know and want to know, stories that are not usually represented in literature. The coming-from-this-moment insistence on being heard and seen reveals the silences and invisibilities of so much literature and media up to that time.

its squalid charm

In 1994 BlackWattle published another anthology, *Fruit*, also edited by Gary Dunne. It included Soldatow's story 'Love Piss'. I have just learned this title is a name for semen. In 1987 there had been a controversy over an art piece by the American artist Andres Serrano, 'Piss Christ', which might have nothing to do with this. Soldatow's 'Love Piss' is a stream of words, some in unpunctuated dense paragraphs, some in short lines poem-like, the method so endlessly changing I can't pick an extract to quote; it's all intensely sexual, perhaps all of it a masturbation fantasy.

Robert Dessaix reviewing the anthology in the *Australian Weekend Review* 4–5 February 1985 says 'There's an in-your-face faggoty frisson to Tim Herbert's writing as well as there is to Sasha Soldatow's, who's [sic] unreadability is somehow part of its squalid charm.'

The anthology, thanks to Soldatow's recommendation, also included Christos Tsiolkas' story 'Bypassing Benalla', developed with Soldatow's mentorship.

Soldatow felt assured of his continued respect and insider status with BlackWattle Publishing, but when the collective declined to publish a novel he had mentored and highly recommended, it was the end of their relationship. The novel was *Loaded* by Christos Tsiolkas. [all about this in chapter 30]

20

nine poets in a room

SBS subtitling 1982–1986

I call it Channel Nothing. [SS, in several recollections]

multiple, various, diverse

Now you'd be able to see free-to-air subtitled foreign films and TV shows at home every night and day. That was an indication of a new sense of Australia in the making, of a massive cultural change.

What did SBS mean at the time to Sasha Soldatow?

It was where the fact of being Russian was his entree and his advantage, and so was the fact of being a writer. It was where a good job was offered to him. Sasha joined the SBS Subtitling Unit in 1982, working there with many other writers and translators. Some he already knew; some became new friends.

The subtitling unit was central to the rationale or ideals of SBS, its rhetoric of inclusion. The subtitling unit became known as the heart of SBS; several longtime and popular presenters began there: among them news presenters Mary Kostakidis and Lee Lin Chin, football commentator Les Murray.

SBS began full-time television transmission in 1980. Special Broadcasting Service. Channel 0. Oh, Zero, nothing. A public broadcaster, meaning one owned by the public, like the ABC. It meant people had more of a say in what was broadcast. It meant no advertising, no commercialism, quality programming, a sense of quality that set it quite aside from the commercial broadcast channels, and its content setting it aside from the unvaried Whiteness of the venerable ABC. Free-to-air television was all there was then. Cable was barely known, and streaming services were not only the future but futuristic.

You might think the purpose of SBS was to satisfy 'ethnic communities' who wanted things in their own language, or cosmopolitans who wanted to see foreign languages in the original. But it wasn't, according to a former managing director quoted in a book on SBS published in 2008. He said:

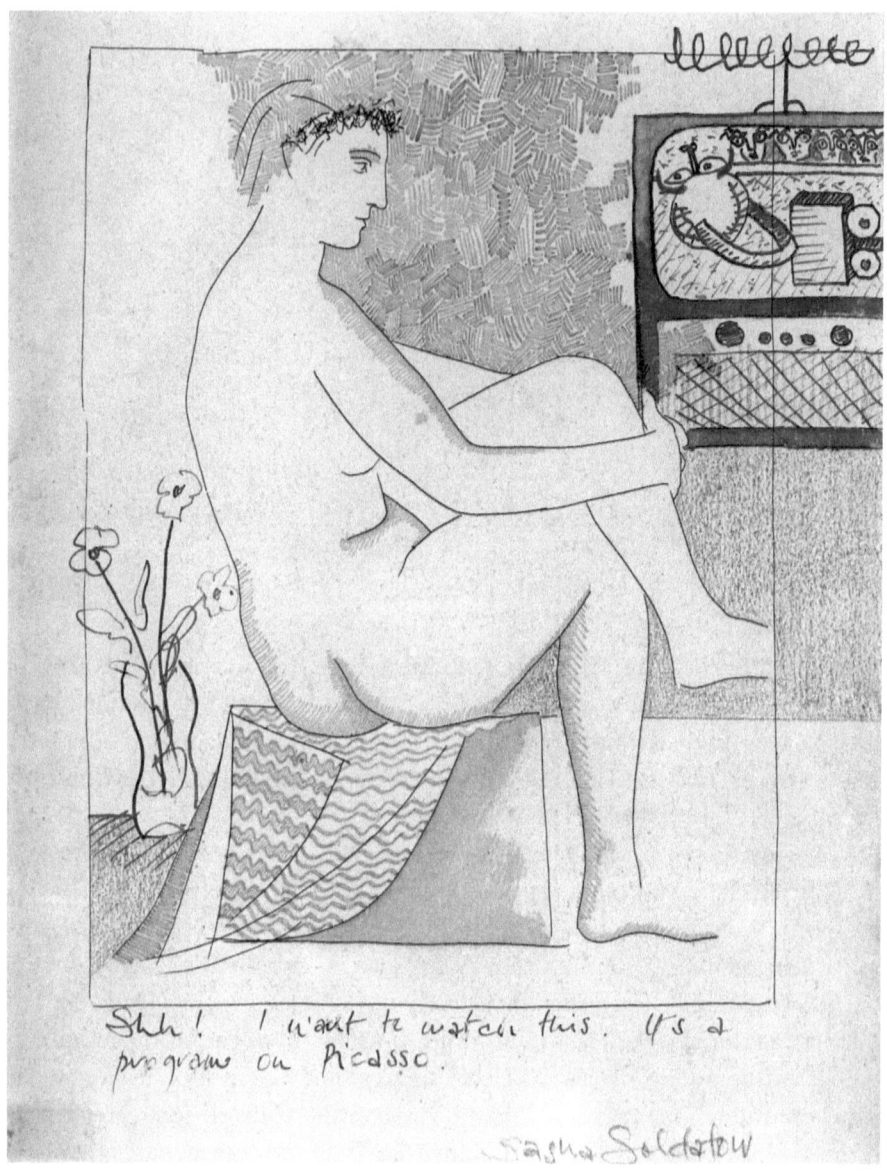

Shh! I want to watch this. It's a program on Picasso.

— Sasha Soldatow

'SBS's ultimate responsibility is to *nation building* [italics in original], to show multicultural Australia to itself; to tell the stories of Australia in the languages of Australia and to unite the nation through understanding and acceptance of cultural diversity'. [in Ang *et al* 2008 2]

I worked in production at SBS-TV when it began. The Anglo guy who fronted a new current affairs discussion program I helped produce didn't think people 'with accents' should be doing the front of camera, TV host kind of work he was doing. The unexamined idea was that some people had accents and others didn't. Never mind the multitude of ways people spoke English even when it was their mother tongue. Still! Even so! This was changing, SBS was the start of recognition that Australians have multiple origins, various first languages, diverse cultural practices. It was the start of the end of Anglo hegemony (though it wasn't really). Anyway, foreign movies at home. Call it nation building if you like.

the best subtitling outfit in the world

It was of course knowing people that got Sasha Soldatow the job. SBS employed many writers in the Subtitling Unit, some were or would become among the most well known in the country. The poet John Tranter told me it was the best subtitling outfit in the world for a long time.

> I walked around the editors' room at one stage and there were nine poets...Martin Johnson was one and I was one and Sasha was one. Martin got me the job there. [Martin's] brain was so good then. They refused to buy the Encyclopaedia Brittanica over and over because they had Martin Johnston. [Tranter interview]

I talked to John Tranter with Lyn Tranter in their house in Balmain, the inner-west harbourside Sydney suburb, now ultra-gentrified, once populated by the working class and struggling artists; in the 1970s Balmain had been the location of raucous poetry readings; of scenes from life related in some of the auto-fiction from the time, often published in newspaper style short story anthologies; of alternative pubs for Push-related drinkers; and of cheaper-than-elsewhere rents for students and counter-cultural types.

Besides all those poets Tranter counted there were other writers working at SBS, including Nadia Wheatley, Sue Woolfe, Gerard Windsor and later, Kate Grenville. Like Sasha Soldatow, they were all employed as subeditors.

The translators at the Unit worked on all the films and other programs not in English. They did not always get the English idiom right. They were translating into English from, usually, their native language; this was unusual; it was more usual to translate *into* your native tongue. So this is where the subeditors came in, nearly all of them writers. There were no rules for how to write subtitles. They developed their art together as they worked, eventually writing their own 'bible' of subtitling.

exacting discipline, precise words, strict structure

What an ideal job for poets, the subediting: the exacting discipline of precise words that had to fit a strict structure. The subeditor would look at the translation; not only its exactness and clarity mattered, but its precise length. A subtitler had to work it out exactly: a subtitle had to be only 23 characters wide, 2 lines of script per window, and you could put them on for a minimum of 2 seconds and maximum of 4.

Nadia Wheatley explains that the subtitlers used video editing machines that could show the film frame by frame, and that was very rare in those days; in those days you couldn't watch a dvd frame by frame or fast forward or back (no one had dvds yet).

> In the days before Twitter only subtitlers worked with characters or thought in terms of characters. You were so focused on characters you'd write *maybe* instead of *perhaps* because maybe has one less character. As people do now with Twitter. [Wheatley interview]

ability to solve the unique problems

Soldatow, already an experienced and well-regarded editor for many writers, soon was recognised in the Unit for his ability to solve the unique problems subediting presented. An example is remembered by Nadia, from the time she was subtitling a German children's series. In this series, extra-terrestrial aliens came to Germany, to the town where the child characters were living…

> …but they looked just like human beings, which meant they looked German. But they didn't speak German. So German children watching it would be able to tell [the aliens] didn't speak German. This wouldn't be clear to an English speaker, but their mouths are moving and sounds are coming out, so you've got to subtitle something, or you'll think the subtitles have fallen off the screen at SBS. So I came to Sasha as my fellow subeditor and instantly he got it. He came up with the idea of using the asterisk and dollar sign [and other symbols] which now seems obvious but wasn't obvious at the time. [Wheatley interview]

I'd seen that kind of usage in comic books and the like to indicate expletives of an extreme nature, where the ^%&#° symbols would indicate what is nicely called curse words. And now could indicate aliens' utterances.

> I always remember it was a great solution and it came to Sasha like that, so he was also a bloody great worker, he was a good colleague in every sense.

He wasn't just naughty Sasha. [Wheatley interview]

Nadia says that it was one of the great things about working at SBS, the new problems the subeditors came across every week or even every day in their work.

Subtitlers — the translators — might call on the subeditors at any time with a query, and it wasn't always a high-level language issue they had to adjudicate.

> For instance a character might be talking about a flower and [the subtitler] would know the name of the flower in Bulgarian but it wouldn't be in the Bulgarian-English dictionary, so you'd go and look and say, that's a hydrangea or that's a frangipani. [Wheatley interview]

problem of the English 'equivalent'

Sasha's skill and love of editing flourished in this environment. Talking about the days in the subtitling unit with some of the writers who worked there was to appreciate the pleasures of discussing the finer points of language and translation with others equally adept.

Jason Johnston, who also worked with Sasha in SBS Subtitling, gave examples of the kinds of issues subtitlers and subeditors would be called on to discuss, and how useful they were to each other. One constant problem, as anyone interested in translation is familiar with, was what the English 'equivalent' was of some term or cultural referent in the original.

Jason recalls other subtitling challenges and the fine way Soldatow was able to help find solutions; of course long talks about such things — exact translations that sounded wrong, consistencies in terminology, the reading they would do around a French historical series — were much enjoyed. Geeking out.

Besides the issues of faithful translation, the subeditors were called upon to consider questions of timing and abridgement, and Sasha was useful here as well. Jason recalls a lot of discussion with Sasha about an Italian comedy, due to be shown one Christmas Day, in which the original dialogue, more or less non-stop, was spoken at breakneck pace…

It took the work of several subtitler colleagues, with a lot of input from Sasha Soldatow, to arrive at distilling each subtitle to its essence.

Only those who care as much about the exactitude this craft required would understand some of the small regrets still remembered:

One occasion where Sasha and I got it wrong — I'm ashamed to say because I more or less insisted on getting my own way in this case — was in rendering 'Maréchal de Saxe' as 'Marshal of Saxony'. In fact, the standard English-language terminology is 'Marshal de Saxe' (he was a Marshal, and he was Count of Saxony, but he was not a Marshal of Saxony). [Johnston email 24.3.2019]

the state of subtitling

The immense and often subtle issues in subtitling are rarely considered these days, underlining the fact of the quality of the Subtitling Unit at SBS in the days Soldatow worked there.

It's worth remembering that until then subtitling — especially into English — was not common, except for some art movies shown at the far fewer festivals they had then, or in very few cinemas. English-language films shown in other countries were often dubbed.

In the present, of course, films, television, screen content of many kinds, can be made anywhere and shown almost everywhere else, so subtitling is more common, but it's not necessarily better done. Fan-made subtitles might sometimes be superior to the studio-made ones. [Billson]

the workplace was an experiment on a micro level

If SBS was an experiment involving the larger culture, the workplace was an experiment on a micro level. And in most accounts, a successful one. Joanna Savill, journalist and then subtitler/editor, tells me that when SBS television began in 1981, everyone was making it up as they went along. It was this bold experiment in multiculturalism, a motley crew of people who spoke other languages, an amazing bunch of people she says. Joanna remembers it as a great workplace, of camaraderie, and enjoyably various assignments.

> You'd be doing a nature documentary one week then the life of Molière. We all moaned and groaned about things but we actually were translating movies and documentaries and working the shifts that suited us, so we had time off during the day, or working till midnight and hanging out with each other. So we had a very fun time and everyone I've ever seen since, we all have really great memories of it. [Savill interview]

Nadia Wheatley says it was an astonishing work environment with all those writers working there. Also she enjoyed the sight of the women from the ethnic communities, even while being clear about her difference from them.

> Women [workers at SBS] would wear fantastic clothing, and shoes, and hairdos. Because they were Europeans and South Americans and whatever. [Wheatley interview]

She made a point of wearing jeans and thongs, and she had two identical black Plumbers Union T-shirts and always wore one of them.

In contrast to the enthusiasm and warmth of those memories, the writer Sue Woolfe, then a filmmaker when she came to work at SBS, tells me her memories of the place are not happy ones.

We met at a café in Darlinghurst, already acquainted through past literary events.

It was a difficult time in her life, and the workplace did not make it easier. But she found Sasha Soldatow very welcoming.

Woolfe was yet another who found in Soldatow a friendliness that touched her. She recalls the pleasures of conversations with him:

> The other thing I loved about Sasha, he was anarchic, he didn't seem to belong to any persuasion, so you could have lovely free-floating conversations with him. We used to talk about all sorts of wild things. Utopias was one. He wasn't committed to anything so he wasn't hamstrung by an ideology so our conversations would be free floating and could go anywhere which was very charming in that cloistered environment. [Woolfe interview]

Gerard Windsor was another writer at the Unit. He describes the workplace as 'a relaxed, chatty place'. It was even as if the SBS subtitling unit was a microcosm of an ideal multicultural Australia, with an end to the enmities of the past elsewhere, in a new context of diversity and commonality.

tensions in the Subtitling Unit

There were, though, certain tensions in the Subtitling Unit. Soldatow was a constant smoker of cigarettes, and in those days people could smoke in restaurants, trains, streets, and at the desk.

> My particular gripe was smoking. The place worked seven days a week eighteen hours a day with no restrictions on smoking, I think 70% smoked, I thought neurotic Europeans. I asked for at least some restriction, I remember getting the general line, there's more pollution out on the street from car exhausts than there is in here. [Gerard Windsor interview]

It might have been the smoking issue that made others remember that Gerard and Sasha did not get on, but Gerard says they got along quite amicably.

reason to stay in Australia

I knew Joanna Savill, used to see her around, through Sasha and other mutual friends who were working in SBS at the time. I went to see her at her beachside home in Sydney shared with her husband and a dog. She recollected her friendship with Sasha with special warmth.

We spoke about those days, about SBS, and how the job she got there made Joanna stay in Australia when she hadn't been going to, and a lot of that was because of her friendship with Sasha. Which began in that workplace.

She went to Italy on a scholarship, lived there for a while to improve her language skills, then trained at the EU as a conference interpreter. The SBS job was only going to be a way to get money to return to Europe.

SBS turned out to be a great place to work. There were day shifts and night shifts; people ate together, bringing in different kinds of food. Firm friendships were formed. The group of people were nothing like anything she had known; she'd had a sheltered life, she says, brought up on the lower North Shore — a notably White, upper middle-class area of Sydney — and going to ANU — a privileged university in the nation's capital.

Soldatow's influence on her life was considerable.

> Sasha did a lot for me, to help me see there were interesting people and ideas and things going on in Sydney. And we were very close friends, the way you are when you work with people, and apart from the people there — this odd crowd of wogs, community leaders, and translators and writers. [Savill interview]

Joanna formed a friendship with Sasha that lasted beyond his time at SBS. He took her under his wing, she says.

> As he so often did, that's something I observed with Sasha all the time I knew him, he took people under his wing; he liked them or he saw something in them. I don't know why me. He would take me to parties and introduce me to people.
>
> And I just kind of became aware of this really interesting world. And I always say — and I told Sasha this when I went to see him when he was dying — thank you, because you showed me a whole other side of Sydney, and Australia as well.

> And very much on the strength of that I decided to stay and not go back to Europe, which had been my plan. I still had boxes of belongings in Belgium and France and Germany and Italy, my record collection strewn across four countries, I hadn't intended to stay. [Savill interview]

And stay she did, going on to work at SBS for many years, moving into production and on-air presentation, with a popular food show produced by SBS, and food journalism and events management.

It all began in that workplace, where Sasha was her portal to a world of parties and people Joanna loved to meet.

> A pack of people who knew each other and were involved in arts, writing, theatre. I remember lots of parties, it was very much the era of parties, lots of parties, and Sasha holding forth, hunched over a bit with a cigarette, and those wicked eyes. [Savill interview]

an anarchist in the union

Nadia Wheatley tells a story about Sasha being shocking; there were so many of them; Sasha being shocking was a mainstay of gossip then. Nadia makes the point that (as Margaret Fink said) Sasha might enjoy shocking people but there was always a politics to what he would say. Nadia wasn't working at SBS at the time Sasha was sacked, but remembers what Sasha told her about it:

> A bunch of women came back from lunch one day and one of them had a wonderful new hairdo and everyone is saying how wonderful her hairdo is and she names the hairdresser, this lovely little man called Luigi or Fernando or some non-Anglo name, and Sasha supposedly, this is his story to me, Sasha screeches: Oh Fernando, I haven't seen Fernando since I fucked him on the Southern Aurora! Which is classic. Classic Sasha. And supposedly people were so outraged he got the sack for gossip. And his line was always that the gossip was about *himself*. Fernando or Luigi wasn't an employee of SBS and the only person he was gossiping about was himself, his own sex life not someone else's.
>
> Whatever the truth of the story, the significance is, Sasha was sacked, and he went to the union. [Wheatley interview]

That was the politics part of it: Sasha was an anarchist who also was active in the union. As Joanna Savill points out, it was a very precarious employment situation; they were on weekly or month-to-month contracts.

Nadia tells me that Sasha had for some time been trying to persuade people to join the PSA, the Public Service Association. One other person in the subtitling unit who had joined was Martin Johnston. One day there was a strike, maybe just that union, maybe various trade unions were going out.

The background of many of SBS employees was what had made them wary of the union, a wariness that could come from different political positions: they might be anti-communist, and so averse to joining a trade union; while many SBS workers came from communist countries (understood as authoritarian), Nadia Wheatley explained, and they had a fear of defying the government by going to a trade union.

When Sasha was re-instated, Nadia tells me, then a whole lot of people joined the union.

The story of exactly why and how Soldatow was fired from his job became fuzzy with time, the degradations of memory, and no one keeping a journal about it.

Joanna Savill remembers that they used to work night shifts sometimes, enjoying a greater freedom at those hours; they did work but they also gossiped. There was always someone charged with supervision at night time. One night, while the supervisor wasn't around, some subtitlers went into one of the bosses' offices to find something, which film they'd be assigned next or who would be editing the film. They weren't supposed to be rummaging there of course. Somehow the supervisor found out and wrote it up in her report, along with other misbehaviours.

> Taking too long at dinner break or gossiping or mucking up in some way. And we did, we did.
>
> Anyway somehow Sasha may have confronted [the supervisor]...he said something quite harsh to her about it. [Savill interview]

Whether for that or for the rummaging or for the gossip, Sasha was sacked.

no longer the heady place

Soldatow seemed to neglect his duties once he had been re-instated. John Tranter said Sasha used to drink at his desk at work, his vodka in a brown paper bag. SBS was no longer the heady place of experiment and invention.

He lost interest, Joanna Savill says, they all did. SBS was becoming more of an establishment organisation, things became more fixed and they weren't inventing something new any more.

Nadia Wheatley, herself a writer, makes the sympathetic point that however attractive the job might be, it also meant, as she wrote in a recollection of

Martin Johnston, 'The creative energy that went into re-writing subtitles left nothing over for real writing.'

There were all those conversations among writers about the endless problem of how to financially support themselves and still have time and energy for writing. Wouldn't a non-writing job have been preferable? But the pay and the hours wouldn't have been as good. And solving linguistic or cultural questions could be intellectually stimulating, as Jason Johnston's examples show. Still, as Nadia Wheatley points out, Jason is a linguist and wasn't trying to write poetry or fiction on the side.

> The short-term nature of a lot of the projects, and the variety — the switching between different shows and different languages and different sub-titlers — probably appealed to Sasha's mercurial nature. But this just stopped you from realising that the place was a trap.
>
> For me, the supreme evidence of the destructiveness of the work is the fact that Martin wrote almost no new poetry in the decade he worked at Channel Nothing. [Wheatley email 5.7.2020]

It's true that Sasha also did little new original work during the SBS years.

> Of course, Martin [...] needed a regular working rhythm. I doubt if Sasha was the same. But I believe Sasha wasted his time and his talents at SBS.
>
> That is not the fault of SBS. But it is a waste, just the same. [Wheatley email 5.7.2020]

Sasha Soldatow would leave SBS when he saw an opportunity to be a full-time writer.

21

we believed in something

Private — Do Not Open 1987

We believed in something. Don't ask me what it was, I'd say I can't remember except — we stuck to each other. [SS *Private — Do Not Open* back cover]

a contract long before the book was complete

It was quite a saga, preparing Sasha Soldatow's first book of collected prose for publication; it's an example of publishing in those days being very different. Though he was essentially a first-time author, and this was a book of experimental short prose pieces, there was the possibility of a contract long before the book was complete. Those were the days!

It's something unlikely to happen now especially in a major multi-national house. The book, eventually to be called *Private — Do Not Open*, was signed up by Penguin, one of the largest, oldest and most prestigious publishers in Australia, before the later mergers that diminished greatly the number of mainstream publishing houses.

It was nepotism, Soldatow claimed years later in an interview with writer and fellow Gutter Club member Gary Dunne in the gay magazine *Outrage*.

> The real reason I got published by Penguin is that I'm old enough to know people in power and it was nepotism. I insist on saying it. It's not a funny joke. ['The politics of the sentence' *Outrage* 1987]

If not nepotism, there is always an element of some kind of luck in any publishing story and Soldatow was not one to ignore that fact. Maybe it was more that Soldatow's work was timely, as his editor Bruce Sims points out:

> In this comment Sasha is big-noting himself in a way. It does help to know a lot of people but Brian Johns and his staff had a policy of trying to cover Australian life in all its variety in the publishing program and that included gays and lesbians. So Sasha's book was partly a way of 'filling the gaps'. [Sims email 4.12.2019]

At the time, Sasha's friend Jane Arms was working as an editor, freelance but nearly full-time, for Penguin Books Australia, and Bruce Sims was on staff. He can't remember who recommended the book to Brian Johns, the publishing director; it might have been Jane or both him and Jane. Arms kept sending Sasha advice on how to get his manuscript, the collection *Private — Do Not Open*, in a state for acceptance for publication:

> It's not bad, but there's just not enough of it, and it doesn't have enough coherence to make it satisfying. I reckon it would be reasonably easy to fix the lack of coherence if you're prepared to write at least four more major pieces. I think the book needs to be at least vaguely chronological so that the reader gets a sense of your development, sexually and politically. In that way, you turn the book into a sort of autobiographical novella. [...]
>
> I think the Penguin view and mine, is that if you agree to write/produce some more they're prepared to contract the book. [...]
>
> If you agree to this, we can talk about what you need to write and what goes where once you've signed a contract. [Jane Arms letter 1.12.1984]

A few months later, Soldatow reported the book was in the final stages of publication process, about to go into page proofs.

> And yes, the expected has happened — the Lit Board has given a grant to its publication, which it never gave to its writing. [letter to Andrew Brophy 16.5.85]

The Copyright page of the book (1987), containing all the standard data including the publisher's acknowledgment to the Literature Board, also has at its foot:

> Author's note: This book was written without the assistance of the Literature Board of the Australia Council.

Soldatow was still counting the rejections he'd received of his writing grant applications.

the politics of the sentence

In June 1985 Sasha wrote to Jane Arms with ideas for the cover of the book (he recommends artist Ken Searle). He and Jane have been friends for a long time, and after some general chat and a music recommendation (the pianist Pogorelich, which he says is the best piano music he's heard in years), he avows his faith in her as an editor:

take your time, and please edit hard. If in doubt, follow your instincts — because ultimately I do think we agree. [letter to Jane Arms 23.6.1985]

That agreement didn't last long.

The next month, Jane Arms, writing on Penguin letterhead, insisted that, far from being ready for publication, there was more work to be done on the manuscript.

But she also offered suggestions and encouragement.

> We're quite a way from having a book. I've done what I can with the language, and I've made a lot of suggestions, the rest is up to you. I still think there are some overwritten pieces that should go if you don't want to work on them [...] Sometimes your writing is simply indulgent with all the faults of the 'new writer'. The fuck pieces are wonderful. They stand up well. [...]
>
> Close up, I don't agree that what you sent me is the final version. When you've cleaned up the edited MS, I think you may need to write a couple of linking pieces. But I can't really tell until I see what you can do with my suggestions.
>
> The consolation for all this is that however the middle-aged body is declining, the middle-aged writing is getting better and better.
>
> Much love [Jane Arms letter to SS 18.7.1985]

Soldatow would not have welcomed the opinion that his writing had the faults of a new writer.

It's both a sign of how different those days were in publishing, and of the strength of the connection between Arms and Soldatow, that there was so much discussion of the manuscript before it was considered ready to be submitted for publication. These days, especially with large corporations, a new writer usually needs to present a final-draft manuscript; in-house editors do far less work on each manuscript; and the marketing department has a lot more say in what can be published.

In August Soldatow typed a five-page letter to Arms, first detailing his ideas and intentions for *Private — Do Not Open*, and for its cover. It's a long list of things changed, taken out, put in again, suggestions for the order of the pieces. The letter continues a day after he began it, with some gentle questioning on the editing Arms has done so far; one instance is that apparently she changed his word 'overseas' to 'abroad'; he would complain about such things:

> [B]ut aust [sic] usage is overseas. If abroad is more international, then what happens to words like flagon — an aust invention not known 'abroad'. Just wonder about that.

> Yr editing was harsh rather than hard. I know all writers feel badly done by when they get their edited MS back, feel defiled etc. That's why I've purposely left it this long before getting back to you. To temper the natural reaction. I feel good that I let this time accumulate because it allowed me to do two things. It made me review what it was that I was really trying to say, and it made me harder on myself. You will see that I have, because of your work, been harsher on myself.
>
> But if feel I want to explain a few instances where we differ on our reading the text. [...] on some occasions I think you misunderstood the nature of the writing. [...] I felt your editing technique was too rigid.
>
> Firstly I think you took my tone out to often. [letter to Jane Arms 6.8.1985]

He began complaining to his friends about Arm's editing, that she was trying to change his style to something more conventional.

In November 1985 Sasha confided his literary woes — none of which dented his confidence in the quality of his work; the woes were due to the failures of others:

> ... Im a fair bit down cos I didn't get any funding again ... I've been doing a lot of readings and tell you what, without blowing my own trumpet, I think some of the stuff I've written this year is fabulous. But it's so different and way ahead of anything else being produced that no wonder the stupid drunken pricks in the Lit board don't have a clue. Nor do Penguin for that matter. It's been no end of trouble with them. They want to cut everything right back, make it into a proper book. They don't understand modern writing. ... [letter to Andrew Brophy 3.11.1985]

In April 1986, Soldatow, while confiding about a new passionate affair (it wasn't going to work out), continues his complaints about his publishers:

> They're scared shitless of modernism... Wouldn't publish Gertrude Stein now... [letter to Andrew Brophy 11.4.1986]

Did he have a point? It is certainly not a book of conventional short stories, with their plots and their turning points and their moments of change. While modernist, experimental writing had flourished at times, though always on the margins, the late 1980s was notably an era of a new conservatism, which affected mainstream publishing.

Still, *PDNO* was published and with the text much as he wanted it.

Years later, Soldatow rehearsed his complaints about publishers:

You give them a platypus. They edit it through and they give you back a duck. [...] I call it the politics of the sentence. It depends on where you place your word as to what voice comes across. ['The politics of the sentence' interview with Gary Dunne *Outrage* 1987]

the last chance to alter anything

On 7 December, Arms sent Soldatow a hand-written note on Penguin letterhead with a promise to have the book (i.e. the edited manuscript) to him by Christmas. Sasha annotated the letter in pencil with the words 'she didn't'.

In January 1986 Soldatow wrote to Arms with a list of twelve points: new changes. He said, 'You should take this as the final MS.' [letter to Jane Arms 20.1.1986]

But Arms could not take that as the final MS. She wrote back with fresh directions and a postponement of the publication date:

> …cannot work from this retyped version. [You] must transcribe corrections onto master copy…reschedule…[not sure] whether or not what we have got here really amounts to a book… [Jane Arms letter to SS 24.1.1986]

That would have been the end of Jane Arms as editor on this book.

> Bruce Sims pulled it together. He's worth a million dollars a week. [...] [SS 'The politics of the sentence' *Outrage* 1987]

Bruce Sims was also a friend from the days at Melbourne University and student theatre. In 1986 he took over as editor for *Private — Do Not Open*.

He and Soldatow for years had been writing to each other. Sims' letters are affectionate, intimate, humorous, gossipy: evidence of a solid, trusting friendship.

The rest of the editing went along without the disagreement that marked Arms' involvement.

> [W]hen Jane and Sasha fell out (surprise, surprise) it fell to me to complete the job which I really enjoyed and, I think, finished with a really good book constructed out of fragments. Jane was mightily pissed off that I stepped in. She felt (I think) that Sasha should have been told he had to stick with her or the deal was off. That kind of ultimatum wasn't Brian Johns' style.
>
> I suspect that she would have finished with a book that was more saleable. [Bruce Sims email 22.2.2019]

Sims added to his reflections on the process of producing Sasha's first book, and his perception of the dynamics at play:

> I meant this to mean that they were both combative personalities, but it was nobody's fault. Some of the problem was Sasha's nervousness about being on a big stage masked by resistance to Jane's very reasonable requests for more and better. [email December 2019]

In December Sims sent Soldatow the first design for the cover of *Private — Do Not Open* (it was not ultimately used, nor was the cover copy) and with it the page proofs.

Writing on Penguin letterhead in January 1987, Sims warned Soldatow this was the last chance to alter anything:

> no restriction on changes at this stage but this is it! Once set — no more changes. [Sims letter 19.1.1987]

Still making many changes, in February Soldatow sent Sims a four-page hand-written letter with notes for the book — name changes, other notes on text, spacing, words, punctuation. [letter to Bruce Sims 9.2.1987]

forty years later, I am struck by how good it is

In the present, Bruce Sims, while I was writing this, reread *PDNO*. It might have been a surprise, but he was impressed:

> Re-reading the book, over forty years later, I am struck by how good it is and how much Sasha, in this, as in many things, was ahead of his time. Compare the stunning (and stunned) response which Christos Tsiolkas' *Loaded* got eight years later. They are very different books but I think Sasha had, in some small way, laid the ground for more explicit gay sex and a different way of looking at relationships. [Sims email December 2019]

finally, a party: the book launch

Done! And now, finally, a party: the book launch.

Penguin sent a cheque for $50 as a contribution towards the launch — Soldatow organised the party himself; naturally he'd do that better than they ever could.

The launch on 2 September 1987 for *Private — Do Not Open* was a big cheerful party held at the Crafts Council premises in Sydney's Rocks district. Everyone remembers the bottles of vodka encased in ice with sprigs of gum blossom frozen inside the ice. That was Margaret Fink's typically generous and stylish contribution, reported somewhat hyperbolically in *The Australian*; in those days Lyn Tranter wrote the literary column under the name Elizabeth Swanson.

(Lyn told me in 2019 that it was meant to be Swanston, like the Melbourne city street.)

> Maggie Fink is a good friend. She turned up at the launch of old mate Sasha Soldatow's *Private — Do Not Open* with a zillion vodka bottles encased in ice. Also frozen into the ice surrounding the vodka bottles were sprays of eucalyptus and wattle. Later in the evening the ice had melted enough for the shoulders of the bottles to be free of their icy casing and the wattle and gum to be just…spilling. Looked great. And Soldatow's book is doing well for Penguin. (Put a bottle of vodka into a giant opened-out milk carton or sliced off-at-the-shoulders orange juice flagon, fill with water and freeze. Then cut away carton or plastic flagon and present bottle of vodka in ice. I thought everyone knew that.) [Swanson 1987]

It was a happy occasion, friends from various spheres coming together.

In November, Sims wrote with the nett sales numbers and reported that he'd seen Jane Arms who broke about twelve months' silence on the book to ask how it was going. [letter to SS 30.11.1987] Looking up those numbers in 2019, Sims says:

> I looked up the sales of the book and I think this is accurate. Nett sales, after returns, are 2234 from a print run of 3448. Hardly a runaway bestseller but quite respectable for the time. Penguin would not have regarded this as a success at that time. [Sims email 18.11.19]

friends wrote warmly in response

It has been said that a writer's books are intended for a small number of people (and their personal letters meant for the world — I'm not saying this is true). Some of Soldatow's friends and peers wrote warmly in response to *PDNO*; the writer Drusilla Modjeska praised the book:

> It's a great book. I'm half way through and enjoying it, and impressed with the way you handle all that difficult contemp innercity stuff, let alone the sex. It's funny + sad + moving + so good to read a man writing about real things, and vulnerabilities. [Modjeska letter 14,9,1987]

Quite likely several people found their intimate encounters with Sasha transmuted into his interpretive prose.

The writer Mark Macleod wrote a six-page letter and enclosed two poems.

> I think the book is terrific [...] [It has] an extraordinary vulnerability and an almost bottomless sadness. That's despite the humour and the very beautiful writing. [Macleod letter September 1987]

Macleod was particularly touched because of a past relationship with Soldatow; he says he was thinking of their relationship and that the breakup was traumatic and upsetting.

these amazing reviews

Soon from Penguin a 'with compliments' slip says 'Thought you'd appreciate these amazing reviews!'

Attached were reviews as good as Soldatow and the publishers might ever have hoped for. They began with a brief but positive notice in the *SMH*:

> ...he [Soldatow] writes like no one else in Australia at the moment [Lucas 1987]

A lot more space was given to the review in *Times on Sunday* (previously *The National Times*). *PDNO* is the Book of the Week, and there is a sizeable extract as well as the sizeable review. Alongside the review is a good cartoon of Soldatow by Michael Fitzjames.

The reviewer admits he has to rise to the challenge of grappling with this book, being made to do so by the paper's editor. But the initial reluctance and sense of the life being depicted as uncomfortably very other gives way to admiration.

> Here was a voice. Here was really good writing, a frustrating sentence that, as well as reminding us of Soldatow's background, has earned him a place in the First-Sentence-Writer's Hall of Fame: 'What were the faces....(for remember she is a mother).'
>
> *Private — Do Not Open* is a Pandora's box of urban life, childhood, sexuality, homosexuality and humour. It closes symmetrically, with another reference to the narrator's background, in *Pleasure*, a prose tribute to the logic of Central European end-of-the-world hedonism. [English 1987]

This, too, could hardly be better, and must have been gratifying:

> ...Advent of an important new literary figure in Australia...Possibly one of the most important new pieces of fiction to be published in Australia this year [Connell 1988]

The book is being taken seriously, reviewed where book-loving people and readers of reviews go, and being assessed in gratifying terms by its first critics. Still, there always has to be dissent:

> PDNO [is] an unsatisfactory read; it is like a sketch rather than a finished painting, fragmentary, tenuous and with a very faint odour of righteousness about it. [Dalziel 1988]

Seeing all that is also to be reminded how much longer book reviews in the newspaper were then, and how many more of them.

talk about ideals and politics

At the time I was editing a monthly publication, *Ariel Book News*, and in the September 1987 edition reviewed *PDNO* and interviewed Sasha. In that interview Sasha returns to his story about the friend who, he says, once called the cops. (This is the David Marr incident told in chapter 17 and Marr did not in fact exactly call the cops.) It is an opportunity to talk about ideals and politics:

> It's not the event so much, it betrayed the fact he wasn't an idealist... That's also behind the story of how I realised how many of my friends, the people I knew, were not idealists. They were pragmatists, or they'd never thought about it, or they'd forgotten that idealism... [SS *Ariel Book News* September 1987]

Naturally in the interview I was a sympathetic, even enthusiastic reader of his book and gave him a chance to articulate his current thinking on politics as personal.

> IB: most writing presents things as definite, as given, as it-was-so. You present the process of becoming, realising.
> SS: I like to think of that as a European sort of thing. [*Ariel Book News* September 1987]

That is one of several places over many years where Soldatow would refer to his sensibility as 'European'.

> You have ideals, but you also have to judge your politics by what you're doing at any particular moment in time, or what you're being pulled to doing. To put it on a superficial level, my politics has now become gardening and eating and socialising again. [SS *Ariel Book News* September 1987]

So, *Private — Do Not Open*, in spite of Soldatow's grievances, made quite a splash, sold well for the kind of thing it was, then went out of print. Penguin sent the last royalty payment, a cheque for 62 cents.

22

the boundary lines of our personalities

Bruce; Bondi years

There is nothing more erotic than success, be it in work or in love. [SS 1996 *Jump Cuts* 168]

to the very end past the end

When one major thing is going well in your life, the magnetic side to your personality is going to be amplified, that erotic charge bestowed by the feeling of success. When Sasha Soldatow met Bruce Pulsford, it was during the happier time with Penguin.

Sasha Soldatow and Bruce Pulsford were to live together for twelve years, their flat at Bondi Beach becoming the site of innumerable parties, lunches, dinners, late nights, drinks drinks drinks.

Bruce remained a close friend and supporter of Sasha's to the very end — past the end; he was executor with Gill Leahy of Sasha's will. He is invariably mentioned in other people's recollections of Sasha.

In his obituary, David Marr calls Pulsford 'the guardian angel of [Soldatow's] last twenty years'.

(Bruce says this is kind but that he was not a guardian angel.)

should have been a sign

Bruce met Sasha at a party in Darlinghurst. It was in June 1986, Bruce tells me; he was about to turn 30 and Sasha was nine years older, close to 40.

> I'm not sure if there was an instant [sense of] connection, there probably wasn't.
>
> He needed a lift home. I lived in South Bondi, in a place I shared with friends; he lived in a flat in North Bondi he shared with friends. I gave him a lift home, we didn't spend the night together, though we talked of catching up again.
>
> One thing I remember, we went to North Bondi from Darlinghurst,

> then on my way back from North to South Bondi my car ran out of petrol! It was two kilometres [from home]. Looking back, that should have been a sign! [Pulsford interview]

But a sign of what? Should Bruce have stopped off at North Bondi or stopped this going any further right there? Or what?

Bruce had to leave the car there until he could get some petrol the next day. They must have caught up soon after that.

> I think Sasha might have phoned me and asked if he could come round. My bedroom [was] the front room of a terrace house. He came through the window. [Pulsford interview]

Through the window. An entrance made to remember.

fell into the relationship

Bruce Pulsford is a good-looking man with a quiet, dry wit and a generous, sociable nature. Contrary to Sasha Soldatow's attention-courting manner, he tends to utter his droll one-liners in a softly-voiced deadpan.

I remember in the early days of their living together I said to Sasha about Bruce, in a we're-old-friends way, words to the effect of, you have got a really good man there, don't fuck it up, and his words back were, with that impish grin, 'Everybody says that'.

> I fell into the relationship with intention and partly not with intention. I was interested in him very much. Can you say 'going out with' with Sasha? We started seeing each other. [Pulsford interview]

Soon after they met, Bruce moved to Kings Cross to a little apartment he had on his own, and Sasha visited more often. At the beginning of 1987 the two of them moved in together, a place in Park Parade Bondi which they rented together.

So they moved in together six months after meeting.

I remembered my first visit to Park Parade. As I went up the stairs I heard the clear sounds of what must have been a solo piano piece; I thought it was someone, probably Sasha, playing the piano.

I arrived at the flat and found it was a CD. CDs were a bit new still, it was vinyl records for quality and cassettes for copying and portability. (Walkmans prepared us for MP3 players with their choice of quantity.)

I'm reminded of Larry Strange telling me about coming down the stairs at Margaret Fink's and hearing piano music so good he thought it was a recording but found it was Sasha playing. Several people mention how well he played.

it all began well

To move in together is a sign of optimism and commitment. In Sasha's archives I find a photograph of the two of them, at a picnic, together, looking young and gorgeous and in love.

Over 30 years later, Bruce is never exactly eager to talk about all this, but kindly accommodates my research. I'm realising again that while I entered this biography project in good conscience — in the sense that Sasha *wanted* his biography written, so it wasn't a matter of a hostile, resistant or merely accommodating subject (which I'd never undertake) — of course other people in your subject's life never wanted to be written about, and I wouldn't blame them.

Bruce came over to my flat — we happened to live a few minutes' walk from each other now — to talk about those days. He acknowledged the ambivalence I sensed as he tried to recollect the early days of the relationship, tinged as these recollections now are with all that came later.

> As you can tell, I'm a little diffident in expressing it too positively, as I've got very mixed feelings about the relationship. [Pulsford interview]

But yes, it all began well; it had been something new for him. As with many of Sasha's friendships, part of his role was to be a kind of teacher. Bruce found him fascinating, and not what he'd have foreseen as his first serious boyfriend; although he'd been sexually active he'd only had 'fleeting' relationships.

> The first few months were good. I thought he was very brainy. He knew a lot of people, he was popular with people. I also liked the fact he was Russian, I liked that, an exotic aspect to him, not a normal Aussie bloke. The physical side of our relationship was never very strong. He interested me in things I had not known about before — he taught me a lot about classical music, he knew a lot about literature, especially Russian literature which I'd only vaguely been exposed to. He had a lot of ideas about, um, I was going to say interior design, about art. He struck me as a very not out of the mould sort of person and for some reason that interested me.
>
> I was a lawyer working for a law firm. I had a car. Maybe he saw me as someone interested in what he was doing. I don't really know what he saw in me. Or I can't articulate it. There's a section in *Jump Cuts*, but I can't remember what that says. [Pulsford interview]

That section in *Jump Cuts* was written ten years after their meeting.

> I live with a man whom I love but we don't fuck anymore. Bruce and I sleep together sometimes, but usually that's when friends are staying with us. We are not comfortable with each other's sexuality and, to be truthful, probably never have been, not having given each other enough physical space in which to explore, though we've been together for ten years. [...]

Chris, many people have said that they don't understand the dynamics of my relationship with Bruce. He's shy about the things we are writing here. There is an imbalance, that's true. Neither of us knows what is happening with our relationship — the boundary lines of our personalities have merged into a common space and it is hard to retrieve something of your own from that space without causing a catastrophe. [SS 1996 *Jump Cuts* 170–172]

Boundary lines of separate beings merging into a common space: that's a good description of what happens in long-term relationships, as far as this outsider can tell. And that would have something to do with why, long after that, there's a sense that the better times are harder to evoke.

I can't speak of the relationship with a great deal of positivity, or I'm finding it hard to do so. [Pulsford interview]

However, of course there was positivity, and Bruce recalled that too.

He was a homemaker, he was a great cook, he collected art, not expensive art, he knew a lot about art, he had a great sensibility about [collecting] tiny things, like pebbles, and tops of bottles — he was eccentric I suppose. [Pulsford interview]

And then there was a new social life to be experienced.

an exquisite gem hysterically funny

Soldatow and Pulsford became known as a couple to new friends.

John Walker, now a retired public servant and academic in Canberra, recalls that Sasha had been to meet him and his then partner Craig Rendell when they lived in Gunning, a small town in NSW near Canberra, first brought there by the historian Humphrey McQueen, who fondly described Sasha, says Walker, as 'not an anarchist, an emotional terrorist'. Rendell tells me they'd heard a lot about Sasha for years from Humphrey and found that Sasha 'endeared himself to everyone'. [email 15.7.20]

Walker now describes Sasha as 'an exquisite gem…hysterically funny…a wonderful human being who sparkled'. Sasha rang him after that introduction, and said he had to go to a nearby town to do research on Harry Hooton, he was with a friend, could he stay. He brought Bruce Pulsford with him.

It was tremendous fun, Walker says. Sasha and Bruce would lip synch to old show tunes, doing the duet to Ethel Merman's 'You're not sick, you're just in love'!

I took a moment to find that on YouTube and imagine the scene. Must have been adorable.

After that they visited every long weekend until Sasha went to Moscow.

his first trip outside of Australia

Pulsford retrieves the fresh bright joy of taking Sasha Soldatow on his first trip outside of Australia, during the romance of the early days. Sasha told him he'd never been overseas, and within two months of meeting him Pulsford arranged a trip to Bali for the two of them.

> Which I paid for. For some reason I thought that was exciting, I was able to help him go overseas, I saw myself, this sounds odd, as a facilitator or something. It was misplaced. But that's how I saw it.
>
> And we had a great trip.
>
> He was a great traveller, interested in people, enthusiastic, took everything in, still enjoyed a drink, drink hadn't taken over like it did later; he was young and good looking, he liked my jokes and I liked his jokes, so that was a great time. The first six months was good. [Pulsford interview]

Of course it was tremendous fun to go to new places with Sasha, places full of marvellous things to see. He had a great eye; he noticed things in a way not everyone did. He enhanced your experience. He was great company, a comely companion.

Sasha will now begin to fashion himself as the well-travelled man, dropping his long-time stance of scorning the idea of leaving Australia.

list of highlights

Pulsford took Soldatow on a second trip to Bali about six months after the first.

> We stayed in Ubud, we bicycled around; as you know there are lots of painting shops, mass produced or not, and he was very interested in those, interested in the food, we had a wonderful time, found a great little restaurant: warung. We didn't do it on starvation so he enjoyed the comfort. [Pulsford interview]

They went on to Java, to see Borobudur. Soldatow created a book about the trips, with sketches and pictures; it took months; Pulsford still has them. He should have brought them over, he tells me, it would remind him why he liked Sasha; he had a wonderful eye.

Pulsford puzzles over the dynamics of the relationship from the vantage of the present:

> I found it fascinating; even though he's ten years older, he hadn't been away and I'd been away a lot. [But] I wasn't a father figure, you can't be a father figure to someone older than you.
>
> I was happy to be able to guide him or put the foundations in place to let him do things. I don't know why I did that. Maybe I wanted his approval. Basically I was just after some love. But, um, love from Sasha came in different shapes and sizes. [Pulsford interview]

Soldatow did not keep an intimate diary; in the notebooks he wrote the names of the places they travelled to, kept tourist brochures, tickets to museums and performances — legong and so on. In Java he made lists of 'three disappointments, five highlights' for himself and for Bruce. Sasha's disappointments were:

> 1 Borobudur 2 white bait in Panjandaran (got sick) 3 Bruce sending off all the postcards from Jakarta museum.

His highlights:

> 1 Museum at Jakarta 2 Pranbaran temple burning 3 See. Buy. Fly. 4 Dance and gamelan practice Puri Mangureganam and seeing the Queen 5 Wooden things particularly ferry from Cilacap to Kalipucan 6 Rich people arriving from Jakarta to slum it in Panjandaran (7 All hot showers)

In Bali, Sasha made a collage from found objects; he called it Bali Hi. Each treasure — seashells, old coins, a rusty old horseshoe — is glued onto an intricately painted panel in a grid of six cells each inscribed with the name of a place in Bali, presumably where the object was found.

He gave this to his friend Joanna Savill, who often came to the Lamrock Avenue parties. She still has it on a wall and we admire it anew, how good he was at this sort of thing, original visual creation, how generously he gave things to others.

idealisations and exclusions in the work of Donald Friend

Soldatow wrote some notes about the paintings they looked at on their trips, including those by famous expatriates in Bali.

The painter Donald Friend enjoyed a stellar reputation. He had moved to Bali and was one of the luminaries of expat society on the island.

He was also known for his household of attractive young men and boys. You would never have criticised him for this, that'd be homophobic. It wasn't a time to separate out homophobia from a concern over pedophilia and cultural exploitation.

> The affect [sic] of the european [sic] artists is noted more than interpreted or evaluated. In most cases they seem not to have been 'good' artists, merely academically trained painters who transferred to an exotic environment. You get the feeling (with FRIEND it's more that you *know*) that there's an awful lot left out of the official Balinese talk about these european artists. There is hardly mention of why they came here. Why they are of importance here — yet justly ignored outside of Ubud, though there were some worse ones in JAVA. But above all there's the observation

that what these euro artists did for B painting was:

(a) idealise the 'beauty' of the people. This involved no representation of the aged, or men with beards

(b) an eroticisation of the women and young boys. Breasts are shown for the first time [more] [Indonesia notebook 28.11–14.12.1986]

I don't know what Soldatow meant by 'official Balinese talk', something he would not have had access to; he could be referring to standard guidebook accounts. In any case, his perceptions about Friend's paintings are uncommonly perspicacious, although apparently undeveloped beyond these notebook jottings. Soldatow was insightful about the idealisations and exclusions in the work of Donald Friend and other foreign artists in Bali. But I doubt Soldatow would have joined in the later denunciation of Friend for his unabashed accounts of enjoyment of sexual relations with the boys and young men in Bali, and the calls to stop showing his work because of it — recent years have seen many serious discussions about not showing the work of 'morally tainted' artists. Soldatow was perceptive on the glamorising of the painters' subjects, but not to make a moralising point, rather to do what he often practised: looking for what is unacknowledged in the gaze, in the representation.

to correct some information

It is amusing to find in Soldatow's letters his copy of a letter sent to the publishers of the popular tourist guide Lonely Planet to correct some of their information.

Amusing because there seem no limits to his desire to correct others, to apply his critical and criticising mind, to do a bit of editing.

great ability to make people like him

In 1988 Sasha and Bruce moved into their next place, the flat in Lamrock Avenue, a place mentioned over and over in interviews as the site of lunches, of visits that went on and on, of all those parties. It was a modest enough two-bedroom flat in a block of eight, half a block up from Bondi's main drag Campbell Parade with the beach on its other side. They didn't go to the beach very much, though. But liked that it was there.

Their home became a site of new social intermingling. They joined their friends, Pulsford tells me, and Sasha was loved by all his friends. Well, not all, he recalls; some were wary of him but Sasha did have a great ability to make people like him; it was remarkable.

Bruce reflects on how much attention Sasha gave a range of people. He charmed people who were different from Sasha's own friends. Bruce says he often couldn't work it out though he was relieved that his friends were comfortable around him, a few even mesmerised. Even those from a conservative Sydney middle-class background. Many came back to see him when he was dying.

> It always surprised me, the range of people who liked Sasha; they could be old, and living in a nursing home, they could be a fifteen-year-old girl learning the piano, or a 40-year-old straight man, a whole range of people: when he interacted with them he impacted on them substantially, very quickly. They might fall away, or not see a lot of each other, but if you asked them later on, they would all say he was fascinating to them. That was a skill he had, he was interacting with them and taking an interest in what they were doing. That at times caused resentment on my part as he seemed more interested in what they were doing than what I was doing. [Pulsford interview]

Margaret Fink was a regular at the Bondi parties, invariably mentioned in people's accounts; for example, literary agent Fiona Inglis first met her there.

> Great lunches, great fun parties, [Sasha] knew everybody, he could talk to anybody about anything, he could charm anybody. He was quite a gourmand. A great entertainer. That's what I remember most, his connections, his joie de vivre, his style of entertaining. It was the good old days, people had long luncheons, lots of wine, lots of gossip, and it went on all afternoon. [Inglis interview]

Megan McMurchy was living in nearby Bellevue Hill at the time, with Gaby Mason.

> Somehow we fell into that circle of people who'd be invited to the parties; always crowded, lots of food, Margaret Fink would always be there holding court; Bruce always seemed to be scurrying around doing the necessities for the catering and so on; Sasha would always be telling wonderful stories and keeping people amused. [McMurchy interview]

Lyn Tranter speaks of Sasha's generosity and great style when putting on parties:

> There'd always be large bowls of mandarines or something like that; it wasn't just cut-up cheese on a board, it'd be a fantastic great brie and that's

all. The aesthetic he had I thought really sensitive, his places always looked stylish. He did a lot of entertaining when he was living there with Bruce in Bondi. Who was a saint, he was a saint. Because Sasha wasn't earning any money he just lived off people didn't he, he didn't work to my knowledge after SBS. Nothing very serious. [Tranter interview]

Sasha Soldatow hosted a party for the Tranters' daughter Kirsten, now a writer, when she turned 21 in 1993. Asked to tell me about that, she wrote a beautifully detailed piece, adding to the testimony of the impression Soldatow made on so many: his looks, his distinctive presence, his hospitality, his bringing people together, his ease with the young, the way he laughed:

> When I think of Sasha, right away I think of him laughing. He had a distinctive laugh, almost a giggle, sort of a chuckle that shook his whole skinny body. I can remember his voice, its campy edge, but as soon as I try to imagine him talking whatever he is saying is interrupted by a laugh. There's a photograph of him that I have in mind, sitting with his legs crossed in a pale shirt that captures him exactly as I remember him: legs not just crossed but almost wound around each other, and those long arms always at an angle holding a cigarette or a glass of something, shoulders raised in a perpetual shrug, as if he was always in the process of folding and unfolding his limbs. He was warm and funny and generous and enjoyed being cheeky. I can imagine that he could have been quite mean when he wanted to be; I remember his tongue being sharp and his eyes being sharp and observant even while he was giggling away.
>
> He was one of those grown-ups who seemed to remember something about what it was like to be a kid, or some part of him had never grown up. I can't remember now exactly how that was apparent to me, but there was a Peter Pan quality to the Sasha I remember.
>
> He hosted a birthday party for me when I turned 21 at his flat in Bondi, which was incredibly kind of him. I probably didn't appreciate it as much as I should have, being a deeply self-obsessed young person, and also consumed with anxiety about that kind of event, but I imagine Sasha would have been patient with that. I remember two things about it: a platter with an enormous, delicious ham of which he seemed extremely proud, and the presence of the late Peter Blazey and his partner Tim Herbert, who gave me a silver bracelet as a gift. I'm not sure if it was the last time I saw Peter, but it might have been. Tim and Peter and Sasha were important to me at that time as queer people at home in the world as I struggled with questions about my own sexuality. In that poetry scene full of straight men

who seem to me now to be always trying so hard to be cool, Sasha was just effortlessly stylish, with his nice shirts and big spectacles. And had a capacity for affection that seems beyond compare. [Kirsten Tranter email 2.5.2019]

Kirsten's 'a capacity for affection that seems beyond compare' is substantiated in Pulsford's account of the wide range of people who returned that affection.

Joanna Savill recalls that at one party Sasha hired an Italian accordion player to make her visiting Italian mother-in-law, with no English, feel at home; she was happily swaying to 'Volare' and people were singing.

> There were people of all ages and stages at the party, children running round, including ours, and friends having a joint in another room. [Savill interview]

not only for parties but to work

Amanda Stewart, a poet comrade from the early 1980s readings, became a regular visitor to the Bondi flat, not only for parties but to work with him there; she produced a radio program that Sasha wrote and presented on Harry Hooton in 1988. [chapter 23]

> I remember that as soon as you'd arrive the wine would come out so some of [my memories] would go down the pluggers with that. He was sort of magical. When we were doing the Hooton program, I'd go around there for lunch, which would go on into the evening, Bruce would arrive later. Lunch would be all laid out beautifully, the bottles of wine on the table, it was like entering into another world. He was so passionate about stuff, very erudite, pedantic, highly critical, and very generous, and you'd get swept up. And the afternoon would be over and you'd have been around the world. [Stewart interview]

Another writer friend, a Gutter Club comrade, Denis Gallagher, was one more of many who would visit during the day; they'd talk about writing, and gossip, and drink wine, and Bruce would come home later from a long day at the office, to, Denis told me, a scene of apparent dissipation; there was no evidence of work done. Though writers could always rightly claim that conversations were a kind of work.

a famous cause of relationship woe

Bruce did a lot of the work in making the home environment attractive and comfortable: adding furniture, painting the place, creating the garden on the back veranda, doing some of the cooking. There was a stream of visitors. While among them might have been interesting, attractive people, many, Bruce says, ended up drunk and overstaying. It was, he points out 'our joint home, not "Sasha's flat" where I was a sort of benevolent "lodger" with an entitlement to sleep in one of the bedrooms'. [email 8.10.21]

What's it like to come home from a demanding regular-hours job at a law firm to find your partner drinking and socialising, with the evidence of a day-long session in your shared space? He resented it at times, says Bruce, felt depressed by it and at the same time powerless to protect himself from it.

Anxiety about money is a famous cause of relationship woe. Although Bruce, with the income from his job, wasn't meant to be the one who had anxiety, he found that he alone was supporting the two of them and the hospitality they offered.

> I was a young lawyer who should have been looking after my own. I was a bit profligate with money, still am. To think I could take on someone else and support him was very unrealistic. Sasha wasn't the kind to ask, can you afford this? He [disdained] interest in money, seemed to disdain earning his own or wondering where mine came from and if it was feasible for me to keep it coming. Which wasn't a positive trait of his, to express it gently. If it was offered he would accept it. I offered many things and paid for them willingly but at the same time it made me worried, and made me resentful. [Pulsford interview]

The resentment was not intense at the time, that came later, especially after Sasha's return from Moscow in 1992.

When and if it might have been perceived, later, Sasha never cared to notice it.

the differences between them

In the present, Pulsford judges the relationship harshly at times. He says it went on for too long.

> We weren't either brave enough or whatever to end when it should have. Probably soon after it started. Probably within a year or two after it started. I was very exasperated with the relationship because I don't think —

> indeed I am completely certain — Sasha was the partner I needed or was looking for. [Pulsford interview]

And now it's more than 30 years later, and those early days can only be recalled through the haze of what came later. There must have been a sense of shared values, to decide to live together, but the day we talk about it, Bruce is taken up with the differences between them. They did share, he says, a basic small-L liberal view of the world, as did the friends they mixed with. But Bruce says while he was more 'traditionally Leftie', Sasha was dismissive of mainstream politics.

> His anarchist world and activities…I tried to understand them but I didn't really understand them. That could have been an indication of our differences. [Pulsford interview]

I wonder if I'd had this talk with Bruce on a different day if he'd have told his story differently. On this day it is tinged with the regret for things not faced at the time. They'd had separate bedrooms from the start of their cohabitation.

> Our intimate relationship wasn't working and I don't think it was in either of our interests to make it work, in a way. My long-standing middle-class upbringing, which Sasha had as well in a funny way, though he had defied it, kept coming back.
>
> I felt trapped in the relationship. It is said to me even up to today that I wasn't more protective of myself and didn't have the courage to end it.
>
> And we would argue a lot. Usually because Sasha hadn't done something or had forgotten to do something or remember something which was important to me, I'd start the arguments, trying to bend him into the sort of person I wanted him to be. Which was a sort of husband. He wasn't husband material; of course we didn't think of husbands in those days…I'm not talking in terms of getting married. I'm talking about something much more basic and more important — I'm talking about two partners making each other the first priority in their lives. I'm talking about a basic loving partnership.
>
> Was I too dull, too un-open to things? I actually don't think I was. I found some of his friends tantalising but also some of them terrifying, some of them impossible for me to connect with. I'm sure many found me impossible to connect with the same way. I guess in any sustainable relationship that shouldn't matter — individuals have their own friends and don't need to become best buddies with friends of their partner. And I think this would have weighed less heavily on my experience with them

if I could trust my relationship Sasha was actually working. Which it was not. [Pulsford interview]

The 1980s was a kind of crisis era

The 1980s was a decade of crisis for gay men in Sydney, in cities around the world, because of HIV/AIDS: the new fear of death, the experience of friends dying, the intensified ostracism and demonisation of gays by much of straight society; the attempt to radically remake how gay men should have sex with each other to avoid HIV infection were suddenly ever-present issues in sex and relationships.

In 1986 Soldatow writes in a letter about his new lover Bruce, 'A lawyer, very thing about AIDS'; he does not elaborate on what 'thing' is. [letter to Andrew Brophy November 1986] Pulsford thinks this means that he talked about HIV and AIDS a lot, not just with Sasha but with other friends as well; it after all was what most gay men were talking about. (As it happens, in the same letter he tells about archiving his papers, and giving them to the Mitchell Library, which is where I found the letter.)

Naturally, safe sex was not always practised at this time, says Pulsford; he himself didn't test till years later; he's not sure if Sasha ever did get tested. Pulsford recalls that Sasha was shocked — and appeared upset — when Pulsford returned a positive test in 1999, after their relationship had finally ended.

Sasha had never asked for the result of his 1989 test, and only accidentally found out his negative status years later after some other blood tests.

another precious opportunity

Besides his first experiences of travel, and a home in which he could fulfil his gifts as a generous host to his own unique mixture of people, the relationship with Bruce, the security of a home that Bruce guaranteed, gave Sasha another precious opportunity. That is, to work on his writing. Sasha had been working at SBS since 1982. By '86 he was only a part-time worker there. And was determined to leave it to pursue writing full-time.

> I remember when we were leaving Park Parade he made that decision — without really consulting me as to how it would work. He was going to do [book] reviews and things like that. He did a few reviews for *The Sydney Morning Herald*. [Pulsford interview]

A bit extraordinary to assume you could make a living from freelance writing in Australia — even then, when there was more paying work — and before long it was clear Soldatow wouldn't be able to pay his share of the household bills. And somehow the dynamic at home became one in which these things were never calmly clarified, clear agreements and plans never made.

> I guess the income from a grant figured as well as a way to give him independence but he never got that, so he had to become dependent, or we slipped into the dependency of me paying the bills. We never really discussed it. I must have said I'll cover the bills from now or something. That was my inadequacy, not standing up for myself, and a sort of misplaced need to provide for someone. People talk about 'co-dependency'; I've talked about it with my psychiatrist, I've never really quite understood it. Is it when two people become dependent on each other for different reasons?
>
> I think we had that in a way. But it wasn't necessarily that healthy obviously.
>
> I think we would have tried to [discuss it] but it would have ended up in a shouting match, and I would have elevated it to a shouting match, often under the influence of wine and things like that. [Pulsford interview]

Some friends remember that when he left for work each day Bruce left money on the table for Sasha.

not interested in the examined life

It seems that the two did not conduct those relationship talks, those explorations of feelings and responses, those sober morning unearthings of the suppressed, sessions devoted to utter frankness, safe vulnerability, the shared search for clarity, insight, resolve, connection, affirmation.

> Sasha didn't believe in psychiatry and he was very dismissive of it, although he read a huge amount, including Freud. But he wasn't into talking about feelings and things like that. And he wasn't that interested in others' feelings as well or their expression of them. [Pulsford interview]

It's interesting how someone so into the Truth of things is not interested in what one might call the examined life, the individual's scrutiny of their inner self, that understanding being potential to understand better the inner life of others.

Medusa thinking
(snakes play up).
27.9.1990.

Sasha would often say he did not believe in the unconscious.

I read psychoanalytic discourse [...] as poetry. By inventing new words and redefining language to express thoughts that have no immediate expression, they therefore in a sense don't exist unless they are first spoken. A play on words, a good image or a profound metaphor is as intellectually rigorous as a mathematical equation. [SS 1996 *Jump Cuts* 178]

Soldatow often employed a dangling participle, okay fine let him; but that sentence requires parsing: it almost clearly means that it is the new words and the redefined language that don't exist until they are spoken. Or that what they refer to doesn't exist until the words do. In this view, psychiatry depends on concepts that didn't exist until it invented them. There's a lot of argument to be had about this (for example, whether aspects of human nature did not exist before they gained a Psychology-made definition).

In defence of this argument, one of the things you would look at is the Diagnostic Manual, that tool of the psychiatric profession, which adds and subtracts, redefines and reviews its various definitions, sometimes quite controversially. Is it always getting closer to accurate definition of all the human mental health disorders, or does the view of what is healthy or not change? And this is not to even touch on questions of cultural relativism and imperialism. The fact of issues like this supports Soldatow's view.

I once wanted to discuss such matters further with him except that it was hard to find a common premise when Sasha always used to insist there is no such thing as the unconscious. He wouldn't budge on this, would refuse to engage with the phenomenon of dreams, let alone motivations, attractions, anxieties and other phenomena that were not created consciously.

Trying to challenge him on this, the co-author of *Jump Cuts* seems to get an answer that puts all irrational phenomena down to physical disarrangement. In Jump Cuts the text layout does not indicate which of the co-authors is speaking, but we can be sure that in this case it is Tsiolkas asking and Soldatow replying:

> **If the unconscious does not exist, where do the demons come from?**
> [Bold in original]
>
> I don't use the word demons, that's your word, demons are not part of my cosmography. I do use the word phantoms, though in a fictional way. I don't believe they exist, either — it's shorthand for a warning that something is out of kilter, out of place, that there's an emotional storm gathering so watch out because your synapses are popping out of pace. But this is a poetic expression, not a scientific one. [SS 1996 *Jump Cuts* 178]

Anyway, there seemed to be no discussion of feelings about the reality that Bruce would always be more than an equal partner, he was the one who provided materially,

> I was an at home patron without having the money of a true patron.
>
> He spent a lot of time in his room in front of his big Apple computer but he also drank pretty consistently and that had its impact. [Pulsford interview]

So, daily drinking was already in place then.

Yes. The drinking was another reason for growing apart.
[Pulsford interview]

working on his grant applications

One of the things Sasha would be working on during this time was his grant applications. A grant is for many writers the only way to get freedom to write; it can also be a vital form of validation.

> One of the reasons he wanted the grant was quite banal, he wanted the money. He wanted the independence. I knew he didn't like the dependency

he had on me. Neither of us did. [Even a one-year grant] would have made a huge difference.

So that was one reason he wanted the grant, but the other reason was, he felt he was an outsider from that, he felt he was overlooked, that he had the same talent as [grant recipients]. And that made it more difficult for him. And [failing to be awarded a grant] made it easier to be overlooked by publishers. [Pulsford interview]

Still, grants for emerging writers were bestowed on people without a large publications list, and Soldatow always was sure there was something personal involved as the rejection count increased yearly. Pulsford noticed how he became increasingly agitated over his failed applications to the Australia Council.

He perceived it [not getting a grant] as a great slight. He was excluded from people who were getting grants, people like — who was that Melbourne author he fell out with? […]

He wanted to get in the door to get what they were getting. [Pulsford interview]

That door would be a legal action. In 1989 Soldatow began asking people for letters of support to send to the Australia Council.

But before he took the step of recruiting a lawyer in an appeal against its decisions, there was the publication of his edition of poems by Harry Hooton. And his first travel to cities of great importance to him, Hanoi and Moscow.

23

problems are flowers and fade

poet of the 21st Century; Harry Hooton 1990

In modern Australian literature, Harry Hooton stands in 'idiosyncratic isolation,' an unjustly neglected writer. [SS 1990 'Introduction' *Hooton*]

endlessly encouraging her stories

In the Acknowledgments in Sasha Soldatow's edition of Hooton's *Collected Poems* (1990) Soldatow writes:

> [A]bove all, my thanks go to my friend Margaret Fink, who first alerted me to Harry Hooton and without whom this book would never have happened.

That friendship began in the early 1970s so, although Sasha probably decided early on to do some work on Hooton, he didn't begin for another decade.

The poet Harry Hooton (1908–1961) became a lifelong interest, even a passion, of Soldatow's. For a long time he planned to write a biography of Hooton. He worked on that for many years, but it was never completed. He did however produce his edition of Hooton's work. And before that, a radio program.

the love of her life

Soldatow wrote the entry on Hooton for the *Australian Dictionary of Biography*. It was published in 1996 and can be found online.

> In 1952 Hooton met Margaret Elliott (later Fink) with whom he lived for seven years at Potts Point. They held regular Sunday soirées. Hooton loved fierce discussion, though often in a humorous and gentle way. There, and in many Sydney coffee shops, he continued to talk, write poetry and work on his unpublished philosophical treatise, 'Militant Materialism'. [SS 1996 'Hooton, Henry Arthur']

Fink willingly talked about Hooton to Sasha, who would have listened with alert curiosity. He often would say about himself, 'I crave details.'

Margaret Fink always said that Hooton was the love of her life.

She told me this again when I recorded her in 2018.

> The most important person in my life [was] Harry. I made no secret of it. Leon married me a month after Harry died and I was in mourning. Rocky [Meirs, known as the Push doctor] had given me nembutal, he said have one of these every night or you won't sleep. I was drugged to the eyeballs. I grieved for two years. Leon nursed me through, he's a prince. I will never forget how patient he was. I'd have irrational spasms of grief. The duration [was not unusual] but the intensity. [Margaret Fink interview]

Hooton was also appreciated by Margaret Fink's close friend since her youth, Germaine Greer. In her 1997 book on Greer, Christine Wallace quotes an archival tape of Greer speaking about Hooton's effect on her life.

> When I last saw him he was dying…but…the power of his soul filled the little room he lay in. And he called me to tell me he had great faith in me… that he thought I was the woman of the twenty-first century. I didn't know what he meant then, but I think a lot of the things I've done since I've done out of a desire to please Harry Hooton. Too late… [Wallace 1997 179]

a particular interpretation of his neglect

Hooton had an unwavering adherence to anarchism, and an insistence on writing in his own way against all fashion and judgment. Enough people cared for his work and for him to sustain this insistence. Whether he sought more of such people reveals an ambivalence Soldatow might well have recognised, identified with.

> Although he searched for recognition, Hooton at heart distrusted success. Now he began to question whether there was anyone in Australia capable of comprehending what he was trying to say. [SS 1990 *Hooton* 14]

In Harry Hooton, Sasha Soldatow found a kind of model. (Did he ever consider their double initials?) Quite likely, Sasha felt kinship with the 'unjustly neglected' aspect of Hooton.

Then there was Hooton's publishing, and his means of support. Apart from his poetry Hooton created a new magazine: *21st Century, The Magazine of a Creative Civilisation* [22].

Hooton had 'various scams' [21] including regular gifts of money from supportive friends.

In spite of those friends, Hooton was not well-regarded by all literary luminaries and gatekeepers. I was told by Nicholas Pounder that when Soldatow, with Humphrey McQueen, met Dorothy Green, a well-known literary critic in her day, and told her he was working on a biography of Hooton, she said only 'Why?'.

At first Hooton was published in most of the magazines of the time, then they dropped him. In his Introduction, Soldatow tells us that Hooton encouraged a particular interpretation of this disdain and neglect.

It was to blame it on his work being 'too vibrant', that it stands out in its 'insistence, its originality and its...tone' [2]. Soldatow insists on the seriousness, and the philosophic purpose, of Hooton's work, even while contemporary prominent poets all dismissed him; in fact Soldatow cites a 'torrent of abuse' from them, quoting Dorothy Green ('we had a crude impulse to put our hands to our ears and scream for god's sake, Harry, stop that noise'), James McAuley ('[Hooton is] an anarchist whose writings were without talent or coherent ideas'), Harold Stewart ('Whitmaniacal verbal sludge') and Alec Hope ('Ogden Nash and water').

It wasn't that Hooton was ahead of his time, Soldatow argues, but that everyone else was behind.

> I have always distrusted the explanation that someone was ahead of their time. It is an absurdity. I would rather argue that Hooton was of his time while the majority of progressive artists and thinkers in Australia lagged far behind. [SS 1990 Hooton 23]

There are echoes of this argument in Soldatow's defence of his own work.

the question of 'neglect'

Hooton claimed that poetry and philosophy are not easily separated.

Still, an idea (or set of ideas) being philosophically interesting even engaging does not of itself necessarily make good poetry, or let's say, the kind of poetry people like, even people who like other kinds of poetry. There is no necessary end to unlayering causes of causes in human social phenomena. The question of the 'neglect' of any particular artist cannot easily be determined. As Hooton himself says:

> The study of each factor in a situation uncovers thousands of others, and each of these separately, others. [quoted SS 1990 *Hooton* 69]

Soldatow's considerations of Hooton's general 'neglect' do illuminate some things that are useful in understanding the reception of poetry — such as, how such neglect is considered, how poets are given rankings in a world with its own rules and preferences, how poets might be read and re-read in a future they hoped for but which was impossible to certainly imagine.

no rules for my utterances

Marie Pitt was Hooton's 'first literary contact' says Soldatow in his Introduction [7]; a friendship conducted only through letters for eight and a half years, beginning when he was 28 and Pitt 67. (Soldatow doesn't quote these letters at all in his book.)

> **Marie Elizabeth Josephine Pitt** (1869–1948) was an Australian poet and socialist activist, also journalist and Unitarian. Pitt wrote very highly coloured nature poetry, once much anthologised; and also wrote poetry in support of the socialist and labour movements. [Wikipedia]

Photocopies of letters from Hooton to Marie Pitt are in Soldatow's archives, some hand-written, some typed.

Hooton wrote a kind of artistic manifesto in a letter to Marie Pitt:

> I will recognise no rules for my utterances. They shall not conform to beauty, delicacy, reason, except by accident. Utterances should not obey preconceptions of the hearer — should in fact do nothing by design but by accident. [Harry Hooton letter to Marie Pitt 21.4.194, typed by SS among other quotations in an outline for a book called *Utterances*]

No rules for my utterances! It could have been Soldatow's credo. (As it is for all original artists?)

Utterances is the title Soldatow gives to an incomplete and unpublished collection of prose in his later years.

advantage of all 'fortuitous introductions'

Hooton's first book *These Poets* (1941) received considerable attention and his circle of correspondents widened. He took advantage of all 'fortuitous introductions' [12]. Eventually he met Miles Franklin, with whom he disagreed, so Hooton reported to Pitt, he calling himself a feminist (this is in 1942) and she insisting she was foremost feminine. (Imagine!) But they became friendly and corresponded for a while. Soldatow mentions only in a footnote that Miles Franklin's novel *My Brilliant Career* became the basis of the film made by Hooton's later lover Margaret Fink, considered a feminist classic in a fresh era of Australian cinema; Hooton and Fink never spoke of the book together. [Fn 56 p 30]

A character in Soldatow's unpublished historical novel *The Gloves of Mr Menzies* [chapter 28] has a brief meeting with Miles Franklin.

Curry Fellowship from the State Library

There was one grant application in which Soldatow was successful. At the end of 1984, Soldatow won the CH Curry Fellowship from the State Library of NSW. He received $2500 and access to the Library's archives of Hooton material.

Hooton's letters and drafts are found in various collections in the State Library. There is a box of Hooton material in Soldatow's archives. Sasha pursued his research diligently, and acknowledged the help of the Curry Fellowship in his book.

Rewording 1987

In March 1987 the Poets Union held a weekend-long event — a conference they called *Rewording* in Glebe, Sydney, with 26 poets named on the promotional poster. They were each given 20 to 30 minutes to present.

Pam Brown kept the published papers; they were gathered as an assembly book.

In this book, Sasha's text is the Hooton readings he presented — several poems, part of the essay on 'Anarcho-Technocracy: the politics of things', and a sample from the transcripts of Hooton's death bed tapes (denouncing motor cars).

The event was recorded. To listen to Soldatow's presentation — he adds his unscripted introduction to each piece — is to have Hooton's words presented with vigour and clarity; Soldatow even sings part of it and makes some of it funny (you can hear the audience laugh).

he had to get it right

Soldatow continued his work on Hooton beyond the Curry Fellowship period. In December 1988 the ABC Radio series Radio Helicon broadcast an episode on Hooton written and narrated by Soldatow. John Tranter was the series producer, and made the episode available online years later.

Amanda Stewart, the producer of that episode, recalls making the Harry Hooton program was very labour intensive.

Sasha could be a bit wearing at times: if he got stuck on something he'd go on and on about it. But I usually understood why and respected him for that. [Stewart interview]

Stewart told me about that the day I interviewed her together with Pam Brown and they spoke about the party Sasha held for his washing machine, and the days of their poetry readings together in the 1980s. [chapter 18]

Stewart had done her degree in Communications at UTS where she became involved in setting up the radio station 2SER, and a program called *GayWaves*, where Sasha had broadcast a poem by Ray Denning in 1979 and his own commentary on 'What Is This Gay Community Shit?' in 1980. At the end of 1982, Stewart started work at the ABC, at first just answering the phone; eventually moving into radio production. She had been a bit familiar with Hooton's work, but, she says, nothing like Sasha, who'd been obsessed for years. He had a massive amount of material, and it would have been useful to him to have her, as the producer, to look at it.

Soldatow was thorough and exacting in the work — admirably but also to the point of occasional infuriation.

That amazing relentless determination in his historical research — he was a fascinating historian. He was always looking underneath, the idea of a seamless history was anathema. Sasha had Harry Hooton's deathbed tapes, about ten hours of tapes, and I had to work with a technician to equalise them, they were very fragile and badly recorded and we wanted to make sure they were preserved, it was a really big production.

Sasha had done all this fastidious research. He had to get it right. [Stewart interview]

The thoroughness, the zeal of Soldatow's labour was recalled with appreciation of just what this took:

He was absolutely meticulous about getting the text right [going] this can't be right there, more there, be accurate, why that word there…One thing I loved about him: he wanted to get a sense of the vernacular of the time, he was into oral history, he was into debunking historical mythologies but not just for the sake of it but because he thought they weren't accurately representing the ethos going on at the time. [Stewart interview]

Naturally, Margaret Fink was an essential contributor, and Stewart, talking with Fink for the first time for the program was as charmed as most people were.

[Margaret Fink] was just unbelievable, brilliant, I could see why she and Sasha hit it off immediately, [she was] hilarious, right down the line, also debunking stuff, left right and centre. For example…I'd say something like, the Push were debating, and she'd go 'the Push no! All they wanted to do was get pissed and go to the races'. [Stewart interview]

Stewart admired Soldatow's thoroughness in his research, and the care he took to understand and represent Hooton's theory.

Harry Hooton had a particular take on anarchism which came out of this theory of anarcho-technocracy. And so Sasha spent a lot of time trying to position that idea, and painstakingly went through all of his texts. You can see him with his pencils …

(Everyone chuckles and repeats 'pencils'.)

…going, I think Harry would have been thinking this. You could see him trying to really get to the core of what the ethos was, what this person was. I think [Sasha] was quite extraordinary like that. He's the kind of historian they want at universities. [Stewart/Brown interview]

Not that he'd likely get a university position, she thought, because of his passion for anarchism. 'Though he'd be suspicious of the word passion as well,' Pam Brown points out.

The erudite, captivating Sasha is remembered, who taught you so much, who always had a fresh take on things.

He was very well read, wasn't he, far better read than I was, so I was beholden, though I'd come in with my own dilettantish remarks. He was so beguiling, seductive on every level, endlessly fascinating, he was always picking away at things wasn't he, undermining anything that seemed seamless, he'd show the contradictions. [Stewart interview]

character was built through joy

On the night of the broadcast in 1988, Sunday 18 December, I was one of fifteen people invited over to Sasha and Bruce's flat to listen to it. We would have eaten well and drunk what we pleased and enjoyed the company and loved the production. My diary noted everyone said how good it was to sit together to listen to a radio program, and that Hooton said that character was built through joy rather than through suffering.

mix of diligent scholarship and empathy

That meticulous research that Amanda talks about is evident in the book that Sasha Soldatow published two years after the radio program, in 1990: *Poet of the 21st Century Harry Hooton Collected Poems*, with an Introduction by Soldatow. It was published by Angus & Robertson, by then a division of HarperCollins Publishers. On the title page it says *Collected Poems* with the subtitle 'Poems and prose introduced and selected by Sasha Soldatow.'

While the term *collected* implies the entirety of a poet's work, Soldatow's Acknowledgments details the many revisions and versions Hooton published of his poems. Soldatow chose to include the poems in Hooton's first book *These Poets* (1941), those in his last book *It Is Great to Be Alive* (1961) and one poem from each of four other books of Hooton's.

Soldatow's work is an ideal mix of diligent scholarship and empathy for Hooton's work.

Margaret Fink would often say that Sasha's Introduction to the Hooton book was the best thing he ever wrote.

> I loved and respected Sash — against odds sometimes, but his work on the Harry book was meticulous. For instance, he dredged up Hooton UK connections which is how I met Harry's niece Dee. We kept in touch desultorily but I was overjoyed when one day opening a parcel (trad postal service then) I found Harry's mother's wedding ring and an accompanying note from Dee saying 'this should now be yours.' I wear it every day. [Margaret Fink email 2.9.21]

we have arrived at humanity

In his Introduction, Soldatow makes the case for Hooton's serious purpose.

> He believed in art as a positive force, and as such, he wanted to use art to change the world. [SS 1990 *Hooton*]

Hooton makes an arresting declaration, his version of an end-of-history moment:

> In philosophy and art humanity is no longer worthy of our enquiry or representation. [...] [T]he humanism which has inspired so many of the great philosophers and artists of the past is a goal attained. We have arrived at humanity. [SS 1990 *Hooton* 67]

That's an excerpt from 'Problems are Flowers and Fade,' from *Things You*

See When You Haven't Got a Gun, Hooton's 1943 self-published booklet, quoted by Soldatow.

It's a densely written piece, a call for discarding the old, arguing that the machine, rather than inherited social relationships, must be a new focus, and demands a new, industrial aesthetic.

to known special people

The invitations to the launch of the book were from Margaret Fink and Sasha Soldatow together. The event was held at Harold Park Hotel, for long the venue for readings, launches and similar literary events — the Sydney Writers' Festival was first held there.

Tom Thompson, publisher at Collins A&R, writing on the publishing house's 'with compliments' card, sent Sasha a copy of the invitation, with a note saying '210 of these went out with 100 postcards to known special people.' [21.11.1990]

Thompson also enclosed a photograph of the book's cover, and some extra copies of the invitation.

We might note that this is in the dying days of major publishing houses still publishing poetry, around the time the 'economic rationalists' were taking over, declaring that each book must earn its keep, and ending cross-subsidising within a publishing house.

reception (at the time)

Melbourne poet PiO sent a hand-written note of congratulations on the Hooton book:

> I've been a great admirer of the man and his work ever since I bumped into a copy of his book at the State Library. I couldn't work out how to steal it though... PiO [no date; postmark 12.12.1990

Years later, PiO wrote again asking if he could quote from Sasha's book. Of course he could!

> There is no problem with copyright — Harry would have loved his writing to be used by anyone and his final letter to his Literary Executors is that, like any anarchist, all of his works can be used by anyone particularly to advance his works and ideas, which, it seems to me, the encl poem does. [SS letter to PiO 25.6.2003]

Soldatow adds his advice on proper citation.

The reviews sometimes were less about the new edition than about Hooton and his work, such as the one in *Overland* by Adrian Rawlins, who chose to quote examples of Hooton's poetry that made the case that he wasn't that good as a poet. That in his time Hooton was 'important as a gadfly and a stirrer', Rawlins did allow. But ...

> But as a poet the long view will reveal him as a small ripple fast receding into the stream's relentless, unruffled flow. [Rawlins 1991]

Soldatow's new edition does not alter this assessment:

> Soldatow suggests it is a pity that the literary establishment ignored Hooton in his later years. But what could they do? The man had nothing to say but endless reiterating of the one point. [Rawlins 1991]

What exactly that one point was, Rawlins did not say.

> [Soldatow's] attempt to promote Hooton as a poet of the future is absurd. Far from being *a* let alone *the* — poet of the 21st century Hooton's aesthetic belongs to the Industrial Revolution (or the London Science Museum era of machines): not the complex technological universe of quarks, computers and fractals. [Rawlins 1991]

Let's hear from the 21st Century then, when quarks, computers and fractals are not the latest words in our complex technological universe.

the theory of Direct Action on Things

In the online poetry magazine *Jacket*, in 2011, Sydney poet Astrid Lorange publishes a thoughtful, appreciative essay on Hooton, part of her archival project:

> I want to try to construct a loose and pliable index of poetry and poetics in Sydney, Australia, collecting materials that have otherwise gone uncollected in official anthological and historical constructs. [Lorange 2011]

Lorange begins with telling of discovering Hooton through Soldatow's book, lent to her by fellow poet, and radio producer, Amanda Stewart, about twenty years after the radio program.

Before discussing the work, Lorange recounts Hooton's biographical details, presenting these as a useful background for an approach to the work.

Lorange quotes Hooton describing his central philosophical premise:

Anarcho-technocracy is the theory of Direct Action *on Things*. It is anarchist, insomuch as it states that all government over men must be replaced by the administration of things; it is technocratic, in that it contends this administration can be encompassed, in this era of increasing technological complexity, only by the technicians. It comprises the other political theories, which in reality, if not avowedly, all have the same end in view. In particular, it comprises and furthers democracy, our own brand of political theory. [quoted by Lorange 2011]

the age of the machine as the proper object of pursuit

The term anarcho-technocracy suggests that if there is to be an elite of technical experts, they should operate according to anarchist principles.

One might see the idealistic early days (all knowledge freely available to all) of the World Wide Web as an anarchic technocracy. One might argue for Wikipedia (which, by the way, offers a definition of anarcho-technocracy) as its best enduring example.

Lorange shows that Hooton offers a vision for this future, recognising that the fear inherent in his program is the fear of a ruling class of technicians:

This is something that must be resisted, he says, for no one need be ruled. Collective campaigns to organise and move matter, under the direction of technicians (those who can 'make a pot, grow a turnip, open an atom' (p.90)), will manifest the modern utopia: an industrial co-operative democracy. [Lorange 2011]

Lorange considers that Hooton's work, whether or not some of it was 'tongue-in-cheek', has resonance and meaning in the present. She engages with Hooton's convictions and politics, as elucidated by Soldatow, as a way into his poetry.

Hooton was critical of modernism

It is curious to consider that for all his calls to 'discard the old', Hooton did not embrace modernism.

Soldatow says Hooton fought against many aspects of modernism, as in its Australia manifestations he saw it as lacking in politics. [18]. And yet in Hooton's work there is much of the experimental and the break with tradition that are obvious characteristics of modernism.

a neo-avant-garde sensibility

So, while when Soldatow's book came out Rawlins dismissed Hooton just as his contemporaries had, there was a better outcome: decades later young poets in Australia with an interest in early avant-garde found a way into Hooton's work through Soldatow's.

Margaret Fink recalls that in the 50s the Andersonians and the academics were scornful of a poet writing about technocracy. But she salutes it:

> Yes! Because he [Hooton] envisaged the new revolution since the industrial one. It's the technological one. He evolved the philosophy when he was thirty you know, you know how you think thirty is old when you're young. That's how old Andy is, three oh. [Margaret Fink interview]

Earlier in 2018 Pam Brown had introduced 30-year-old poet and academic Andy Carruthers to Margaret Fink. Carruthers was interested in experimental poetry in Australia and this led him to discover Harry Hooton, and to find Soldatow's Introduction essential. Fink was impressed with Carruthers' understanding of Hooton's work, which had never been widely taken up, not in his lifetime or later.

> The thing is, he [Andy] found Harry through the work and realises Harry is ahead of his time, that's what visionaries are. [Margaret Fink interview]

Hooton's poems have the hallmarks of the poetic avant-garde:

> Relocating such work, or better, historically situating it, bringing it to the *formative center*, will require a large-scale reconsideration of works that exist outside the conventions of Australian verse. [Carruthers 2017]

Certainly if this reconsideration is to take place, Soldatow's work would be, and was surely intended to be, a compulsory source.

his zest and drive against complacency

Hooton is a poet who has been read 'for decades and decades' by the prolific and highly regarded Australian poet John Kinsella, who included Hooton's poem 'Word' in the *Penguin Anthology of Australian Poetry* in 2009, and considers Soldatow's selection 'vital'.

> hooton is interesting to me in terms of his zest and drive against complacency more than for his machine vision of liberty. he and i would have opposite views re humans as 'masters' over all (i am a vegan animal

rights person), but he wrote against the grain of middle-class complacency and has amazing moments of verbal transcendence. i argue with him in poems [...] and of course i would, but as a fellow anarchist if of a very different bent, though also of the far Left, i feel empathy with his anti-violence of people against people and his belief that no person should have power over another. [John Kinsella email 18.6.2020]

he has poems i object to, and then poems i think do something unique, especially in terms of the staid old manner of australian white male hetero colonialist writing (from which the world still suffers) that got 'officially' sanctioned. so, it's not all bliss, and plenty of arguing, but it can't be forgotten. [John Kinsella email 18.6.2020]

24

because I have to

legal action against OzCo 1990

Although I can spend many nights drinking wine and speculating whether my history with the administration of the Literature Board has been affected by my thematic material, my politics and homosexuality, there is no evidence that can prove it one way or another. [SS letter to Melissa Range and Sigi Curnow 18.2.1991]

what is this literary community shit?

In 1990 you could not have had a conversation with people in the Australian literary world without a discussion about what Sasha Soldatow had done. He had taken legal action against the Australia Council for failing to award him a writing grant.

All the writers I knew argued about this at some time. Should he have done that and why not? Are grants to be treated like a lottery? Or if you think decisions should be transparent, accountable, what should be the clear criteria?

Australia's richest government-funded grants body could seem like Roman nobles at the Colosseum, deciding artists' fate with a thumbs up or thumbs down.

Australia is a small country by the measure of population and so the sum of literary people is numerically small. They are as riven by factions, disagreements, rivalries, prejudice and favouritism as literary people seem to be anywhere and if you want to call their collective self a 'community', I would echo Sasha perhaps and ask, 'what is this literary community shit?'.

'Why is he doing this?' Betty Riddell asked me once. 'Tell him not to. Does he know how much this is costing the taxpayer?' She had sat on the Literature Board at times. She told me she didn't like Soldatow's writing; it was 'too dirty'. I replied writers should speak the unspeakable.

People kept asking why. 'Because he can,' was George Papaellinas' reply, so I heard.

'Because I have to,' Sasha told me.

I remember a surrendering shrug when I repeated that one; it was a reason to which no amount of reason had anything to say.

I did not see it the same way as Sasha did. I had been rejected many times also, meanwhile having produced three very favourably reviewed books by the end of 1990, also writing annual grant applications. I did not receive a year's writing grant until 1993 and not from the Australia Council until 1994. I also thought it was manifestly unjust and that I was being wrongly undervalued.

But I thought something like: if you apply to their organisation for the grant that is theirs to give, you are in effect agreeing to go by their rules, and accept their decision. Or anyway, fairness inevitably always had its limits. And sure, the people on the Literature Board then probably liked the kind of writing we did not do. Also, how much time do you want to spend on this? Also, it was a game of chance, the application, a lottery. Also, all that did not concern the muse of Literature.

But people who sat on the decision-making bodies did not want it to be seen as a lottery, or why would they be having meetings, and reading and assessing and discussing, maybe disagreeing, maybe agonising, arriving at maybe everyone's second choice because everyone's first choice was different?

But Sasha was certain it was a case of unlawful discrimination and improperly conducted assessment; and it was true that his work was as good as any new writer deserving support, and probably different from the kind of writing that won grants then.

The choosing and administering of grants is not supposed to be a personal process. But of course it is, it's people judging and ranking the work of other people; what artist's work is not part of their personhood, their sense of their self? It was called a 'peer assessment process' but the only sense in which assessors were one's 'peers' was that they were also identified as writers.

many worthy authors are inevitably deprived

Receiving his latest rejection in November 1989, Soldatow appealed to the Australian Society of Authors. The letter was answered by Executive Officer Gail Cork.

> As a general policy, the ASA does not intervene in any matter which involves value judgments on the work of its members. This is particularly so in the case of Literature Board applications in which only about 18% of applicants are successful and many worthy authors are inevitably deprived of assistance. [Cork letter to SS 14.11.1989]

Cork went on to say that in spite of possible problems and inequities, the Board was believed to be basically sound; and invited Soldatow to provide specific documentation if there were something inherently amiss with the Board's assessment system.

prominent writers addressed letters of support

The money a grant gives you is of great importance for someone who doesn't have any, the opportunities it gives you can change your life, but it always felt

like what Sasha was doing it for — applying, contesting the results — was not only about the money.

It was something else, too, that he wanted, felt entitled to. Something like validation.

The 1989 decision was particularly galling as Soldatow had written to everyone he knew or knew of who might have some standing with the Council to support his application.

Several prominent writers addressed letters of support to Literature Board director Tom Shapcott, making the case for Soldatow's originality, talent and dedication, and in some instances for special consideration of his case.

Kate Grenville: [...] Sasha Soldatow is an original and innovative writer; his collection of stories *Private — Do Not Open* was striking in the way it broke new ground not just in subject-matter but, more interestingly, in form. [...] I am sure that a writer who had been exploring many different media and many different kinds of thinking, in the way he has, is more likely to produce genuinely original and significant work than writers who are content to repeat conventional approaches [...] [letter 'To Whom it May Concern' 20.10.1989]

Suzanne Falkiner: His talent is particularly original, and he is working in a genre that is barely explored and widely understood in this country. [letter to Tom Shapcott, Literature Board 13.11.1989]

Jan McKemmish wrote three pages, praising Soldatow's writing and saying the grant rejection was 'beginning to look punitive and unfair'.

Tom Shapcott replied to Jan McKemmish on 31 October 1989, outlining the protocols of the grants procedure and saying Soldatow 'is not the only published writer to be consistently rejected'. A version of that letter probably was sent to all who wrote to Shapcott.

Some wrote to emphasise how invaluable grants had been to the development of their own well-received work.

After the Literature Board rejection. Sasha sought more letters of support for his intention to appeal the decision, writing '...thirteen rejections in sixteen years...What may have started as joke has now become a scandal.'

By now, Sasha was sought after by many writers as an editor and advisor; and his valuable, even transformative work as an editor was attested by other writers. Gillian Leahy wrote about his help in writing and producing her prizewinning film, which led to more financing of her next project. She said, 'I have always regarded him as a better and more experienced writer than myself.' [letter to Director, Literature Board. 12.11.1989]

Margot Nash wrote about Sasha's 'intelligent and helpful' work on her film *Shadow Panic* and said, 'Outrageous and daring, Sasha's work is an integral part of a literary culture intent on surviving.' [letter to Australia Council 2 November 1989]

Laurin McKinnon, writing as publisher at BlackWattle Press pointed out Soldatow's unfunded achievements.

going to take this as far as he could

Soldatow asked the Literature Board for better feedback, an explanation for its decision. But when you ask the Board why you were turned down you'd only get the predictable, same replies: limited funds, very many applicants, a rigorous procedure correctly conducted, difficult decisions made properly.

Soldatow obtained the meeting papers of record through the Freedom of Information process.

He began talking to lawyers.

He was going to take this as far as he could.

The grounds of Sasha's case were that the Literature Board had not correctly assessed his application.

it was clearly an outrage

The refusals had become part of his identity, his sense of himself. From early on, in every biographical note submitted for any purpose, Sasha began to include the number of times he had been rejected by the Australia Council. The blatancy of citing the number of rejections in every biographical note seemed to have a clear meaning. It was clearly an outrage, this writing must be recognised, and that's what you were meant to think when you looked at his writing and his plans for writing.

In the two pages of Acknowledgments in his Harry Hooton book, Soldatow ends 'The Literature Board of the Australia Council has, over the last six years, consistently rejected all applications for funding.'

How differently might things have gone if Soldatow had received a grant by then? It might have changed everything forever.

It is true that sooner or later any writer who wants to be published needs encouragement, and it's true that encouragement can produce better work. Somewhere, at some point, considering any life, we must wonder about sheer luck, the place of luck in this life, in anyone's life, in life in general. You might argue about the degree of luck's power, but there's always an element of luck.

Soldatow's starting to make a point of drawing attention to the rejections might have seemed like a kind of dare to the assessors. Resist or submit.

However much he sometimes felt under-valued, Sasha never seemed to doubt that he should be taken seriously. He was certain the repeated refusal of his applications meant that people were trying to silence him, to deny him his seriousness, to deny him the circumstances necessary for a writer to work.

> Sash never doubted he was fascinating, never. Whatever he doubted about his life, his friends, whatever, he never doubted that what he was doing was compellingly interesting. For somebody somewhere at some time. [Marr interview]

And therefore the grant applications, and the appeals for money at other times. And therefore the certainty that any refusal was palpably unjust, personal, indefensible.

my talent and my pros pects

It was hard for a lot of people to get by in the 1980s, especially people starting out as writers or other kinds of artist. (Not only then, of course.) At some point you make a choice, burn bridges. No more full-time jobs, no more thought of sensible careers. Because of longing for, needing, periods of total immersion in the work, the uninterrupted concentration.

But as a consequence you have to live on precarious freelance work.

Meanwhile, back then, like now, if you didn't have a patron, whether it was a grant or some other source of funds, you got paying work. The poets usually had jobs.

An outrage, the very idea, so it seemed to some who looked around and saw that there were people who didn't need to. So unfair! Who to blame?

a Judicial Review late next week

Sasha found support at home, talk about luck. Bruce Pulsford recalls

> [Sasha] was getting knockbacks, and, as someone who would care about someone would do, I'd disparage the Australia Council on his behalf: obviously they help the elite. It was the time of the Keatings as well. [Pulsford interview]

WIKIPEDIA [W]riters received almost a quarter of the money handed out under the short-lived, controversial and uniquely generous Australian Artists Creative Fellowships. The 'Keatings' paid $11.7 million to 65 artists between 1989 and 1996.

> That used to rile me, you'd find well off authors, I won't mention [a name], getting 150 thousand, who already had a second house, it seemed to me very wrong. [Pulsford interview]

Sasha spoke to John Basten, then already a leading lawyer, who was also a friend, and he agreed in 1989 to take on the case, and not charge him. And Bruce's own law firm said he could work on it for free also.

In a gossipy, often bitchy letter to his loyal friend George Papaellinas, Sasha included an update on his Australia Council action:

> I'll get the Bored over and done with. No, they didn't even consider my appeal, which is very stupid of them as I've subsequently found out the right of appeal is enshrined in Common Law, though I like the fact that they refuse to have anything to do with the Common, let alone Law...We take out a Judicial Review late next week, touch wood...[letter to George Papaellinas 14.12.1989.]

The application for a Judicial Review was made.

homophobia was part of it

There were rumours that Soldatow had sent as part of his application the nude picture of himself on the red sheets posing like Marilyn (for the poster of Rock-n-roll Sally) which was considered self-defeatingly provocative and imprudent. There were rumours that the refusals came down to homophobia. That was not an issue raised in the legal action.

Soldatow's friends and supporters often suspected particular prejudices were at play:

> [...] I do agree that you've got something to gripe about; can this possibly be anti-gay or anti-anarchist prejudice? One is tempted to think so. [...] [Sylvia Lawson letter to SS November 1989]

An insider in arts bureaucracies told me that there was definitely prejudice against Soldatow, and basically it was homophobic. A Chair of the Literature Board in the 80s would have social events with people on the Board and writers they supported would be part of that social scene. The bureaucracy insider says the Literature Board had its own insiders and from conversations with the Chair formed the view that there was in those circles prejudice about Soldatow's work, an attitude of antipathy to him — based on his flamboyant, provocative out-ness, his love of disruption — and homophobia was part of it.

A harsh dissent is expressed by David Marr nearly thirty years later.

> Being a writer is hard! But stow the homophobia stuff, if he'd had runs on the board it wouldn't have mattered how queer he was, but he didn't have runs on the board, there was no reason to give him a grant, why would they give him a grant? Looking for my copies of his books, and going through my bookshelves, that are a mess, I look at all the books that were published in those years while he did nothing. Why should the Australia Council subsidise somebody who was all talk, he was just all talk. He had a picture of himself as a great writer, profoundly a genius and he lived it but he didn't work. But he did not work. [Marr interview]

Marr's assessment of Soldatow's work ethic was too severe; Sasha it is true did not keep regular hours at his desk, nor obey the dictum of Flaubert (who hated the bourgeoisie) to live in a regular orderly way like a bourgeois so as to be wild and original in your work; not at all; but Sasha did work obsessively in his own way, at odd hours, often very late at night, and long conversations with other writers, however much alcohol went with them, can be part of a writer's work.

Also, Marr is now looking at a slender body of work, and at things that had been published after the time Soldatow began his legal action. In spite of the large number of rejections, in 1989 he was still counted as a new writer, an 'emerging' writer in some ways.

His performance and text-based work took place on the culture's fringes but it was not less substantial in amount, ambition or quality than the work of new writers who were being officially encouraged.

In any case, from the earliest time of providing biographical data, he always made a point of saying his grant applications had been rejected 5, 6, 7, 12 times...

> Suicidal. It was suicidal. You just blamed people for what was in effect their not doing what you wanted. Sash was incapable of saying, well I don't have enough runs on the board to get the kinds of grants that they give or, you know, these things are a bit of a lottery, it's nothing to do with me; there are all sorts of ways of dealing with it, but he would sort of strike the martyred Russian pose of being misunderstood. [Marr interview]

headline writers toiled

The first action in the case was to apply for a Judicial Review.

The press reported Soldatow's action and headline writers toiled at their craft.

> DOGGED WRITER TAKES FIGHT OVER LATEST REJECTION SLIP TO COURT [Jennifer McAsey *The Age*, Thursday 1.3.1990 p5]

> AUTHOR TO LEARN WHY GRANT WAS REFUSED [*Sydney Morning Herald* 20.4.1991]

> 'SHUNNED' WRITER SUES GRANTS COUNCIL [Simon Kent and Rachel Loos *The Sun-Herald* Sunday 02.12.1991]

That was a five-page story, including comments from writers Frank Hardy; Thomas Keneally; Ross Fitzgerald; Rosemary Creswell; Colleen McCullough; David Williamson; Georgia Savage; John Sligo; Morris West; Elizabeth Jolley; Blanche d'Alpuget; Margaret McClusky.

In that Sunday newspaper story, Soldatow was quoted

> The Literature Board...was almost totally closed off under the directorship of Tom Shapcott in the 1980s...[*Sun-Herald* 2.12.1990]

Literature Board Director and poet Tom Shapcott wrote two typed pages directly to Soldatow in response; the letter comes from his own address but was sent in an Australia Council envelope. First he detailed the procedures for the assessment of grant applications, then ventured some more personal advice:

> [...] Because one of my more difficult jobs was to sign all the letters emanating from the Board, I think you have confused the administrator with the executor. [...]

> As for your own case you must concede at least that your own publishing history is infrequent and mostly quite recent. To be a star of literary café society in one city is not in itself an automatic guarantee of success in a nationally assessed and highly competitive 'competition' which is based almost entirely upon the actual samples of work submitted for examination. [Shapcott letter to SS 5.12.1990]

With some further defence of the fairness and good results of the procedure, Shapcott ends

> I am writing this so that my views may be recorded. [Shapcott letter to SS 5.12.1990]

And a yellow post-it note is attached, its hand-written message saying

> The article was good publicity for your Hooton book, eh? Tom [Shapcott letter to SS 5.12.1990]

lawyers were at work

The Judicial Review case went on, the lawyers were at work.
'Suing the Australia Council' is how people talk about it though it was not strictly speaking 'suing'.
Sasha was given legal advice by his partner. Bruce Pulsford neither encouraged nor discouraged Sasha's actions, but helped him to do what he insisted he had to do.

the case had two basic aspects

When I interviewed John Basten he'd been a Judge in the Supreme Court of New South Wales since 2005; he's said to have a distinguished academic career too. In 1989 he had been a lawyer in the Frederick Jordan chambers, considered fairly progressive at the time; Basten has called it 'as diverse and congenial a community as one could find at the Bar'. [Swearing in Ceremony of John Basten QC]
He speaks with the delightfully measured and articulate diction of a quietly successful lawyer.
Basten had known Sasha socially; as he puts it they were 'members of a social community'.
He recalled that Sasha had put in a number of applications for a writing grant and was getting frustrated.

I think he might have known that he'd been shortlisted on occasion and he wanted to know why he wasn't getting a grant when others were and he thought he was doing good enough work to justify a grant. So we talked about what he could do.

Sasha thought he had been unfairly dealt with and thought he was entitled to a better explanation than he'd got. I'd read stuff he had written, he was a perfectly competent writer at least. I thought the problem was interesting from a legal perspective: it was interesting how much transparency you could get from a process that was handing out public money to individuals. It may be a very subjective judgment who gets it, but ultimately some people are successful writers and you'd expect experts to pick them at a mid stage of their career. [Basten interview]

Basten told me he had found the case an interesting variation on his experience in judicial reviews. He used to do work of a similar kind, judicially reviewing decisions of government authorities, especially the Commonwealth.

Not that Basten rushed into the case, he told me; Soldatow had to persuade him to take it on. Once Basten did agree, Soldatow applied himself with marked diligence to presenting the case in the court's own terms.

Obviously this was a provocative step in the art world but he did it. He was very articulate of course and could be extremely persuasive, he was no fool. Certainly in this case he wanted to develop an argument so he worked it out pretty thoroughly.

I guess it's a different process [from doing creative work] but certainly Sasha was very focused about this, very focused, he knew exactly how he wanted the points raised. [Basten interview]

the zeal, the application, the focus, the dedication

It was a different order of work from Soldatow's work as a writer, and approached in a different mode. The zeal, the application, with which Soldatow studied the relevant laws, the focus, the dedication he applied to presenting a winning case, after winning over the lawyer to his case, are notable. From his earliest correspondence with Basten, his notes and accounts of documents are meticulous, thorough, obviously painstaking. Masses of legal paper, masses of correspondence, were all carefully filed. Basten explained the process: in his appeal Sasha sought reasons for the decisions under the Administrative Decisions Judicial Review Act. The reasons he was given were, not surprisingly, fairly bland, ticking boxes. Large number of applicants, limited number of grants, shortlists, chosen on merit.

> And Sasha said, that doesn't tell me anything, and I said, no it probably doesn't. And we decided to review the decisions to refuse him, I guess in 1990 or 91, and we went before a Federal Court judge. [Basten interview]

John Basten's previous work on judicial reviews had been about things like reviewing migration decisions. He had not previously worked on reviews of decisions to do with arts and culture, with their peculiar imperviousness to objective measurements. Both legal and public interest factors interested him.

> I think it's fair to say we didn't find any previous cases which sought to review decisions like this and particularly on the basis of lack of adequate reasons.
>
> There's no objective standard to be applied especially in an artistic field like fiction; judgments will differ of course.
>
> I think it's a spectrum. You get decisions made according to readily applied criteria which can have some objectivity; on the other end of the spectrum you get decisions made on criteria which will be malleable, everybody would have a different view. And [Sasha's] was on that end of the spectrum obviously.
>
> The issue was really interesting from a legal perspective and perhaps the public interest: how do multi-member bodies justify evaluative decisions like who is a good writer and who isn't? [Basten interview]

Basten says that the case had two basic aspects: merit, and panel decisions:

> One was the very subjective nature of the criteria applied to merit. The other question was how you explain a panel decision. Because different people on the panel might have different reasons. I don't think that problem really washed with the court because we [courts] are used to sitting on panels. The High Court has seven [members]. [Basten interview]

As for the argument made by many that by submitting an application you are in effect agreeing to accept whatever processes take place, whatever outcomes will be:

> I don't think that's right. If you apply for a grant you're entitled to having it dealt with according to whatever legal standards exist, and if they publish their criteria you are entitled to having it dealt with according to those

criteria. And then the evaluative element is hard to articulate but they have to try.

I think Sasha had got to the end of a line in a sense because he'd had so many applications knocked back. It wasn't as if he was saying to himself, maybe the next one will be okay, I've just published something, maybe next year I'll do better and therefore I don't want to risk appearing difficult and so on. I think there's always a reluctance to undertake litigation if there is some other way to go about it. You may feel you've been done an injustice but to go to court and expose yourself to the possible disapproval of your peers is not easy.

In a way you are being judged by your peers for that sort of grant.

I don't know if people enjoy that kind of work [assessment]. [...] If you have to give reasons why you accepted X and not Y, people may not do the job. The job becomes harder and more unattractive to those required to do it. [Basten interview]

This is the problem. When it comes to artistic merit, it's not easy to give a rational, verifiable argument or evidence for your assessment. If you look at a lot of art you can respond at once to a new artwork in almost an instinctual way; if you read a lot of literature an evaluative response to a new piece of literature arises before you ever might rationalise your response; if you listen to a lot of good music, you recognise good new music. The art is teaching you what is good by teaching you to like new things. Also, of course, you'll never get unanimous agreement on the worth of any work, not even between people you might say are equals in taste and experience. Also, for some people good music is only music they already know as good music. So it's tricky, the question of articulating your judgment.

That was the problem that we foresaw, that the court wouldn't ask people to articulate their responses. But the other side of the argument is, if you are handing out public money, you should be able to say why this response in this case and not in that case. And if you're an expert in the field you should be better than the rest of us in explaining a response. I would have thought that's generally true. [Basten interview]

Talking about grants and prizes, people will often agree that there cannot be a rational objective selection procedure, that it will always come down to a matter of taste.

There's a kind of absurdity in calls for more 'accountability' in such decisions. Why not just tell the truth and say, these are various humans exercising their taste, and taste, as the old saying has it, cannot be disputed?

In 2020 English writer Julian Barnes said writers nominated for a major literary prize should treat it as 'posh bingo'.

no certainty of success

Basten felt at the time there was no certainty of success in the case. But succeed they did.

> The judge basically said, it's not enough to say other people had greater merit, you have to give reasons, and it's not enough to say different people on the Board had different reasons for choosing others in place of Sasha and others.
>
> I think that was a valuable decision [by the Judge] because it did require a level of transparency in the way Arts grants were being handed out. It's a bit like school essays, or university essays, you give people grades but you have to be able to justify [those grades] and you do it by writing often quite lengthy comments on the bottom of their papers. [Basten interview]

The case was heard by a single judge, Judge Davies.

> I thought it was bold of the judge to take it on. And they [Australia Council] didn't appeal. I think they revised their protocols, and tried to do something more substantial where reasons were sought. I remember nothing about the aftermath. Did Sasha get a grant? [Basten interview]

Sasha did get a grant, the following year, 1991.
I asked John Basten if this case had been good for his career.

> I think it was a fairly minor [case]. It was fun. [Basten interview]

not the end of contention

It certainly was not the end of contention, private and public, over grants given with public money. For example, in 2018:

> I believe the Australia Council['s...] working culture is silo-based, myopic and disconnected from many of its constituencies. I believe it can neither understand nor read nor respond to the artistic trends and cultural movements that shape Australia's identity in the 21st C. In many ways it represents and replicates our political class. [David Pledger *Daily Review* 9.8.2018]

And contentions, private and public, over grant decisions would go on as long there was as any grant system.

The decision in Soldatow's favour, his victory, wasn't going to keep him contented with the Australia Council's procedures for very long. He resumed threats of legal action in 2001. [chapter 36] But for now…with the grant he had some freedom. Of course Sasha was going to travel somewhere. This was the best use of a writing grant — some new experience.

25
famous secular trees

Hanoi, March–August 1991

I av got ze grant of $22,000 yippee. Though this is not going to stop me from whingeing... [SS letter to Sue Howe 20.10.1990]

Sasha decided to go there as well

When Sasha Soldatow finally received a one-year grant for writing from the Australia Council, he decided to use the money to do some travelling. His old friend Sue Howe, from those days back in Newtown and Camperdown in the early 80s, in Ferndale Street, and the Dada activism of *The Only Sensible News* [chapter 13], was now a teacher in Vietnam. Pam Brown, also a good friend of Sue Howe's, had gone to visit her, and Sasha decided to go there as well.

Sue had written that she loved everything about Hanoi, that she was 'quite happy here'.

Sasha and Sue had been writing to each other since she left Sydney, chatty warm letters, meant to amuse and confide.

> Here at the Central C'tee Guest House you [get] only cabbage and bean curd. I supplement my diet with cognac. After hating everything for a few months I am now quite happy again, and only hope it lasts. Reading D. Lessing doesn't help. I hope you write a cheerful book. I also hope you come here, because there's lots of places you'd love, but I'll understand if you don't.
>
> I am making progress in the language at last. My teacher is a doctor & she entertains us with tales of Germans coming to her clinic with terrible gonorrhea and her with no rubber gloves. She says 'If you frequent V.N. Girls, very dangerous. Translate please.' The verb 'to frequent' is very useful.
>
> ...The Embassy staff here are (mostly) reluctant about everything except their 'entitlements'. It is scandalous but this will not surprise you. You must enjoy your grant & get several more. Love to Bruce and you. [Howe letter to SS 9.12.1990]

Sasha wrote to Sue to announce his plans. The letter is full of bitchy gossip, about Patrick White's recent death, other grant winners, mutual friends.

interest in Vietnam began with the war

Soldatow in Melbourne and Howe in Sydney in bygone years had attended the massive demonstrations against the war in Vietnam.

From 1962 Australia had sent troops, including conscripts, for the purpose of strengthening the alliance with USA, which had long occupied Vietnam, and was accelerating its military actions there.

In spite of its Federation and independent nationhood in 1901, Australia remained in many ways a de facto colony of Britain but from the Second World War onwards the political, military, economic and cultural relations with the USA became more important. In Leftist and artistic circles there was a mix of anti-Americanism on one hand and on the other an enthusiastic consumption and imitation of the USA's counter-cultural political actions, writings and art, and of course music.

Understanding something about that war created or strengthened a great deal of nascent political interests and tendencies in our generation. Many of us would say as Sasha did that something profound and lasting happened to us discovering a truth that government spin tried to hide: it was an illegal, vicious war. And there were ways to show that you knew it:

> The Vietnam War brought me to political consciousness when I was sixteen in a way that no books had. Rowdy unpopular demonstrations, quiet sit-ins, all-night vigils and the confrontations, conversations and arguments filled in the rest. I got my political education on the streets of Melbourne. My parents tried forcibly to take me away from all these activities, for behaviour such as this was not the manner in which the aspiring middle class behaved, particular those from a migrant background, but it was too late, I was alive with rebellion and have never looked back. [SS 1996 *Jump Cuts* 6-7]

The opposition to Australia's military involvement in the undeclared war in Vietnam grew.

It sparked interest in knowing more about what really was going on there, at least in people like Sue Howe, who knew many of the Vietnamese who had arrived in Australia in the 1970s, the so-called 'boat people'; she taught a lot of Vietnamese kids in the Sydney suburb of Ashcroft.

> I just felt very attached to the place and their struggle, and the kids who came too. I was in the Australia Vietnam Society in Sydney, and we had

projects in Vietnam. It was a communist front. As things were in those good old days. [Howe interview]

A friend in the Society was also with Australian Volunteers Abroad, an Australian aid project, and told Howe they were putting teachers in Vietnam. Would she like to go and teach English there? She didn't need asking twice.

She took a year's leave, thinking she'd be gone for a year.

Many a long life as an ex-pat has begun with thinking it was just for a year.

I'd most recently seen Sue at her home in France, which I'd visited a few times while living in Turkey; she was visiting Sydney in late 2018 when she told me about arriving in Vietnam in September 1989. It was a place that felt very 'other', and was very different then, in the early post-war period, in a way later tourists might hardly glimpse. Saigon was very quiet, there were only bicycles, there weren't any cars.

It was at the start of Vietnam opening up. Sue worked in Saigon (its post-1975, post-liberation new name Ho Chi Minh City had not caught on) at first, and after a year or two in Hanoi returned to Saigon. She told me about working at the Foreign Languages Teachers Training Institute, speaking with much warmth of her students who would become teachers of English.

It was during her time in Hanoi that Soldatow visited. When the idea of travelling to Vietnam became a possibility, it was to the north that you'd want to go.

meet you in Hanoi

When Soldatow planned his visit, Vietnam was still a place very few tourists even thought of going to. Soldatow wrote to Sue Howe that he had made his booking; he also mentioned that on the way to Hanoi he'd stop for a week in Saigon, where somehow he had a contact, a couple of piano players who had studied in Moscow and spoke fluent Russian. Then he planned to take the train — 50 hours, he said. [letter to Sue Howe 7.2.1991]

Pam Brown was already in Hanoi when Sasha landed in Ho Chi Minh City, in the south. (She wrote about it in her blog [Brown 2006].) To help prepare Sasha for his visit, Pam sent him a cassette tape and booklet on the language.

all the joy and excitement of history

Sasha had last seen Sue Howe in Venice in 1989. Although until then he had always failed to get a writing grant, Soldatow had been awarded the use of the flat in Venice administered by the Australia Council.

In those days, if you were granted this residency, all you were given was the use of the apartment. No money for travel or expenses was included in the bequest.

There had been a fund-raising party for Sasha to help with his expenses for the trip. In his archives there is a flier, 'Benefit for Sasha Soldatow' dated Saturday 11 March [1989] with the Newtown address; and a small State Bank 'State Saver record book' in which Soldatow wrote 'Venice/USSR fund book' and listed names of friends and dollar amounts.

In 2020 Denis Gallagher found his diary from that time and sent me this:

Sunday 12/3/89 Sasha's farewell and benefit at Wendy Bacon's house in Newtown was a jolly conversational affair with not one note of amplified music. Old faces included Pam Brown, Sue Howe (who together with Inez Baranay organised the evening), Martin Johnston, Darcy, Denise Hare, Tassio and Tim Herbert there, Gary Dunne and Laurin McKinnon not. On display, a 'reliquary' curated by Sue Howe which represented the multifaceted Sasha — performer, pamphleteer, poet, writer, flaneur and pinup (the 'Marilyn' Sasha was on display). Inside a wardrobe were selected items of S's clothing. I bought his shortie pyjamas for $5 after having to fight off Jill [sic] Leahy. I also won the raffle, a deal of grass. [Gallagher diary shared via email in 2020]

I had no memory of that party let alone organising it with Sue, whose own memory is vague. She had already paid for Sasha's airfare. Sue visited Venice, staying in the flat with Sasha, who was travelling with Bruce Pulsford.

Wendy Bacon and Chris Nash were also briefly in Venice while Sasha was there, and Sasha cooked for everyone, including some Italian guests. Susan Varga and Anne Coombs happened to be in Venice for a short while also, but have only a faint memory of seeing Sasha there; he noted a couple of dinners with them.

Sue Howe and Bruce Pulsford left Sasha in Venice, after Margaret Fink joined them. Margaret then took Sasha to Moscow. That was his first trip to Russia.

This trip caused a rupture in their friendship.

Soldatow describes a sad and deprived world

With Margaret Fink as his host, Soldatow would have been comfortably accommodated in Moscow. This was not mentioned in a long letter Soldatow wrote to his mother and step-father in June 1989.

In it, Soldatow describes a sad and deprived world: no one eats well, there are radiation fears (the Chernobyl nuclear reactor explosion had taken place in 1986); he misses cafés and bars; he says he would not live here, but would like to return, now that he has made contacts, to see the interesting changes that are taking place. His tone is curiously stilted, authoritative in the information he offers, as well as somewhat complain-y over the lack of familiar amenities and comforts (bars, plentiful fresh food).

Sasha was like Margaret in this way, he would never share the view that to travel was to agree to live in the conditions local life provided wherever you were. But he did decide to return to Moscow and live like a Russian.

So we might see here the beginning of an inner conflict that the return would render full-blown — how to reconcile the desire for another place with the desire for familiar levels of comfort, comfortable levels of familiarity? What living conditions can you choose, what does the choice imply, what are its consequences? Travel some more and find more questions.

Soldatow's mother and stepfather, who would have been sure to find interesting the reports from the capital of the homeland, if that word can be applied to the USSR, received at this point Soldatow's most detailed description of the new conditions there. His informants were people he met socially:

> Moscow. Dear Lily and Val, it's not good news from the USSR, the country is poorer than we think. Perestroika, if anything, has turned into a farce. That's what the people I've met have all said to me. Not that they hate Gorbachev, rather he's admired and quite liked by most. But you get different opinions depending on who you talk to. I'll tell you how each group talked. In Leningrad we had some talks with speculators, though they would not call themselves that. What surprised me about them and about some other people we came across was that they were religious.
>
> These people had a car and didn't seem to need of anything, but I must say they lived in the smallest rooms out of the centre in high rise flats that were modern but run down dreadfully. [SS letter to Lily and Val 12.6.1989]

As for food, the good things were expensive and hard to get.

In Moscow one person said to me that Perestroika [restructuring] has only had an effect on one class — the intelligentsia. They now live reasonably well, all have cars and don't fear to tell you what they think. But they still won't come to visit in the foreign hotels. One man who did met me outside and said he had his passport and would have to get permission to go through a side door. When I took him through the main entrance with no trouble he almost fainted. ORANGES — Margaret said to tell you the there were oranges in Leningrad from Cuba but we never saw them on sale. In Moscow we bought 8 oranges for 15R, so it's true you can get things, but you have to know where and be able to pay. It sounds depressing and partly it is. [SS letter to Lily and Val 12.6.1989]

Already the certainty of return has set in. Not one meant to be forever, under the circumstances, but curiosity and the sense of good material has been aroused. He has made contacts, it will be easier to return, and he'd like to, soon...

...not because I particularly feel at home, but because the life here is changing, and it is very interesting to see first hand. I would like to get out of the major towns next time, see the smaller cities and on to the other countries like Georgia. But any thought of living here — forget it. It's not the one would miss the luxury — it's just that it takes such a hell of a long time to do anything. And the pollution is as bad as in Jakarta. I chatter away in Russian which is sometimes a problem because they don't believe I'm a tourist so I have to wait in long queues. And it's been more interesting than this letter sounds, but so frustrating and very poor. Love Sasha [SS letter to Lily and Val 12.6.1989]

This is all written to his difficult mother and the disliked stepfather, presumably to be shared with the rest of the family. The tone is one of scrupulous reportage and of course he kept his carbon copy.

disappointed expectations of the other

Margaret Fink and Sasha Soldatow fell out for a while over their shared first trip to Moscow. Back in Australia, each told friends, many being common friends, of the other's failings as a travel companion.

I don't recall what Sasha's grievances were. More recently, Margaret told me, as she told David Marr when he was researching the obituary, that Sasha 'sulked'.

Margaret did all the research. He wasn't a good travelling company, he would sulk. She was doing a piece for Vogue, that's one of the problems with Sash...maybe that was tricky. [Marr interview]

Meaning it was 'tricky' because it wasn't he who was writing the piece.

The falling out was short-lived, there was too much shared history, too much enduring admiration and affection, and there was the work on Harry Hooton.

a little trepidation also

Sue Howe returned to Sydney after the trip to Venice, before going to Vietnam for the first time. Sue welcomed Soldatow's plan to visit, though there was a little trepidation also — she knew more than one side of Sasha. She was sufficiently established there by then, and looked forward to some fun company. But...

> But I did think, oh my god. Because you know how he could be incredibly confronting and a bit indiscreet with people, and I thought, I hope he behaves himself, which was cowardly of me but you do think that don't you.
> When you're a teacher there [in Vietnam] you are respected and you make so much more of an effort than you need to do here [in Australia]. So [I thought] I hope he doesn't get too up front with senior party officials. [Howe interview]

Howe did not take for granted the respect she was shown as a teacher there, and was acutely aware of how poor people were in general.

She asked Sasha to bring books and red wine from Australia.

a sensitive resident foreigner

Sue made Sasha's entree into Vietnam easy — he wouldn't have gone without someone who could — but he failed to be alert to her cues on behaving as a sensitive resident foreigner. She made some introductions:

> There's always someone who's willing to help out, show around, be the translator. So he rented a room in someone's house. And people would say to him, why don't you get a cleaner, why don't you get a cook. And he'd say, no, I'm too poor. And I found this scandalous, he could have easily. And he'd drag out the old egalitarian garbage: I don't want someone to clean my house. And I'd say, you can pay them just a tiny amount, for five dollars a week someone would do it. But he never did. [Howe interview]

This indignation is understandable; this attitude to cleaners seems derogatory, a failure to honour and reward a type of work, its professionalism. That mightn't matter in Australia, where not employing a cleaner you could afford was a point of pride for some, but in the context of Hanoi then the preference was a direct refusal of the least you could do. And this was just one example. He would go to the markets and buy up a large quantity of something — quail eggs, for example — something he wouldn't use, just because he thought it looked pretty, not seeming to care these things were costly and precious to the locals.

Sasha was not an exemplar of how to live in another culture, not now, not later. He was so insistent about being political in all areas of life, yet it seems his politics could warp a moral ethos.

> And in Vietnam they desperately needed any little bit of money and that would have helped somebody and he could have had a cook and he probably would have learned a bit about cooking. It didn't seem to occur to him: in a poor country, the first thing is, be generous. [Howe interview]

Known among friends for his generosity, Soldatow apparently couldn't perceive the different ways there were to be generous in this new cultural environment.

Sue remembers that they went together to the lovely Temple of Literature but doesn't know what Sasha mostly did in his time there; he would have pottered around the market and cooked, he certainly chatted to students and other people he met. Probably, she says, he had a life she didn't know about. He wrote postcards and letters; always looking out for paper products and quirky ways to amuse, he sent notes on pretty paper to Margaret Fink; one tiny hand-written note accompanied a length of lurid pink toilet paper.

He liked that first brief visit enough to want to return, in fact he soon decided Hanoi was one of his favourite cities.

> Tuesday 2 April 1991.
>
> Dear Inez, I am now in Chiang Mai in Thailand where Bruce joined me on Sunday in Bangkok…Vietnam is indescribable. HCM City I got quite lonely in — couldn't find a hotel, stayed with a family, that turned out to be illegal. Saigon is not really my kind of town so I passed quickly onto Hanoi. Best thing I did. Saigon was that unbearable full-sun blue sky heat all day — 3 showers at least weather. Hanoi overcast all the time, some drizzle, but mostly pleasant. Pam and Sue and I got around on bicycles all the time — talk about work! For a start, five flights of stairs at least 5 or six times a day, or seven or ten…Sue put us to work — we did English classes, made tapes of conversational english — I even took a Russian conversation class. …Hanoi is still one of those places where everything is saved and reused — throw out a bottle and it's gone within minutes, get a plastic bag and you have to keep it for the poo paper. …Will tell you more when I get back (after a rest). Lotsa love me.

fundraising for Vietnam June 91

After her visit to Hanoi, back in Sydney Pam Brown organised a Reading at the Harold Park pub, held on 25 June 1991, called Fundraising for Vietnam. It was to buy books for young students there. Pam had met many of them and knew how much they needed access to books. The reading featured many poets and other writers.

After his visit to Hanoi, Soldatow decided he'd return very soon. It was arranged that he'd bring the books with him.

In 1997 this operation would become the basis of a falling out when Soldatow publicly exaggerated his part in the whole mission, claiming credit for its organisation. In her rebuttal of his claims, Brown pointed out that he hadn't even been at the 1991 Reading; she hadn't even asked him to participate. [more in chapter 33]

out of this place for as long as possible

Soldatow had barely returned to Sydney before he was planning a return to Hanoi of limited time, then a return to Moscow for unlimited time. People were telling him it was a great idea to spend longer in Moscow, it was the most interesting time to be there. Gorbachev was still General Secretary of the Communist Party, though not for much longer, and the world was watching the destabilised politics of the Soviet Union, which were only going to become more dramatic.

He wrote a long sparkling letter to Sue: he wrote to her about a trip to Thailand with Bruce; about an illness; then news of his grandmother dying, with an amusing account of his family's behaviour.

And then Sasha laid out his plans for his return to Hanoi and Moscow, with what was left of his grant money.

> Now for my real news, I read your letter, went to bed, and woke up this morning having made the decision to waste the rest of my grant on getting out of this place for as long as possible [...] In July I will revise *The Gloves of Mr Menzies*. Then, after handing it over to a publisher, I thought I would go away for as long as the money lasts. [letter to Sue Howe Friday 24.5.1991]

He would come back to Hanoi for a short while in August then take the Aeroflot plane to Moscow.

> Because I do miss Hanoi and I want to go back to Moscow on my own. [letter to Sue Howe Friday 24.5.1991]

poetic memoir

Soldatow wrote of his time in Hanoi in his book *Mayakovsky in Bondi* (1993) in a form one might call poetic memoir. [more in chapter 29]

'The Magnitude of Beauty', one of the eleven pieces in the collection, is about Hanoi. The first part ends with the date 30 August 1991. The narrator, Soldatow, is enchanted by Hanoi and some of the young students he befriends there, and records his adventurous forays into the cuisine of Vietnam, where every single living thing is potentially food.

> During the glowing heat of the day, walking stupidly out like an Englishman without a hat I buy 333 beer and 555 cigarettes, then at lunchtime eat eel and frogs legs and devour gigantic snails at local restaurants. Minh laughs at my distaste as I'm presented with a still-beating snake heart and a glass of fresh blood. He shows me how to eat it; down it all goes, hardly touching a taste bud. Later at the markets, I photograph pigs ears and the offal of their dismembered carcases [sic]. These are the bits of meat that wake me early every morning with their intermittent screaming as each pig is intentionally bled to death. Everything here is used, everything kept. But the Red River continues to move slowly on its way, oblivious to me or to the animals that have to be slaughtered so that I can eat tomorrow. [SS 1993 *Mayakovsky* 16]

Soldatow recounts more conversations and excursions with the students he met through Sue Howe, viewed with a mix of an amused fondness for their exoticised charm and a pedagogic need to correct their English. They take him bicycling.

> 'You must observe the trees, Mr Sasha. They are very famous secular trees.'
> 'That is not how the word is used,' I say to Mr Hop as we stream past.
> 'I will show you in the dictionary,' he says. 'You will find the word *secular* there mean very old. But do not mind about the meaning. You must not miss seeing these famous secular trees.' He points them out as we cycle past. They are majestic. [SS 1993 *Mayakovsky* 20]

Indeed, that meaning can be found. Uses of English that are non-standard, antiquated or hybridised can be relished in the non-Anglo world.

There is a wonderful moment of the two of them contemplating a painting:

> In the Fine Arts Museum there is a painting by Le Huy Tiep called *An Illustrated Story*, dated October 1986. You come upon it in the very last room of the ground floor, a section which is devoted to modern, mainly

correct-line, social-realist art. Not unexpectedly, like in the Historical and the Military Museum, we are the only people there. On the other hand, this is the first time the boys have been in this museum. Knowing more of the exhibits on the upper floor, they are keen to explain to me, and see, the preserved remnants of their ancient culture, though they quickly tire of this show and tell; apart from the reverence, they are not very knowledgable about their own history. They're modern kids.

The painting comes as a bit of a shock. It is large and quite stark. Pictured across the bottom is a desolate scene of smoking bomb craters. Above it, a huge expanse of brilliant blue sky and, falling out of the blue, in an extraordinary manner, as if unconcerned, is a burning Mona Lisa.

'This must be a very outstanding painting,' says Mr Hop, sensing my attention.

'Yes,' he adds. 'It is very modern in its theme. There is much to recommend it.'

'Have you finished?' I say.

'For the moment, yes,' says Mr Hop. We look at each other. I adore Mr Hop. We are like secret conspirators communicating through layers of meaning. [SS 1993 *Mayakovsky* 20]

From his second trip to Hanoi, Soldatow went on to a very different environment.

In spite of the dismal circumstances he had reported in his letters from the first short trip, he wanted to return to Moscow. This time, to live like a Russian, he said.

It would be a life-changing time if, as is inevitable, in ways impossible to foretell.

26

a country of poetry

Moscow, to live like a Russian

On my first visit to Leningrad and Moscow in 1989, I felt like a very strange Russian-speaking tourist who both did and didn't belong. It was as if I understood the jokes but couldn't tell them…Almost instantly I understood…that I was not and could never be a Russian. [SS 'The Third Rome' 1993 Mayakovsky 59]

to live like a Russian

That understanding in 1989 might have been instant, or perhaps it was instant only in retrospect. To fully test, comprehend, accept its actuality was the theme of the months in 1991–92 in Moscow.

In 1989 Soldatow had made his first short trip to Moscow with Margaret Fink and began to plan a return to Moscow, but this time alone, as a free agent, not as a tourist but to live there, to live like a Russian.

Sasha's dreams and aims for this return were for a new life. He told me in Sydney, 'I'm going to be Party Fun again.' He would have a vivid, rich social life. He would argue and joke all night long, spinning ideas and laughing with new comrades, all of it in Russian perhaps. He would write, write a lot, a lot of new work, important and satisfying work. He wrote in English but who knows. He would be read, his works bought, passed around, discussed. He would meet everyone important, interesting, well-connected; he would be watching and listening down in the streets.

Any of it, all of it, might have been possible. Some of it was down to luck, which is apparently the ruling principle of our lives. If the rest of it was down to something else, what was that — character, will, persistence, fate?

I want to live like a Soviet person

From Sydney Soldatow wrote lively, flirty letters to someone he apparently hadn't met who could advise him about his upcoming trip. He had found a place to stay:

> I have a room in Moscow and an invitation which is all being organised through this Russian guy, Max, who lives in Manly and who I'm meeting for lunch on Wednesday. It's his room, but I'm not sure where it is yet. I'm bringing my map... [letter to Jim Jenkins 3.6.1991]

A few days later he knew a little more about where he was going, but not quite what to wear:

> My flat is in <u>Filevskii Park</u>. They don't want to take any rent (though I insist — how much should I pay? 40 American dollars a week?), and now I learn that Max's grandmother will move out for the duration of my visit so that I can have it to myself. Mad. I don't really know what I'm getting myself in for. All of Max's friends are hooligans, drunks and drug addicts [...]
>
> What should I take to wear in winter? [...] A big coat. What sort of trousers? I don't think I should be seen dead in thermal underwear. [letter to Jim Jenkins 11.6. 91]

Sasha had of course made sure of meeting Australian journalist Monica Attard, then stationed in Moscow. Faxes were sent back and forth about the complex arrangements in those days for obtaining permission to visit the Soviet Union. It was not a popular tourist destination. It required an invitation from a Russian.

Before email, before smart phones, fax transmission was the fast, immediate way to contact people. (Faxes faded fast, but Soldatow photocopied some for his archives.)

He asked Attard for assistance in his arrangements for arrival.

Attard was as helpful as she could be. The *ovir* was the local government office handling immigration, and it provided visas, though it could not be made to hasten its often very slow procedures. Somehow about six weeks later Soldatow's arrival in Moscow was scheduled.

He asked how much to pay the taxi, where to stay on his first night, if she wanted anything from Vietnam.

Attard had told him he was welcome at her place if he needed a place to stay.

> And he said no no no, I'm renting a little Soviet apartment, I want to stay there and live like a Soviet person would. And I said, cool. And it turned out he was actually renting an apartment in the next suburb to me, not very far at all, a K and a half away. It was small, a tiny little Soviet apartment, two rooms basically, old and rickety and probably things that didn't work, and he was on his own. He came and it was the dead of winter, and we met a couple of times, and got on like a house on fire. [Attard interview]

I am not at peace; there has been a coup

Soldatow's second stay in Hanoi preceded the move to Moscow. In a piece written about that time in Hanoi, he mentions in a single sentence some anxiety or foreboding about what is happening in Russia.

> I am not at peace; there has been a coup in Moscow.
> [SS 1993 *Mayakovsky* 16]

That August 1991 coup was an unsuccessful attempt to take power from Gorbachev, an episode in a tumultuous series of events that had the world riveted to reports from behind the so-called Iron Curtain and made Australians in particular aware of the frontline reports from ABC journalist Monica Attard.

people often shed their souls

Soldatow arrived in Moscow on 2 September 1991 and on 11 September wrote to Pam Brown that he was in 'a country of poetry'. This is what he was here for, these raptures, the closeness to the poets he had always loved, a place where intense emotions were freely expressed.

> [M]y thoughts for this week have been of poetry. You wouldn't believe, can't even imagine, and I feel I can hardly explain how much this place is a country of poetry. Maybe this is my own nostalgic silliness and will pass, I don't know. I am reading Bulgakov in russian [sic] for the first time. Hooton was right there is no distinction between prose and poetry — there is only the poetic imagination — everything else is bullshit. I have a picture of Anna Akhmatova by my bed. It is a severe painting, knowing life-strong eyes tinged with both reality and sadness, her strong high-hooked nose passing down to the most loving lips I have ever seen in a painting. Children read her poetry on the radio and I weep, embarrassingly and uncontrollably, and I don't know why, except for the beauty of the language. In the background of the painting, which is blue, there is a blue haunting face of a man — I assume it's Gumelev, her poet-lover, shot two years later (the painting is dated 1922). There is a Gumelev poem which has a line something like:
> Snakes shed their skins, people often shed their souls. [SS letter to Pam Brown 11.9.1991]

But besides being a country of poetry it was a country of hardship, and already Soldatow's idea of living like a Russian was wavering; he was not, after all, a Russian and did not want to share the hardship of everyday life with everyday Russians. The letter continues with some details of these hardships:

> Life is very hard here, harder even than I imagined. But I am not despondent, awkwardly happy is probably the best description. On Monday I went shopping at the stalls they set up at the local Metro. I bought half a kilo of black berries — I thought they were black currants, but they weren't. The seller weighed them out but I of course didn't have a bag to put them in. Don't you even have a piece of paper to wrap them in? I asked. No. An old woman close by, hearing our conversation, gave me a small plastic bag, saying — it's clean, it's only had bread in it. I took it and thanked her. She moved away. I watched her for a minute or so, going from one stall to another, asking the prices. Instinctively and out of gratitude I pulled some roubles from my pocket, and trying to be unobtrusive as possible approached her pressed the money into her hand. As I started to thank her for her kindness, she let out a howl which I completely misunderstood. I thought it was the money, but it was her hands — they were arthritic — my attempts at thanks had physically hurt her. I vanished as quickly as I was able. [SS letter to Pam Brown 11.9.1991]

He was realising how distant he was in mentality even while being among those who should have been his people. This realisation, though it had arisen early in his days in Moscow, continued to disturb and complicate his already complicated relationship with himself, his idea of himself as Russian.

> Russian I might feel somewhere deep down, but though I speak the language I understand nothing yet. I am in a foreign country which I feel should be my own, but I am really dispossessed. I am still a displaced person and always will be — but that is not new knowledge, I have simply relearned this. [SS letter to Pam Brown 11.9.1991]

As we so often keep learning the same things about ourselves?

To Margaret Fink, he wrote a long letter about the dissolving of his certain sense of who he was and what he was here for. (Paradoxically perhaps, ego-dissolution can be a step towards a new sense of the self.)

> ...It's hard to turn your mind around here, for me now, into a Western way of thinking. Life here is a constant battle against the obvious and there is nothing to do, but my days are filled with incidents, which take up hours and sometimes weeks. I have stopped being a tourist — I now live here for a time, and that has pushed me deeper into my own self, which

> I resist because the only response is to go into depression or become cruel. Cruelty is just under the surface — I've never known how close it was. I've gone through so many variants of sanity — feeling pity, shame, anger, worthlessness, pride, but they are all responses to a culture that has collapsed. I can almost no longer talk of me — me keeps on disappearing into a vacuum of nothingness and it is a daily struggle to resume a sense of identity. Humanity, the knowledge that you are a person — I have to remind myself of this every day. Every morning when I wake up, before I get up, I have dream-sleep conversations with my close friends in Sydney and Melbourne. If I do not do this I cannot face the horrors of the day. [SS letter hand-written to Margaret Fink 15.11.1991]

Increasingly he would write of those 'dream sleep conversations'.

The letter goes on to describe some of the people he has met through Monica Attard, who became important touchstones for his formulations about his life here. He especially liked Natasha, a close friend of Monica's (who is a constant presence in Attard's book) — kind-hearted, and also an unreconstructed communist.

> [Natasha] said tonight of the kids on the streets, I don't feel pity and I don't feel anger. They are incapable and won't help themselves, but they have to learn something else apart from selling pornography on the streets. I hope they starve — then they'll see and understand what to do. For all her dogma she at the same time holds to ideals of personal salvation. A little story. Natasha recently went to Paris, through her work, as a film specialist and when she came back she returned full of confusion. 'In Paris all they try to do is make people's lives happier and more interesting.' She couldn't understand or eat the food — artichokes, asparagus, snails — all she craved was potatoes and to return to her dogs. [SS letter hand-written to Margaret Fink 15.11.1991]

He passes up the chance to reflect on the formation of his own cravings. He will keep on insisting 'our' lives are better.

> I have a russian [sic] friend, Zhenya, he's 22, straight, but he reads and thinks and is excited by modernism. You must remember that this country stopped in 1927 and just went backwards so there are words which are common to us — like Dada, surrealism, atonal music, anarchism, existentialism etc that have no meaning here. Feminism is almost incomprehensible. Tonight on the phone, he said he wanted to have a literary conversation, about Hemingway. I've finished reading him, and

I now understand what you mean when you said he is macho. It's a new concept for me. This is a boy who said to me — you can't come here and expect people to change because you think they should, just because you think their lives are not good enough — what makes you think your lives are better? — But they are. –Then you are all egotists. [SS letter handwritten to Margaret Fink 15.11.1991]

Sasha says our lives are better, but what are the ways Zhenya does not think so? It's left to us to wonder.

The letter concludes with a story he would repeat in other letters and eventually in a published piece:

A last story — a ding-bat woman in red sq was wandering around with a sign in English: 'Defend and save us Connie Francois'.

Tomorrow I will talk with you in my dream-sleep. When I can no longer do this, I will come home. Love, Me (an australian) Sorry for being so heavy. [SS letter hand-written to Margaret Fink 15.11.1991]

the difficulties of Soviet life

Writing to his old friends in the gay writers' group in Sydney, Soldatow told more of the difficulties of Soviet life, from his position as an on-the-ground observer, with a vivid set of anecdotes:

Wednesday 13 November 1991

Official Gutter club report from Moscow. (Am I the only one who writes the GC letters — why don't youse lot travel, you big sissies. I tell you what it makes you THIN.)

Well youse, Im sick to death of writing believe me all this is true as I recount the total and absolute collapse of a once great nation, of starvation and food shortages and moral degradation and the absence of any relationships as we know them. Hardly anything exists anymore and what still survives doesn't work. The culture has all but vanished and I waver between heartbreak and total mystification the whole day (it gets dark here at 3.30 no kidding). In retrospect some of it can sound funny but at the time it's just indescribable horror after horror, and you laugh or more often burst into tears to allay your shock. And winter has not set in yet (though I've had my first taste of ice and snow, which I quite liked and then slush and dirty wind — I actually prefer it when it snows as it's warmer) and food riots have already become a reality and civil war is a genuine fear because it is almost inevitable. The people are angry, afraid, mean, sly and dangerous. Nothing of my street training has prepared me for what I have to go thru here. For a start I stand out like a sore thumb. Even when I dress a bit more like a russian and I've picked up on the moscow slang, what gives me away is my demeanour — I don't take no for an answer, I am pushy, and most of all what gives me away is my eyes. I look at people, my eyes still sparkle instead of looking dead, and I have a smiling look about me. The locals have all been taught from an early age — look down, you'll never find something if you look ahead at the horizon. [SS letter to Gutter Club 13.11.1991]

Once more, that realisation that returns over and over as if fresh each time.

(Explanations — there is so much to explain — First, I came here with a fantasy and have only just recognised the reality. Second, I am not a russian even though I bridge the gap somewhat. Third, I always have known I am a dollar on legs, but this life here has pushed me further, I am a Westerner, specifically an Australian, and about a week ago said to myself, stop. I was with my friend Zhenya who's lovely, and we had just been to the Pushkin Museum and wanted to go somewhere just to sit and chat. Eight closed cafés later, and we were now getting hungry, and this is the exact centre of Moscow mind you, no coffee, were open, nothing — and I say lets go to a Pizza Hut. We go to one of the four in Moscow and the queue is about a hundred long. Stop, I say to him, I will not stand this degradation any longer. I'm an Australian, a human being. [SS letter to Gutter Club 13.11.1991]

So for Soldatow standing in line was experienced as 'degradation'. And flaunting this sense must have marked him out not only as a foreigner but one who insists on his privilege.

He would repeat, in Russia and elsewhere, this idea that 'a dollar on legs' was the inevitable perception of him in materially poorer countries.

The letter continues to recount the tough conditions, the sense of apartness from the people around him, and a constant sense of threat.

Instinctively I know I must sever myself from these people. In the centre of Moscow I am scared. Stripped of everything valuable that I have on me, and I mean literally stripped, I am worth more than one year of wages for an ordinary person. They call it russian mafia here. Im almost getting to the point where I will not go out after five if im not with someone else, preferable a russian. It has become this bad.

Thursday. Sorry that this is so heavy but this is a heavy time. [SS letter to Gutter Club 13.11.1991]

Standing in lines, the sense of threat, the not belonging, all of it soon overcame his sense of 'a country of poetry'. How could he escape the worst of it and still remain?

I'm coming to stay with you

There was a way.
One night, Monica Attard got a phone call from him.

Very very late, saying, come and pick me up. I said what's the matter, he said, I can't stay here, I'm going to go, I'm coming to stay with you. [Attard interview]

She found him at the side of the road, with all his goods piled up next to him in the snow.

And I had a very big Western-appointed apartment, two big apartments made into one, with lots of room, and hot water. And one month turned into two turned into a year. It was a very long time. And we had a great time. It was great for me, great for him; my friends became his friends and we had lots of adventures. [Attard interview]

Soldatow reported to others only that his flat 'fell through'. And that he loved being chez Monica. 'She's not only a companion, she's a soul mate,' he wrote to Pam Brown. [30.9.1991]

Attard was a working journalist, with the ABC since 1983, and she already knew Russia, spoke Russian. She was in the job she had wanted for so long. It had become evident that when the ABC opened its bureau in Moscow in 1989, when events in Russia were news everywhere, Attard was the journalist to be sent there.

I went to meet Monica Attard during the last weeks of her time as Head of Journalism at Macleay College; she was soon going on to be Head of Journalism at the University of Technology, Sydney. We sat in a meeting room at the College near Central Station in Sydney. I hadn't met her before, but she was a legendary name in our lives for her reporting from Russia, that is, from the Soviet Union as it reached its final crisis.

At Monica's apartment, Sasha revelled in its comforts, in meeting people, in conversation, fraternising, sociable drinking. This was more like living the dream — not the dream of living like an everyday Russian, that dream had been set aside; this was a dream of being in the thick of things, amidst an international group of people deeply involved in politics, in reportage, in analysis, in comfortable surrounds, with plenty of alcohol, where he could be both host and guest.

> There was a period of time my apartment was like a refugee camp. When the coup happened [August 1991] they came to stay. I had people from Tajikistan, Uzbekistan, Georgia; you needed traffic lights to be in there. Always someone. My closest friend was Russian. I just got used to having lots of people around, I'd get up and go to work, come home and someone had cooked a meal and that was fine. People would arrive and it was like you were the embassy; instead of the embassy they'd go to Monica's place: 'oh you're here, okay you're coming to stay, okay you can come and stay.'
>
> Sometimes they'd been booked in hotels and still come and stay. Or they'd come to dinner. [Attard interview]

Attard's illuminating book [1997] is about friendship in Russia as well as the political events and reporting. Her description of the quality of friendship there would have chimed with Soldatow who often averred that friendship was his highest value. 'Friendship for me is sacred,' he said in an interview. [Machon]

The main subject of discussion then was the failed coup in August.

> By dawn the coup attempt was over.... But no one could be sure...David Marr had arrived from Leningrad and we nutted out the possibilities. David wondered whether the hardliners had hated Gorbachev so much throughout his six years in office that they'd listened to nothing he'd said, seen nothing positive in the relaxation of party oppression. [Attard 1997 196]

an unplanned, unexpected reunion

While Sasha was still living in the little Soviet flat, soon after his arrival in Moscow, Sasha experienced an unplanned, unexpected reunion. It was just a few weeks after the coup, which must have only intensified everyone's emotional state.

When we talked in August 2018, David Marr told me, after the recollections of his earlier relationship with Soldatow, about his arrival in Moscow. Marr's biography of Patrick White had come out in June 1991, after six or seven years of work, to 'a huge amount of hoopla', and while that had been pleasing and reassuring it was also exhausting. Marr planned to go to England to see his publishers there. Then he wanted a holiday. Somewhere exotic, where he'd go alone. Somewhere no one mentioned Patrick White. He decided on Russia, and made the booking on the cruise from Helsinki to Leningrad. It so happened that his old friend the theatre director Neil Armfield had met a young Russian man, who could meet Marr in Leningrad, to help with translating.

> The ship came in, there was Oleg on the wharf, he took me to his flat which was in one of those godawful Russian suburbs, rather like that bit of Redfern you've gone to live in, and took me on the underground of Leningrad, and we went up some huge escalator, and he said, we get out here, we went out, and he said, this is the Nevsky Prospect and I burst into tears. All those Russian novels, everything! [Marr interview]

Everything Marr could have hoped for: the romance of being here, the echoes and ghosts and memories of great literature, the complete otherness of the place. At first he was free to immerse himself in this new experience. He says the first few days were completely thrilling, wandering around Leningrad, dealing with getting a meal in Soviet Russia, all that.

And then everything about his time in Russia changed. One day, when they were in one of the galleries, some American tourists were asking anxiously, are they going to let us out?

> I looked over to the guard on the door and said, there doesn't seem to be any problem. And they said, no, haven't you heard, Gorbachev has been overthrown. That's how I found out. And I thought oh fuck that's the end of my holiday. I'd been working for the ABC so I contacted the ABC in Sydney, and they said, we knew you were there and were trying to get hold of you, thank god you're there, now this is what we want you to do. So I started work. From Leningrad. And the first order [from Sydney] was: we've heard that the navy is marching on Leningrad to depose the mayor, Subchak. And I said, okay I'll see what's happening and I got into a taxi, with Oleg interpreting.
>
> And it was heaven, the whole thing was fucking heaven.
>
> We're tearing around Leningrad in a Russian taxi playing American disco music, gathering information on the non-invasion.
>
> Then I was given the order to go to Moscow and make contact with Monica Attard. So, I started working for Monica. What then developed was kind of intense intimacy. [Marr interview]

David already knew Monica, but in this environment all relationships were marked by the particular intensity of closely sharing such tumultuous times; hardship and joy combined, there is such an intensity to life in a place fraught with total political and social upheaval, its indefinable danger.

And Sasha was there.

> Well this was a Sasha scenario come true, revolution going on, we're in Russia, Russia was his beat. I'm reporting, trying to make sense of what's going on. Monica is radio and she's feuding with the television people, [with a] split in the ABC. Her apartment is filling each night with gloomy intellectuals smoking and drinking, it was heaven. [Marr interview]

I don't doubt Marr got that right, that it was heaven for Sasha to be in the thick of all of this.

> [...] The fact of the matter is, I said, come on Sasha what about it, and we fell into bed, and it was pretty good, we had a wonderful time. I would go over to the flat, sometimes I'd have a hotel, and he'd come to the hotel, he talks about that in *Mayakovsky in Bondi*. It was terrific, at the time the whole thing was just fucking terrific. [Marr interview]

rapturous and tormented

Soldatow in rapturous and tormented tones writes of an intense brief love affair at the age of 44 between two who'd been lovers fifteen years ago. The 'intense intimacy' of the moment that Marr mentioned is poetically elaborated:

> *They were in Moscow*
> *There was a revolution*
> ... Like an ancient incantation of wonder, like a spell which unexpectedly introduces a new-found wisdom into his life...
>
> How much he longed for an experience of how love and politics could suddenly strike out of the blue, come together and mix, bind, meld, then resolve their opposing natures in one passionately fragmented moment.
>
> Moment, month or mouth, it did not matter.
>
> This intense, mysterious unity was one that'd he'd only read about in books, never expecting to live through the poetry of such a time.
>
> Such a lifetime.
>
> Yet, in a momentary passing, in the sudden death of an empire, he rediscovered his own need for a future.
>
> A brief resurgence of an ideal.
>
> Something that might cover past mistakes.

A joy that would leave you speechless.
The need to fill an empty house.
And one final resolution, an admission to loneliness — to live with and then die in the arms of a longtime lover. [SS 1993 from 'Critical Mass' *Mayakovsky* 25-26]

Lines about gathering autumn leaves create a kind of elegiac mood. The piece ends:

And there was no revolution, not really.
Maybe just a slight commotion.
An unfulfilled domestic dream.
Silly fights about emotions.
Too much practical advice
The death of a wish.
Whatever, it burnt my heart away like a snowflake.
[SS 1993 from 'Critical Mass' *Mayakovsky* 27]

David Marr also uses an image of burning.

We had a lot of fun. But it was burning itself out as far as I was concerned. And certainly the expectations that he writes about in *Mayakovsky*, that I would somehow throw over my life and join him on this great adventure — just crazy, it wasn't going to happen. I'd just scaled this peak in Australia by writing this great big fat biography, and I didn't quite know what I was going to do next, but it wasn't going to go on an adventure in Russia. We did a *4 Corners* [TV] show, then I came home. And the unhappy aftermath of that is what Sash writes. It's not inaccurate, I was saying, I have work, but he makes work sound as though it's doing something dirty in a factory. My work was writing, my work was reporting, my work was trying to make sense of what's going on. [Marr interview]

Again, Soldatow did not think someone else's work mattered as much as the relationship he wanted to have, the mutual devotion and surrender. And as Marr saw it, the end of their fling left Sasha to deal with his persistently obvious outsider status there:

And anyway it showed we were terribly different people. And there was Sash left alone and finding himself completely at sea. Sash and I were only there together for three weeks. He had another six months. It was very clear that he was not remotely at home in Russia. Not remotely. [Marr interview]

he broke apart

Soldatow writes that he broke apart when Marr left. He writes that he is finding the place hard, physically and emotionally...

> ...and of course it did not help that as soon as I arrived from the airport who should open the door but David Marr and we fell into bed together for the next two weeks...I was the only friend he could open himself to about his gross insecurities and fear [...] and then he left and it was as if nothing had happened. I felt used... [letter to Jim Jenkins 12.11.1991]

Soldatow's intimate letters turn up repurposed as parts of his published prose. A typed letter to Marr of several pages, written over several days, with a phone call during its writing, is a draft of what later appears in *Mayakovsky in Bondi*. Soldatow makes declarations that do not appear in the book:

> Dearest darling you...David, I have never felt this with a man before. [letter to David Marr 24.9.1991, typed, several pages]

Soldatow says he has been writing good and very good poetry. He declares his love.

> You've broken my heart again. [letter to David Marr 24.9.1991, typed, several pages]

In a letter back to Soldatow Marr acknowledges what the two of them experienced.

> I was as open, as candid with you in Moscow as I've been with anyone in years. To your rebuke that it was not good enough I can only reply [with] thanks for making it as extraordinary as it was for me. I'd run away from Australia because I was afraid of losing myself in the gush and self-promotion after the book came out. I was in a dreadful state [...] everyone told me what a golden time I was having, & I was swimming in self-loathing and confusion [...]. I told you all about this. It was a godsend for me you were there. For a couple of weeks something quite bizarre and wonderful happened: I was brought back to earth by being whisked off my feet. Then things fell apart. [...] There isn't a soul I've told so much to in years. [Marr hand-written letter 27.10,1991]

Marr goes on to tell, in friendly leisurely tones, about the seaside cottage outside Sydney he has retreated to (fire, friend, music) before he goes on to give his assessment of the manuscript Soldatow asked him to read, the long-worked-on novel *The Gloves of Mr Menzies*. [chapter 28]

anguish, recrimination, erotic fantasising, taunting

Soldatow seemed to think that Marr should stay with him, travel in the region with him.

Could he really have expected that? What on earth would make him expect that? Only the force of his own feelings, his desire. Perhaps some attachment to the moment.

To the satisfaction of having an immediate, responsive person to be with.

The piece in *Mayokovsky in Bondi* (1993) about this brief romance in Moscow is full of passages of anguish, recrimination, erotic fantasising, and a kind of taunting:

> [E]very time I've had to deal with journalists I end up coming out of it feeling a bit of an ignoramus. I seem to always pick out the wrong material. Youse deal in facts and turn them into quick stories — I deal in impressions and turn them into slow writing. They are two different processes. It's like confusing art with life. [SS from 'Critical Mass' 1993 Mayakovsky 28]

After attempting a phone call, Soldatow continues to insist on his own better values:

> David, I don't know what you want…You call your priority work. Is that so true for you that you will pursue work to the exclusion of your friendships? You have always something else to do or somewhere else you must go whereas I will drop everything for people. That has always been the difference… [SS from 'Critical Mass' 1993 *Mayakovsky* 29-30]

It sounds like the Sasha of old that David described, the one promising that his way was the superior way, the way of freedom. No one who has work they love that is going well wants to drop it for the sake of prolonging a fling. In that view, a good partner will step aside, understand, and let's see later. But Soldatow did not regard Marr's work, his calling, as one whose compelling Muse mattered as much as his own compelling Muse who called for something like ecstatic submission, renunciation of all else. Good poetry would come out of it.

Sasha might, if he had been someone else, have decided the separation left him more time to write. After all, he knew he was living in an amazing time, well positioned to report on events fascinating the world.

Soldatow's writing shows its own kind of ruthlessness. Whatever happens, that's your material, use it. The method of writing letters from whose copies you create text for your next book.

In a kind of cold rant he writes about what were in his view all the profession's moral and ethical failings, which included, and now does it not get bizarre?, a table full of journalists not being interested enough in the rose he had brought to it (expecting what, all conversation to stop in a swoon?). Soldatow even says that journalism is 'a vile profession'.

In our day how vital it has clearly become to value and defend the work of journalists.

Even written then, this vilification is indefensible.

Apparently a few people who saw the piece in draft form had severe reservations. Soldatow wrote to his trusted friend Margaret Fink for her opinion, as he had been told, he said, to drop all references to David.

> [...] not for legal reasons as there's nothing defamatory, but for reasons of 'ethics and morality'. I don't know what he means by this, that's why I'd like you to go through it — I'm not at all concerned by what David will feel, but then, I can't really see why people find this piece to be too confronting, [...] I don't find it objectionable. Do you? [SS hand-written letter to Margaret Fink 30.6.1993]

Whether or what she replied cannot be found, but anyway, it stayed in.

an intensity whose purpose I have never understood

In *Jump Cuts* (1996) Soldatow tells of the only four people in the previous four years he's had sex with.

> David is a former lover and a friend for over fifteen years. Our intimacy is strong but reserved — that acts to bring out an intensity in me whose purpose I have never understood, but this intensity has twice destroyed our friendship, put it on hold. We won't sleep together again unless we both change drastically, which I doubt is possible — we are the same age. [SS 1996 *Jump Cuts* 171]

So, here he attributes to his own intensity the destruction of that relationship, while in the former writings he blamed David for not being in tune with his, Sasha's, needs and desires, or his unquestionably correct position on things.

> I'm reading his sad aftermath of the fling we had in Moscow in 1991 in *Mayakovsky* and it's clear to me now reading that — was he expecting me to just throw over my life and go off on an adventure with him? — well fuck him — I'm a writer, a journalist, I work; but he was always free for an

adventure and the fact of the matter is we loved that in him till it became sad. [Marr interview]

great television really

Meanwhile, the astonishing events in Russia were being heard and watched all over the world, and those of us who followed the news from Australia were knocked out by the reporting by Attard and Marr.

We saw the celebrity biographer and the wonderful Monica Attard on '4 Corners' last night. We get the proper news from Monica Attard's radio reports….Great television really…Monica Attard was out on a rooftop in a leather jacket with the light wind. [Pam Brown letter to SS 3.9.1991]

The letter is full of more warm and witty chat and gossip, and the declaration that Pam had 'given up the fags […] I really have this time'.

exploring and treasure hunting

On happier days, Sasha enjoyed exploring and treasure hunting in the local streets. His good eye, his self-assured taste meant that he swooped on objects others would overlook, and found things that delighted him. And he could speak Russian, of course, which made all the difference.

It was a heavily accented Russian but it was good Russian, grammatically correct Russian, not like mine which was street Russian because I learned it from my friends, but he spoke perfect Russian and would get a real thrill out of it … [Attard interview]

Another thrill was to poke his head in the doorways of the shops they passed and discover things. He was excited to find a nearby shop that sold paper, you could even ask for a certain thickness of paper. And they also sold pencils, imagine Sasha's joy. This at a time of deficit all over.

As for Sasha's core-shaking discovery that he wasn't really Russian …

That happened early and fast, within a few weeks of him moving into that place in Philosophy Park that Max had organised for him, where he realised, no thanks, I don't want to live like this. So that was the first iteration of it, the kind of physical discomfort living like a Soviet person. [Attard interview]

Now he was living in Monica's ABC apartment, as someone well placed in society. He would have had to reflect on this preference, if he ever reflected in this way, and on who he thought he was now.

> From there [came] on the slow realisation that hardly anything about him was Russian at all, apart from the fact his parents had been born Russian.
> There was no touchstone. He could speak Russian, he studied the literature, but it didn't make him Russian. [Attard interview]

hugely amused then immensely pissed off

It takes more than speaking the language to fit into a culture, and Sasha did not want to change the way he responded to things, the way he revolted against standing in line, doing things the way they were done there. Attard talks of the Russian mentality of the time: this was a totalitarian system; either you work out how to get around all the many rules, or you simply submit. But he would not. As Attard describes it, Soldatow, at first an amused observer, became exasperated, even outraged at the standard procedures at a shop:

> You would decide what you wanted, then you'd go to the counter and a girl with an abacus would work out how much change you'd have to be given for the money that you had…He was hugely amused when he first arrived then immensely pissed off by it. You'd go into a shop and there'd be ten thousand items of the one thing as that had just been produced by a factory and he'd be amused by that and talk about it in detail and watch people as they navigated around the ten thousand items of the one thing. Then it got to him. [Attard interview]

His frustrations in the shops point to something that one can extract from many of Soldatow's travels: a lack of adaptability. For all his modernism he never embraced the ethos of not judging others on one's own terms.

Soldatow's constant conflict between his soon-abandoned yet somehow retained goal of 'being Russian' and his preference for the identity and privileges of the foreigner was never resolved.

And meanwhile, he was there at a really hard time…

> …deficit and no money, no jobs, unhappiness, confusion, your world thrown upside down if you were a Soviet citizen; the regime had collapsed, the country had collapsed.
> Russia was always intense but particularly then. [Sasha] absorbed a lot of that intensity but didn't know how to deal with it, if that was being Russian it wasn't him. He socialised less and less with Russians and more

and more with foreigners, which was kind of surprising. He'd talk about it, usually drunk, but talked about it a lot. He found it at first really difficult because he felt he had failed, but eventually rejoiced that that wasn't what he was like. [Attard interview]

It must have been somewhat confronting for him that Attard was more attuned to, knowledgable about, assimilated to Russianicity than he. She'd been going to Russia since 1983. Her problem was the opposite to Sasha's:

> I don't have any Russian blood but I felt I was Russian, sometimes I felt too Russian for words. I think [Sasha] understood early on that nothing about him was particularly Russian and it's a ridiculous notion and he didn't really want to be Russian in the end. I think he got to the point where [he thought] it's not for me. And that would have been hard for him to accept. [Attard interview]

a Russian drinking another Russian's vodka dry

And of course Sasha drank, increasingly he drank more. And he drank whatever there was to drink, wherever he could find it.

He kept a hand-written note Monica left for him one day in the apartment. She said a friend was upset as she found her vodka had gone; apparently Sasha and a couple of others had drunk it all. Monica wrote, 'I think, basically, it breaches a few cultural norms to be a Russian drinking another Russian's vodka dry. Boruja says he'd like to talk to you about it. I'm staying out of it.'

Those tricky ethics: you should let anyone drink all your vodka — that's what I imagine Soldatow would be arguing. No possessiveness. If it had been his vodka, he'd have shrugged it off if someone else drank it. But it was someone else's vodka. He drank way too much, Attard says.

> I'd leave him at nighttime on the couch with his bottle of whisky or whatever and I'd get up in the morning and he was ready to have a chat. It was exhausting. It wasn't [exhausting] for a long time, it was wonderful for a long time. I genuinely loved Sasha but he was exhausting. [Attard interview]

Sasha loved to cook and often made meals for everyone at Monica's. There were parties every week. Sasha would invite anyone he knew.

> He could party till the wee hours of the morning. I was younger then so it was easier to deal with. It was wonderful until it wasn't. [Attard interview]

tough words enclosed

In October 1991 his loyal sensible friend Pam Brown wrote on the envelope of the letter she sent:

> Look out — tough words enclosed.

Tough enough, and with excellent advice:

> I hope that you have resolved your sadness. That is that you have caught the train to parts of Moscow that are completely strange to you & walked about them with your eyes wide open & with your irrepressible curiosity leading to new images and new ideas.
> There really is no point in sitting in a flat weeping over old lovers who are already engaged in their own futures. And whatever happened between you and the celebrity biographer would probably not be altered nor improved by your returning to Sydney to knock on his door.
> You are actually living in the reality of your chance-in-a-lifetime to do some writing for your future. So why not do it!! Otherwise the alternative would seem to be to return home, dry out and get a job. I do love you but that's all I can say. Love Pamela x. [Pam Brown hand-written letter to SS 16.10.1991]

more parties! and more flings

Soldatow, never a good traveller on his own, did not venture beyond the areas he was taken to by his friends.

> It was like he was a bit scared, he didn't like to go to areas he wasn't familiar with on his own, which was probably why he never travelled while I was there, a bit sad. [...] The closest he came to tapping into an artistic world is when Belvoir [Theatre] came, and they were Australians. [Attard interview]

In October 1991 Sydney's Belvoir Street Theatre travelled to Moscow, with their production of the play *Diary of a Madman*, adapted from Gogol's 1835 short story, directed by Neil Armfield, featuring actor Geoffrey Rush. The troupe stayed at Attard's apartment. More parties! And more flings. Soldatow travelled to Leningrad (as it was still called, and the name he always insisted on) with the troupe. He wrote to a longtime confidant 'I have got over the David thing' and tells of falling into bed with one of the visiting Australians.

Soldatow made friends with musician Matthew Fargher from the troupe; they kept in touch. Back in Australia Fargher wrote 'After Moscow it's hard to believe life is hard anywhere in the West.' Later [nd, postmark 17 November 1991] Fargher reported a meeting in Sydney of 'the Belvoir crew...and I left feeling somewhat depressed and not altogether surprised at the cynical negativity of their experience of Russia.'

once you're dead you won't be able to drink

A chapter in *Mayakovsky in Bondi* is titled 'Zhenya'. The epigram at the start is a kind of paean to alcohol by Marguerite Duras ending

> What stops you killing yourself when you're out of your mind is the thought that once you're dead you won't be able to drink any more.

Soldatow's piece speaks first of an early Russian film that records the execution of three revolutionaries, then of the statues removed from Moscow.

It's a beautiful story, full of restrained feeling and unrestrained feeling, passages about various moments with the young Zhenya, sometimes called 'you' sometimes 'he', about art and about drinking and most of all about the explorations of their perceptions, the narrator's and Zhenya's, of what life is here, here in Moscow. Zhenya says, 'I am as much an alien here as you are' [85] for he had grown up in a small village.

This young man, who drinks prodigious amounts of any alcohol at all, who has his own different responses to the art they look at, who objects to Soldatow's insistence that life in the West actually is better, who walks around Moscow with him, to art galleries and to ruins, in the dark and the rain, confiding, baring his soul.

> We walk, Zhenya and I, and I touch him, innocently, my Zhenya. It is a touch not totally devoid of sexuality but it is an allowable sexuality. [...] Clear as day, if I had fathered a child, this would be the boy, my son, my angel. [SS 1993 *Mayakovsky* 85]

Soldatow's observations here are full of fascination and tenderness. He writes of three generations in Russia:

> The first one is already too far gone. [...] They are too tired, too worn out from facing the consequences of the experiment. Then there are the parents, the people who are my age. The ones who worked their guts out for something they were told would be a better life and then read one day, in a foreign newspaper, that they had lost everything [...]
>
> Then it is your generation, Zhenya. Some of you will slip through, more by mistake than by chance. [SS 1993 *Mayakovsky* 87]

Monica Attard tells me that Zhenya was one of a group of young guys who'd taken her under their wing and shown her a side of Moscow she'd never have seen as a correspondent. And Sasha became friends with them too. Zhenya's story was tragic.

> Zhenya actually committed suicide. [Sasha] was very close to Zhenya, and Zhenya died not long after Sasha left Moscow.
>
> Zhenya was really young, 20, 21, and he was gay but not out because he couldn't be, his family would not be accepting. His father was a journalist with *Red Star* magazine which was a military magazine, so there were familial circumstances that would have made it difficult to come out.
>
> Sasha took on his pain, he took on everybody's pain. He was the agony aunt, everybody would have a whinge, a cry on his shoulder. He was very fond of Zhenya, he loved Zhenya and there was a lot to love — Zhenya was a beautiful kid. It was very easy to think you could fix people's problems, you were a Westerner, you had a passport, it was easy to think you could fix people's problems. [Attard interview]

I will tell you the true state of Russia

During November 1991, Soldatow wrote many letters from Moscow, trying to describe what he saw around him as Russian society was thrown into crisis, examining his own state of mind in that confusion of exhilaration and horror in the intensity of his experiences.

Sasha wrote to his mother, his tone somewhat different from that he used with other people; it's more sedate, more apparently wanting to please. He tells how Russia has changed him.

> This will not be a pleasant letter to read because I will tell you the true state of Russia [letter to his mother 1.11.1991]

He tells about going to Leningrad: 'not as bad'. He reports that the rouble was then worth 6 cents. He offers details of the horrible things he has written of to others. He repeats his story about the beggar woman.

> Two months in Russia had turned me into one of them, cold, hard and brutal. At that moment I had turned into an animal with no human feelings. [...] I have arrived in Moscow at a time of great crisis. I want to observe it...I am living through historic times, but as a Westerner. I am not Russian. I am an Australian. All that exists for me is the Russian language — everything else here for me has died. And the Russian language here in

Moscow is also deteriorating. They don't speak Russian, they speak slang. And the youth are only after money — 'golden rain' they call it. And for this money they are prepared to do anything. The KGB has turned into Russian mafia. And the people have turned greedy, and I can't blame them.

There is more in that vein. He concludes on a tender note.

I have bought you a very beautiful Russian woollen scarf. It is gorgeous. I will wear it because I cannot send it out of the country by post, so you will have to wait till I return — it is lovely. This is most of me [sic] news. Please don't worry about me — I am fine. Love and kisses to everyone, and to you especially. Me. [letter to his mother 1.11.1991]

missing you from such depths of my being

Soldatow writes to Craig Rendell that he is missing Bruce Pulsford, the partner left behind, in that relationship whose boundaries, whose chosen future, had never been clearly delineated.

> I have started to miss Bruce heaps — I think this time apart was necessary and will bring out new qualities in our relationship, or at least that's what I hope [letter to Craig 1.11.1991, 2 pp typed, carbon]

On the same day he wrote to Bruce:

> Moscow. I am missing you from such depths of my being that it is almost overpowering. Oh, of course I've missed u before this, but it was different, a kind of travelling distance which you get when you're moving about for a little while... [letter to Bruce Pulsford 1.11.1991]

He writes about the awfulness of life where he is, then ends on a note of passion and intimacy.

> When we meet up again, I am now insistent that we solve our fucking, our relationship became a bit of a haze — I am now able to see through that haze again and have rediscovered, no, that's the wrong word — surrounded myself again with the intense love that I have always felt for you. Miss ya more than I can express, love, love, love, Me. [letter to Bruce Pulsford 1.11.1991]

The relationship, so ill-defined yet so tenacious, wasn't over exactly. Bruce would come to Moscow for Christmas then take Sasha to Paris. Sasha returned to Moscow, and Bruce to Sydney. Telling me this, Bruce reflects on how young he really was then, only 35.

> We should have been more articulate about what we wanted from each other but we weren't. But my understanding was he would stay in Moscow indefinitely. [But] he never asked me to pack his stuff up or send it to Moscow.
>
> I was very heartened, I thought it was very positive. He was having a great time. But for his dependency on someone to stay with, he would have stayed there indefinitely. [Pulsford interview]

one of the greatest anti-climaxes of the twentieth century

On Christmas Day 1991, Bruce Pulsford arrived from Sydney for a visit, bearing a ham for a festive Christmas meal with friends held at Monica Attard's apartment. Attard writes of expecting nothing more than the feast and some rest that day, when something momentous happened.

> The Sydney-based winter Sasha Soldatow was staying with me in Moscow and we'd invited over some friends [...] to indulge for the day.
>
> We'd just settled into a post-gorging slumber when one of the greatest anti-climaxes of the twentieth century took place. Mikhail Gorbachev, president of the Soviet Union, appeared on television to announce that the Soviet Union would soon cease to exist, and that he was resigning. That was that! The Soviet president had thrown in the towel. Max, Sasha and I went to Red Square that night to watch the red hammer and sickle flag be lowered over the Kremlin for the last time. But by the time we arrived, it had already been replaced by the Russian flag. [Attard 1997 213]

That was the place in the world everyone was listening to that day.

Radio was still the most important medium for instant news then — not so much TV. And there weren't even mobile phones, let alone the idea of having a camera, that also can take video, in a device in your hand about the size of a cigarette packet, that everyone calls a phone.

Attard describes the New Year's Eve celebrations in the Square six days later going on just as they always had, where the thousands of people gathered there seemed 'oblivious to the real portent of the occasion.'

Soldatow did not speak directly of these events. It wasn't the kind of work he did, reportage. He would rather tell stories about what people in the street were saying.

His Moscow diary for that New Year's Eve says only 'Red Sq.'

And the next day, Bruce took him to Paris.

So, whatever is going on with Bruce, he is still the friend who will take Sasha to Paris.

Bruce thought Sasha was going back to Moscow indefinitely, and Sasha must have thought so too.

a better time in Moscow

Returning to Moscow Sasha realised he had made some friends, learnt his way around a bit more. He was unlikely, alas, to take Pam Brown's advice of venturing out alone, taking trains to unknown parts. Still, he got out into the street sometimes, he had companions, he was meeting people. People kept saying it was the most interesting time to be there, people would be envying him for being right there at right that time. He reported his improved state of mind to Pam Brown:

> [...] a better time in Moscow, seeing it more benignly, I can't say I'm in love with this country but I'm intrigued with it in a way that continues to keep me here. [letter to Pam Brown 13.1.1992]

There certainly was a lot to be intrigued by. And here he was, fantastically well placed to observe events as sweepingly transformative, as tumultuous, as historically significant, as the Revolutions in 1917. Here he was well sheltered, protected by a woman he had called a soul mate as much as a companion. Here he was well connected, comfortable, passively supplied with a stream of visitors with their gifts of experience, stories, gossip from connected circles, who could be counted on as conversationalists; there was debating and drinking into the night. He could speak Russian with Russians and English with everyone else. He loved to cook for people and people were there to cook for, enjoy his food, and participate in that bonding magic of breaking bread together. He didn't have to think about getting a job, or, anyway, apparently he managed not to.

That major realisation, that he wasn't really Russian, had come early, it was a recurring theme in his letters; it must have been assimilated to some extent and had the potential for deep exploration.

The promise of a good life in Russia must have bloomed again.

He might have had a big sad end to a dramatically romantic fling, but it gave him something to write about. And other flings had followed and more were likely.

He might have found a form in which to pour his experience, his singular, eccentrically studious way of looking at things, his idiosyncratic flow of language and attention to details when his writing was at his best.

It could have gone on.

But then came the fall.

27
the past is unpredictable

Moscow after the fall

I broke my leg in Moscow. I snapped the top off my femur, a complex break. It was 2.30 in the morning and minus 15 degrees. [SS 1996 *Jump Cuts* 211]

it's pretty icy out there

The story of how Sasha broke his femur bone at the hip begins with all the people who came to Monica Attard's Moscow apartment — they came to stay, or they came to dinner and ended up staying even if booked into hotels, or they came to dinner and had to return to their hotel later. One night it was a visiting curator from an Australian gallery, and Sasha cooked a meal for everyone. Then the visitor was going back to his hotel and wanted to walk to the corner to get a cab to take him there. Sasha went with him. It was cold, there was snow and also ice. Attard remembers saying 'you be careful Sasha, it's pretty icy out there', then she went to bed. When she got up in the morning, it was to a knock on the door.

That was the building's concierge, and he had Sasha in tow.

On his way back, Sasha had slipped on the ice. Walking and crawling on the snow in the earliest hours of the morning he had made his way as far as the building, and could go no further.

> And that was the beginning of the end. He was bedridden and the medical services were virtually non existent. [Attard interview]

Sasha was taken to a local hospital in Moscow, and underwent some surgery, under less than ideal conditions. Then he was left in Monica's care, and that of a group of friends, who cared for him, taking it in turns to make sure he had food. More disaster. For example, one day there was no one else at home, and he had to go to the toilet. When he'd made his way there he slipped and somehow pulled the lock on the door and couldn't get up again to unlock it. So no one could get in there to rescue him. Eventually Monica's friend Max climbed out onto the balcony of another room, this in mid-winter, to climb to the next balcony, Sasha's room, where he could enter and release the lock.

night after night after night after night

Monica told me a story about another visitor — someone Sasha also was dazzled by and in a way he didn't always like.

> He had the most perfect and beautiful writing, monumentally intelligent and talented. I think he was one who just turned up on the doorstep; he was going to do a bit of study in Moscow so he had an apartment. And he spent a lot of time with us. Everyone loved him, he was a beautiful boy, young, 25 or 26, a beautiful personality. [Attard interview]

> He spoke beautiful Russian, he fitted in, he was around a lot, he got along with everybody. Although he didn't drink he'd talk with Sasha endlessly; he and Sasha got on extremely well.

> What used to upset Sasha was that [that man] was way more Russian, he was deeply insightful and profound and understood himself and understood people around him. He'd talk to someone for half an hour and know them and know all their weaknesses, which is very discombobulating. He and Sasha spent a lot of time together. [Attard interview]

And it was Sasha who'd been called The Russian by his friends in Australia. And yet his friend Monica without any Russian heritage was more at home here than he, and now this brilliant and loveable Australian man was considered way more Russian. Attard says that would have been hard for him to accept. Sasha wasn't going to stay in Russia forever because he didn't love it enough.

Attard sums up Soldatow's time in Moscow. For the first months he was there they had a great time.

> It would have been hard to imagine a life without Sasha Soldatow. He was a hoot. He would lift you up on his wings and carry you off to some faraway place and you'd just have a nice time. [Attard interview]

Until he became depressed. And it got worse.

> David [Marr] leaving was really hard for him. From that point onwards Sasha began the slow decline, that became a rapid decline, that became a fall in the snow, that became a broken hip, that became having this grown man unable to do anything at all. [Attard interview]

The drinking and depression were already a problem even before this broken hip disaster.

> It was exhausting. You can't party that much and work. I was really worried about his drinking, it just didn't stop. It was night after night after night after night. He'd sleep in the day after drinking all night. And that would trigger bouts of depression. At times it was really hard. Living with someone who's depressed and crying and you can't help them. Until it was hard it was great.
>
> He'd get really depressed about different things — at times about things in his own life, at times about somebody else, because he absorbed everyone's pain. I found it difficult. I had a lot on my plate, four years of revolution. [Attard interview]

writing about that pain

His staying with her had been 'fantastic until it wasn't' and now Attard often felt deeply frustrated. It was like looking after an elderly parent, she says. She was lucky to have a bit of help.

> There was a time when he wasn't leaving the apartment because he was drinking and wallowing and crying.
>
> I'd ring David [Marr] and go, help, I don't know how to deal with this. David would say, he's got to come home.
>
> So I was looking at this thinking, it's either that Sasha is going to stay here in bed for the next few years, while this resolves, or he goes home. [Attard interview]

That wasn't going to be easy to arrange. He didn't have insurance. He didn't have a job to go to. And now he was often in physical pain.

And that was on top of being what Attard compassionately saw as a man who absorbed the pain of others. Which meant more pain for him, and an impediment to writing.

> Instead of writing about that pain he just absorbed it and let it sit there. What it did was just sink him into depression and drinking and I don't know that he wrote very much at all in Moscow. [Attard interview]

Living in Moscow at the time was a goldmine of material for a writer, but Soldatow did not have the method of regular, solitary writing sessions. Nor detachment.

His error was, I think, [that] he immersed himself into people's lives rather than observing and writing.

He didn't have the detachment and that was his downfall in Russia. I don't know about elsewhere but in Russia.

The lack of discipline of writing I think was a big problem for him. [Attard interview]

I think now of Graham Greene saying a writer needs an icy splinter where others have a heart. I'm not saying this must be true but yes Attard does have a point, no matter how involved a writer is in their subject matter a degree of detachment is required for the writing. (Some people find that therapeutic.)

Anyway, Soldatow wrote enough that his next book mostly included his Russian experience, and would be praised for his unique perspective and felicitous phrasing. [chapter 29]

Sasha wasn't particularly political

Attard talked about Soldatow, who did observe what was going on in the streets, as not being interested in Kremlin politics.

She said, Sasha wasn't particularly political.

I was astounded, that seemed like the last thing anyone would say about him.

Well, he was into gender politics, she said, and more interested in the impact of Kremlin politics on everyday life: he had been looking at the suffering in the streets, the food shortage, the amazing rates of inflation. Her job on the other hand was to understand Kremlin politics, and she would have ten-hour conversations with people about it. Sasha wasn't into that.

> But Sasha was into the impact of politics on people's lives and that's what he talked about. [But] that was a negative, that distressed him, and it was a burden on him. I don't even think he found it intellectually stimulating, he just found it emotionally draining, because he could see the terrible impact it was having on people. [Attard interview]

Attard's memories of the time are still acute and deeply felt. The Soviet Union had collapsed and Boris Yeltsin was in power. And capitalism was introduced...

> ...with a thud, without restraints, it was gonzo capitalism on steroids, and it was awful, it was really ugly, and hard, and brutal. And [Sasha] watched all of that. All our friends were struggling. My best friend, who he

knew because she was there all the time, Natasha, she was a committed communist, he watched as her world kind of crumbled. At the time it was hard, nobody could understand why: this used to be free, this used to be guaranteed, this was the way we used to live. They saw personalities changing, people becoming focused on themselves and their own well-being instead of everybody being on the same boat, sinking. People's lives were changing. Sasha used to sit up all night and talk to Natasha about it as well. [Attard interview]

It was all right for Westerners, as Monica Attard said, but it wasn't all right for a lot of people, nothing like all right.

On December 25 1991 the Soviet Union collapsed and in January 92 they freed prices for the first time in 70 years. So there was galloping inflation, and deficit of almost everything because the [Soviet] republics decided to starve Russia of fresh produce and Russia of course doesn't make much itself or grow much itself. So it was pretty tough times in terms of availability of produce; there was a palpable sense of anger when prices were freed because all of a sudden money was devalued and there was a queue a mile long to buy bread. You'd get to the top of the queue and the price had gone up. In the market you'd say, how much for a kilo of tomatoes and it was 3,000 rubles and the next guy said 5,000. [Attard interview]

Westerners working there were paid a stable salary, but it was really hard on locals.

That was a time when the elderly populations were struggling to eat, no pensions were being paid as the state had gone bust, their children weren't being employed as the state had just collapsed, people were emptying out their apartments and taking [their things] onto the streets and selling them. And Sasha was there for all that and seeing it and probably that's what he was writing about. [Attard interview]

Sasha was in physical pain, and other kinds of anguish. Incapacitated by the broken hip, which had been treated ineptly, he no longer went out exploring, talking to people on the street and in shops and markets. The pain of people's suffering could be felt, however, even in the comfortable ABC apartment, as he heard of hopes shattered, spirits devastated. Hunger. Greed. Not what their best hopes had been at all.

People like Natasha and others had hoped that the change would be the one articulated by Gorbachev [...]: perestroika is economic reform and glasnost is social openness. I think that all hoped that socialism would be preserved, the best of what they had coupled with better socialism, social renewal and openness and freedom. And totalitarianism would subside and they'd carry on. [Attard interview]

But that didn't happen. Gorbachev was overthrown, the Soviet Union collapsed. Which no one was quite prepared for, at any level.

Experiencing all that makes Attard understand the present era. From the outside, she tells me, people look at Putin and think he's terrible because he wants to take Russia back to the Soviet days. They don't understand why people agree with Putin that the collapse of the Soviet Union was the greatest geopolitical disaster of our times.

I have decided to go home

Among his papers is an undated hand-written note for Monica by Sasha.

> Wake me up when you get up. I have decided to go home. Within the week. Me. People I want to see before I go. [Soldatow hand-written note 1992]

A list of names follows. And where, exactly, would he go? Home to Australia, but where specifically? Bruce Pulsford got a phone call from Sasha one night...

> ...this terrible phone call one night, it must have been on a mobile [number]; I was at a friend's. He said, you've got to meet me at Sydney airport in two days time, I'm in a wheelchair. I said, I can't meet you, he said, you've got to meet me.
>
> I went out to the airport to meet Sasha being wheeled out by a [flight attendant].
>
> I knew about the fall. It must have happened quickly, the downturn of events after the fall because I'd heard about the fall; I think the operation which went wrong happened fairly quickly after that.
>
> I was the obvious person to come back to. [Pulsford interview]

Back to the Lamrock Avenue flat. None of this was what Bruce had seen in his future. He had thought he had a different life ahead of him. But now Sasha was back living with him, as if everything was meant to be the same. Sasha was severely incapacitated. There would be more surgery.

> But it was another six years before I had the courage to leave the place. Probably '92 to '96 were the worst years of my life. [Pulsford interview]

Bruce Pulsford during that time was extremely busy at work; he had a new job as the lawyer for the Writers' Guild, he worked for the Refugee Review Tribunal, he had started his own business as well.

> But there was no real joy at home, so I put on weight, drank a lot. [Pulsford interview]

Their terms of their relationship had not ever been clearly delineated. This didn't seem to be the right time to start. Bruce tells me they 'weren't a functioning couple'. They hadn't really talked about their understanding about whether they were monogamous. Bruce assumed, he says, that like many gay men the unspoken 'contract' was they could have sex with others. And that held the risk of more contact with someone else. An intimacy, a new relationship. Could have happened to either of them. And eventually Bruce moved out of the Bondi flat to live with a new partner. But he let Sasha stay on there. A friend helped them work out the terms.

> Sasha hadn't really contributed to the upkeep of the house. George Papaellinas, he was around; he was a very useful broker between me and Sasha, I remember, we had a rare discussion. George said, can you give Sasha some money, and I said, I can't really, because I was very heavily in debt, I'd been paying rent, the mortgage, Sasha is not the only one irresponsible with money, I was also irresponsible with money, none of it was sustainable, I had to sell the place. It made me realise Sasha and I had been together for twelve years by then, so that was a partnership [...] even if not a functioning one, so he might have been entitled to something [legally] but he didn't push that. [Pulsford interview]

Sasha stayed on at Bondi for two years before the flat was sold.

After Sasha's return to Sydney, Bruce reported on his dire condition to Monica by faxes addressed to her at the ABC office in Moscow. More hospitalisation, more surgery was called for.

> Well, it seems Moscow ice must be bloody hard as Sasha has found out he has to go to Sydney Hospital asap for what the doctor has called major surgery on his hip. S has asked me to let you know[...]
>
> It seems the operation next week only has a 5% of working and if it doesn't he'll need a hip replacement. He's been in a huge amount of pain but, with the standard amount of gentle prompting/voracious ear-bashing he at least went to the doctors and has found out just what is wrong.... [faxed letter to Monica Attard 19.2.1992]

As he had been doing in Moscow, Sasha for a while continued to be mired in his pain and misery.

He alienated some of his friends, some irretrievably.

He also enjoyed new friends.

But although some of the time he was the depressive, non-functioning person, he did put together some of his writings from Moscow for the volume *Mayakovsky in Bondi.* He mightn't have kept regular hours at the desk but he was able to mine his own letters and notes and memories to great effect.

And he returned to another rewrite of, or at least some fiddling with, his epic novel *The Gloves of Mr Menzies*, again sending it out for critical readings and publishers' consideration.

28

a confusion to you all

The Gloves of Mr Menzies

Taking advantage of Miles Franklin's thoughtful letter, Amelita decided to go around to seek her advice on how to sell her grandfather's emerald. [SS from *The Gloves of Mr Menzies* 1990 MS 80]

I want to talk about it

To return to Soldatow's only novel, and to look at the responses to it, a novel never published but important in the author's life, tells us about the reception of unruly works, and about Soldatow's unyielding sense of himself and his writing.

Sasha had begun the novel he would call *The Gloves of Mr Menzies* sometime in the 1980s; the earliest hand-written notes about it in the archive are dated December 1986. He worked on it on and off for years, until near the end of his life.

In 1988, Soldatow had a contract from Pan Macmillan publishers, and wrote in biographical notes of the time that his novel would be 'coming out soon'.

He began sending it out to friends, for those pre-publication readings of drafts that can be so useful to writers.

In a 1990 letter I tell him I've read it and want to talk about it. I have no memory of that reading. I know I was unable to be as fully enthusiastic as I'd have liked to be, but had little to no confidence in my response and little to no experience in the language of manuscript assessment (some years later I'd begin to have all too much experience in it, once I began to publish my own novels, to teach creative writing in universities, and take on paid mentorship and manuscript assessment work).

I don't remember if we did talk about it. I looked up to Sasha as a writer and probably suspected that if I wasn't crazy about the work it was me missing something.

And yet, almost (but not quite) entirely, his early readers and advisors also had misgivings.

a family epic in three parts

I have a 1990 typescript of the novel in three parts.

A family epic, each part is set in a different era. Amelita, also called Nellie, is in each part, and emerges as a kind of main character, though a curiously inconsistent one.

Here I attempt a summary of the plot, or at least note the novel's main events, and this will be unsatisfactory; I want to keep it short but tell enough for you to follow the comments others supplied:

Part one 'Ave, Australia 1939-1942'

Victor Brown goes to his secret meetings in the city, from his country home, to meet with other members of 'The Bunyip Club', a nationalist organisation. His wife Amelita, or 'Nellie', a house-wife, whose marriage 'prevented her from nothing' [19], has an affair with the milkman, Henry Evans, 'Heaven' to her, and becomes pregnant.

Part one ends with Nellie going into labour.

Part two 'Pastoral 1956'

Nellie had twins she named Dido and Mussolini. (So they must be fourteen now.) They all now live with her sister Oriel at Oriel's rural property Chirrup. Oriel has had an international career as a model and is endlessly wealthy. Oriel 'missed a European kind of company' and befriends Sonja, an eccentric old Russian in the town; also she is courted by Jack, a local farmer. Oriel meets Sonja's friend Henry Lippard at a very fancy catered lunch Sonja holds for him, desires him, and disappears with him to Sydney for ten days and tells nothing on her return. Which is when she makes her proposal to Jack: they are to be together but live apart. Sonja in her advanced age goes to Sydney to live with Henry. Nellie takes up various pursuits, like 'Tao and Buddhism' while Oriel tells stories to the children. Dido is into witchcraft, and learns Nellie's previous name. Nellie is scared of her own daughter. Henry briefly returns; Sonja is dead; Dido flirts with him. Dido begins to menstruate; Nellie's attempt to explain this to her is incomprehensible, Dido has hysterics, Oriel has to take charge. But after all it's not menstruation. (An unlikely twist and for what?)

Part 2 ends with a fierce bushfire approaching.

Part three 'Deus Ex Machina 1986'

It's 30 years later. This part starts with a transcript of a phone conversation; evidently it is a coded talk about surveillance. Dido is returning to Sydney by plane, with one of many false passports. She is high up in a drug smuggling operation; a courier is arrested and Dido manages to thwart those following her; Dido is wanted for drug trafficking. Nellie is persuaded to sell her house, unoccupied for 40 years. Henry Lippard was involved in Dido's drug traffic world.

Now living in Kirribilli, Nellie has wealth but also guilt as Oriel had died in that bushfire and Nellie inherited her (implausibly extensive) wealth. Everyone is now wealthy.

Mussolini is all about guns, hunting, cruelty. Even his shooting friends desert him. Later he goes by Farlap, which was Oriel's name for him. He becomes a family man, and allows Dido to shelter at his rural property (she arrives by plane).

Nellie is a mess, takes lots of pills, bullies and threatens; she's suddenly and briefly in Venice and suddenly back in Sydney, suddenly involved in radical action. It's the Vietnam War era, Menzies in power.

A lot of very dramatic events take place — an explosion, revelation of murders, Nellie is knocked unconscious by falling birds.

Part 3 ends with a funeral for Musso, Dido going to a Remand Centre, and Nellie going home the long way.

Epilogue. ['Formerly Prologue']
Dido has been in jail for 22 months, studying philosophy, existentialism, quoting Camus, pondering the end of history and surrealism.

by the way, something curious

It's odd to come across, by the way, something curious in this 1990 manuscript: an incidental reference to the fact that early on, Victor, on his honeymoon in the Blue Mountains 'slipped and cracked his femur in two places, landing in an inadequate country hospital' [19]. After Sasha's fall in Moscow (in early 1992) this reads like an uncanny coincidence if not a presentiment.

Sasha liked the title

Sasha liked the title and would not be dissuaded from using it. To Australians, the name Menzies recalls the Conservative, Royalist Prime Minister, whose second term in office began in 1949 and lasted until the late 1960s, so he was the figurehead of political authority for a generation; in spite of the cultural shifts his party stayed in power until the emphatic change heralded by the landmark election of Gough Whitlam in 1972. Towards the end of the novel Nellie, part of an anti-war demonstration, with the subterfuge of disguise as a graduating university student, meets Menzies:

> [...] As old bushy-eyebrowed Mingus offered his congratulations, she grabbed him instead and pinched him hard inside the palm, whispering under her breath, 'You should learn to wear gloves. Murderer. We will save our sons regardless.' [256]

So maybe that's the part that should unite the whole?
I can find no other link between Menzies and gloves.

Menzies' last year in office was 1966; Australia entered the American war in Vietnam in 1962; it was Menzies who increased the number of troops in 1965 and anti-war protests began then, but were small until the 'moratorium movement' later. Soldatow made sure you checked your historical knowledge.

A later reference to Menzies can be found in an email Soldatow wrote in 2004, writing about his 1970 university graduation, and a moment of grand condescension:

> The PM Menzies did award me my BA at Melbourne University and, as he shook my hand and handed me my bit of paper said (I swear to you this is an accurate quote, who could forget it?) — 'It's good to see migrants making good.' You know that stunned silence which prevents you from replying with an appropriate retort. That was speechless me. [email to Ian Harrison 23.3.2004]

'what's a legong?'

On 10 October 1988 BlackWattle publisher and editor Laurin McKinnon included an extract from *Gloves*, in *Cargo* number 5.

I laughed when I read McKinnon's question in his acceptance letter: 'What's a legong?' I had noticed on my first reading, and remembered, Sasha's phrase 'legong-dancing hands' in a description of the new-born twins; Sasha had been to Bali with Bruce Pulsford the previous year, his first trip outside of Australia. His character Oriel's experience is summed up in a couple of sentences whose employment of cliché does not clearly signal any kind of irony:

> 'Oh, heavens,' she breathed as she went ashore, recognising it at once as the island of perfect tranquillity and sense. Bali enraptured her soul with its festivals and sacred ceremonies. [136]

The bio note in the *Cargo* issue says the novel is 'to be published by Picador in July 1989'.

In 1989 *Meanjin* published an extract. Soldatow and editor Jenny Lee exchanged proofs and edits.

Another acquaintance and Soldatow published each other in periodicals they edited. Soldatow published Raymond Willbanks in *Cargo*; Willbanks published Soldatow's 'Prologue' from *The Gloves of Mr Menzies* in *Antipodes*, a USA journal about Australian and New Zealand literature and culture, in Vol. 5. No. 1, May 1991.

six words can take a while

In 1991 Soldatow announced to Andrea Stretton (1952-2007), an arts journalist and book reviewer:

> Contract for a novel 'The Gloves of Mr Menzies' signed 1989 with Pan/Picador. Nearly nearing completion (six words to go!) [SS 16.1.1991 fax to Andrea Stretton]

Six words can take a while. But Pan never did publish the novel.

basically good but needs more work

I read the novel again while working on this book. I'd sum up my reaction as 'basically good (readable, original) but needs more work'. It makes me want to talk with Sasha about it, read it with him present, ask does he intend a certain effect, how to make more of it if so. One thing I want to talk about is the authorial voice: remarks occasionally come from the author — 'clever little shit', 'oh let me tell you' — but not often enough for this to be a method or style of the book. I'm all for defying the conventions of narrative but it has to feel purposeful and controlled; these matters always must admit an element of subjective response — the conditions of readership are many — but there are ways to talk about them.

Sasha did not engage with the questions other writers did ask him.

readings that followed

As Sasha wrote to Sue Howe when he got his grant in 1991, he planned to revise *Gloves* before he departed Sydney, and 'hand it over to publishers' before returning to Hanoi later that year and going on to stay in Moscow.

He was advised not to do that just yet.

Literary agent Barbara Mobbs wrote Soldatow a warm friendly letter in response to the manuscript he sent her, along with pages of notes — not something all aspirants to representation will be granted. Mobbs offered an astute reading, with detailed points with examples on what she considered didn't work in the MS. Mobbs for a long time was the valued agent to Patrick White and several other acclaimed Australian writers. Still Soldatow dismissed her reading as lacking understanding.

Not that she was necessarily always right but that happened over and over with readings that followed.

> As a whole, I found some of the characters wonderful and was swept up with where they were going, but the pace is inconsistent, as are some of the characters themselves. [...]
>
> I was left with the feeling that you were trying out too many ideas and letting a lot of them hang loose without a direction and without ultimately adding to a solid shape/body of text. [Barbara Mobbs letter to SS 27.3.1991]

Soldatow kept sending it out anyway.

'I thought it was stunning'

The friends in Gunning were a beacon of encouragement.

Sasha sent a copy to Craig Rendell who wrote back 'I think *Gloves* is wonderful' and even added details.

> ...a great story well told. At the end of part 1, I marvelled at the apparent ease and economy that you had drawn the characters of Victor & Amelia. It still seems so effortless, and continued to be so throughout the other two parts. [...] As you know the third part is weaker and needs some work; as I mentioned there [are] about three areas which are more like drafting instructions for you. [Craig Rendell hand-written letter 9.7.1991 3 pp]

Nearly 30 years later, John Walker, who had often been with Craig Rendell host to Sasha and Bruce in Gunning, told me that while he couldn't recall specifics he did recall that he thought the novel was great, a meditation on Australian history, stunning. He says it was not accepted for publication because 'they couldn't compartmentalise it'.

also turned it down

Writing on CollinsAngus&Robertson letterhead, publisher Tom Thompson, an old friend, turned it down, also taking the trouble of attempting to analyse the effect of the work:

> While there is much to enjoy, we really feel it is much too long to hold a reader's attention. The problem lies in the fact that these characters are

comic reductions. As obvious cyphers you are not asking the reader to believe in these characters, yet you are asking us to believe in detail that real things happened to them. [Tom Thompson letter to SS 26.7.1991]

In August 1991 Soldatow offered *Gloves* to literary agent Caroline Lurie. His outlining of his woes with Penguin and A&R publishers is not in the least diplomatic.

> David Marr spoke to you about my novel last week. Here it is. [...] This book has already had a small but checkered history. Pan/Picador took it on and paid me an advance of $2,500 three years ago, then early this year cancelled my contract when the company was taken over. They do not want their money back and as far as the contact goes, I am back to a clean slate (I don't know why they did this, it all seems a silly and wasteful decision on their part). [SS letter to Caroline Lurie 11.8.1991]

Saying 'they don't want their money' back is a self-serving interpretation of the resigned acknowledgment from James Fraser, then publisher at PanMacMillan, apparently admitting defeat after trying to recoup the advance:

> I have to face the fact that we won't be seeing the money so let's just call it quits and this letter will serve as official notification that the agreement between us dated 5 October is no longer valid. [James Fraser letter to SS 24.4.1991]

What happened at Pan? Surely they would only ask for the return of the advance if Sasha had not delivered according to their agreement. Anyone I could find who worked there at the time can't remember.

Soldatow's letter to Lurie continues:

> Next, Tom Thompson of Collins knocked it back, again I'm not all that clear why, though I enclose his letter. Did he think it was some kind of allegory? [...] At the present moment the book is with Bruce Sims of Penguin who likes it [...]

There's a great deal more. The leisurely, chatty tone of the typescript letter reminds you this is before email, texting, online submissions with strict templates. The letter ends:

> I think it's a really good novel and a cracking good read too.
> Hope to hear from you soon, somehow or other.

No reply from Caroline Lurie can be found. In the present, Lurie, who retired as a literary agent in 1993, cannot recall the novel or what she might have replied.

Just two months later, Sasha had returned to Moscow and experienced the tumult of his reunion with David Marr, amidst the tumult of current events there.

However unhappily their fling in Moscow had ended, David leaving, Sasha trying to make him stay, back in Australia Marr took the time, and made an effort that few friends would make, to read the manuscript with painstaking care.

> I wished I liked the book but I don't much. There might be all sorts of reasons for this that aren't to do with the writing. I don't like novels that are full of magical and unexplained events. Coincidences end up, for me, no more than coincidences. And eccentrics live by rules of their own which most of the time are just eccentric. So this isn't my kind of novel. [David Marr letter to SS 27.10.1991]

Marr discusses his own tastes, which favour realist fiction.

Marr says he made notes as he read. He kept noting, 'I don't hear Sash speaking.'

Marr goes on to make specific points, and says again how unhappy he is to write this. On a positive note, he points out some great images in the novel:

> Nellie in the seaweed, the glowworm cave with Dido, Oriel finding her mother in the Paris demonstration, the conception of Victor and Rossini. Victor hunting. These are wonderful things. But I wish I were reading those wonderful things you tell of your family (reworked of course into fiction), of your life and of the places you know, — stories to which you bring so much (everything I suppose) of yourself.
>
> [...]
>
> Wish I wasn't saying what I'm saying but I'm no good to you if I don't.
> Love

Jan McKemmish, author of the novels *A Gap in the Records* (1985) and *Only Lawyers Dancing* (1992), was also for years a much appreciated teacher, advisor and mentor to many writers. In a letter full of kind, loving advice, she pinpointed an aspect several of the readers of *Gloves* agreed on: like Marr, she said that the novel didn't sound like the Sasha whose voice was so distinctive in his earlier writing:

> I've always worried that Menzies hasn't got any of you in it. Sometimes, especially when writing a story you need to work, indirectly, fictionally, about yourself, what you know...Anyway you are lucky to have Bruce being so supportive, domestic labour is a joy, non intellectual, physical, the perfect companion to art... [Jan McKemmish undated card]

The consensus of readers who knew his other work seemed to be that the lengthy novel did not sound like Sasha, while it was the pieces that did sound like him, and therefore like no one else, that had always delighted and astonished them. Us.

The next rejection came from Allen & Unwin.

> ...a surprise, mostly a really interesting one. I enjoyed wending my way through The Gloves of Mr Menzies but I don't feel enthusiastic enough about it to add it to our fiction list. [Annette Barlow letter to SS 21.10.1991]

Editor Barlow added a few specific yet oddly vague criticisms.

It's like that with so many of the readers, they couldn't quite pinpoint what it was that didn't quite 'work' for them. It was a strange absence in the work. For those who knew his other work, that absence was the authentic, unique voice.

Shall I go on?

Publishing and literary acceptance are strange to contemplate, the factors largely unpredictable, debatable. It is possible that a reading of the novel today might meet with more general enthusiasm. It is possible that an independent publisher, defying the risk-averse mainstream, might want to add it to their list.

this is my intention

Writing to literary agent and old friend Lyn Tranter from Moscow, Soldatow refuses to find any worth or point in the critical readings he has received, and berates 'all of you in the trade' for their lack of understanding of his literary purpose and accomplishment.

> This is my tally of responses — 4 negatives, 2 interested, 4 positive. [...] All of you, in the trade, so to speak, point to the same things. You go to the book as if you're expecting a normal novel. Okay, a positive criticism, which I accept. Except it isn't a novel at all, it's an Australian response to an anti-novel. The word <u>novel</u> acts as a confusion to you all, because you've learned to expect something specific from a novel and I don't give

> it to you. I'm not going to and I don't want to write another <u>Monkey Grip</u>. That's all old hat, from my perspective.
>
> Listen, maybe I am very very wrong in my understanding of what I have written, but my gut reactions say to me that I am not....I know what I am doing with this book. It is all very carefully structured [...] [SS letter to Lyn Tranter 12.11.1991]

The next day, Soldatow wrote a letter headed 'Official Gutter Club Report from Moscow' to his writers group in Sydney. After recounting more of the ills of life in Russia, he returns with unwavering defensiveness to *The Gloves of Mr Menzies* and the critical readings he's received.

> You all point to aspects which you regard as deficient. But what you have to understand is that I know all this — this is my intention, it is not an accident. [...] You know me well enough to know that in my writing I will not let one paragraph go by without a huge amount of critical analysis and structural thought — I don't just dash things off. [SS letter 13.11.1991]

He repeatedly insists on his intentions.

> (The word intention will unfortunately crop up over and over again.) [SS letter 13.11.1991]

But he never considers that one cannot read according to a writer's intention, intentions which a reader might only deduce from the text.

> I don't satisfy your expectations — well again that is my intention. [...] You've got too used to the simple. [...] As to my <u>voice</u>, you have forgotten that it is an erratic voice that needs to keep changing. [...] I know that my book is not perfect, but, having finished it, I cannot radically restructure it. [SS letter 13.11.1991]

Used to the simple? Really? Several people say Sasha's time in Russia was a turning point; maybe because of the broken hip, or maybe in any case. It might have been where his alcoholism passed the point of no return.

Had anyone previously noticed an inability to accept, at least *consider*, good quality criticism?

From this point on, Soldatow seems to be intransigent.

None of it, nobody's reading that was less than wholeheartedly enthusiastic, was considered by Soldatow. Not readings by other writers, not anyone whose work he might have admired or at least approved of, not a single point was conceded.

Soldatow simply rebuffed Marr's reading without any thanks. Marr's response:

> Sash you are a patronising twerp. Why get me to read the mss if you think I'm the illiterate dodo you describe — wallowing in easy novels, wanting only the simple texts? [David Marr letter to SS 24.11.1991]

There's a lengthy reply from Sasha defending his work — as if by pointing out how he wanted the novel read, he would make his critical reader see it all differently.

what kind of readerly pleasures

In December 1992 Soldatow wrote to Amanda Lohrey, sending a manuscript of *Gloves*, asking for her comments. (She told me Sasha had once given her the best editing advice she ever received [email 1.6.2018]). She too wrote in careful detail her responses to each of the three sections, unable to be positive.

> Cut adrift from any discernible genre the blackness and absurdity of it didn't make any sense to me. Is it meant to be absurdist nihilism? What kind of readerly pleasures do you intend for your readers? [Amanda Lohrey letter 1.2.1993]

There is always the possibility that new readers might be more impressed than those quoted here, especially without looking for the Sasha voice they already knew. In the days of Reception Theory, it is never question of right or wrong readings, but of *how* texts are read, what goes into shaping their reception, how that reception is to be understood.

It might be that this unpublished novel could be a basis for an exploration of the themes of literary merit, of strange works, of the dynamics of assessment, of the politics and fashions and expectations in reading and reception.

Maybe some writers yearn to write in a form that doesn't really suit them.

the rejections kept coming

On 11 January 1999 literary agent Fiona Inglis at Curtis Brown wrote that she liked *Gloves*, but had some criticisms, and gave her suggestions for rewrite/'polishing'. She did however agree to represent Soldatow.

When I spoke with Inglis in 2018, she didn't clearly remember the book, but is certain she'd never have sent it out if she didn't think there was a chance of it getting published. Though she was a 'baby agent' in those days she had worked for many years as a reader and editor at Allen & Unwin and HarperCollins.

Inglis sent out the manuscript to publishers, but the rejections kept coming, including one from publisher Angelo Loukakis at Simon & Schuster:

> It sits in some unhappy place near the realms of black comedy or political farce [...] but to me is too uncertain in its mode or tone. [Angelo Loukakis letter to Fiona Inglis 21.3.2000]

Inglis wrote to Soldatow that they were 'running out of options'.

Apparently Soldatow kept on revising *Gloves*, if never conceding he'd received any useful advice. As he'd said to Caroline Lurie, he didn't want to make any structural changes.

Jump Cuts co-author Christos Tsiolkas told me he had read a full draft of *Gloves* and really liked it. He said he was surprised it wasn't published.

While most responses to *The Gloves of Mr Menzies* continued to disappoint him, Soldatow's next published book, in which his unique voice was indisputably present, met a great reception.

29
beautifully crafted literary gossip

Mayakovksy in Bondi 1993

I agree with Mayakovsky — write what has to be done and to hell with the consequences. [SS 1993 *Mayakovksy* 106]

suggests disillusionment with the Left

Speaking about the title of *Mayakovsky in Bondi* in the *Sydney Star Observer*, Sasha Soldatow said he chose it because it's euphonious.

> He means, 'It sounds good.' He adds, 'It suggests disillusionment with the Left. Mayakovsky was disillusioned. And besides, he's such a strong creative figure in the twentieth century.' [Machon]

And more than that: if Mayakovsky is in Bondi these days, in Australia's famous beach-side suburb, he is where Sasha is — beside him, inside him, do we take it that Soldatow himself is the Mayakovsky of his time? Feels he is, wants to be, wants to be seen to be? Was there ever a Lenin figure for him?

> For Vladimir Mayakovsky, the giant of Soviet propaganda poetry who fathered the Futurist art movement in Russia, the revolution meant freedom from the church and the monarchy which had dominated Russians' lives. Out with the old, in with the new was his cry and that of [...] the Russian avant-garde who looked upon Lenin's revolution as a way of radically transforming life in Russia. [Attard 1997 72]

Mayakovsky wrote an epic poem about Lenin. Apparently it was applauded at workers' meetings, but the great man himself was not impressed:

> Mayakovsky sent a signed copy to Lenin, who said it was 'rubbish, stupid, stupid beyond belief, and pretentious'. [Pinkham 2017]

my sentences and paragraphs the way I do

The cover of *Mayakovsky in Bondi* is a striking design featuring a large red star. The book was published in 1993 by long-time associate BlackWattle Press.

In the *Sydney Star Observer*, Soldatow speaks about why he chose to publish with BlackWattle, saying he prefers the editorial freedom he is allowed there, not resisting a dig at the mainstream.

> There is no way this book would have gone through the editing process with a major press. I would never have been able to construct my sentences and paragraphs the way I do.
> Australian publishers take your voice back to blandness.
> [SS in Machon 1993]

There's nothing of blandness in this work.

the highest hopes of the Revolution

When you look at poems by Mayakovsky (1893–1930), the appeal to Sasha Soldatow is evident in titles like 'A Slap in the Face of Public Taste' and 'Ode to Revolution'. Mayakovsky stood for the highest hopes of the Revolution — true freedom, renewal, new forms of art, a new society of comrades. He had a glorious career — fame and popularity, followed by imprisonment and a death supposed to be suicide.

Mayakovsky's suicide, imagined as losing a game of 'Russian roulette' was not disputed in this volume, although there have always been rumours about it; years later, Soldatow's view was that this death was not suicide. In an email of chat about various poets he says he has a photograph recently released of Mayakovsky dead in his chair.

> All the stuff about him playing Russian roulette is rubbish, putting a pistol to his mouth and blowing his brains out. He was shot directly thru the heart — murdered. It's quite clearly so tho I suspect it's a posed photograph and that he was carried to be 'officially' photographed. After all he was living next door to the Lubianka. It makes sense of what Russians said to me — better to be taken from the top of the building than to be taken from under the street. [SS email to George Zisopoulos 29.10.2001]

eleven chapters

Mayakovsky in Bondi contains eleven chapters, with material I have already quoted extensively.

The first, 'Requiem', offers that first sentence remembered more than the rest of the book: 'I am trying to remember what my father's cock looked like.' This is the piece first published as 'Memento Mori', admired by David Marr [see previous chapter] as an example of Sasha's distinctive writing at its best, using his most personal experiences as material.

The second chapter is set in Hanoi, telling among other memories of the conversations with 'Mr Hop'. [chapter 25]

Seven more chapters are set entirely or mostly in Russia, in Moscow specifically, anecdotes about people in the streets, conversations in those so very tough times.

Here, his letters to Marr and others are repurposed for these pages.

One chapter is a fantasy of licentious letters between Rimbaud and Verlaine.

The Epilogue is simply a few lines from Brecht:

And I always thought, the very simplest words
Must be enough. When I tell it like it is
Everyone's heart must be torn to shreds.
That you'll go under if you don't defend yourself
Surely you see that.
       Bertolt Brecht 1956
[quoted in SS 1993 *Mayakovsky* 119]

The penultimate chapter is Soldatow's translation of the heart-scorching poem 'Requiem' by Anna Ahmatova; pointing back to the (renamed) title of his first chapter suggests another kinship with a significant Russian writer, this one undergoing horrendous suffering in the post-revolution era of Stalin's Great Terror. [all about this in chapter 38]

there is something 'European'

In an interview Soldatow, talking about Mayakovsky in Bondi again, claims there is something 'European' about the kind of work he does.

> I couldn't hazard a guess as to the genre, I don't think it has one. And I think that's very European. It's not autobiography, it's not memoir, it's not pure fiction, it's not a scholarly text, it's not philosophy, it's not journalism and yet it's all of them. [Kiley 1993]

It's still hard to publish a book that can't easily be sent to its genre-category shelf in a bookshop, especially with a mainstream publisher, and even in these days of autofiction, cross-genre and hybrid works, with lists of emerging genres popping up on bookchat sites.

Soldatow's description suggests a rarely recognised genre:

> 'I'd like to think of it as beautifully crafted literary gossip,' Soldatow says. [Machon]

Soldatow also outlines some plans for his future books in the interview with Dean Kiley in *Burn*. Quite ambitious plans: this is to be the first of a four books; he'd like to write a biography of Ho Chi Minh. He insists on how crafted, deliberate, he considers his writing to be:

> I think something I'm always doing in writing is I'm having a dialogue with history. [...] I'm told I write English in a Russian way. [...] I write rhythmically and I can hear the singing of the language. [...] Poetry happens among the politics. [Kiley 1993]

the book was about friendship

To launch the book, Sasha Soldatow asked his old friend and comrade from back in the Victoria Street squatting days, Meredith Burgmann, a frequently arrested political activist, who had introduced him to the Builders' Labourers Federation [chapter 7] during the time of the Resident Action Group. Burgmann had in 1991 been elected to the upper house of the State's parliament, the New South Wales Legislative Council. When she retired in 2007 she had been the longest serving female presiding officer in Australia.

Burgmann told me about the launch, referring to notes she had kept from that time.

I did point out I was not the appropriate person to do this, I couldn't get into the sexual stuff [in the book]. His descriptions of masturbation and everything I found very disturbing. I said [in the launch speech] I thought the book was about friendship and that I was very happy to consider myself Sasha's friend.

One of our ongoing jokes was that Sasha and I wanted to meet everyone in Sydney by the time we died but we realised we were doubling up so we decided to divide it up but no one wanted to do Western Suburbs. [Burgmann interview]

Sydney's Western Suburbs (where I grew up) were considered by people in the city and the more 'leafy' areas to contain nothing desirable, nowhere worth going to and no one worth knowing. Burgmann tells me that in fact as a dutiful member of the ALP she spent quite a lot of her political life there and came to love parts of this unknown territory.

[At the launch] I'm laughing about our pact about knowing the whole of Sydney and how badly this was impacted when Sasha broke his leg because he just couldn't get around. It must have been awful for him.

I say he might think the book is about love and lust but I say it's about friends. [Burgmann interview]

Soldatow himself said that for him friendship is sacred.

That's above everything else. Mind you, that's a very Russian characteristic. [SS in Kiley 1993]

Burgmann said another reason she was asked to launch it is the book is intensely political and her connection with Sasha was so political.

It's about his notion of a just society. It's important [that] the book includes the brief glimpse of Hanoi then concentrates on Russia. [Burgmann interview]

Burgmann points to Soldatow's perspective from the political philosophy that he never modified.

His writings on Russia, Burgmann said, gave her a better idea of what was happening in Russia than three years of reading newspaper articles.

Burgmann's launch speech speculated on the gender issues and personal issues the book made her think of. She said that while the book might be gay lit, it's also like a lot of feminist writing:

I talked about Fay Weldon, Fay Weldon was big at the time and if you read Fay Weldon it's all about women not being loved enough. And there's a bit about that I felt in Sasha's book and I think Sasha always felt that, in his relationships he felt he was never loved enough.

I didn't know much about his relationships. For someone so open he was very private about them. [Burgmann interview]

the first and most important readers

The first and most important readers of a new work are the writer's friends and fellow-writers.

Gutter Club member, poet, activist, and writer Ian MacNeil (1946–2011) in a hand-written letter to Soldatow:

> I have just finished Mayakovsky in Bondi. Last night, reading it in bed, I thought this is almost unbearable like the Kreutzer sonata, that tautness. Your intensity saves your desperate truths from outrageousness [...] I think you enact the dreadful anxiety and comfort of disintegration — Moscow. PS BlackWattle should get you to do all their covers. [Ian MacNeil letter to SS 23.11.1993]

Those other writers are a writer's best readers, even better when they get you:

> I've just finished reading 'Mayakovsky' and mate, this is terrific work. I've got pages full of quotes from your writing. This is compliment! The requiem framing of the work is a slicingly powerful thing, a beautiful act. The whole work is so suffused with wisdom and patience...the idea of dying, of 'older', of love. [...] Such a dignified work, and frankly, Sash, the Zhenya part is brilliant — wise and politically sophisticated as well as emotionally so. [...] [George Papaellinas letter to SS 4.11.1993]

Reading *Mayakovsky in Bondi* again, perusing it for quotations to use in this work, I find the book a brilliant, idiosyncratic gem.

I thought I'd tire of looking at it but keep finding passages I find striking, and the sense of that distinctive voice, its confidence, those arresting images ideas arguments anecdotes; there's an underlying feel of a purposeful shape, the way modernist pieces might let the contents make the shape.

'glorious aphorisms and epithets'

The reviews must have been gratifying. Michael Sharkey, a poet, at the time a lecturer in English at the University of New England, wrote about the book thoughtfully, with misgivings about the worth or lastingness of some aspects, but on the other hand...

> Happily, the lapidary style of the work, and a plethora of other topics which emerge in the course of travel-diary entries, elegiac poems, imagined letters between Rimbaud and Verlaine, and reflections on writing lend the whole performance the tone of a philosophical meditation. [...]
>
> Along the way, Soldatow's prose is peppered with glorious aphorisms and epithets. The Mayakovsky Museum is a 'monument to constructivism as interpreted by the secret police' [...] [Sharkey 1993]

There was a little demurral at *Australian Book Review*, too, at first, but this review also decided that the up-front shocking bit belies the better aspects:

> Do we really need some phoney shock element to attract us to the writing of someone who has been around as long as Soldatow? The author's fumbling recollections of his father's cock in the opening sentence to *Mayakovsky*, and the quote on the back cover about the smell of fresh semen [...] don't do other sections of the book justice.
>
> [...]
>
> While the Moscow sections open doors onto a world many of us will never visit or come close to understanding, the most glittering piece of writings is pure and wicked invention. 'Like Verlaine and Rimbaud' [...] rings gloriously true. [Tina Muncaster 'Getting on heroically' *Australian Book Review* [month and year not shown]

Others had no demurral:

> [T]he biographical seems decisive, the fictional rings true, and gossip is iced with the sweetest of poetry. [...] [Machon 1993]

What is brimming with poetry, prose, autobiography, fiction history, fantasy, wit and humour? 'Sasha Soldatow's new work of fiction. [Susan Robbins]

Those glorious aspects of the book derived from Soldatow's distinctive, personal voice. The reception of the book must have fortified his confidence, as a writer and as a reliable advisor to other writers.

30

always trust the reader

Tsiolkas, *Jump Cuts*

Something happens when the past, in this case mine, is resurrected. It comes to be redefined according to others' needs. In this process, the mundane disappears. [SS 1996 *Jump Cuts* 53]

re-invigorated, newly alight

That resurrected past, redefined for an other's needs, the disappearance of the mundane, this lay ahead when Sasha's new reality was being back in Australia, back in Bruce Pulsford's flat in Bondi.

He put together the pieces he'd worked on for his book *Mayakovsky in Bondi* and that had been published and there'd been the launch party in 1993, where Meredith Burgmann called him the John Reed of the Push.

He had plans for more writing; he had not given up on *Gloves of Mr Menzies.*

But for a while he gave in to the tendency to sink into the slough of despond, and with the shattered hip-bone — more surgery, more anaesthetic — was more clearly in physical decline.

And maybe that's why for a time he was too drugged and passive and sulky either to work consistently or to delight his old friends. He was drinking heavily; in those months after his return he seemed to be descending too far into dejection and lethargy, complaint, self-pity.

At least one old close friend terminally lost patience with him. Many stopped calling.

And yet there would be another period of intense productivity, even joy, in creative work. There would be the next book. He became re-invigorated, newly alight with creative fire.

Because of Christos Tsiolkas.

a million butterflies going crazy

Tsiolkas' first letter to Soldatow was formal, polite, tentative. 'Dear Mr Soldatow' it starts. Undated, its hand-written annotation by Sasha is 'received 5.3.93'.

Tsiolkas included some work he'd had published, including a brilliantly-written review of the film *Romper Stomper*, spoke of his plans, and asked Sasha for advice. He ended

> I'm waiting for your reply with a million butterflies going crazy in my stomach. [letter to SS undated March 1993]

Soon after, the two met at a dinner given by a mutual friend in Melbourne. Tsiolkas told me about it in Sydney in 2018; he was in town for the Writers' Festival and came over to Wendy Bacon and Chris Nash's house in Newtown, where I was staying, with a bottle of white wine. I'd only fleetingly met him before; I hadn't been living in Sydney in the 90s.

He told me that the person responsible for the meeting was George Papaellinas. Papaellinas had edited *Harbour*, a multicultural story collection, in 1993 and published his own story collection *Ikons* in 1986. Papaellinas was important to Tsiolkas as one of the first Greek-Australian voices. Tsiolkas had been writing literary short stories and sending them to Papaellinas, whose generous response led to a friendship.

> This was before social media. He moved to Fitzroy during that period we were getting to know each other. And he invited me to dinner, saying, I have a friend I really want you to meet, Sasha Soldatow. [Tsiolkas interview]

Tsiolkas was excited, as he had read *Private — Do Not Open* when it came out in 1987, and thought it was 'phenomenally good', remembering long conversations with a housemate 'over countless drinks and a thousand cigarettes' about what this book meant to him. Already impressed by that, Tsiolkas found himself impressed and fascinated by its author. Sasha was a great storyteller, and not only that...

> ...He represented to me a way of being a political gay man that I really needed to find at that time. I'd been active in politics but the whole HIV-AIDS period meant we had to seriously think through what it meant to live in a homophobic culture. Apart from Wayne — that is one of things I do share with my partner, Wayne is an anarchist — because of my anarchism slash socialism, I didn't really feel I had a lot of people who felt that way about what was important. And Sasha represented that. And I was seduced and in awe. [Tsiolkas interview]

Soldatow tells of the effect Tsiolkas first had on him in the book they later co-authored.

> ...After we'd corresponded for a while and talked over the phone quite intimately I didn't know who to expect as you came into George's dining room....I didn't expect you to be drop dead gorgeous, and my immediate sexual attraction confused the shit out of me...[SS 1996 *Jump Cuts* 228]

Later that very night they kept saying to each other 'I love you.'

you are a born one

Sasha willingly devoted time and thought to giving his new friend the best advice and guidance he could.

In a letter to Tsiolkas later that year, you recognise that recognition by a teacher of writing, an experienced writer, finding in a student or new writer seeking advice such a certain talent, the voice of a real writer, however raw, inexperienced, stumbling, unformed, that extra care must be taken in the response.

> Hey you I love you and I don't care who knows it not even you. Why do you write so differently in your prose to what you write like in your journalism? Tone or style or is it rewriting? I said to you that you were a natural writer but you don't write english, but there you are in your articles and you have the tone and style down perfectly. It is hard to be an artist and I'm not sure it can be achieved if you are not born one. You are a born one. [SS letter to Christos Tsiolkas 25.10.1993]

With a new writer who's a born one, you want to say only, keep doing what you're doing. You don't want to be prescriptive, that new voice is too precious, it should form as it must. You just want to encourage them, help them see their strengths, show how much you believe in them.

Soldatow's letter contains advice useful for any starting out writer. (And from a position of openness, respect and even humility that might be useful for some teachers of writing.)

> I am not sure which way to push my remarks. One of me says edit him hard to make him make sense, fix his commas and grammar and meaning. The other one of me says let him splinter, shove him out of his education, let him go along his own wog constructions of English. I love you because you push into new directions and because you have the power not to respect what I tell you. Don't trust me. You are always right just as I am

in my writing. But you must hold tightly to your own self. And I found you wandering in the pieces you sent me, but maybe you are writing things so new that I cannot see it yet. It is a possibility. Tell me if you are. Though, you never have to know what it is you are going to write. Just write it. Write and then rewrite it. But you have an ambivalence with the reader. You don't think we'll understand enough. That's why you pummel the message into your pieces. Don't. ALWAYS TRUST THE READER. The reader is always your friend. The writer is always your enemy, and you are the writer and you know too much. That's why you must learn to edit yourself. That's the hard part, that's where the really hard slog comes in. Eight or nine drafts and then some more. It has to be perfect because you are perfect and I am too and so is the reader who will not accept anything less. Why should we.

I am going off to reread your email more closely.

My leg aches, don't know why. [SS letter to Christos Tsiolkas 25.10.1993]

For a moment the body makes itself felt. That pain wasn't over.

But Soldatow will go and read again what Tsiolkas sent him, and say what he thinks. Specifically, directly, and with certain advice.

The letter continues:

Later. I'm going to be tough. A lot of what you sent me reads like notes for further expansion. I like Pasolini [title of a piece] a lot but it needs work. And Cargo [magazine] will take Letter from Year Zero, though I want to play with that too. (They'll prob take Pasolini too on my say so.)

What is a wog? You use the term as if everyone knows, but some don't. Explain, then explain the significance, then tell me about pride, eh?

My secret agenda…I am thinking here you should get together about 30,000 words and do a book in about a years time. So I'm looking at your stuff as possible selections for a book. It's not out of the question. Think on it.

You have a problem with titles. You're too literal. You give the story away, often even the punch line. Titles are hard. They come to you at unexpected moments. Wait for them. Trust your intuition.

You use wog and fuck too much. It's like you're repeating yourself, which you are.

Make your themes richer.

I have a lot of things to say which I'll do on the copies which I'll send back.

Don't weep, just work.

LOVE ME [SS letter to Christos Tsiolkas 25.10.1993]

friends heard about his new friend and protégé

Soldatow's friends heard about his new friend and protégé.

Margot Nash remembers well when Sasha was really excited, telling her he'd met this young writer he thought was incredibly talented.

Susan Varga recalls when her book *Heddy and Me* was coming out in 1994...

> I went for the first time to a Gay and Lesbian conference at Balmain at the Writers Centre and Sasha said, 'keep an eye out for Christos' — that's Christos Tsiolkas — 'as he's just starting out and he's worried and shy, so say hello to him and tell him you're a friend of mine'. I did all that. At that stage Christos was quite shy and tentative. [Varga interview]

Tsiolkas took careful note

Tsiolkas took careful note of his new mentor's guidance.

> Here is a rewrite of 'Bypassing Benalla'. Most of your suggestions I've included ... [Christos Tsiolkas letter to SS 16.8.1993]

The story 'Bypassing Benalla' came out in the anthology *Fruit*, published by BlackWattle in 1994; it also included Soldatow's story 'Love Piss'. [chapter 19]

The two men wrote to each other constantly — Tsiolkas in near-indecipherable handwriting, Soldatow in typescript which he as usual kept carbon copies of.

Tsiolkas had been working on a novel as well as the stories and before long showed that too, a work still in progress. Soldatow had no doubt about its worth. Or what would happen next.

it's a sensational book

Sasha told Christos it was a 'sensational' book and that BlackWattle would publish it.

> [...] I would like to do the edits and, since I know BlackWattle's shortcomings, I'd like to generally interfere (you know me). But on these conditions. That if you don't agree with me and what I suggest, you will say no, no way, tell me to get fucked, and, if I go off the tracks, you'll even fuck me off. There's not much to edit. Just a bit of tidying up. I want nothing to ruin our friendship though, but I want a working relationship where we're both allowed to argue. But it's <u>your</u> book and you always have the ultimate say. [letter to Christos Tsiolkas 28.1.1994]

Tsiolkas responded with keenness and gratitude.

In the confident expectation of an immediate and enthusiastic response, the manuscript was sent to Laurin McKinnon, publisher at BlackWattle, producer of those ground-breaking gay anthologies and novels, of Sasha's *Rock-n-Roll Sally* and of *Mayakovsky in Bondi*. No immediate reply came.

Meanwhile Tsiolkas continued to confide his plans for new work, including a novel about vampires. That was the germ of what would be *Dead Europe* (2005). Soldatow was always enthusiastic. Tsiolkas continued to confide his literary thoughts and his state of mind during various intimate and artistic travails; the two men continued to express their love for each other.

On 22 March 1994, Tsiolkas sent Soldatow the revised manuscript of his completed novel, now bearing the title *Loaded*, saying he was happy with this title, very. Its previous title was *Novel with Soundtrack*.

On 13 April 1994 Tsiolkas was still waiting for a response from BlackWattle. On 17 April 1994 Tsiolkas wrote again to Soldatow attaching a copy of his letter to Laurin McKinnon. He still hadn't heard from him.

a rift that never healed

Eventually BlackWattle rejected *Loaded*.

> It was very much a slap in the face because the collective said, the guy can write but it's racist and homophobic. It was a really hard thing to hear, and I think a mis-reading of the novel. An element in the Left is [the idea] that there is a correct representation, there are good and bad. [Tsiolkas interview]

In response to historical homophobia and silencing of queer voices, the leading gay publisher of the time — its publishing decisions made by a collective — apparently insisted on positive representations of homosexual life; Tsiolkas' main character, in a portrayal of shocking authenticity and empathy, is still struggling with confusion and self-loathing on his way maybe to liberation.

This rejection marked a falling out between Soldatow and McKinnon, a rift that never healed; it was also personal:

> Since you seem unable to even be polite to me these days, I am asking you to repay the $500 personal loan made to you some time ago.
>
> Your on-going preference of actively working against me (and BlackWattle) would seem to preclude any positive reason for my personal support of you financially. Your attitude seems even more unusual in that

BlackWattle seems to be the only outlet who is publishing your work at the moment.

This loan matter does not affect any on-going relations you and I have through BlackWattle, those relations will continue to be positive and professional.

I would appreciate your check at your earliest convenience. [Laurin Mckinnon letter to SS 1.3.1995]

There is no record of any such cheque being made, sent, or received.

Sasha turned up with the manuscript under his arm

However, of course, *Loaded* would go on to be published, and with a big splash.

Somehow, in the following decades, it was said that Christos Tsiolkas' electrifying first novel *Loaded* had been picked up from a slush pile — that legendary place where both works of genius and total duds go to die.

Pity the unknown novelist whose work is sent in to a publishing house and put on that pile. It'd be lucky to be even glanced at; it could be assessed in that glance by the kind of clueless reader it was never intended for. But *Loaded* did not come out of a slush pile.

In 1994 Jane Palfreyman had just been appointed as Publisher at Random House. She had heard of Sasha, she told me, but if she'd met him it had been only in passing, until he brought her the manuscript of *Loaded*. She was still so new in her job that there wasn't any furniture in her office and they had to sit on the floor. There'd been a bit of press about the appointment, and she thinks Sasha would have thought, there's someone in a big house looking for projects, and that was true. Quite probably without prior arrangement Sasha turned up at Palfreyman's new Random House office to see Jane Palfreyman in person 'with the manuscript under his arm'. Turned out it was good timing.

> I don't think he did a really big pitch. It was just more, you know, I've got this promising young writer and you're a young publisher. I was a bit more open, not as busy. These days if someone wants to talk about a manuscript I say I'm sorry I don't have time. I read it and loved it, so we just very quickly did a deal, and the rest is history. And I asked if [Sasha would] like to edit the book, which he did…he'd have worked on previous drafts; Christos will tell you that.
>
> It was more of a line edit by then, from memory; it was a long time ago. The manuscript I remember I thought was really good structurally, just fantastic. So that's where all that started. [Palfreyman interview]

a commercial and critical success

Loaded was published in 1995. It was a commercial and critical success, and quite soon after negotiations followed for a very fine perfectly-cast film adaptation, *Head On*, released in 1998.

Years later Tsiolkas is quoted pointing out that his novel came out the same year as two other notable Australian works of queer fiction, Dorothy Porter's *The Monkey's Mask* and Timothy Conigrave's *Holding the Man* and this was because of a new generation of women in publishing. Before then:

> 'There were some fantastic publishers before them, [...] [but] they were a generation largely of men, whose politics had been formed in the 1960s and '70s, and I think they didn't understand queer. They were the same generation as those people in the gay and lesbian press who said to me 'this book is racist'. Jane wasn't terrified of the word 'wog'.' [Cosic 2016]

Sasha, though he too was from that older generation, did understand queer, though he never used the term about his own sensibility or identity.

> Sasha Soldatow says he's too old to be queer but he likes the term anyway. 'Queer is not me. But I'll stand on the sideline and applaud. And you can always ring me up for bail.' [Machon]

collaborative project, *An Autobiography*

Meanwhile, even before *Loaded* was published, Soldatow and Tsiolkas had embarked on their collaborative project, a book called *Jump Cuts*, subtitled *An Autobiography*. Autobiography singular. In a text structured as dialogue, it is not indicated which of the two voices is speaking and is not always easily discernible; there are passages where both are in total accord, passages of fascination with their generational differences, passages of intense disagreement. The book was written in an intensive period where Soldatow moved into the house Tsiolkas shared with his partner.

By then, their short-lived sexual affair was over, but the friendship continued to be intense and intimate. Tsiolkas says that when he met Sasha he and Wayne were committed to non-monogamy, but that wasn't working.

> There was a year when Wayne and I split up over that; we were falling into a heavy drug use and we had to be away from each other to get clean. But we did get back together and Sasha was a really good friend during that period.

I made the decision [that] it was destructive for me and destructive for him to continue to be lovers. That decision was a tension for a while in our relationship. It seemed to me the right one to make. When Wayne and I got back together we started living in Collingwood and Sasha came to stay with us and that's when we wrote *Jump Cuts*. That book is his and mine but it also belongs to Wayne in a way. This small workers' cottage in Collingwood, we were drinking like fishes, and Wayne was going to work, but he seemed to think, it's important for these two men to write this book. And the fights, the arguments in *Jump Cuts* are the arguments we had. [Tsiolkas interview]

Sometimes those arguments were fierce, hostile; the relationship was also very volatile.

At times it was quite savage. When [Sasha] was drunk he could be really mean. Partly it's my responsibility, I would come late to things; there was a dinner at a mate's place, I was late, and it was before mobile phones. And Sasha was in a foul mood and laid into me verbally, it's funny now, he was angry, he was, you are worse than Stalin. And my friend Jeana said, Sasha, think about it. And [someone] was in a corner crying. So it was volatile. After that period I cut off the relationship. I was angry with him. [Tsiolkas interview]

Soldatow always fell heavily when he fell in love, and it wasn't easy for either of them when Tsiolkas insisted on a non-sexual collaboration.

We developed a really close friendship. I think there's a great weight I carry because I know he did fall in love with me and I do love Sasha but my conflict was, my love is Wayne. It's in *Jump Cuts*. I was much younger. I wish I was more honest with him in some ways. But I do think we were really honest with each other which was terrific. I hope he knew how much I loved him. [Tsiolkas interview]

Tsiolkas readily acknowledges how much Soldatow meant to his career.

He was instrumental in my formation as a human being on this planet and clearly I owe so much to him in terms of the success I've had now. [Tsiolkas interview]

It's a success that keeps on growing; after several other novels, Tsiolkas' tremendously ambitious and compelling novel *Damascus* was published in 2019.

a deep loyalty to feminism

Tsiolkas shared with Soldatow a deep loyalty to feminism, and understood its importance to him, learnt from him an understanding of its link to his anarchism. They bonded over their agreement that of all politics the most transformative and central was feminism.

> I think Sasha's commitment to that was much greater than mine, that was a defining politics for Sasha. It's in his writing. An understanding of how gender worked informed how his anarchism was, rather than the other way round. What makes his work so beautiful is it's shaped by that relationship to feminism. [Tsiolkas interview]

But he did not know how Soldatow's life experiences had forged that importance. Tsiolkas says that Sasha didn't talk much about his university experience or family.

> Because the relationship with his mother was not good there's some mystery here to examine.
> By the end we could laugh at each other, at the anarchist vs socialist stuff. I think I had both [socialism and feminism] that came from a sympathy that came from being gay, and from looking at my mother's life and the damn unfairness of being born a woman in this world and that affected every choice she made. [Tsiolkas interview]

a kind of united Europe

Differences of class, and of national, religious and ethnic backgrounds were not as important to children of immigrants as their sense of something shared in their families, their personal histories. Tsiolkas says that one of the connections they had was to do with being an immigrant child.

> ...That European-ness is a romance he had in the sense of what being a writer is and what a writer does. [Tsiolkas interview]

Throughout his life, Soldatow would use the term European to describe his sense of himself, his sensibility. Children of immigrants, of Sasha's generation, while all non-Anglo might have all had different ethnic/national backgrounds, but, as I wrote about my schooldays' friends, we formed a kind of united Europe, long before we had heard of any European Union. [Baranay 2011]

unexamined family dynamics

But Soldatow and Tsiolkas also had formed different relationships with their families: Soldatow's more fraught and defiant, Tsiolkas' more close and forgiving.

Soldatow often got along well with his friends' mothers; this is one example:

> He really admired my folks. One of the loveliest memories from early on, he was going to meet my mother, and he brought her a present of caviar. And in that silly young foolish way I was [I said], she's not going to know what caviar is, she's a working-class woman. And he presented it and her eyes lit up and she was, oh caviar I haven't seen caviar for so long. And it was such a lovely moment. And I remember him turning to me with that wicked little grin: See! It's in a lot of his writing, he really did admire and have a lot of affection for my parents. My mum was very taken with Sasha, she felt protective of him.
>
> And yet Sasha was angry about my relationship with my family; we'd have some of our most stormy arguments about family. There was something clearly not worked out in his family. [Tsiolkas interview]

The arguments seemed to be about Tsiolkas' greater closeness to his family of origin. The complexities of Soldatow's relation to his own background defy easy understanding, but unexamined family dynamics and religious cultural traditions played their part.

> There's the weight of Orthodoxy, even though we're both atheists. [Tsiolkas interview]

generational difference in their experiences

A generational difference in their experiences was also a factor in the arguments. Tsiolkas says he doesn't know what it was really like for that first generation of post-war immigrants, but knew it was harder. When he came into an active political life, he says, consciousness around migration, consciousness of how race and ethnicity work, was already really being discussed.

But that talk had not taken place in political circles when Sasha had been young.

> When I listened to Sasha talk to older Greek Australians, older Italian Australians, older Turkish Australians, [I learned] they didn't have that

> [discussion] in the Left, the Left was almost silent about that. It must have been isolating. [Tsiolkas interview]

Indeed. In Sasha's generation, you only talked about these issues with other immigrants, other first-generation children of immigrants. The Left, like all of mainstream culture, was dominated by the Anglo-Celtic, the largely unquestioned universalising norm of Australian life, in which immigrant identity was not, in the days of Sasha's youth, a part of this Left's sense of itself. [also see chapter 6]

Tsiolkas grew up in a political family. Next to the usual icons of the Greek Orthodox culture, there was a photo of Gough Whitlam. Whitlam represented the first time an Australian politician talked about immigrants as part of the nation.

In the Vietnam War years, when Sasha's family was harshly disagreeing about his coming out, and he was going to the 'moratorium' demonstrations, his family would have gone along with the Australian government's collusion with the USA war in Vietnam, as did anti-communist European immigrants in general.

family's politics, family dynamics

Even for his intimates, it wasn't easy to talk about Soldatow's family's politics, or any of the family dynamics.

> It was a really tough conversation to have with Sasha and he would get really almost aggressively angry when I questioned him. He felt betrayed by his mother for the remarriage.
>
> I think we on the Left can be guilty of using politics to hide behind, we make it political when sometimes it's emotional. [...] [Tsiolkas interview]

his protégé, one who was worthy of him

That intransigence of Sasha's — that conviction in his own assailed rightness, that sense of being misunderstood — that dynamic was put to rest with Tsiolkas. Christos was his protégé, one who was worthy of him, with his knowledge of Russian cinema, his political passions, his own brilliance and transgressiveness. Sasha could take pride, he had as it were midwifed *Loaded* into existence, and now he was the co-author of a bold new book with a rising literary star.

Jump Cuts contains vivid passages about being young and curious, the kind of curiosity that makes you fearless, finding out so many things about people, about art, the world, for the first time. Loving to feel your mind stretched and changed; the feeling of talking about things that really matter to you with someone who really wants to know, someone who is making observations that do and do not support the received ideas of your time and place and identity, the meaning of what you observe; extreme candour over sexual fantasies and acts, or extreme fantasies of sexual candour. There is the immense difference between a generation for whom sex was liberation and one for whom sex always was tinged with fear; in other words, how HIV has changed us.

As the two writers exchange snippets of travel observations, personal history, tales of discovery, claims to enlightenment, fierce political convictions there may be at times the whiff of competitiveness. But because they are of different generations, and value each other and their friendship, it never becomes malicious. There is a strong sense of wanting these stories, anecdotes, opinions, to be set down, put on the record.

Usually you can figure out which of the two is speaking, and enthusiastic readers stop minding if they can't. This arresting statement on politics might have come from either author:

> Proudhon, Marx, all social theorists, have not answered the question of what to do with those of us who refuse to give according to our means. It is with this gaping silence that my dissent from politics begins. [SS 1996 *Jump Cuts* 315]

The book sparks an enticement to enter into the conversation. There are issues that in general everyone talks about with people close to them — love, age, family — while some are based on more esoteric shared interests and devotions — Pasolini, Godard, Proudhon. The prose feels both written in a rush of feeling, and pared to its essentials.

In *Jump Cuts* Soldatow wrote his own history, made his personal mythology manifest, chose and shaped his credo and his repertoire of anecdotes.

the failure of his generation

Soldatow considers the liberation movements of the 1970s, considers the failure of his generation. Things have not been made wonderful. Some things were not known.

For the homosexual movement, he says, two things were important, one to do with identity, one with what ideology conceals:

> First. To define an identity you need to create one. So we embraced the word *gay*. We didn't realise that in the political process of doing this, we were also closing off other options, in defining ourselves, we restricted ourselves.
>
> Second, and this is from hindsight. Because we were political activists, we intentionally cut ourselves off from old definitions. [...] We began to structure a small enclave and planned political actions, but the hidden agenda was that we were all on the lookout for sex. [SS 1996 *Jump Cuts* 197]

He goes on to talk about writing his 1983 pamphlet *What Is This Gay Community Shit?:* its main argument now expressed in new language:

> I wrote that the emerging gay community was dismantling a whole history of radical political actions. So-called community aspirations were taking over from the preceding debates of sexual politics, debates that involved both women and men attempting to renegotiate and reinvent the temperament of gender. Simply put, the whole gay community thing was twaddle... [SS 1996 *Jump Cuts* 198]

Jump Cuts must make (at least some) impassioned young writers want to carry out a similar project (they may be doing it). Maybe they're doing it in whatever other forms people might be working in or are about to be.

From 2018–2020 musician Anthony Pateras [b. 1979] produced a radiophonic interpretation of *Jump Cuts* with composer-performer James Rushford, their music and readings combining 'to reflect the complexities embedded in the text'. [Pateras email 3.11.21]

Jump Cuts got noticed

Jump Cuts came out as a book, a paper book. In 1996 there was not yet the reach and plethora of alternative media and platforms that attract users and experimentation. Anyway, the general notion that new media would entirely replace paper books soon began to evaporate in the face of the evidence: people love books; young people often prefer to read paper books than screens; reading on paper is a qualitatively different experience than reading from a screen. And more recommended for better engagement with the text.

It's also true that *Jump Cuts* was a paper book released in what is called a marketplace with an uncountable immensity of competing products of the same type. That's how you talk about books in late capitalism.

Jump Cuts got noticed because: there was nothing like it around; the main newspapers reviewed it in their books pages and that's what everyone read who was interested in books in those days; Tsiolkas was getting famous and Soldatow in a different ways in a different world had been linked with fame; and their pairing was intriguing.

the writer must believe there is pleasure

Self-indulgent is a term I've heard a few people use about Soldatow's writing: his own prose collections and *Jump Cuts.*

I think 'self-indulgent writing' means that it seems more for the writer's pleasure than the reader's. Still, the writer must believe there is pleasure to be found in their text or they wouldn't seek a reader.

The writer must be the first to know their text as a desiring text in order to offer its desire to others.

The term indulgent is used in the online discussion quoted below, and even by its publisher Jane Palfreyman in the 2018 interview when I mentioned that Tsiolkas' agent Fiona Inglis said *Jump Cuts* would not be publishable now.

> No. Maybe. [Pauses] Seems a bit indulgent now: why do these people's opinions and pursuits kind of matter; I think it's a really interesting book but probably the economics of publishing these days […] Probably if Christos wanted to do it down the track with someone else I'd probably be unable to say no [laughs]. [Palfreyman interview]

Naturally after the success of *Loaded,* Random House was always going to publish *Jump Cuts.*

> I don't think anyone else in those days would have or could have published it. It was just lucky in those days I didn't have a big publishing menu of things I had to get approved. It's an extraordinarily idiosyncratic book that I'm glad got done, I've got a copy I look at sometimes. [Palfreyman interview]

rekindled an area of disagreement

The editing process of *Jump Cuts* brought out Soldatow's adamant side and rekindled an area of disagreement:

> It was an insane project. He [Sasha] was infuriating during that process. Just being dogmatic about things. Yet again we ended up on the floor of my office, with Bernadette Foley who was the editor, having these furious arguments, Sasha wanted to say that a friend of his had been having an affair with a nine-year-old and I said you can't say that, it's a disgusting

wrong relationship and an abuse of power and all that, and he's, no no no the child loves it, the child...anyway there was screaming... [Palfreyman interview]

This was not the first time Sasha's views on pedophilia made most people firmly draw a line. [more on that in chapter 32]

the co-written book was introduced to the world

Tsiolkas fondly remembers the event when the co-written book was introduced to the world, one of the happiest memories from the years with Soldatow. The launch was held around the corner from the house where it had been written. They invited everyone they knew. And as they were going to do a lot of signing Wayne made them a wonderful gift, a potato stamp for book-signing.

rampantly sexual and scabrously raw

An early review of *Jump Cuts* by Peter Blazey came out in *The Australian*. It's as if the review were written for a handful of people to discuss (this can also be the case with reviews published in New York or New Delhi or London). Blazey and Soldatow were friends. Blazey was one of the three editors of the anthology of self-styled 'transgressive' short stories *Love Cries* published in 1995 and, after a tumultuous life would publish his memoir *Screw Loose* in 1997; it was posthumously republished in 2019. His gossipy review discloses an intimate knowledge of the authors; it's referred to in the following online discussion.

> Written in a white-hot day-and-night three-month spree, in a Collingwood cottage, *Jump Cuts* is one of the most unusual books of the year. It was composed by two people who are the terrible twins of Australian queer letters. There's Greek-Australian Chris [sic] Tsiolkas who at 30 is the *enfant* while Russian Australian Sasha Soldatow, at nearly 50 is the *age* (if not the *enrage*). They have joined together to produce 'an autobiography', but it is more a joint rave, a queer dialogue, a commination against the patriarchy, and a screaming match conducted verbally and over their joint computer. Looking at its rather portentous chapter headings — Revolution, Ethics, Love, Aesthetics, etc — *Jump Cuts* is probably intended to be an addition to that growing genre of introspective meditation a la Drusilla Modjeska and Robert Dessaix. But it is rampantly sexual and scabrously raw in comparison.

> The title comes from Jean-Luc Godard's attempt to simulate 'real time' in the film *Breathless*, so the book becomes a dialogue between a Dionysian Rimbaud who thinks he can get away with murder and a self pitying Slav solipsist who knows he can't. Unsurprisingly, they soon become unstuck. (And Soldatow, middle-aged, in a ten-year relationship and bourgeois despite protestations, is very much the Verlaine.) It climaxes with an angry spat over pedophilia. Soldatow approves while Tsiolkas doesn't. In between, they give their views of sex, love, politics and the meaning of life. [Blazey]

Blazey discusses at some length some of Tsiolkas' revelations about his formation and dwells on Tsiolkas' contribution for a few paragraphs; the review goes on with a slight demurral then more enthusiasm, first mentioning the lack of any clear indication which of the writers wrote which bits, which Blazey didn't mind, but he complained of what was not there, not resisting the impulse or obligation to gossip:

> The problem was the lack of humour, of camp banter. The book's stern relentlessness is due to political differences and the fact of Soldatow's guardedness due to being in love with Tsiolkas. They had a one-night stand a few years ago but nothing since. Tsiolkas has a live-in lover to whom he retires every night. He says to his partner Wayne, 'Hold me', and childlike he falls asleep, while Soldatow, Myshkin-like, sleeps alone on the living-room floor. [Blazey]

Not camp enough for Blazey, but he summarises the whole with quotable praise:

> Yet the book's stringent honesty is compelling, as is Soldatow's impressive polymathic cultural awareness. It is shot through with apt film and art references as well as brilliant, apposite quotes in large type from authors ranging from Gertrude Stein to Anna Akhmatova...
>
> *Jump Cuts* is both marvellous and frightful; it is both a curate's egg as well as a curette for septicaemia society. It will make some people throw up but it will change other people's lives. I wish I had read something like it during my 20s. [Blazey]

destined to become the 90s book of quotable quotes

Jump Cuts was reviewed in other serious venues for the serious general reader in terms which must have been gratifying to the authors. And even for those days — notice how much longer reviews were — this was a lot of reviews upon its publication.

> [...] a collective autobiography which must surely be destined to become the 90s book of quotable quotes, the hip version of an Oxford reference book. [...]
>
> Moments of great clarity and simplicity intermingle with elaborate and complex ideas to offer perceptive truths and a philosophy of life that challenges currently accepted notions in a striking and origin way. In fact, Soldatow sees the current age of conformity as a personal affront [...]. Perhaps the fusion of the complex and the simple present throughout the book is best summed up by Soldatow's 'Thinking is never simple, though the best thoughts are', and Tsiolkas' reply: 'Maybe. But the expression of a simple thought can be difficult.' [Simon Clews 'Soldatow, Tsiolkas and Godard' review of *Jump Cuts*, *Australian Book Review*, August 1996]

The reviews continued to be very positive, in a range of publications:

> ...The writing is appropriately edgy...uncompromising moments of literary and personal bravery...a densely textured slice of life. [Miller, Campaign:]

> I like these people. I enjoy the fact that they think and write about their lives, that they throw themselves into their ideas and learn frothier mistakes, that they have the guts to write it down and share it with unknown readers...[McCulloch, *Screaming Hyena*]

> This is a sticky, messy, deadly serious, deadly playful, sometimes infuriating, often exhilarating book. [Hawker, *The Age*]

There were also glowing reviews in the *Sydney Star Observer* and *Rolling Stone*. [Chapman; Barney]

And there's always got to be one from someone who refuses to be impressed:

> It's too easy to be cruel about JC. And I suppose one oughtn't to say anything worse than that it is silly and the two people responsible for it have made themselves out to seem like bores. [Richardson, *Sunday Age*]

online discussion of *Jump Cuts*

At the time, several people involved in Australian literary life who were also early adaptors to online life frequented the electronic mailing list AUSTLIT.

> FROM McKenzie Wark
>
> I find it a bit self indulgent — I wonder if its editor didnt quite have the nerve to tell these boys to pull their heads in. But overall, its such a rare pleasure to read two thoughtful and passionate people writing about books, music, boys, more books, politics, aesthetics, etc.
>
> Interesting that the point where their sensibilities intersect is Wilde's 'Soul of Man' essay.

> From: Pam Brown
> To: 'Australian literature discussion' AUSTLIT@banks
> Subject: Jump Cuts
> Date: Wed, 31 July 1996
> X-Listname: <
>
> McKenzie Wark asked:
>
> Is anyone else reading Christos Tsiolkas and Sash Soldatow's _Jump Cuts+?
>
> Yep. Ive read 'Jump Cuts' and in the context of Australian 'Gay' writing it's a terrific book. If only because it dares to embrace POLITICS in a romantic way.
>
> These days, it's impossible to act politically in the way Christos and Sasha intend — which gives the book a kind of sad, not nostalgic tinge — these days activists can lose battles at anti-runway rallies and picket their own institutions in protest at funding cuts — that's about it — as Sasha S. says in the book — something like this — Everyone knows the pen isn't mightier than the sword — if it was we'll be writing our heads off...
>
> Of course there are some loony pretensions in a book like 'Jump Cuts' — but it's full of energy, openness, ideas, carefree posturing, love, sex, and the design makes it, at least, a refreshing interlude in the autobiography bookshelf. (If that's possible — an interlude in a row of books??)
>
> Pam Brown

The online discussion continues, rich in bitchiness and gossip.

31

i need my friends to frighten me

The friendship becomes destabilised

I have frequently said, in half jest, friends are totally dispensable, there are more where they came from. [SS 1996 *Jump Cuts* 310]

we have to watch out for envy

By the time *Jump Cuts* was published, *Loaded*, published just a year earlier, was considered a successful book. Although Soldatow had been his mentor, Tsiolkas was more the focus in much of the reception of their subsequent collaboration.

> I knew Sasha was writing, but [only] in dribs and drabs. You know what it's like, I often say that one of the things we have to watch out for as writers is envy and that was in the mix. [Tsiolkas interview]

With hindsight, Tsiolkas reflects on Soldatow's difficulties at the time, including his sense of his own reputation. Soldatow was still counting the rejections from grant applications and failing to get published.

There was ambivalence in Soldatow regarding Tsiolkas' ongoing acceptance, his works with established publishers, gaining a mainstream readership; Soldatow was proud of his protégé, but as we've seen he both desired and despised this kind of success. Tsiolkas says it was hard for Soldatow to stop being the *enfant terrible*.

Some of their conflict was based on the differences in their relationships with their respective families. Tsiolkas increasingly grew closer to his family of origin, speaking of their origins and struggle with pride and compassion, while Soldatow's embattled family dynamics never arrived at peace.

> My mum was very taken with Sasha, felt protective of Sasha. And yet Sasha was angry about my relationship with my family; we'd have some of our most stormy arguments about family…He'd get angry: you just want to be a good Greek boy. [Tsiolkas interview]

The year after *Jump Cuts* came out Sasha began to complain that Christos was neglecting him. He wrote in a rather muddled letter:

> I need my true friends to frighten me, frighten my soul. Not too often as that can be destructive. Maybe that is a role you can't perform, but I need that confrontation, which is ultimately commitment. Perhaps I'm asking too much. [letter to Christos Tsiolkas 20.3.1997]

The typescript ends:

> We have to establish a new relationship. [letter to Christos Tsiolkas 20.3.1997]

A Post Script in handwriting says that Sasha wasn't going to send this letter but he will

> because I have no secrets from you.
> You sometimes have to make me feel special — but that's my problem — to love me is not enuf. Sinfully, Me [letter to Christos Tsiolkas 20.3.1997]

It seems that the kind of intensity and close involvement that got *Jump Cuts* written could not be sustained, but Sasha found that hard to bear.

The letters the two exchanged now seem to be veering between the old affection to a new dynamic. Soldatow was sounding needy, complaining of neglect, not showing any new writing.

And yet, later in 1997 when Soldatow returned to Hanoi he carried music mixtapes that Tsiolkas had made him for his journey, and photographs with a warm message on the back: 'I'm glad we love each other'.

But that wasn't enough. From Hanoi he wrote about how much more he wanted from Christos.

> It would be so much easier if I could say these things in person, but I am in Hanoi and you are in Melb and letters and phone calls are not the same. My dear friend, I know that we will never be lovers — this not even a possibility. But I want to be more than just close friends — I want to live in your heart just as you live in mine. Is this a love letter? I suppose it is. But it's just that sometimes I feel you neglect me or simply take me for granted. My dearest one, perhaps I am asking you to be my best friend, but then I might be asking too much. But my desire is for something more intimate, though this could be distance talking. [letter to Christos Tsiolkas 14.9.1997]

Is it an emotion or a trait? What is jealousy? Well, there'd be a lot less literature without it.

Forgive me for saying this but you will understand. I am jealous of your success. [letter to Christos Tsiolkas 14.9.1997 faint blue carbon from Hanoi]

That jealousy was probably made worse because Soldatow wasn't able to find a publisher for *The Gloves of Mr Menzies*. This exacerbated the old sense of being overlooked, misunderstood.

That is my problem to handle, but everything I write from here is either rejected or amended in a form unacceptable to my voice. Except for my articles in Campaign which are run without a change. No one is in the slightest interested in me being here, nor are they interested in my skills. It's as if I don't exist. [letter to Christos Tsiolkas 14.9.1997 faint blue carbon from Hanoi]

He wasn't only complaining though, he also shared what was going on in his creative life; he had new projects also.

But I have taken up painting with a fury, and I've started my next book. You were correct on disencouraging [sic] me on the original title, but I will use it as a quote. It is now titled The Grief of Knowledge. I now call my writing 'autobiographical fiction'. [letter to Christos Tsiolkas 14.9.1997 faint blue carbon from Hanoi]

Autobiographical fiction would soon be known as auto-fiction.

The two kept on writing to each other; Tsiolkas sent a ripped poster from Italy with a letter about his travels on the back of it later that year.

By 1998, Tsiolkas passionately expressed a desire to be free of Soldatow's complaints and demands.

On a form dated 30 March 1999 Soldatow was applying for temporary parking on his Bondi street for Tsiolkas, so they had made up.

Soldatow's influence continued

Soldatow's influence continued; in 1999 Christos sent a card thanking Sasha for recommending *Three Uneasy Pieces*, the last book published by Patrick White (1987). Tsiolkas would go on to publish an excellent book on White in 2018. It's a novella compared to David Marr's epic biography, but Marr himself acknowledges the value and new insights offered by Tsiolkas' familiarity with the Greek Orthodox tradition he shared with White's long-term partner Manoly Lascaris and the influence of that in White's work.

increasingly Tsiolkas had to estrange himself

The two continued to send letters and postcards to each other, and to read early drafts of new work. But increasingly Tsiolkas had to estrange himself, and that affected Soldatow badly.

Cards and letters from Amanda Lohrey include a card congratulating Soldatow on his protégé Tsiolkas. Her effusive praise of him might not have been the most welcome thing to hear after her harsh though kindly well-considered response to Soldatow's *Gloves* in February 1992. [chapter 28]

In the early 2000s, Soldatow's letters to Tsiolkas increasingly are complaints that his name and reputation are mud, that he is lost, seriously lost, feels abandoned. He mentions the drugged state from his pills. Now it is Tsiolkas who becomes like a wise elder, offering advice, and the promise to have a talk with serious plans.

how bad it could get

Jane Palfreyman continued to be Tsiolkas' publisher even when she moved to a new publishing house, their friendship becoming closer. For a while she stayed friends with Sasha as well, and met Bruce Pulsford; she and her husband were invited to dinner and to parties at the Bondi flat.

But then there was the time where Christos had been invited to talk about his new novel *Dead Europe*, an event at the Sydney Writers Festival in 2005: Christos in conversation with Malcolm Knox.

> And at question time Sasha stood up and said in his wavering voice, that kind of wavering voice that he had, he said, I really feared for you, I really feared for you, I thought you'd taken on more....
>
> I think they'd been a bit estranged before that and this was a kind of hijacking of the event and I was furious about that.
>
> [Sasha] was patronising, he was saying, I was afraid you wouldn't be able to pull this off but you have, but he said it in a roundabout patronising kind of way. It kind of completely derailed the event, it seemed very selfish to me, so I had words with him afterwards. And I don't think we quite made up after that. [Palfreyman interview]

Tsiolkas, however, recalls that event as a reconciliation; they hadn't been communicating for a while. He was nervous about what Sasha would think of *Dead Europe*, afraid he might hate it.

[...] And he said, I started reading it, and the first three pages are just advertising. It was all bits from critics on my previous books, and I was, oh he's just going to rip me a new one, and then he was just so generous in his response, and this was in public at a forum in the Sydney Writers' Festival.

And we were friends again.

Dead Europe would not have been possible without Sasha's influence; he said you have to understand the virulence of this hatred in the European consciousness. [Tsiolkas interview]

It wasn't always easy or fun, now, being friends again with Sasha.

Then the alcoholism, going to rehab with him, when he went to hospital in Sydney, and thinking I really hope this is going to work. [Tsiolkas interview]

The rehab period was before the next hip operation in Sydney because he had to get clean to undergo surgery. But Soldatow didn't stop drinking for long.

It's what killed him really. I loved the world with Sasha, I loved going to that flat he and Bruce had in Bondi, talking all night, we'd be lying in bed there just laughing, laughing, lots of laughing, a beautiful intimacy then he'd be up in the morning and into the red wine. What made the relationship change, I couldn't be around his rage when he was really drunk. [Tsiolkas interview]

Anyone who knew Sasha for long soon had to talk about the use of alcohol, an ever-increasing, ever more debilitating use.

Jane Palfreyman told me a story about how bad it could get.

I think that [alcoholism] did drive a lot of his narcissism, paranoia, jealously, particular with Christos, I saw a lot of that. In Adelaide [Writers' Festival] I introduced them to Colm Toibin who was a friend [of mine]; he was very keen to meet Christos — [...] taking the three of them out together and watching them, watching Christos and Colm sparking off each other and Sasha getting more and more insistent about being the main voice of the conversation; it was quite sad to watch...[Palfreyman interview]

In an interview in 2010 Colm Toibin describes meeting Christos in Adelaide twelve years earlier:

We found ourselves laughing at the same things for a week. Nobody else was laughing at this stuff. We'd look at each other and shrug and keep on laughing. [Knox]

Later that night Soldatow was hammering on Palfreyman's hotel room door...

> ...like four o'clock, just really upset, you know that Christos would like Colm more than he liked him, just really baby stuff, he was just drunk and sad, in that situation there was nothing you could say. And Christos was dazzled by Colm as most people are and it was the familiar versus the new. That was my most formative memory of him, it was so emotional, I just spent three hours till the morning going don't worry don't worry, thinking I could kill you. I felt really sorry for him; I really wanted to go to sleep. [Palfreyman interview]

After Soldatow died Tsiolkas acknowledged the difference he had made to his early work, and, now knowing what comes next, reflected on the joys of writing and the perils of a career. [Tsiolkas 2009]

about a year before he died

In spite of the rifts, Christos did keep in touch with Sasha. He was pleased to remember a lovely evening with him about a year before he died, sharing a certain sacrament.

> I'd just gone and scored some E from some friends and had it with Sasha. He was living in Redfern at the Council flat he had. It was the night of the London bombings. [7 July 2005] We sat under the little blanket looking at the news and just having a great conversation and laughing. It's good for me to remember that. [...] We were old friends then...we were making jokes, the way you laugh at horror, the way you have to laugh or else; we were in stitches because they had footage of all this horror, but they still had the stock market reports in the bottom left hand corner! We were like, this is how absurd the world is.
>
> I never knew Sasha as a big drug taker, but those lucky accidents happen. [Tsiolkas interview]

A year later Christos attended Sasha's death bed in hospital.

Like others who knew Soldatow, remember his reliably unique, honest and insightful response to things, Tsiolkas often wonders what he'd make of artworks and events today. Once there'd been a time he could share certain cultural discoveries with Sasha, such as the time he'd been working at the State Film Centre from 1992 to 1997 and had access to all the 16 mm films there. One of those films was *Army of Lovers* or *Revolt of the Perverts* by a

German queer filmmaker, Rosa von Praunheim, who had gone to the US in the 1970s when he was been offered a residency to teach at UCLA. He had asked his students to make a porn film, write, produce, direct, shoot and star. Tsiolkas remembers telling Sasha he'd love to do that too but… Of course that wouldn't have been possible in this place, in these days. And today's world, its manners and media and mores so different; what would Soldatow say?

> I still have conversations with Sasha about all this, I would love to have his perspective now, this whole social media stuff, this outrage culture, his perspective on same sex marriage. I can see us laughing at how conservative things have become. Because of his love of youth he would probably caution me, don't get conservative in your old age. That generosity he showed to me. I think he would have been a marvellous teacher. [Tsiokas interview]

32

how can you talk this way?

that issue

There is a great deal about ordinary living that is hidden. [SS 1996 *Jump Cuts* 241]

they violently disagreed

In *Jump Cuts*, the two writers find points of convergence and points of difference but there was one issue on which they violently disagreed, and never found any common ground.

Sasha Soldatow never backed down from his assertion that children could have sex with adults of their own volition and enjoy it, and that their consent was real.

faintly strange and disturbing

I remember a man and boy at a barbecue Sasha asked me to, in the garden of a house in North Bondi in the late 1980s; the boy was, I'm not sure, about thirteen, the man well past his youth, and they were affectionately entwined on the lawn, and it was known that they were lovers. It seemed faintly strange and disturbing but there seemed no clear thought or position to confidently take; who could censure others' relationships, and it didn't seem like anyone else's business really.

That party was in the house that Sasha shared with Geoff Adlide and Robyn Laurie. I talked at length by phone with Geoff Adlide, now living in Amsterdam. He doesn't recall that barbecue in particular, but he had been involved in the issue.

He spoke about the way Sasha had an influence on him.

> Sasha taught me, in a sense, to be open-minded about this stuff and to think through what does developing sexuality mean, what does consent mean, what does it mean you hit this magical age of sixteen and suddenly you're able to make decisions. [Adlide interview]

Adlide was working at the ABC at the time, and had started to make a documentary on a pedophile group from Melbourne. Sasha introduced him to one of the activists, who went by the name of Emu. (Emu is on the program of some of the readings events in Sydney.) Adlide went to Melbourne as a radio producer and interviewed Emu and some of the other men and some of the boys. The project was to make a radio documentary for the program *Background Briefing*.

> In the end it never went to air; it was never completed. The reason was, right from the beginning Emu and the group had agreed they'd be interviewed and I had to agree and I willingly did that if their lawyers felt this could be problematic I'd agree to it not being broadcast, and at some point lawyers pulled the pin on it, before it was actually finished. I don't know if the tape even exists. [Adlide interview]

It most probably doesn't exist; tragically the ABC has not kept archives of its programs from the pre-digital age.

Adlide and I discussed the strength of the taboo against talking about childhood sexuality. Sasha isn't around to be challenged with the argument that allowing the fact of the sexuality, or sexual feelings, of children does not ipso facto make the case for adults having sex with them. Childhood sexuality cannot be the same as the sexuality of even a post-pubertal young person let alone that of an adult. The imbalance of power alone should be a moral impediment.

Sasha never backed down from his position that even a pre-pubescent child can consent to sex with an adult.

> He liked to provoke a crisis, to provoke a controversy. He taught me a lot in ways of thinking — not that I accepted everything he said, but it was super interesting. [Adlide interview]

to complicate this matter

It's harder to make firm rules about someone who has reached puberty, which is a kind of adulthood — first decide at what point it is reached. How exactly do you decree a universally applicable, legally enforceable age of consent? These things do have to be reconsidered.

There are some serious propositions around these days to lower the voting age, to even as low as thirteen, which is going to complicate this matter.

So it is all to the good that one must not stop at the first impulse in how to respond to the idea of an adult and a child having a sexual relationship that is apparently consensual, whether that is an immediate sense of horror, or an inclination to wonder if ever it might be all right and whether it's all the outrage that causes the harm.

But I think there is only one thing that anyone who has ever cared about a child can reasonably conclude:

There is no way that a child can meaningfully consent to sex with an adult. That is as absolute as anything can be.

And of course sex without consent is assault, whatever terms it's carried out in.

But Sasha would not agree.

And the more that his point of view outraged people the more he stuck to it.

how can you talk this way?

In the *Jump Cuts* dialogue, Soldatow and Tsiolkas begin to talk about sexual curiosity, the sexuality of children, the dynamics of an adult aroused by a child, the important difference between desire and action.

> I think every time an adult has sex with a child even if they imagine it as consensual, the possibility that it will be understood as abuse, as rape, cannot be dismissed.
>
> The first lesson I learned about sex was that you can't fuck whoever you want. Desiring sex with a child does not make someone monstrous. But committing sex with a child is irresponsible, is cruel. I perceive it always as an abuse of trust. [Tsiolkas 1996 *Jump Cuts* 238]

And the reader like Tsiolkas is assaulted then with Soldatow's outburst: *How can you talk this way?* It goes on and ends:

> I have listened to the boys involved with older men in a complicit sexual relationship. This is not rape we are talking about here. It is an equality, between a nine year old and a thirty-five year old. [SS 1996 *Jump Cuts* 240]

The book then records that the dialogue broke up here. Tsiolkas was angered.

> You can't dismiss my difficult grappling with the subject of paedophilia [sic] on the testament of one nine-year-old boy and then pretend authentic experience means nothing to you. [Tsiolkas 1996 *Jump Cuts* 245]

almost all his friends

This issue is one on which almost all his friends parted intellectual company. Probably this made Soldatow only determined to stick to his guns: he was not one to examine himself in the face of an appeal to see things another way. And usually when people were shocked by him it only meant they could be shocked.

Meredith Burgmann recalls that while generally they saw things the same way, years after their friendship began, years after they became comrades at the Victoria Street squats, she and Sasha did have this disagreement, and while she continued to disagree with him, she was kind about his motives:

> We were discussing pedophilia. [Sasha] ran his line: what was wrong with it, it didn't hurt anyone, you know the line he ran, and you could tell he was wanting to get a rise out of you. I had him to lunch in at Parliament [House], after 1991 which is when I went into Parliament. And we had this argument — not really an argument — he was saying it in a very loud voice in the Parliamentary Dining Room and you could tell he was almost hoping to cause a scene, to say stuff like that when there are a lot of journos and conservative politicians around. But it was part of Sasha that he wanted to poke people into thinking about things. And he always had pretty good arguments for things he said even though they were shocking. [Burgmann interview]

Soldatow at age thirteen

My own sense is that Soldatow did not experience sexual desire for children, which, maybe contrary to what some might expect, gave him a more disinterested concern for supporting the expression of this kind of love and desire; I suppose he saw this support as an aspect of liberation from the social control of desire, from oppressive or life-denying power over free expression of sexuality and love.

If there's any value in his position, it is in making one consider and clarify one's own.

Soldatow liked to give support to the condemned and persecuted.

What he had experienced though, apparently, was desire as a thirteen-year-old himself:

> Would you fuck a thirteen-year-old if they asked you to?
> Would you take the initiative if you thought that they wanted to be

fucked but were too scared or embarrassed to say so?

I ask this because at the age of thirteen there was nothing more that I desired sexually than to be fucked by an older man.

Looking back, I now regret that it didn't happen.

Knowing all this, I am forced to ask what I would do with thirteen-year-old in a similar position.

Is art anything that takes you out of the contracted certainties of everyday reality?

Stop. [SS 1973 'Fragments']

What he does not consider, not in this piece nor in general, is whether desires that are fantasies should be fulfilled necessarily. Whether a thirteen-year-old should be given what they want (he'd probably say yes).

articles and papers on pedophilia from early 1980s

Soldatow kept articles and papers on the issue of pedophilia from the early 1980s.

His archives contain typescripts, printed articles, and newspaper cuttings. There are some early essays by Terry Leahy, who examined the phenomenon as a serious academic, including 'positive experiences' of sex between adults and children, and the ethical issues involved.

long correspondence with the man known as 'Emu'

Soldatow had long had a correspondence with the man known as 'Emu', who confided in him with apparent assurance of sympathy and assistance.

In July 2000 Customs seized a parcel and refused Emu permission to import a book and magazine. Emu's three-page letter to Sasha details the points — some finely argued — that his appeal will make. Apparently Sasha has agreed to give evidence. Emu thanks him for his help, saying it means a lot to him, that he feels very isolated on this issue. [letter 5.4.2002]

Banned material sent to 'Emu' again was seized in the following years, and eventually appeals in Emu's case were finally lost in the Supreme Court eight years after Soldatow's death.

cross-generational relationships celebrated in art

A more on-Sasha's-side view, citing generational differences and a nuanced perspective sympathetic to Soldatow's, appeared in a review of *Jump Cuts* in *The Age*:

Nowhere is the frustration of the older man against the rigidity of his protégé's thinking better displayed than while discussing the issue of pedophilia. While Tsiolkas remains focused on power, manipulation and abuse, Soldatow echoes Freud when he argues for the recognition of infantile sexuality. He reminds Tsiolkas that cultures the world over are shot through with cross-generational relationships celebrated in art to this day. While Tsiolkas threatens to reduce this highly complex issue to a political cartoon, his friend argues on behalf of adults who pursue consensual, loving, nurturing relationships with pre-pubescents, to the benefit of both parties. In today's climate, it is a brave argument, eloquently stated.

At this point the two voices fuse into one. It becomes difficult to know who is saying what. We are privy to an internal monologue which almost tears itself apart with the contractions and minefield that surround the topic. For me it is the high point of the book. [Kakmi 1996]

how street-wise are you?

Sasha continued to take an interest in the matter and to defend his unchanged position. In 2002 he wrote in response to an ABC Radio broadcast to presenter Sandy McCutcheon, but it's not clear whether the letter was sent. He points to what was missing in the program he cites; though insistent on the importance of experience like his, or his interpretation of it:

> My objection is the 'spin' you have taken on — I know, abundant reading of books and newspapers, fragments of information through yourself and your researchers, and listening. A personal question, though I suspect I know you as best as you reveal on radio — how street-wise are you; how much do you listen to and wander around watching? Not much, I imagine. I don't want to be offensive, but it seems to me that your information is at best second hand and biased.
>
> Let me tell you about me. I am 57 and have been openly gay forever. Everyone knows; it is no secret. There are things about sexuality that my close friends and their children, whom I've know since birth, cannot discuss with their parents. Girls are slightly different — how many times have girls come up to you (usually about four) and erotically rubbed their thighs against your legs or (about seven) provocatively sat on you, moving themselves, knowing there is a cock between your legs? They are not quite as innocent as we are taught to expect. Possibly they do not know the

consequences of their actions; probably they know that I will not fuck them — they trust me, as do their parents who equally trust me, considering this quite normal as a progress of growing up. I may exist in a society which you know nothing of. Girls, it seems to me, mature emotionally and sexually easier than boys. Then they have a very hard time in their adolescence, both genders. Girls grow breasts and menstruate, which, if they are lucky, some woman in the family or female friends recognised this. Boys don't have this passage — I was masturbating since I was six or seven and no one recognised this. To tell you the truth, I would have given myself to any man who would suck me or fuck me. This is what is missing in your programme. [letter 4.10.2004]

The program can be found online:
https://www.abc.net.au/radionational/programs/archived/australiatalksback/child-pornography-and-paedophilia/3431346

a strange addendum in the present

It's a strange new dimension to the debate that since *Jump Cuts* there has been unearthed, thanks to great investigative reporting and brave testimony, the grim reality of forced sexual relations by adults, in particular clergy in the Catholic church, on under-age children. Some of those accused, and even tried in courts of law, are people in very high positions in their institutions and therefore are one of, or are close to, some of the most rich and powerful men in society, and these men, in spite of convincing evidence and stringently arrived-at verdicts, rush to defend them, freely accusing witnesses of untruthfulness.

What would Sasha Soldatow have made of all that?

33

exchange between cultures involves many dilemmas

Hanoi 1997

The exchange between cultures involves many dilemmas. Some of them can prove very disconcerting. [SS 1997 'Undertow' in *Campaign*]

he sought new correspondents

The moment my visa came through I was off. Couldn't get out of the place quick enuf. [SS letter to SB and W [initials only on copy] 16.5.1997]

In May 1997 Sasha returned to Hanoi; in spite of his post-Moscow unwellness he had successfully applied for a well-funded trip.

I'm here in Hanoi for six months at least on something called an Asialink residency to do anything I want to in the field of literature, to link the two countries together, so to speak. Truly, there's nothing I'm formally meant to do except 'occasionally be diplomatic'. Well, I thought as I took the money and flew, you've chosen the wrong person. It's like an extended holiday in the most humid place on earth. [letter to Tim Cribb and Peter Starr 11.5.1997]

In Hanoi Sasha wrote long letters, as usual keeping a copy. He chats about funerals, death, life in Hanoi, changes he's noticed; he says it hasn't changed very much in the six years since he was last there.

It has become a bit more expensive by which I mean a little less cheap. The architecture of the city is still grand, and the scale, despite modern developments and renovations, is still perfect. I don't mean only the French colonial midlands, though some of them are very lovely. I mean the common domestic architecture. The place works. Despite the new economic rush. [letter to SB and W 16.5.1997]

He wrote that he'd taken up painting, and begun his next book. [letter to Christos Tsiolkas 14.9.1997] But most of the work he did in this period in Hanoi seems to have been writing letters, and not only to old and recent friends; he sought new correspondents. Soldatow wrote to the author of a book he admired, Michael S. Dobbs-Higginson, author of *Asia Pacific: Its Role in the New World Disorder* (1994).

> I was intrigued by your almost insistent hypothesis that the US would eventually splinter in some way. [letter to Dobbs-Higginson 6.5.1997]

Prescient! Soldatow's letter includes a brief biography of himself and the advice that MDH would find it useful to mix with artists.

Dobbs-Higginson replied, with three pages of typescript, thanking Soldatow for his 'generous and thoughtful letter' and responding to points he had made. Encouraged by this reply, Soldatow wrote more personally, confiding to this man he's never met whose letter was not personal, telling of his dreams, of his talks with Emma Goldman in the night.

a kind of lucid dreaming

Since his time in Russia Soldatow often mentioned his not-quite-asleep dreams of talking to people who have died, those he's known, and those whose work he's known, like Goldman. It's possibly a kind of lucid dreaming: the dreamer is asleep but able to direct their dreams.

> Interestingly, my father, who died in 1961, refuses to visit me. Nor does my Russian friend, Zhenya, who died at the age of 26 of a drug overdose — in a typical Russian way his cause of death is recorded as 'died of depression'. He hovers in the café across the road, but when I go there he has left. [letter to Michael Dobbs-Higginson 27.8.1997]

Why is he telling all this to someone he doesn't know, and who doesn't mix with artists?

> Why am I telling you this? In part it is a response to your generous letter. In part it is coming to an understanding of the worship of ancestors, something I am only just coming to grips within myself. Something to do with the fact that I will live in Hanoi for as long as my money lasts. [letter to Michael Dobbs-Higginson 27.8.1997]

I found nothing more about Soldatow coming to grips with a worship of ancestors within himself.

The correspondence does not seem to have continued.
Soldatow had written of talking to the dead in his dreams in *Jump Cuts*.

I often talk to Emma Goldman in those late, quiet, night-time hours when I wake from sleep and write in bed, tossing with my thoughts. She's been dead for years, but always makes the effort to hear me out. Impatient as ever, with so much work that has to be done, bristling with irascibility, she still makes the effort. I asked her once — was it worth being alive? She answered, yes! with the force of a volcano erupting. Then added — this is our condition, our obligation. Human beings are not very rational, not even necessarily sensible, but instinctively, being human we all must know when things are wrong. [SS 1996 *Jump Cuts* 37]

These talks became a theme of his life, for all his refusal of matters spiritual or psychological.

his thoughtless posturing

Soldatow wrote in more than one letter that he kept hearing that the Australian Ambassador to Vietnam was very good, and so he hates her. Is this actually pointless contrarianism? Contrariness can have value, it shakes up assumptions, invites reconsiderations. It's often the case that something that most people seem to think bears some skeptical examination. But to hate someone only because 'everyone thinks she's so good'? So here the biographer must be wary of getting judgmental. We're at a time where Sasha is infuriating, alienating, and boring some of his best friends.

Sasha frequently wrote reviews for the *Australian Book Review*, then edited by his friend Helen Daniel (died 2000). Daniel sent him several requests to write reviews even when he was in Hanoi, discussing how he would get the books. He did review several books for the publication. In May 1997 *ABR* published a long letter by Soldatow in which he claims to have been one of those who organised a reading and obtained books for Vietnam; he made the detailed point that he could not get any help at all from the Australia Council for the cost to transport them.

In June 1997 Daniel wrote to him to ask if he wished to reply to a letter published in the June 1997 edition from Pam Brown, refuting his claims. There's no sign that he thought he might.

Brown's letter pulls no punches. It's come to this.

Dear Editor, In the May issue of *ABR* Sasha Soldatow credits himself with 'begging, borrowing and buying' 75 kg of books for the Women's Publishing

House and the Writer's Association of Vietnam in 1991. I must refute this. Soldatow had absolutely nothing to do with the project. I did an extensive mailout asking writers for assistance and many responded generously. I organised a benefit reading at the Harold Park Hotel from which I raised several hundred dollars. I did not ask Soldatow to participate and on the night of the reading he was not present — he was accompanying Margaret Fink to a gliterati dinner in honour of the Miles Franklin Award.

I selected and bought the books, paying due attention to requests from the Vietnamese organisations. Tom Thompson, then publisher with Angus & Robertson, generously donated any books I selected from his list. I packaged the books and, as Soldatow was passing through Hanoi on his way to Russia, asked him to oversee the freight. I gave him the money to cover costs. For many weeks I had no idea whether or not the books had made it to Hanoi. Months later, Soldatow sent me a photo of himself posing with one of the Vietnamese groups and that was my receipt, I suppose. The 'friend who owned a motorcycle' is Le Dai Minh who had worked at the Australian Embassy and who generously ferried the books and Soldatow to the destinations.

Never at any stage of my project did I ask the Australia Council or any other funding body for assistance, in fact, I wrote to the Literature Board to inform them of the literary exchange I had engaged in and activities subsequent to my visit to Hanoi. I received a gracious reply from Sandra Forbes, then Director of the Literature Board.

One other point is that if Soldatow was asking for $500 to freight some books up to Hanoi he must have had at least a quarter of a tonne in tow.

Soldatow's ire in relation to the Australia Council is well known, he once sued them into granting him over $20,000 and still he shows extraordinary gall in asking them for more. But to have used my independent project as evidence of his supposed artistic generosity is just completely beyond the pale. Soldatow might be 'sick to death of the Australia Council'– I'm sick to death of his thoughtless posturing. [Pam Brown letter published in *Australian Book Review*, June 1997, 4]

In the magazine the letter is followed by:

(Ed's comment: Sasha Soldatow is currently in Vietnam and I was unable to contact him for a response to this letter in time for this issue.)

They made up of course. In 2006, Brown adds more text to her obituary after Sasha's death, recalls their earlier time in Vietnam, and adds:

Some years later (I think in 1997 when Sasha was returning to Vietnam for an AsiaLink residency) he claimed, in his inimitable manner, in the pages of the *Australian Book Review* to have been solely responsible for my altruistic project — an undertaking that had taken considerable time and energy to co-ordinate. Subsequently, Sasha and I engaged in a minor public stoush in the correspondence pages of the magazine. Sasha had a way of bragging about 'his' radicalisms that was sometimes unthinking. Of course, after a couple of months silence, we reconciled. [Brown 2006 'In Hanoi']

collaboration made in heaven

While some of the old friendships back in Sydney were ailing or on hold, this period in Hanoi also brought a couple of new Australian friends into Sasha's life. One friendship lasted; one did not.

Oliver Strewe was already a well-known professional photographer, specialising in travel photography. I knew him slightly when I went to talk to Strewe in the Bondi apartment he'd lived in since the 1970s, where one room was full of his archives. Strewe had been introduced to Soldatow because they were both about to go to Vietnam. Strewe soon saw in Soldatow an ideal collaborator, for work that would be easy to place, which they first discussed in Sydney, meeting in a nearby Bondi restaurant.

The collaboration was made in heaven, Strewe said. He knew a few editors of colour magazines and had lined up a few jobs for them to do in Vietnam. Strewe had been to Vietnam in the past with the English writer Simon Winchester. This could be a collaboration as good as that had been. The editor of *The Australian*'s Weekend Magazine, Candy Baker, was a friend of Strewe's and keen on his doing the stories. Strewe also had done work for the Qantas magazine who wanted more.

Strewe arrived in Hanoi with his assistant Ernie, who had travelled with him around the world for years, photographing for books and magazines. Soldatow was already there, and had found a hotel for them. He was living around the corner, boarding with a family.

They soon planned their first story, Eating Out in Hanoi. The research of course was tremendously enjoyable. They went to restaurants, to a cooking school.

> I took a lot of photos, he made a lot of notes, and we had a really good time, sitting out in restaurants, eating good food, drinking good beer. We'd start out around 10, with a couple bottles of beer. [Strewe interview]

Strewe himself didn't drink in the mornings, he was 'quite disciplined'.

Strewe's photographs would be delivered on his return to Australia. Soldatow had made his notes for the story about eating out in Hanoi to be sent to the editor of *The Australian*'s Colour Magazine.

A new story soon became their next project when Strewe got an offer he couldn't refuse. He was in another hotel with Ernie when a guy came to them, saying he had a travel agency, and proposed a deal. He would provide a car in return only for some photographs. They'd go for a trip around the north. A four-wheel drive, and driver, and their only expenses would be hotels, which then were incredibly cheap to foreigners.

Soldatow was part of this expedition; he was going to write the text for a travel piece. Strew showed me some photographs: Sasha sitting with some people from the hills of northern Vietnam, Hmong people dressed beautifully in distinctive colourful woven clothes. Soldatow must have loved it all, he made his companions laugh, and they saw other marvels, in an area barely known by foreign tourists at the time, driving to Dien Bien Phu where the French had been defeated by the Vietnamese in 1954. They must have discussed the importance of this event to the USA intervention that followed, but mostly Strewe remembers what a great time they were having, laughing, talking, eating great food.

> [Sasha] was funny, really funny, he made Ernie and me laugh the ten days we were together, that's a long time day and night with someone. [It was] the three of us and the driver, the driver was very quiet.
>
> We got some beautiful photographs.
>
> We had some incredible light, up in the mountains, I can remember the light, the low light in the afternoon, people walking down the road.
>
> We went to nightclubs, and did karaoke, and it rained, and we had a wonderful time.
>
> And we went to Ha Long Bay, down the coast, I'll show you [photos], it's in the north, it's pinnacles in the sea, rock, limestone I think. We hired a boat, with a sail, it was the three of us, and three or four crew, and we were sailing around, and it was really beautiful and calm. And little boats would come up to us with fish which we'd buy, and we had a good cook on board.
>
> Sasha kept beautiful diaries and notebooks. [Strewe interview]

So far it was a happy trip, even idyllic.

things got weird

Then, it all changed. Things got weird with the crew on the boat.

> Sasha is obviously gay, so they thought me and Ernie were gay, and they thought they could make extra money out of us. They were gonna sorta, sell their bodies basically, and it got really heavy and nasty. They were poor young men. One of them pinched me on the thigh, it really hurt. Ernie freaked out and locked himself in a room. Me and Sasha were sleeping on the back of the boat. It got tense: what's going to happen. We were out on the water, out at sea. We weren't sure what was happening and it turned into a them and us sort of thing. [Strewe interview]

Soldatow later wrote about this incident in one of his columns for *Campaign* magazine:

> We were on a boating trip in Ha Long Bay, six men on a boat in one of the most unbelievable natural wonders of the world — old volcanic islands which thrust upwards out from nowhere in a sea of pure green, pure magic. We anchored for the night in a desolate bay.
>
> The captain produced some turpentine hootch which we tasted, though mainly threw over the side while no one was looking. And then, among men, sexual innuendo came straight to the fore. Oliver was wearing a white handkerchief around his neck, to prevent sunburn while photographing. Suddenly he was referred to as 'missy, missy'. Called madame. Was told that the cook (male) was not married, followed by a lot of ribald laughter. At first we dismissed these advances. Then it became serious. TV magazines with cover photographs of sexy women were produced and their mouths covered over with a hat, covered and uncovered, covered and uncovered — the meaning became transparent when the young cook sat next to Oliver and pinched him very hard on the thigh. Things then turned nasty, then turned very silent. We aborted the trip the next morning. [SS 'Undertow' *Campaign* October 1997]

It had happened on the first evening of what was meant to be a longer trip. Strewe says Soldatow had to be forceful and argumentative to get the crew to take them back. And then there was an argument about payment. Soldatow describes this scene in his 'Undertow' column [1997], concluding

> We left what we thought to be a reasonable amount of money. Negotiations are difficult, particularly when alien issues such as sexual harassment are involved — the West and the East are both infidels to one another. You

simply have to put it down to a fact of life (though you are never sure if you have acted properly...) [1997 Undertow]

No, how could you be sure you did 'act properly' in a situation like this? People were very poor, unused to tourists, their actions likely to be from some desperation rather than calculated criminality, and misconceptions about Westerners not unknown. Soldatow's actions seem somewhat stingy, and not like him really, to be punitive and vengeful.

Anyway, Strewe soon returned to Australia, pleased with the photographs he'd taken, fabulous photographs from North Vietnam. All that remained was for Soldatow to submit his text. And somehow, that didn't turn out well.

> Sasha sent a story to Candy [Baker, editor] about eating out in Hanoi, written on a typewriter, [but] impossible to read, three or four pages, things were crossed out, it was in a dreadful state. She said she doesn't have time, it would have been hours and hours of editing. So she rejected it.
>
> I looked at it, it showed he was pretty chaotic. She's under enormous pressure, he's under no pressure, sitting for hours in his room in Vietnam. [Strewe interview]

I contacted the editor who, twenty years later, does not remember that time. Strewe got someone else to write it up and eventually sold it as a picture story. Strewe recalls too that Soldatow was having some conflict with the people he rented from; he doesn't know what that was about.

When Soldatow returned to Australia he behaved in a way that made no sense to Strewe. Or to anyone.

> He came back to Australia and rang up and left a funny message on the machine abusing me for being treacherous and all sorts of things.
>
> And I left it on there and played it to a few people; it was quite funny and abusive and crazy. I rang David Marr and he said, don't worry he's fallen out with everybody.
>
> They published the story but hadn't used his words. He must have known it wasn't up to me. And he must have had correspondence with the editor.
>
> And I never saw him again. And I live just up the road. It's sad. Because we had a wonderful time together. [Strewe interview]

But Strewe returned to the hours of travelling, looking, laughing. Enjoying. As always the case with Sasha, however much things might turn sour later, the charm of his conviviality and talent to amuse created a lasting fondness, and the stronger memory.

'do not throw knives through windows'

From Hanoi, Sasha wrote to Bob Ellis, Sydney journalist and author, reporting on his dismal entry to Vietnam, a letter with funny tales of woe, and White Traveller complaints. [letter to Bob Ellis 12.5.1997]

As it happened, Bob Ellis' son Jack at the time was planning to go to Vietnam. Jack had begun a university degree at the Conservatorium of Music in Sydney, and planned a trip with a friend in the semester break. Jack called Sasha on the number his father had passed on, and Sasha encouraged him to travel up to Hanoi after landing in Saigon.

It turned out a welcome introduction on both sides.

> I think he's t*riffic [sic]. We took to each other the moment we met. [SS letter to Bob Ellis 10,8.1997]

I'd met Jack Ellis at Sasha's flat in Bondi, it must have been the late 90s, when I'd only be in Sydney on infrequent visits, and I knew Jack was a new friend Sasha was fond of, or adored more like it. I had last seen Jack at a barbecue party in early 2007, where Jack told me he'd think how much Sasha would enjoy things like this party and then get angry at him for having died. In 2018 I went to talk to him at the apartment in Sydney's inner west he shared with his partner and their child, where Jack worked on his music and his writing. He told me the story of his friendship with Sasha, which began in Hanoi, or really with the phone call before he arrived:

> I said, do you want me to bring anything. He said, bring Scotch because it's really, really expensive here, like $100 a bottle. So I brought a big bottle of Jamiesons all the way up to Hanoi and arrived at his flat, and we got along famously straight away. We drank pretty much the whole bottle of Jamiesons. [Ellis interview]

Sasha lived above a shop, a grocery or mixed business run by a family, and you had to walk through the shop to get to his place upstairs. A woman there taught private English lessons to children.

> One of the phrases she used, that delighted Sasha, was, 'Do not throw knives through windows' and you'd hear these people saying, do not throw knives through windows.
>
> He was by himself there and it was just a typical Sasha place, he found things and put things up. [Ellis interview]

Soldatow did not learn what he did not think he needed to know; his 'not good with money' trait exaggerated in foreign currency.

He made this strange decision not to understand the economics of the place so what he'd do, he'd just go down to the shopkeepers and say, I want that that that; and he would just fan out this wad of dong [the currency] and the shopkeeper would just take the correct money and he'd never know what it is. [Ellis interview]

They went to a shop that sold whisky, and there Ellis quickly understood Sasha's zero error.

I looked and said, Sasha you fucking idiot, whisky's not $100 it's $10. [Laughs] And I'd lugged this big bottle all the way from Australia. [Ellis interview]

how much they laughed together

Sasha's flat had a balcony overlooking a busy street, near a place where the 'moto' (motorbikes) waited.

Jack gets up and does a heavily limping lop-sided walk.

They'd be talking to me, and say, you're going to meet, and they'd do this limp. He broke his leg, I think in Russia, and it had been badly looked after and I think what made it so bad, he had a frightening experience with the operation, I think he had to have it twice, and as a result of that [causing] fear he never had the pin removed; he just wouldn't go back [to hospital]. And as a result the pin faded away his whole hip and that's why he had to have a hip replacement eventually.

He was frightened of dying. He was frightened of the anaesthetic. He was a strange anxious fellow in that sense; on one level he was very philosophical about death and mortality, on another level he was running scared. [Ellis interview]

I asked Jack about the basis of the two of them getting along so famously. As so many others do, he talked about the honesty of their conversations, and how much they laughed together. Laughter, people remember laughter with Sasha, he had the gift of striking a note of shared humour.

Total honesty straight away, we felt like kindred spirits straight away pretty much. And we just laughed, we laughed so much, we had a similar sense of humour. I only spent two or three nights in Hanoi and that was it but when we got back, we reconnected when he was living with Bruce in Bondi. [Ellis interview]

Jack Ellis often visited Sasha in Bondi, and would become one of his most treasured friends and important supporters in the following years.

34

people going past

back in Bondi 1997–99

I don't write to communicate, I write to record, to utter, to verbalise, to express. I write to be read. [SS 1996 'Self-Portrait' *Meanjin*]

have you thought of writing backwards?

Sasha had returned to the Bondi flat after his fall in Moscow; he lived there through periods of intense lows and highs: more surgery for the broken femur; the publication of *Mayakovsky*; first working with Christos Tsiolkas. He returned to live here again after his stay in Vietnam in 1997.

Bruce Pulsford was still there when Sasha held his 50th birthday party there later that year.

The filmmaker Helen Grace filmed some footage. A lot of longtime friends can be seen, and some new ones. Among friends and offering hospitality, Sasha is looking relaxed, in his element. Not the slender sprite of yore, now a tubby older man, genial, expansive; as always in button-down shirt and large-frame glasses.

Sasha is shown chuckling away, seeming tremendously amused by what he and others say. People with a reputation for being funny can say not-so-funny things as if being funny and it sounds funny. Sasha is caught on sound and video talking about how he gave advice to someone who had thought of a great ending for something they were writing, but didn't really know what came before; he said, 'Have you thought of writing backwards?'.

at the time and in retrospect it was magical

After their meeting in Hanoi, Jack Ellis became a regular visitor in Bondi, sometimes bringing friends with him, certain of a warm welcome.

> What Sasha liked in me and my young friends — and the fact we were young guys partly, he's a gay guy — we were musical and played in bands. We'd play gigs in the city then turn up. Because he had this wine-based

sort of rhythm, he was often up very late at night or early in the morning, and we'd roll up and have a lot of fun. [Ellis interview]

This did not make still living there any easier for Bruce Pulsford. In early 1998, Bruce moved out; his sense of responsibility for Sasha remained, however, and he kept on paying the mortgage, giving Sasha the place to himself for another two years.

Sasha's party persona was now far less often his face to the world; his decline had become evident to his old friends, and they stopped coming by. That 50th birthday marked the end of the parties era. Gillian Leahy is one who says she feels she failed him in his final years:

> It was a thing everybody couldn't handle, watching him kill himself. And the denial — he'd have the shakes and he'd say it's the valium. I'm not saying it wasn't, it was also the DTs I'm sure. He'd get up at four o'clock, drink, write, crash out, drink again, then argue with Bruce. [Leahy interview 2020]

Some people still came to visit. Soldatow greatly enjoyed the company of Ellis and his friends who in turn were entertained by Sasha in more than one sense. Soldatow still retained the gift and dedication to friendship. Jack Ellis speaks of those times with much warmth. A golden time, he says.

> We had this wonderful few years, we'd sit on the couch and look out the window for a while, and we'd have a long conversation about the people going past. And we'd go and cook food, and he'd constantly put the dishwasher on, he just loved the dishwasher. [Ellis interview]

There was also his 'beautiful aesthetic' as Ellis puts it; Sasha created visual pleasure out of found objects wherever he lived. And there were some visitors, and his loyal longtime friend Margaret Fink still took him out:

> Maggie was always good to him so once a week he'd be out with Maggie having a fancy lunch, just having a good time. [Ellis interview]

Ellis began to understand how Soldatow's day unfolded, now from a later perspective.

> His rhythm, I hadn't quite realised the extent of it, till I lived with him [later], but his normal day, he'd wake up about four o'clock in the morning and start drinking and he would just slowly have a wine then tune into those early morning Radio National shows, *My Music* and all those BBC kind of variety shows, and go back to sleep and rise again around ten, and set about his day, doing whatever he had to do, nothing much. [Ellis interview]

A few years later, writing to Jack Ellis in 2003, in shaky handwriting, in 'constant residual pain' after surgery, Soldatow writes with warm appreciation about those times:

> Looking back on Bondi it was a kind of arcadia that can never be repeated or resurrected. I don't know for you, but for me at the time and in retrospect it was magical. I truly mean that. [SS to Jack Ellis 15.8.2003]

commentary, opinion, reflection

As for the writing, Ellis recalls that Sasha announced he had finished *The Gloves of Mr Menzies* 'a few times' but couldn't find a publisher. In 1997 he published the piece on culture clash in Hanoi in *Campaign*, one of his 'Undertow' columns in the magazine.

Those columns continued the work he'd done in his 'Wild Card' columns in the *Sydney Star Observer* in 1993-94: he was free to choose his themes and write his mix of commentary, opinion, reflection. His work was published exactly as he wrote it; he enjoyed the implicit respect from the editors.

when Sasha's problems began

There was the possibility of more creative collaboration with his talented new friend. Soldatow always wanted to do some work with him, Ellis says. When Ellis attended the Conservatorium of Music, he'd often go and stay at Sasha's for three or four days and write out the score, and play on his guitar. Sasha was fascinated by that, and would talk about doing an opera on mobile phones.

That all seemed promising, but sadly there was no real development on Soldatow's part, and without rancour Ellis recalls that stage as frustrating.

> He'd announce he'd written something new and that I would set it to music, but it was the same one. It kind of stalled. He was a frustrating collaborator, because he would announce some masterpiece, and then it would sort of not appear or just continue to appear in different forms. [Ellis interview]

Sasha seemed not to have made plans for the inevitable day when he could no longer stay on in the Bondi flat. Bruce Pulsford did however have to sell the place, and had postponed doing so for Sasha's sake, giving him more time to get used to the idea. But Sasha never acknowledged that he knew that he would have to move on. Bruce couldn't keep it up and in 1999 the flat was sold, and it had to be emptied.

But that took a while and it was not the end of Bruce taking care of Sasha, far from it.

Bruce says that that's when Sasha's problems began.

> I felt guilty, maybe I shouldn't. But I knew with Sasha there was never a Plan B, he'd never make a plan B, [even when] I'd be talking about the need to sell the place.
>
> When I'd moved out, he used to come to my place in Darlinghurst and I'd let him stay and sleep on the couch, but I didn't want him to think it was a place he could move into. It was very hard to get him to acknowledge that it was over. And I felt bad about that. He wasn't a person who'd meet you half way. Some would say, he was just out to gouge you in his own way, use you in his own way, but I saw it, probably not to my benefit, as someone who was quite lost, and that touched me deeply. So, taking him out of the house was a very difficult thing, that's why it took me eighteen months as I got further and further into debt.
>
> And it would have been some demand from someone and I realised I had to sell [the flat]. But it was sad because Sasha was so vulnerable. [Pulsford interview]

a year of heavy drinking

As early as 1982 Soldatow wrote about his heavy drinking in a diary; quite likely it's a piece he did not show anyone

He was still young enough then, 34 — if only *just* young enough, if getting into the dangerous years — where heavy social drinking was normal and might not cause concern. Heavy solitary drinking might, by definition, not be seen by others and who was going to say it was any of their business?

He addressed 'you' in this diary entry; maybe himself, maybe an imagined reader, maybe the reader of a planned future piece that this would contain. It's written in short lines, as if a poem.

> I have been changing lately. It's about time. Let me tell you about it. A year of heavy drinking /
> Has left me with a short-term memory loss/
> but that's okay /
> it's scrubbed my mind /
> of who fucked who /
> and other trifling gossip. [1982 diary 29.1.1982]

Every year was a year of heavy drinking.

I had a lucky escape

The accident in Moscow, the surgeries and the pain and the alcohol and the pills and the wanting more than Tsiolkas did from that friendship, the alienation of other friends, were affecting Sasha badly.

One day his old friend Mark Macleod was going to have lunch with another writer friend, and Sasha asked if he could come along. Arrangements were made. It had been a long time since Macleod had seen him, not since their break up when Macleod had made Sasha get out of the car in the rain. [chapter 14] Macleod says he was shocked to see how much Sasha had changed physically.

> The tremor that had always been there in both his voice and his body was now undeniable. He had always drunk pretty keenly (vodka mostly) but it seemed to have left its mark. He started to cry, and embarrassed both Jenny and me by launching into an explanation of how he had always felt about me and how much he regretted the breakup. [...] I have to say that although I was touched by his honesty? sentimentality? I came away thinking that I had had a lucky escape. [Macleod email 10.11.20]

Reflecting on that in the present, Macleod knows there was nothing he could have done.

> That sounds cruel, but I would never have seen myself as a 'rescuer' and he would never have wanted to be 'rescued', but his deep seated unhappiness was longstanding and I don't think writing, or alcohol, or sex, or partying had really helped him to deal with his emotional demons, and I wasn't the right person to help support him through it. [Macleod email 10.11.20]

I don't want to hear about this

Soldatow's behaviour at the time exacerbated the alienation from some of his oldest and even closest friends, who were tiring of hearing the same things from him, no longer sympathetic to his complaints. Even Pam Brown:

> I thought, I don't want to hear about this, you ruined the flat that Bruce is going to have to fix up to sell;...when Bruce moved out, [Sasha] filled the flat with bits of wood, I didn't go there but Bruce told me. That was Bruce's property that he needed to sell in order to live and have his life, not to give to Sash to fill up with bits of wood! The collecting went too far! [Brown interview]

And that's when the only place Sasha was invited to stay was on a farm near a distant country town, Casino.

Bruce Pulsford suspected that Casino was not going to suit Sasha, but Bruce was no longer able to provide Sasha with a home.

Jack Ellis helped Sasha pack up his stuff, and somehow it was all moved to his new, distant accommodation.

35

let me tell you about salad

a farm in Casino

It is scary to become the past in your own lifetime. [SS 1996 *Jump Cuts* 55]

the story of their meeting

Needing a new place to stay, Sasha moved to, of all unlikely places, a farm near a country town called Casino in the north of New South Wales. It belonged to his longtime friend, the anthropologist Inge Riebe.

They first met in Sydney just after he'd arrived in 1972, at the Push hangout, the Newcastle pub.

> She came straight out and asked me for a fuck. I said, 'I'm gay'. I thought of myself as a prominent Gay Lib activist. 'So what's the problem?' she replied. She won me over with that argument and we had a short affair. [SS 1996 *Jump Cuts* 197]

That story of their meeting was one he liked to repeat; he told it in his exuberant 1992 piece 'Party Fun' in *Outrage*, in the context of the early gay scene and what counts as a fuck. The account in *Jump Cuts* is in the context of a discussion about the problematics of defining identity; that to define an identity you create one; that definition is restriction.

I spoke with Inge Riebe in her Katoomba home in mid 2018 (and a few times afterwards). She told me she had been working in New Guinea at the time but was coming back to Australia every couple of months to see her mother, and she first met Sasha one of those times. He was very beautiful, she said. And she knew what she liked.

> He was one of the few men I know whose penis actually matches the skin of his body and I find that very attractive. I find very pink penises very worrisome. And he was entertaining. We got on right from the start. [Riebe interview]

Sasha Soldatow and Inge Riebe found in each other someone who equally enjoyed frank and informed discussions on sexuality. For Sasha the fling with Inge was never going to go on to a longer sexual relationship.

> I liked it, it was great, but to him, it meant he was gay, sadly for me, I'd have been happy to go with it. It was also quite nice to have the relationship as it was. There was no problem with erection or doing or coming, but somehow his sexual object was men. [Riebe interview]

She recalls that he told her he'd never slept with a woman before; memory is tricky; Soldatow had talked in public about sex with a woman; several of his friends knew he had slept with a woman in Melbourne, and some know of at least one other heterosexual encounter.

in other respects she was quite other

In some respects Inge was like him, intellectual, argumentative, political, certain in her views. In other respects she was quite other, with an interest and practice in a spiritual discipline. Sasha Soldatow scorned anything to do with any notions of the spiritual. Inge enjoyed defending her serious study and practice in Buddhism. Sasha found it anathema, she says. But he'd attack it the same way she did: how can a rational person take this stuff seriously?

> So we'd always manage to get to another level. He also called me a bit of a queen, in the sense of a royal, who had to have things her own way. [Riebe interview]

I think you're a sensible person

They kept up their discussions as Inge moved back to Australia permanently in 1981, and eventually bought the place in Casino, an area she had come to know through the father of her daughter, who came from there. The friendship continued into the decade following their meeting. That decade when that strange new disease was beginning its ravages. At times it was as if suddenly a mysterious plague had cursed us and it was urgent to share information and observe the meanings made of this. [chapter 19] Riebe had been away, probably in India, during the time the AIDS scare was at its worst and remembers meeting Sasha on her return:

> I hugged him and kissed him on the lips, and he nearly burst into tears, he was so happy; he said people now would avoid kissing [a gay man]

on the lips. It was interesting, that period of being the pariah who could give someone AIDS. I said, I know you screw around and I think you're a sensible person and would be careful. [Riebe interview]

If she had kissed him on the lips in a self-conscious way, Inge said, he'd have picked that up. It was her unself-conscious spontaneous as-usual warm greeting that struck Sasha. No one who moved in or intersected with gay circles could not have known what superstition, cruel invented rumours, wilful ignorance there was around HIV in the 80s.

conversations about gender and sex

And Sasha was a friend who loved talking about gender and sex, terms that have, especially in recent decades in our culture, been charged with philosophical enquiry, from the works of esoteric theorists to the expressions of the crassest popular culture.

This too would mostly have been in the 1980s:

The other thing I really liked was a lot of our conversations were about gender and sex. To me, because he was a man, because he was homosexual, because he was a thinking homosexual, he thought a lot about the sex act and what it meant; whereas I found men generally were pretty gormless about all that. [Riebe interview]

Because she is a woman, because she is an anthropologist, because her thinking on these matters went far and deep, Inge had a store of esoteric knowledge and eccentric preference. And Sasha loved talking ideas, examinations of intimate matters, personal testimony.

Those who clearly and frankly wanted to know everything about sex found out more than most people do.

Sex was, among other things, politics.

The other things included pleasure. He has been called a hedonist (e.g. by Pam Brown in 'Vale Sasha' in 2006). Pleasure did also interest Sasha, but he really got going on questions of the politics of sex, the politics of gender.

Presumably he discussed the finer points of pleasure with other men, but in Inge he found an intellectually challenging woman with equally passionate interests, one with whom he had a unique sexual history, a friendship whose origin story became one of the oft-told tales in his repertoire, one his myths of himself.

And again, think of the era. No internet. Information about sex was far more successfully hidden and distorted and mangled. In Australia the intellectual class was dominated by an Anglo culture of puritanism, rarely acknowledged as such. Lefties, radicals, outsiders often could be as squeamish about sex, as unimaginative in its practice as the uptight conservatives they opposed.

Academic rigour and queer subject matter had barely stepped out together.

Heteronormativity had barely been named, or not yet, let alone widely acknowledged and examined. Queer desire was frequently denied, quietened, nipped in the bud.

But it was where a new kind of thinking was taking place.

Even while Freudian ideas of the superiority of genital sex to other kinds were pervasive, they were also subject to the silence of privacy, ignorance, and similar constraints and so were not very widely openly challenged.

But they were being challenged.

Such is the value of the margins.

the problem at the heart of anthropology

Sasha was curious about anthropology and met others in the discipline through Inge. In an apparently unpublished piece from 1979 he delves into his unease with what he learns from, or about them, after a discussion with an academic who has just done field work in New Guinea. Soldatow was frustrated by all that this person was unable to tell him, did not seem to know. It was a problem of language, he decides; the anthropologist was not using the everyday language 'of real life sitting around drinking coffee and chattering.' Where, by implication, more truth and depths of understanding about people emerge. The initial quest based on interest in human nature becomes the need to produce preservable books and articles.

> This is the problem at the heart of anthropology. You can only show that you have gathered important and impressive information, data that you then play esoteric games with, projecting various intellectual systems of interpretation and explanation onto. [SS 1979 'An example of social relations under capitalism']

Soldatow posits that the societies studied become destroyed by outsiders — anthropologists, missionaries, imperialists — and their 'secrets' are gone; all that remains is the collection of data, which becomes the bible about that lost world.

> But this bible is dead. The secrets contained in it is not of the same order as real life. [SS 1979]

a room for him at her farmhouse

The friendship with Sasha continued; Inge visited the Bondi flat where Sasha lived with Bruce Pulsford whenever she was in Sydney. Then when Sasha had to move out, Inge built a room for him at her farmhouse.

It would not have been quite the kind of place where Soldatow easily felt at home. But it was a home. And many local people visited. One thing Casino did provide was opportunity for a favourite occupation: making meals for others.

> I love cooking. For me it provides endless pleasure. But not for myself. When I am alone, I hardly eat, perhaps some fish fingers from the corner store.
>
> My truly favourite occupation is planning a big dinner. And the shopping, buying, slicing, cutting, preparing. Strangely, I don't have much fun during the dinner — it is the generation of a surrounding for others which provides the pleasure [...]
>
> I dream cooking. Endless boring dreams of cutting up onions. Over the past twenty years, there have only been, at most, three days in a week when I haven't sliced an onion. It has been a daily preoccupation, and now a nightly one as well. [SS 1996 *Jump Cuts* 314]

Inge like others testifies that Sasha was a terrific cook. Several people, talking about Sasha, would repeat that line attributed to Oscar Wilde, that he had put his talent into his writing, his genius into his life. 'He was what in German we call a *Lebenkunstler*, a life artist,' says Riebe.

At the farm, Sasha would stay in at the house. Riebe rode horses but he never did that. She was doing a lot of work with Aboriginal people, and would bring some of the elders over. Sometimes there were visiting lawyers.

Soldatow's more usual occupations were not available, like a wider social life, receiving his own visitors, poking about in city stores, acquiring his op shop finds.

the wonderful thing about Buddhism

Inge's involvement in Buddhism continued through all these years; she led retreats, and began to work on some translations of Tibetan Buddhist texts. It's the more esoteric philosophy that she's involved in, rather than everyday observances in, say, Thailand. She says the wonderful thing about Buddhism is that it's a philosophical system that can't be defeated by argument.

Which meant it was not available to Sasha's way of arguing.

> [Sasha] thought it was about reincarnation and attachment to some kind of spiritual development. I was saying, that's not what it's about, this is what it's about. And he'd say, then why do they do all that ritual? And I'd say, but the human mind likes that.
>
> One of the most impressive things: they do these week-long puja things where they make these sand mandalas. It takes three monks three days to make one, and it's incredibly beautiful, and it's there for the whole of the ceremony and then [makes whoosh sound]. [Riebe interview]

And it's gone. And there you had a demonstration of non-attachment and impermanence, calmly destroying a painstaking, unique artwork you just made. The traditional sand paintings in the Australian desert similarly are painstakingly, precisely made, but not made to last.

So that was probably an argument for ritual.

And the arguing would go on, what fun.

There is no evidence that Soldatow considered such ideas any further. He had travelled a little in Indonesia and Vietnam by then but was never attracted to what might roughly be called Eastern ways of thinking.

not much of a cultural relativist

As remarked before, Sasha Soldatow was not much of a cultural relativist — he generally resisted examining his responses in cultural terms; he was not for examining how he was shaped by cultural assumptions, habits, preferences.

Inge pinpointed this aspect of his character also, talking about some of the discussions they'd have at the farm, and her experiential knowledge of some Indigenous societies, which required her to see some behaviour without the kind of judgments they'd arouse in the world more familiar to Sasha. They talked about anthropology quite a lot, she says.

> Sometimes I thought Sasha's cross-cultural basis was not as good as I'd have liked it so we would have arguments about that, but they'd be always at least intelligent arguments. He just didn't get, I think, that behaviour was culturally determined to some degree. He had some principles that he thought were correct or right, not in a disciplinary sense, but in an idea way. And the idea that this may not be how it works in this culture, and that doesn't mean these people are what you'd think if they were like that in our culture, they were in a different milieu, that didn't go down too well. [Riebe interview]

She says that Australian Indigenous culture has a phallic orientation but isn't patriarchal in the European sense. It might look like that, because you see men doing things that if they were in the White environment you'd think they were being patriarchal.

Soldatow might have remained unconvinced by her arguments, but there were ways he did argue with Inge that she appreciated and feels the absence of.

> Sasha was one of the very few people who could call me on things close to the bone without me getting cross. It's one of the reasons I miss him. People would say to me, how does he get away with saying that to you and I'd say, that's Sasha.
>
> [An example:] When he came up to the farm my partner was an Aboriginal man and [Sasha] made some very cutting comment about my position in that relationship — something like I had one foot in and one foot out which was very close to the bone and very undesirable to be said. Because it was Sasha, I realised he was right. [Riebe interview]

Sasha did not record those arguments, alas. He did not like it at the farm at Casino, at least some of the time. He said it was awful.

He wrote to Margaret Fink criticising the people who came to the Casino farm — 'them' — their terrible diet, the way 'they' don't bring things to the house where hospitality is offered, that they don't invite him back. He most certainly never was a cultural relativist.

In a phone conversation in 2020 Inge said that Sasha's whole raison d'être was to judge others on his own terms. And what was irritating was, Sasha did have a good bullshit detector, so on the one hand he picked out well and correctly her partner John's phallocentric behaviour.

But the Elders there had to be met in a different way, their way; a way opposite to Sasha's way.

> They present by giving you nothing much and waiting to see what you're going to do. [...] Sasha never had the sensitivity and time to [...] get past that point and think, here's a person who actually might have something I might be interested in. [Riebe interview]

While it's understandable that he was suffering from missing the familiarity of city life and accustomed society, it seems sad that he never examined his use of 'they' as in this letter describing his life at the farm:

> Dear Margie, I am here almost by myself on and off for the next two months — Inge is on some Buddhist retreat in Canada and Tibet — I ask very little of this side of her, and John is in and out on his Aboriginal business. I'm

not surprised that Darcy was an octoroon, this is the only place I've been to where there is a genuine Aboriginal-non-Aboriginal mix though the local mob, the Bundjalung, have maintained an identity despite everything, one which I am only beginning to fathom. (If you detect a bit of cynicism, it sure's there.) Whitey culture and history might be an explanation to their difficulties, but it's their diet that's killing them. MEAT! I've never seen such MEAT-EATERS — beef'n'pork. Trust them to live in the Cattle Capital of Australia. Meat, white bread, milk tea and sugar, sweet biscuits, jam, coke, corner store vanilla custard, tinned ham, and lashings of butter. They'll come at rice, but not that keen on brown. And salad, let me tell you about salad. A few came around for Sunday lunch to say goodbye to Inge. At 3.15 for lunch. I cooked and was truly pissed off. Sat in my room tinkering with my files. Said, everything's ready. I'm not angry, I've had lunch. Emerged. They didn't know what to do with the salad. Didnt like it but made a small effort. It had some parsley (home) rocket (home) coriander (home) bits of red lettuce (not yours yet, it's just coming up) chinese cabbage and something that looks like bok choi, tiny fennel (yum) beetroot tops and a bit of english spinach (all home). COULD ONE ASK FOR MORE? Yes, more white bread.

I hate to say this, but they're not generous. You know, all the times I've cooked and they've come around — no one has ever brought anything. I have never been invited to anything, but then I am not useful to their causes; the conversation always revolved around THEIR culture, which is interesting at first, but pales on repetition. No one has asked me who I am or what I do, though I'm sure I have been on the gossip. [SS letter to Margaret Fink typed 26.6.2000]

Soldatow saw only one way to judge taste: his way. He did not examine his understanding of how one's taste is formed, or seek insight into how people of quite different culture won't engage in the same way you expect, or wonder if one reason might be fear of being judged for it, of making a wrong approach. Who would ask someone so judge-y into their homes?

Inge Riebe understands that Sasha did not feel it was an equal relationship with the elders coming to the farmhouse. From her point of view, those people were giving her unbelievable amounts of information and took her to their sites; in return hosting a meal for them was nothing. But Sasha wasn't getting what she was. She can see how it was for him. She links his non-tolerance to his greater qualities.

There is an element in the idea of tolerance and relativity and allowing people to be something from their own position that directly confronts Sasha's sensibility about what is — I don't know — aesthetically correct. There's a rightness [for him] which is a mix of slightly ethical but mainly aesthetical. [...] That's why his writing is so good. [...] If you're going to deal with people from other cultures, tolerance is unfortunately a necessary element before you get anywhere. And he didn't have that tolerance. But his not having that tolerance was also part of his incisive cutting through shit capacity...That's the context to put his xenophobia rather than ordinary racist shit. [Riebe phone 12.3.20]

Sasha was not in the best of shape

Inge knows that Sasha was not in the best of shape in Casino. She did not understand just how much at the time. It's only with later knowledge that she says one of the problems was that Sasha was on 'unbelievable' doses of valium, as well as alcohol.

> Because of Russia and the leg. Even before, I always knew Sasha drank, in the sense we'd have red wine together, but it never occurred to me that he had an alcohol problem, he was never an unpleasant drunk, I don't remember him ever really being drunk. I had no concept of him drinking. And the valium I didn't really know about. And he came to the farm with the sorrow over the Bruce thing. I did begin to wonder, as my stepfather had left me a whole lot of liqueur and whiskeys and I did notice they all disappeared but I never thought that was a bit weird. [Riebe interview]

Not realising the extent of his addictions, Inge enjoyed his company, and felt it was safe to leave him at the farm when she went on her next retreat.

> The only person actually living in the house with me was Sasha. And Sasha put on great dinners, and spent a lot of time writing, or sharpening pencils, and it worked pretty well. I was happy and everyone was amazed he was saying these things to me and I enjoyed it. Apart from the fact of the valium, and he was trying to go off it. I ended up going to India, as I went to India most years. [Riebe interview]

But that, going to India and leaving Sasha at the farm, turned out not to work out so well:

And if I'd had any idea of the valium and the mess I'd not have gone or I'd have taken him with me. But he had the place and the only problem I saw was that he didn't have a car and I put it on John that he was responsible to see Sasha got lifts to wherever he wanted to go and he was fine with that. Sasha though then tried to go cold turkey on the valium, he was taking enough valium to kill a cow, the doctor said, and he ended up in hospital, and I'm in India. [Riebe interview]

It wasn't clear exactly what had sent him to hospital.

Whatever symptoms he got by going off the valium and the grog too fast. And the doctor said he should take smaller doses and wean himself off. [Riebe interview]

It's not quite clear why then it was so difficult for him to leave the hospital. He was all ready, his box packed…

…but the phone thing with John didn't work and he was obviously in quite a bad state. And I've talked to John about it and said you should have been there, and John said, 'He rang and I went but he didn't wait.' [Riebe interview]

Sasha might not have realised it wasn't like calling a taxi in the city and expecting it in ten minutes.

So Sasha walked out, and had that as a horrible memory, that he didn't get the right service when he left hospital. [Riebe interview]

Somehow he got back to the farm; somebody would have given him a ride.

There is no evidence that Sasha sought medical supervision or advice for withdrawing from valium. An information site on addiction and detox advises:

Benzodiazepines like Valium are some of the most difficult drugs to go through withdrawal from, due to the severity and duration of withdrawal. For the majority of Valium addicts, the initial acute withdrawal lasts for an extended period of time, up to 90 days. The post-acute withdrawal phase is also often a difficult process as it may last from 18-24 months. [Addiction Centre]

some regrets and some puzzles

And soon after that, Sasha had moved again, and Inge began to realise the extent of his afflictions, leaving her with some regrets and some puzzles.

> I was still in India, and he then went to live above that pub [in Melbourne], which was a horror, by the time I came back. And I rang him and tried to get him to come back, but by that time he was quite bad, that was not long before the doctor said it's too late, your liver is done.
>
> And one of the reasons I feel so bad, I feel personally immensely guilty, I should have recognised that he had a problem, how did I not see it? And I should have made sure there was someone who understood it, because John and [the others there] didn't understand it, or I should have just taken him with me to India. That was a possibility, I had a good spot in India, it was fine, it was safe.
>
> The thing I don't have a handle on is Sasha and his addictions because I denied them, or they didn't come up for me to deny. I guess we lived in a world when people's drinking wasn't seen as a problem — did we even have alcoholics in the Push?
>
> He'd be drinking while cooking and at dinner but it all seemed normal range to me in those days. When did he drink all those weird things? — not when I was there, and that was all spirits. I can get the addiction but I find it infuriating that he didn't say to me he had a problem. I wasn't going to be moralistic. Maybe he was hiding it from himself. [Riebe interview]

Apparently Sasha was still working on *The Gloves of Mr Menzies* at the farm. Inge always valued Sasha's writing, and believes he deserved more recognition.

> I had a very high opinion of Sasha as a writer and when [others] got so famous I was, [they're] not half the writer Sasha is, I got so cranky. That's why it's great you're doing the biography as he never got the acknowledgment he richly deserved. [Riebe interview]

Sasha in a desolate landscape

During Sasha's time at the farm, Bruce Pulsford visited him there. Bruce had been having a holiday in Bryon Bay, which, he says, was near Casino.

It's not all that near, quite a long drive, and quite another world. Byron Bay, with its gorgeous beaches and its fame as a centre for surfers and hipsters and New Age-ish businesses, is full of trendy boutiques, beach resorts, yoga studios, smart restaurants featuring vegan options.

The road distance to Casino is about 80 kilometres; Casino is an inland country town, that celebrates itself as the centre of beef production. Indigenous people make up about 10% of the population, and nearly 90% are Australian-born. It's a tough part of the country, with frequent drought and the threat from nearby bushfire.

Bruce went for a day, and was left with an image of Sasha in a desolate landscape.

> It was a ramshackle place, it had some washing machines in the front yard... [Pulsford interview]

We tend to think of Buddhists as having a 'zen aesthetic', all minimalism, abundance by absence, tranquillity, neatness. A farmhouse in the Australian countryside is not likely to achieve that.

As Bruce remembers it, there had been conflict between Sasha and Inge, or perhaps it was just the sense that for all their like-mindedness her very different commitments, and the isolation from familiar surroundings, left him feeling very alone.

> I remember leaving, I remember him standing there, in a dry field, wearing a red and white striped shirt, one of his favourite shirts, standing there in the Australian landscape, like a figure in a Drysdale painting. Yeah, incongruous; he seemed a bit lost there. And he was.
>
> The lack of somewhere to live, it is just so undercutting. It really is. I haven't experienced it, I hope I never do, a lot of people do, it's terrible. And to care about Sasha, I didn't really have an answer for him. I couldn't fund him into his own apartment. [Pulsford interview]

Sasha left the farm in Casino, and now where could he go?

36

on the verge of being scared

Melbourne 2000–02

don't go back to where you've lived before [SS nd 'Seven Songs']

stop it or else I'll faint

When he first returned to Melbourne, to his mother's house, Soldatow, probably invigorated by the change to a familiar urban environment, for a while sounded bright and spirited, giving advice, connecting people.

If it was difficult to get on with his mother, it added to his repertoire of stories about her. And about how he was right.

> I lost my savings card in my room because my mother insisted on tidying up. [...] She had also ripped up two of my shirts because they were just rags with holes in them and who would be seen out wearing them? I wear them as pyjamas or with jumpers over them. I went crackers — we don't speak any more — just a polite hello — and she said, I'll buy you some new ones. No. I don't want cheap Chinese shit for fifteen dollars made by twelve-year-old girls who earn ten cents a week. The shirts you ripped up cost $120 and have lasted over ten years. 'Stop it, stop it or else I'll faint.' I couldn't help myself — you've been threatening to faint for fifty years, faint now. [SS email to JR [only initials shown] 22.9.2001]

And so on. To get away, he took the chance to mind the cat at his old friend Bruce Sims' place while Sims was away for a week, from where he wrote a cheerful letter to Margaret Fink saying he was walking 'like normal'. [27.9.2001]

That was a brief break from the reality that he really had moved back to his mother's house in Melbourne, that he had nowhere else to go.

After his mother's marriage ended in 1992, there was a protracted battle over property settlement. Lily kept the Vermont house while Valentine Sadovchikoff went to live in the Daylesford house, which meant Sasha no longer had access to it.

The place had always been a getaway he enjoyed, on his own or to invite friends to, where his only complaints had been when the family turned up too.

So now there was no getting away. That relationship with his mother was always marked by criticism, each of the other. Sasha wrote to Susan Varga about her racism, the long-time anti-Semitism replaced with 'anti-Moslem crap'.

At this time Soldatow's main medium of correspondence is email but sensibly he relies on prints-outs for his archives. He and Varga keep telling each other how they hate email, hate the internet, hate screens: a stance some of this generation seemed to think was virtuous.

Sometimes he is cheerful about where he is; writing in February 2002 to his longtime friend from the Push days, Liz Fell, about living with Lily (and Peter, a short-term partner of Lily's who had moved in), about life in the suburbs, he said, 'I'm actually finding it quite amusing living here.' More often, he admits how out of place he feels, as the unreconstructed radical and critical observer among old friends whose lives have changed a lot:

> Bristling with ideas but lonesome in Melb — it's not my city and all my old friends have children whom I've known since birth and now they're 28 with fucks and I'm sick to death of lunch parties where everyone is now an academic who has views on the GST and how expensive it is to send their kids to private schools (I arks ya) and almost all their marriages have busted up (what did they expect, to spend their whole life sleeping with the same person?) And here we go again, regressing to being a bit apprehensive of me because I'm gay and still hold to radical and idealistic ideas. They've lost their previous lives but can't quite understand what they've lost. [...] They own things, but that's a fragile delight. [letter to James Cristina 3.3.2002 2pp typescript]

'A fragile delight' indeed. He offers some acerbic observations of suburban life to another friend:

> I'm stuck in the outer suburbs and no one that I know of has written about their paranoia — all the windows and doors in the suburb are double-locked — just in case, of what? [...] My bedroom window looks out on an impenetrable fence and next-door's windowless red brick house. My mother commented I should close the curtains 'just in case someone looks in'. [email to Jane Mills 22.10.2001]

And so on.

A long poem written at the time 'Seven Songs' speaks about how it used to be, this street and house, and how it is for him now:

> my room is a mess
> I have always lived on the floor
> but I know where everything is
> unlike this mausoleum
> (the unfamiliar family home)
> which is the rest of the house
> where nothing can be used

And there's a repeated refrain:

> no one cares if it's tied with string
> or plastic rope
> as long as it appears tidy

Seven Songs: don't go back

'Seven Songs' is the first poem in a poem cycle Soldatow called *A Second Star*. He continued to work on his writing during this period, including this uncompleted but carefully outlined work; there are some completed poems and indications for the remainder.

> don't go back to where you've lived before
> the palm trees have been cut down
> the house is now six apartments
> with a driveway through
>
> the buzzer rings
> the buzzers ring to let you in
>
> no more sixty year lemon trees are left
> with their thorns
> and the garage is some kind of
> enclosure now for rubbish bins
>
> the buzzer rings
> the buzzers ring to let you in

The piece is full of the details of his life back in the suburbs he grew up in, back living with his mother who aroused such intensity and ambivalence in him, such annoyance at her ways, such empathetic attachment over the history she bequeathed him:

5.
my mother is cleaning grapes in the kitchen
hundreds of them
taking out the rotten ones
bought every Friday
when shopping in the Dandenong markets
where it is cheap.
listen to this tape, I say.
'I can't, can't you see I'm busy?'
as if she's preparing food for hundreds
at some blockaded city in the USSR
during the war

I take the upper hand
make her a real coffee
sit her down —
(it isn't easy to do, stuck in her ways).
'Only for five minutes'
she says, irritated

it is Bella Ahmadulina
who is her own age
and speaks her poetry
to her for over an hour

her poems are to Pasternak, Mandelshtam,
Marina Tsvetayeva, Anna Ahmatova
September and October
in Leningrad

she sits and listens to her own White Nights
she sits and listens in her own White Nights
while a late summer still rustles
like a carnival outside her windows

A footnote explains the reference:

from Anna Ahmatova, *Requiem* (my translation).
[...] The hot summer rustles
Like a carnival outside my window;
I have long had this premonition
Of a bright day and a deserted house. [22 June 1939 Leningrad]

[more on *Requiem*, and Soldatow's translation, in chapter 38]

waiting for a rain storm

Another poem in this cycle 'Kristallnacht' also proceeds with deliberation to contemplate details of living in the present, treasures from the past accompanying the threat of coming global atrocities:

> The night sits patiently with me
> as Montserrat Caballé and Maria Callas sing opera songs of female madness
> music from Aida, I Puritani, Il Pirata and Anna Bolena —
> I put some Art Tatum and Mario Lanza on for quiet relief
> waiting for this dirty war
> to begin; the continuation of WWII which
> despite all treaties and signatures
> never really finished —
> though some people on the wireless call it WW Four.
>
> In this cautious autumn summer
> with the trees just barely green
> the late summer flowers just aflower
> waiting for a rain storm to breeze in.
> Red rain is predicted
> from the dark clouds of morning which don't break —
> the occasional drizzle
> brings only lightning strikes
> to bushland trees, free fires
> with a hundred houses destroyed
> not to mention all the dead
> and a thousand grisaille miles to come.

Soldatow is a real writer: one for whom writing is, simply, necessary. In this work done with his health failing, his circumstances so uncongenial, unkind, the writing still is somehow imperative; it is precise, purposeful, principled.

The incompletion of 'A Second Star' is sad.

advice that will not be heeded

Bruce Pulsford wrote from Sydney, gently remonstrating with Soldatow for not having followed the advice to fill in forms that would help him obtain public housing, promising to keep helping him to do, and venturing to give frank advice that will not be heeded:

> SHORT LECTURE COMMENCES HERE You should — no MUST — think about doing something about going off the booze again soon. You may not have noticed it — my guess is you have — you're not processing thoughts and information very rationally at the moment [...] You know the only ones who bother to lecture you about this are the ones who still love you and care about you [...] [Bruce Pulsford email 6.9.2001]

Pulsford urges him to take notice and repeats an offer to put Soldatow in touch with people who can help.

Soldatow wrote back at length, trustfully confiding his worrisome state of mind, saying it's been the worst eighteen months of his life and ending

> And what it's not even a year since my ops but my moods and concentration change from half-day to day. [...] To be brutally honest, I'm on the verge of being scared at what is happening. I have lost control over myself and you know what that means to me. Don't know nuffing [sic] any more. Enuf for now. Lotsa love, me. [email to Bruce Pulsford 7.9.2001]

renewed his grievances against the Australia Council

In late 2001 Soldatow renewed his grievances against the Australia Council, threatening to take legal action again. When once more Soldatow had not received the grant he applied for that year, he claimed that the Council had not followed the directives of Judge Davies in 1990. In October he writes to the Council in combative, contemptuous tone:

> [...] Why send out five pages of PR rubbish and then later say you haven't the funding to send out a report on individual reports? [...] If I am not satisfied by the Council's reply, I will continue to resolve my litigation. [...] I am doing this for the common good; your boards have to become accountable, not hidden behind secrecy. [...] Maybe I don't attend the correct parties or launches/lunches. Get real and stop being a closed fortress. [...] [SS letter to Gail Cork, Australia Council 29.10. 2001]

In her replies, Gail Cork, then Manager, Literature, at the Australia Council, employed a polite, restrained tone.

> I'm sorry the outcome of your New Work application was not what you were seeking. It was an extremely competitive grant round and your disappointment is shared by many.
>
> Your email contains several damaging allegations, I will respond to each in turn. [Gail Cork email to SS 30.10.2001]

Cork goes on to point out that all applicants are told how to contact the Program Officer to discuss their reports, and refutes another allegation:

> It is inaccurate to say that 'only pushy people...can access this information'. Many applicants, many of them not at all pushy, take up the invitation to discuss their application directly with a program officer. Others prefer not to know the details of their ranking and scores; it can be gratuitously upsetting, particularly for those who scored poorly. [...] . [Gail Cork email to SS 30.10.2001]

Sasha did not care if his disappointment was 'shared by many'. There was only one of him. He seems to believe he was uniquely discriminated against; he seems to think he was specifically rejected out of an animus to his very being.

Soldatow replies a few days later with a very long email. Evidently he has been brooding. He hurls insults. Assessors are 'compliant morons', according to him (does this contradict his desire to be given a high marks assessment?)

He does not apologise for his mistakes, and actually says *I don't deal with underlings* in reply to the suggestion that he like every other applicant is invited to discuss his reports with a program manager.

Seeing this material makes it clear how different it is this time from the 1990 legal action. There is no meticulous study of the applicable regulations, and it doesn't look like anything that a sober lawyer could be persuaded to support.

> A reply to my correspondence with Gail Cork. [..] 'Your email contains several damaging allegations...' Damaging to whom? My further applications or comments? Is the Council above criticism? A while ago I wrote a letter to the Board suggesting various changes. Did I get a reply? Check my file, or has it been systemically destroyed as 'All notes are destroyed at the end of the [funding] [sic] meeting.'? I think you are treading on very specific legal obligations here — in effect the Funding Bodies are destroying any path to an explanation or review of decisions. I am glad you included this detail because the Council (if this is a directive) is acting highly illegally. I challenge this and put the Council on notice. [email to Gail Cork 5.11.2001]

That sounds like a threat.

> You write: 'Firstly you state there is nothing in the Assessment Meeting Report which indicates that an applicant can request details of their individual application report'. [email to Gail Cork 5.11.2001]

A long quotation from Cork's email comes here, and in reply Soldatow does not restrain himself:

> I don't deal with underlings. It is not a matter of a 'request' or an 'invitation'; it is an obligation on the Council's part. So don't give me all the crap about 'gratuitously upsetting' and some sweetener or being kind or providing a 'service'. We are not 'clients'; we are applicants and have the right to know. The Council might like to work in mysterious ways — I call it self-protective and authoritarian. What is your salary to provide this nonsense? [email to Gail Cork 5.11.2001]

There is a great deal more in this vein.

Emails show the time; that would be 2.36 in the morning, when that was sent. That time of day — night, really — is not noted for its calming rational effect. Of course, Soldatow is drinking while writing this, because he always is (but in spite of the illogic and insolence he gets his punctuation correct).

Gail Cork must have been working late later that day; her reply is marked 18.09 (I'm not sure the time marker on emails is always accurate).

She knows not to engage with the pugnacious tone and the slinging of insults.

With some polite acknowledgment of his demands, she goes on to clarify how files are stored and that his will take up to a fortnight to retrieve.

She then clarifies the categories of applications for New Work and points to the clear explanation of these categories in the handbook, then requests a clarification:

> While your emails leave no doubt as to your dissatisfaction with the Board's assessment process, it is not clear to me what you expect or what the Board and/or I might do to satisfy your present enquiries, short of awarding you a grant. If you could be more specific as to your expectations, I assure you I will do my utmost to assist.
>
> I will contact you again when the information from your archived files is at hand.
>
> Thank you for your courtesy. [Cork email to SS 3.11.2001]

Surely thanks for a courtesy hoped for rather than received. Perhaps it is an instance of the irony Soldatow accuses everyone there of entirely lacking. Cork was probably right that awarding Soldatow a grant would be the only way he might, only might, consider himself satisfied with the outcome of his 'enquiries'. In any case he never does tell her just what his expectations are.

In a personal letter a few days later, Sasha tells an always supportive friend about this new battle. He seems self-satisfied, he seems to expect approval as he quotes from his own emails. He seems to relish this — this is where he's putting his energy now. This is where the obsessive, painstaking side of his working self is employed.

Soldatow kept it up.

> Late 21 November 2001 to Gail Cork etc.
> Unless I hear from someone within 48 hours, not some underling, I have no option but to resort to legal action. It is not my preference. You must reform or drop dead into the confused oblivion which the Council has been acting in for years. I repeat, I have nothing to lose; the alternative should be obvious. With no respect, [SS email to Gail Cork 21.11.2001 22.35]

The tone was not likely to be productive. How deeply emotionally invested Soldatow seems to be in the Australia Council — he sounds as if he's having a quarrel with his family. His demands for attention, his posture of entitlement — it's hard to know where this originates. In the deep secret recesses of his mind, his psychology, there is a combative and intimate relationship between him and the Australia Council, personified by whoever he's dealing with at the time.

The calm legalese of his 1990 action is no longer employed.

If ever he considered a diplomatic approach, that idea had been truly abandoned.

He is now giving full voice to an extraordinary petulance, throwing out insults and making threats.

He wrote 'late' along with the date at the start; hard to know what late means to him, and why this detail needed to be noted. Certainly Soldatow was not one to know to refrain from pressing Send on an email written late at night.

Soon after, Soldatow once more threatens legal action.

> We go to court. Your advice has been very clever, extending the time after 28 days for me to lodge an application to the ADJR, but I am informed by them that I can extend the time. In your communications you have given me conclusions but no reasons. You ask why I am doing this — it was quite clear from the beginning the Council has not followed Justice Davies' direction. I will tomorrow lodge an application with the Federal Court. You will no doubt be informed. [SS email to Gail Cork 28.11.2001]

Inevitably, Sasha called upon Bruce Pulsford for legal advice and support, and obtained the services of a government solicitor. An application was made at the Federal Magistrates Court of Australia in Melbourne for an order...to review the decision of [the Australia Council] and claims 'that the Australian Council acted illegally on 25 October 2001 in my application and rejection for may application for a literature board grant.' [lower case in original] [Reasons for Judgment, Federal Magistrates Court of Australia, June 2002]

A great deal of paperwork was undertaken. Numerous affidavits were drawn up, sworn and signed. Evidence was gathered. And finally, the application was dismissed. The applicant did not appear in the hearing. The 'Reasons for Judgment' document is fifteen pages. The applicant was to pay costs.

Soldatow's costs were assessed as $3,009.92 (including $2,400 for counsel's fees to draft submissions, prepare for and appear at hearing); the Australian Government Solicitor advised that

> In the spirit of negotiation, we are instructed by the respondent to accept the all in sum of $1200.00 in settlement of the respondent's costs and disbursements. [letter to SS 13.8.2002]

What was going on in Soldatow's life? This is the time he is back in Melbourne, at first having to live with his mother. Things are not going well.

The rage and frustration, the sense of injustice, of not getting his due, seems to call for some psychologising about the family dynamic. But no explanation for any person's ideas and behaviour is ever definitive.

Of course a writing grant would have been the road to freedom, to being able to go wherever he wanted to go — at least until the money ran out.

the sensibility and the intellect and the breadth of understanding

Contributing to the brighter side of the early days of the return to Melbourne was a new avenue of support for the long-cherished ambition of writing a biography of Harry Hooton. Soldatow enrolled to do a PhD back at Melbourne University, 30 years after he had graduated.

He wrote to a few people about his discoveries of his own records as he proceeded in his application. To his step-sister Olga:

> An interesting thing has happened — I had to put in my university results from 1967–1970 for my scholarship application and of course I had no idea of what I did. Well, I paid my 20 bucks to find me in the archives and blow me down, second year I came top of History, which I didn't know, and I won an essay prize for a Russian essay which I knew nothing about (because I didn't attend many lectures). But the best thing was to find out

I had three 'unspecified honours' [...] for subjects which I did not study! [email 7.12.2001]

Repeating the discoveries of his undergrad achievements to Susan Varga, he also writes that people tell him he must have pulled strings to get Joy Damousi to agree to be his supervisor.

No strings had been pulled. Somehow Soldatow found out that Joy Damousi would be an ideal supervisor, and went to see her.

I visited Professor Joy Damousi in her office in a splendid new building at Melbourne University in April 2019.

She had not previously met Soldatow, or even heard of him, when he came to her with his proposal for his thesis on the life of Harry Hooton. She readily encouraged him as a mature-age student very keen to come back to university to do his thesis. She thought it was a great project:

> First of all the time was right to open up that area of study; [Hooton] has attracted a bit of attention but not a lot in terms of scholarly work. And Sasha I thought was the perfect person, he had the sensibility and the intellect and the breadth of understanding of the work and the creativity to create a context for that work. [Damousi interview]

That was a Sasha who still presented his sharp-witted, charmingly knowledgable, congenial side, and the project began promisingly.

> So I was really excited. I encouraged him, I said, you should put an application together. If I recall correctly, there'd been a gap since he had studied, so I would have made the case [to the university, to admit the candidate]; you say, this person is competent in terms of who they are and what they've done and their work since formal study. I thought that [Soldatow's proposal] was a great idea, so he signed on and we started the supervision. [Damousi interview]

Eighteen years have passed since then, but Damousi remembers him; she says the meetings with him were really interesting and engaging; he had great ideas, and a passion for his subject with a depth of understanding that was rare in PhD students coming in for their first year.

> You see a lot of students, a lot, and you don't remember their names, but I remember him, and it was less than a year, but it was really memorable, he was really creative and very engaging.
>
> I met with him once a fortnight, that's our standard meeting, maybe once every three weeks. He got ill over that period obviously but in the

early stages he was very excited and very engaged, very intellectual, very erudite. It was very engaging for me as a supervisor. [Damousi interview]

To undertake the study of Hooton and his life, Soldatow would have to cast a wider net, to study the times he lived and wrote in.

Absolutely and that's what we would have initially been discussing: set the context, the cultural context, this when additional historical material would have come into it. Probably we didn't get that far beyond that. [Damousi interview]

It had all begun so well. Then Soldatow began missing appointments, and eventually no longer turned up.

He was in decline and it was obvious at certain points — losing weight and slowing down quite a bit by the end of it. I just kept encouraging him, saying, take it easy, see what you can do, it's okay....But at certain points he had to cancel and couldn't come to appointments. [Damousi interview]

realised his decline

Soldatow himself realised his decline. When he was asked for advice on writing — Sasha's reputation as a good editor and mentor remained — he replied that material should be sent without delay, and confided his situation, adding something like a boast about his accomplishments:

send anything quick because I've got an enlarged liver — drinking and taking valium since I was 19 — and I think they want me to detox which means I'll be uncontactable for seven days while they play sickiatry [sic], own yr own life and painting therapy — they'll get a surprise when I tell them I'm represented in the ANG, the AGNSW, have exhibited at the Pompidou centre, Los Angeles, Moscow, Leningrad and most recently Hanoi. [email to Alexxk 14.1.2002]

Has he really exhibited in the Pompidou Centre and in Los Angeles and in Russia? Why would 'they' get a surprise, what difference would any of it make? This is in an email replying to someone he hadn't met who wrote asking for advice about writing.

drink happened

Talking of all the great things about Sasha there is much to remember and then the talk always goes to how broken he seemed to become, what happened? Drink happened, says Christos Tsiolkas.

> It sapped his imagination and it sapped his will. Partly it's part of the romantic notion of the artist that was part of Sasha, that genius takes flight whatever condition you are in. But to write is to work. [Tsiolkas interview]

The work, you've got to love the work more than you love other pleasures which often feel more like pleasures at the time. So you have to love something that isn't always pleasure, is more or less of pleasure for various writers.

That's what writers who keep on writing often say, writing is work, it requires its set hours and its sacrifices. A kind of addiction, perhaps?

Addiction to substances though can be a contentious area of definition.

I had one of those conversations about Sasha with the historian Humphrey McQueen, who later wrote to me:

> [A] stray thought occurs. In *Man Against Himself*, Karl Menninger distinguishes chronic suicide from acute. He puts alcoholism into the former. It has two of his characteristics of suicide: a desire to punish which turns into a desire to be punished but lacks the wish to die. He also suggests that the means for either type indicates why. [Humphrey McQueen letter dated 21.3.20]

Allow me to leave this kind of speculation right here. The literature of suicide and addiction is vast and various and in any instance cannot, in this writer's view, deny or solve an ultimate mystery at the core of human being-ness.

it was not a happy place

It wasn't only Sasha seeking refuge at his mother's house, his brother Michael had recently separated from his wife and also fetched up there.

Michael's daughter Natasha, who'd told me how tough her grandmother always had been [chapter 6], was then instructed by Lily to disown her mother, who Lily blamed entirely for the break up.

> Of course I was never going to disown my own mother and my father was disgusted that she would ever say that. I was so angry with Lily I wouldn't speak to her for a long time. My mother and father loved each other right

to the end but my father's story is much like Sasha's, he was an alcoholic. [Natasha Soldatow interview]

Natasha went to see the two brothers once at her grandmother's house.

And it was awful, [Lily] had started to sort of I don't know lose her mind a bit I suppose, and they would play on that, play jokes, but there were these three people on misery road and it was not a happy house. She still didn't want to speak to me, she didn't want to welcome me into the house. It was only because Dad and Sash was there that I was allowed. I know, sad isn't it, very bitter. [Natasha Soldatow interview]

Natasha and Valek told me that Lily even threw her sons out of the house, even called the police to evict them. Michael died first, Sasha in 2006, and Lily after her two sons. As Lily had left everything to her sons in her will, it was then rightfully meant to pass on to Michael's children, but a bitterly contested challenge to the will came from their cousins before things were settled. Had he not died before his mother, Sasha would have inherited enough to solve his financial woes.

like being in Italy

Around the time that Sasha stopped going to meetings with his PhD supervisor, he found a room back in the thick of things in Melbourne.

In handwriting, on the back of a card of Patti Smith's album *Land*, he wrote cheerfully to his old friend Margaret Fink:

Tuesday before May Day 2002. I've moved! I'm in a pensione (hotel) right smack in Lygon St Carlton. No postal address or phone yet — so it's the e-mail. I love it — like being in Italy. Saw Baise-moi — was the only person in the audience who laughed. Love Me. [postcard to Margaret Fink May 2002]

Still, he welcomed being rescued from that room, and the chance to return to Sydney.

37

we write for each other

Cremorne, Redfern, final years

So what is it that I admire about my days? The answer is their unpredictable constancy. The work that lies at the core of my living, which can so easily be defiled, that work is my abundant witness. Don't go easy on me, but judge me by that, judge me by my curiosity. [SS 1996 *Jump Cuts* 311]

only get one carload

After their happy first meeting in Hanoi in 1997, Jack Ellis remained a good friend of Sasha's when they were both back in Sydney. Jack helped Sasha to pack and move when he left the Bondi flat and moved to Inge Riebe's farm at Casino, where, Jack understood, Sasha was very isolated. Then when Sasha moved out of his mother's place in Melbourne and lived in a room above a pub, Jack talked to him on the phone, and worried about him.

> I knew he was down there drinking too much. Living in a pub is no good for anyone especially Sasha. [Ellis interview]

Jack decided to act. He was living in Cremorne, a suburb on Sydney Harbour's North Shore. A flatmate moved out. Jack thought this might be an opportunity to get Sasha out of Melbourne. He discussed it with his then girlfriend Monica.

> To her credit, she loved Sasha too, we agreed we could subsidise his rent. So we made these calculations, how much [rent to charge him], and it was only about $30 a week, so not a huge amount. [Ellis interview]

Jack and Monica were young, they had starting-out kinds of jobs, being clear on just what you could afford was necessary.

Jack knew Sasha couldn't get up to Sydney on his own. He offered to pick him up, but warned him he could only get one carload.

After an overnight stop, Jack arrived at around ten the next morning and found the pub, called Percy's. Sasha was sitting in the bar drinking beer. Sasha took Jack upstairs. He had a single room with a shared bathroom, and a single light hung from the centre of the ceiling. There was a bed and a desk and nothing else. He'd packed his stuff into boxes and wrapped his paintings in newspaper. He took Jack to lunch in a courtyard of a nearby house, 'a strange Mafia-esqe place', with a table of old Italian men playing briscola.

Jack slept on the floor among the boxes in the very small room. The next day they loaded Jack's Volvo station wagon with Sasha's boxes and paintings, and drove back to Sydney, again stopping for an overnight stay in a pub in Holbrook.

> There was a full-size submarine on display in the park across the road from the pub. We walked all around it and I climbed on top to look out at the view. [Ellis interview August 2018; email November 2019]

the rhythms of Sasha's daily life

Back in Sydney, when Sasha moved into the house in Cremorne, Jack became familiar with the rhythms of Sasha's daily life, recalled now with a kind of tenderness: the drinking, the radio, the lucid-dream conversations.

> He had a routine where he'd rouse around four in the morning, he always had by his bed a bottle of wine, a glass and a big jug of water, with all of the discarded fruit peelings of the house, lemon peels, bits of mint, an evolving jug of water. So he would alternate drinking water with wine all day. He listened to the radio incessantly, particularly Radio National early in the morning. You'd come in and he'd be lying like a kind of pope lying in state [arms crossed across the chest] and he'd be engaged in these intense mental conversations with people; they were often provoked by things on the radio, with people on the radio, or with old friends [...], this kind of elaborate mental dialogue.
>
> I knew it wasn't real but he'd report his conversation with my dad for example and it was exactly what my dad would have said. It was almost like he was engaging in some kind of telepathic communication. [Ellis interview]

It had been a while since Sasha had had a good kitchen at his disposal. Food preparation was as important here as everywhere else Sasha stayed; it was his territory, it was a pleasure he was pleased to offer. He'd make the dinner most nights. Jack and Monica went out early to their jobs; Sasha went out later to shop.

Shopping, cooking, that was his day, a bit like a Babushka.

He'd walk to the op shop in Mosman almost every day, it was his exercise routine, but it was difficult for him because it was before his hip replacement.

He'd often come home with something like three new forks [or] with little vases and glasses and bottles, and framed pictures. He'd stop at the greengrocer and buy something for the house. Then he'd arrange the herbs or fennel fronds in the kitchen like a cascading Caravaggio still life. He'd punch the pictures out of the frames and hang the empty frame on the wall until he found something to put in it, often they'd just stay empty. [Ellis email November 2019]

Sasha's food choices could be a challenge to his housemates. Once he captured a lot of snails and 'purged' them in a tub on the back veranda. On the day it was time to cook and eat them, he found that they had banded together to move the heavy dinner plate off the plastic container so they could escape.

So he wrote this fantastic article about that, called A Great Tragedy, and it was all about the French bistros of early Sydney, and it was about capturing the snails to eat, and them escaping. [Ellis email November 2019]

He'd cook these kind of rustic French/pan-European kind of dishes. One he used to do — chicken cacciatore à la Provence, he'd say it was called. And he'd do a 'rat' which was a ratatouille. And you'd come back home and there'd be these soaking fatty European stews sitting on the bench warming up, and you'd try to put them in the fridge and 'no! This is how they're meant to be!', half fermented. They were always really yummy. If you bought cheese, even in the summer, you'd have to leave it out, there'd be cheese kind of migrating across the bench top [laughs]. [Ellis interview]

And there was a garden, and where there was a garden Sasha gardened. Jack planted a patch of corn in the corner of the back yard and Sasha tended it, picking snails off each day. There was the time he harvested the corn, but Jack and Monica didn't come home for dinner...

We'd tell him if we weren't coming but he'd forget, so he sacrificed the whole crop of corn as a way of punishing us for not coming home! [Ellis interview]

Sasha got on well with the little dog, Gotham, and would sit out on the back desk with Gotham, smoking, reading.

It was delightful, Jack tells me, to have Sasha living in the house. The two shared a creative time. Jack was writing songs. Sasha working in visual media as he always had from time to time. He created a few paintings, and collages made from the paper and tickets from the cinema, theatre, or ferry that he still collected. And he was curious about Jack's music and would give feedback. Sasha must have loved being in Cremorne, with his kind and interesting young hosts, who'd have people around, and give parties. Not that he had the same party energy he once had.

> His catch phrase at the time, he wasn't that well, at three or four o'clock, he'd say, I've overdone it. He'd have to go to bed for a while because he'd 'overdone it', and the whole time he was sipping red wine all day. [Ellis interview]

Nicholas Pounder recalls that it was at this time that Sasha told him 'only ring me between eleven in the morning and one pm'; it was such a contrast to his usual 'anytime' that it made Nicholas worried about Sasha's state.

attempts to help

Sasha spent a lot of time in bed. At first he might have been going to rest and recover just for a while, then do something more active.

The age difference might make you think Sasha's affection was paternal but Sasha didn't really do paternal. Jack Ellis says they were more like loving brothers.

> One aspect of our relationship that I think vexed him a bit, I was always trying to help him, get him somewhere to live or something like that, and sometimes he felt I was hassling him. [Ellis interview]

There were reasons for these attempts to help.

> I've got kind of a fairly fatalistic attitude about what people do with their lives as long as they're happy about it. The hard thing is if they're unhappy, not satisfied, and not doing anything to change it. And that was the aspect that was frustrating. He'd express a desire to change things or reduce his drinking but not do it. He'd still occasionally go and have lunch with Maggie [Fink] but there was less of that.
>
> I feel I'm speaking ill of the dead… [Ellis interview]

As Sasha would say:

> (Bugger the moralism that says it is not polite to speak ill of the dead.) [SS 1996 *Jump Cuts* 143, this line also in 'Suicide or Self-Deliverance?' 'Wild Card' 6.5.1994]

...but his drinking was out of fucking control. He'd actually reduced his drinking but he was comfortable drinking three bottles of red — a day, yeah. Not [expensive] if you drink the crap he was drinking, spending $20 a day on three bottles of wine. [Ellis interview]

The effects of that were complicated by the other addiction, the valium. He was taking a lot of that as well.

Jack at some point realised that Sasha was a valium addict, a serious addict, that he'd been prescribed the drug at age seventeen (in some accounts at nineteen) and never stopped taking it.

Sasha would express his desire to get something published.

And we'd say okay why don't you do a little pitch, a proposal, and we'll help you get it to them. And we'd say weeks later, how's it going, and he hadn't done it. He'd say he wanted to do things but not do them. [Ellis interview]

using letters to get back into writing

What Sasha did work on was writing letters, and sorting his papers into folders, the ones in the boxes in the Mitchell Library at the State Library of NSW. (Ten boxes had been deposited in the Mitchell Library in 1996. The rest of the collection of 40 archive boxes would be deposited after his death.)

He'd say 'I've been working all day, I've been writing letters to people. It is work because I archive them.' And he obsessively maintained his phone directory, he'd ring people up and say, is this still your phone number, I'm updating my teledex; he had pride in having everybody's phone numbers.

At this time it was almost like he was preparing for his own legacy, he spent a lot of time filing. So, great you're doing this [biography]. [Ellis interview]

Sasha filed his letters according to the name of his correspondent, not by date. In one (crammed) box there's an index of all the letters in each folder in that box.

From Cremorne, Sasha wrote letters about the drugs he was taking, which included Capadex: 'still experimental' — it's an opioid painkiller, no longer prescribed — and confided his state, while trying to sound upbeat as well:

I'm still in a bit of a mess and don't want to bore friends, just return to the Sash I was (which could be more boring). I'm lonely and for once in my life don't know what to do about it. Can't find meeeeself — not the inside which I know only too well, but the outside which I appear to have lost. Nevermind. At least in the midst of life I am not in Perth. [letter to Ian Harrison 20.7.2003]

and who are you writing for

Jack also witnessed the effect on Sasha of his long estrangement from Christos Tsiolkas. He says it broke his heart.

When [Christos] is there in front of you he's the most engaged, caring and listeny human being. But at that time, he used payphones and didn't want to get a mobile. And he didn't have email, so Sasha wrote him letters. Christos's writing was going well and maybe he felt a bit besieged by people. So I think Sasha fell into a sort of crack and he gave up trying to communicate to some extent, out of pride. [Ellis interview]

Jack also remembers the event that publisher Jane Palfreyman and others have spoken of, where Christos Tsiolkas was speaking about his new book *Dead Europe*, and Sasha was in the audience.

Sasha was a total mess, I've never seen him so upset and distressed. He was trembling, literally trembling; he got up to ask a question, but he made a long statement that was irritating to the room, a long quotation, about the book and why there was so much advertising at the beginning of it. But the question that he got to eventually, was, and who are you writing for? And Christos said, I think we write for each other. Writers write for each other, we write for other writers. And it was a nice line, and I think that's what Sasha was doing, he was writing for other writers. [Ellis interview]

Writers writing for each other, however, was not in the spirit of the times.

Jack Ellis understands Soldatow's troubles in getting published and recognised as due to two main factors. One was his reputation of being difficult in terms of editing: he was known to be 'very emphatic'. And the other thing was what had become publishing's guiding principle, the 'market'.

You can have these excellent creative literary works...you have these very enthusiastic editors: yes, we really think it's great; then you have one of these fabled marketing meetings, and some 24-year-old person is, what's the market, and they'll say we've got a cookbook from [a sports celebrity], we can see the market. [Ellis interview]

So many stories about publishing decisions made in the marketing department. Soldatow was writing to an 'audience', a readership, that was very small. That actually used to be okay, once.

I last saw Sasha

It was during this time that I last saw Sasha. Fittingly, it was at a party. I gave a party at a pub in Woolloomooloo for my self-published omnibus reprint *Three Sydney Novels* — the three novels had gone out of print and rights had reverted to me. The first of those novels was the one Sasha had edited long before it was published.

> [I]n the restaurant after the pub party there were two big tables of animated people, all of us eventually moving around the seats, a convivial meeting of various people I'd known in various eras and locations. At one point Sasha and I had a chance to have a moment and we sat and looked at each other, and finally, very dryly, he said, So, success at last. As you see, I said the same way. That night, he met some new people — he did always rejoice in meeting new people — and charmed them to bits with some of the stories out of a repertoire that I might myself not have cared to hear yet another time, partly because it was not very heartening to see his more recent alterations.
>
> It was you and me left at the end that night. You were staying with Bruce in Darlinghurst and I dropped you off in a taxi. You insisted on being left at the corner, but had a lot of trouble just getting out of the cab. You refused to let me walk with you to the door. That stiff, unsteady, slow walk. The driver was really worried about you, and we did not drive away until you had turned the corner to the house; as for what was the matter with you I could not answer.
>
> The last thing I said to you was, Sasha darling do take care of yourself and the last thing you said to me, laughing, was, I probably won't. [*Really Talking*]

the only way to end the situation

In a pattern familiar to those who know his story, the charms of living with Sasha began to sour.

> He was pretty cheerful but even if someone's cheerful if they're drinking that much and lying in bed, it's a bit draining to be around. We'd be in

the front room watching television, and he wasn't much interested in television. So we began increasingly to have separate lives. [Ellis interview]

Jack and his girlfriend found Sasha resented this.

Once he said, 'there's only one side to you two and it's the outside.' It meant he felt we were a little clique and he was the outsider. It became frustrating. [Ellis interview]

Harry Hooton There is only one side to every question and it's the outside. [quoted by SS in letter email to Geoff Adlide 27.11. 2007]

So frustrating that eventually the only way to end the situation was for Jack and Monica to move out of the flat. 'We did a Bru on him,' Jack says, 'We moved out of our own place because it was easier than getting him to move out.' Jack and Monica left on an overseas trip.

you have truly changed my life

Once settled elsewhere, Soldatow contemplated what Jack and Monica had done for him. On 11 September 2004 he wrote to them with understanding and appreciation:

Thanx youse a lot. I love you both, not in that order! (a feeble joke). Honestly, you have truly changed my life; I mean that not flippantly but honestly. Though I am still basically an anarchist there is a part of me which is almost 'communist'; I wait for the next 'five year plan' to happen and surprisingly it has again. One day I will document all my five year plans, not that they were planned like in the Soviet Union style. But they've been consistent and happened regularly. If there's been one constant in my life, it is — just wait. Something will happen which I won't expect. Jack, you finalised one five year by bringing me back to Sydley [sic] — for that I am eternally grateful (which always reminds me of cleaning out the remains of a fire last night). Expert as I am in words (well that's what I think) I cannot express my gratitude (horrible expression) in any other way. Except you cleaned me out of the personal grate I was in. You may be more intuitive than I was at the time. Perhaps always — I don't want to use the love word between us — it is redundant. Sure, conversations, laughter, humor and sometimes arguments (infrequent) infused our friendship. Still does. So the word 'love' is almost impertinent to use. I'd rather say something like FOREVER and leave it at that. [SS letter to Monica and Jack 11.9.2004]

a wonder which I have never known

Once more it was Bruce Pulsford who came to Sasha's rescue, organising a government housing flat for him in Morehead Street Redfern in mid 2004.

> I'm tempted to change the name of my abode to Less Mind Street — every morning when I wake up, I look out and see hideous high rise buildings and think, am I living in Moscow? [6.10.2004 typed letter to Mister Wood and Christina McKinnon]

As it happens, since 2018 I live in one of those high-rise buildings — not hideous inside; good view — opposite some fancy new low-rise apartments built where the crumbling old flats Sasha last lived in had been.

In Redfern, Sasha realised and admitted how very dependent he'd always been on others. He reports learning that his new phone number came with recent new features, and a realisation of his habitual dependency, amounting to ignorance of everyday matters:

> [...] [I]f I'm not here, hold on and you can leave a message (I don't know how I got this service). I realised the other day that I've never lived alone, always leaving small facts like these to others who know these things and I've never learned how to pay a bill. [...] [letter to John Fink 17.8. 2004]

Sasha continued to write many letters here, and part of his writing and focus was the new experience, in his late 50s, of living alone, finding, as anyone who loves solitude knows, a new experience of the self:

> It's a bit strange having my own home, forever, it seems. Should I feel like a home owner? I feel quite a bit disoriented occasionally, only momentarily — when I reach for my glass of night water and it's not there, on the other side, or my glasses. As if I don't know where I am — sometimes various places in Melbourne, Sydney, Hanoi, Naples, even Moscow or Leningrad. I don't think I've ever lived alone before and can do as I please — have a piss in the nude. I hear phantom voices interrupting my privacy as if I'm in some other place, the clack of feet of other people going to work, calling me to breakfast or lunch or wondering if I want to go out. Oneness is the word. It is a wonder which I have yet to get to know, in fact have never known. That there is no interruption or expectation — there is only ME doing what I want. Still, and I think I've told you Nina Hagen's quote — 'Future is now.' Perhaps in time I might get irritated with this but that is a later concern. At the moment I like the solitude — strange for someone like me. It's like I've

always given too much of myself (and to be totally truthful) have expected the same from my friends. [27.7.2004 to Ian Harrison]

to get back into writing and concentration

Soldatow writes to old friends, new acquaintances, people he hasn't met. He confides, pontificates, recalls, advises. He tells people about physics, art pieces, art history, flowers, correct word usage, words they should know, the 'history wars'; he offers stern advice about health, details of his own doctor visits boasting of his special treatment, critical accounts of concerts, further points to be made after a conversation. He writes to ABC Radio luminaries Sandy McCutcheon, Andrew Ford, Phillip Adams, Geraldine Doogue, Julie Rigg.

One of the letters contains a parenthetical anecdote about taking LSD:

(Once, and only once, I took a tab of LSD, had five valium carefully positioned just in case, didn't know how I would react, it was in Kangaroo Valley. Everyone had gone to bed and I spent about seven hours talking to the wood fire till someone yelled, 'Sasha, will you just shut up, we're all trying to sleep!' By then it was a beautiful misty dawn. Haven't got a clue as to what I was talking but next day the valium were still in place. Someone started to say, 'Next time...' Well, there was no next time and my friend the fire was out.) [25.10.2005 to Gavin McLean]

Sasha wrote that he was using letters 'to get back into writing and concentration'. Letter writing as work was a kind of freedom; the writing took him to wherever his mind went, often to questions of writing itself:

I hope you enjoy my missives. They bring back so many memories which I am translating into writing, letters sometimes not accurate — partly fiction. I'm sure you don't mind — if you do, well fuck you — you don't have to read them closely, if at all. I hope they give you a fragment of a larf tho. You don't have to keep them; I keep copies. They are, after all, MY JOB. Without this there is nothing much else. Oh, my god, have I really said this? Yes! I can't live without WORK, whatever it is. (I also can not live without my friends.)

[...] I'm trying to finish a work called 'Beyond Love' which leaves me slightly nervous. Why? Because I don't know what I'm talking about, don't quite know what I am trying to express. And yet I KNOW. It's a strange contradiction; knowing something that you can't put into words or paintings — even music fails. All of them (and film) fall into interpretation, which are a form of solipsistic mutilation. [letter to Ian Harrison 21.9.2004]

He received heartening expressions of fondness and understanding from his loyal long-time friend George Papaellinas, who, while confiding the worsening of his own health with multiple sclerosis, was warm and encouraging towards Sasha:

> Jeez, you've had a tough year, but you're properly and well-seasoned. You've handled it! Good on you! You're a hero, however ideologically problematic the very idea of a special person is, a leader. Greeks have always been 'into' heroes, ever since Homeric Bronze Age times. [letter 10.2.2004]

his new neighbourhood

Typically curious and active, Soldatow began to know his new neighbourhood, advising a neighbour on what to plant in an urban front yard and how to trim a tree, sending letters of complaint about the state of the building and noisy residents. When there began to be talk of demolishing the building and relocating all of the residents, he decided he was going to plant a Wollemi Pine to delay or prevent the demolition. [Ellis email November 2019]

Sasha wouldn't stop talking

In Redfern Sasha lived as he always had, decorated the place in his own idiosyncratic way. Sasha's niece Natasha always visited Sasha when she was in Sydney, including at Redfern. His place was just what she expected...

> There were papers everywhere, he had this beautiful table that was covered with artworks and books and dead flowers, and he was always so hospitable, so he'd been to the market and bought prawns and other things, and we sat on the floor of his apartment and ate and talked and drank wine. He was how I always remembered him to be, you know eccentric, funny, we could talk and talk, he had the ability to talk like there was no one else around. [Natasha Soldatow interview]

And Sasha had a unlikely companion, Natasha recalls, one he cared for:

> I remember we were sitting on his carpet in that little room and this little mouse came out in the kitchen. I saw it run across the floor, and Sash said, oh he's a friend of mine, and this little mouse came and sat with us, in this little circle, and Sash gave him a prawn and he sat there and ate it. [...] And

Sash said, the last one I had some bastard killed it, it used to live behind my oven and a friend came and shoved my oven back and squashed my little mouse, and he was really sad about it, that his original mouse had passed away. And this was his new mouse. [Natasha Soldatow interview]

What did Sasha talk about to his mouse?

Sasha even held a party at his Redfern flat, only a small party now; many old friends had dropped away.

'Liz Fell still turned up, Bruce still turned up. Maggie, but she was increasingly impatient with him near the end, same reason everyone was, failure to help himself,' says Jack Ellis; he and Sasha were kind of best friends in that period. There was one particular visit to that flat:

I know exactly what day it was, 17 March 2005, because I had my first date with my wife, Alice, and we had planned to have a picnic but it was raining so we met at the Powerhouse Museum and basically had a pub crawl till we got to [near] Sasha's and I rang him and said, I've met this girl and what are you doing. So I brought her round. And I had my yoga mat and swag there so I could always stay at Sasha's if I needed to. So we arrive and Sasha starts talking...and at some point I kissed her and we were having our first kiss there on the swag on the floor of Sasha's living room and Sasha wouldn't stop talking and at some point I said, fuck's sake Sasha shut up can't you see we're having our first kiss. [Laughs] That was thirteen years ago. I'm glad she got to meet Sasha. [Ellis interview]

That was the flat where Christos Tsiolkas visited Sasha for the last time a few months later, and had the night on ecstasy with him watching television, and as everyone who'd been close to Sasha did, tuning right back in to the sense of un-dissolvable intimacy and irrepressible laughter that he created.

Jack Ellis continued to visit Sasha in Redfern. Mostly their relationship took place at home, they almost never went out. But Jack remembers the last time they went out together. Sasha rang him, saying he had free tickets to go to the Five Dock RSL to see the Tarantella performed and would Jack go with him.

And this woman did a fantastic version of the Tarantella. And Sasha got up and danced! Danced sort of like this. It was enchanting. At his funeral I played the Tarantella and told the story of that last time. [Ellis email November 2019]

one day Bruce Pulsford was worried

One day in 2006 Bruce Pulsford was worried that Sasha had not picked up the phone for a while. He went round to the flat in Redfern. What he found made him call an ambulance at once. Sasha was taken to St Vincents Hospital where, falling into a coma, he spent the last days of his life.

38

memory becomes a moral category

translating Ahmatova

Anna Ahmatova was one of the greatest poets of the 20th C. Requiem *and* Poem Without a Hero *simply stand out as almost unique in Russian and world literature. The problem with a lot of her work is that it is very difficult to translate.* [SS typescript notes in folder 'Ahmatova']

The final piece in his prose collection *Mayakovsky in Bondi* (1993) is Soldatow's own translation of *Requiem*, the devastating long poem, or poem cycle, by Anna Ahmatova. She wrote and rewrote it over years. It's an account of the sufferings of Ahmatova and uncountable others in the times of the Stalinist Terror (1935-41), beginning with her experience of standing with others outside a jail where her son was imprisoned, waiting, for seventeen months, for news.

Speaking about his choice of this translation for his collection Soldatow said, speaking of his own work as a dialogue with history:

> I close with my translation of Ahmatova's *Requiem* partly because she is a survivor and radical form is forced upon her because of it. [SS in Kiley]

In this interview Soldatow says he still feels he has the identity of a DP, a displaced person. All DPs are survivors of some kind; not that they all turn to radical forms (some strive for assimilation, acceptance, passing). But for Soldatow the radical form and his identification with displacement are inextricable.

> **could one ever describe this? I can**
>
> The hour has come to remember the dead.
> I see you all, hear you, feel you
> [from *Requiem* by Anna Ahmatova, translated by SS]

To remember the dead, to remember the atrocities that brought about their death, to remember suffering, to remember and remember — that is what *Requiem* demands. Who doesn't want to turn away, who doesn't want to be free from thinking about all that horror, who hasn't had enough of knowing the worst that humankind has done to its own — but *Requiem*'s language is so compelling, forceful, arresting, that the reader must bow to the imperative to pay attention. For this is what they insist on, the survivors, of Holocausts and Terrors, of concentration camps in the present, that people should know.

> During the frightening years of the Yezhov terror, I
> spent seventeen months waiting in prison queues in
> Leningrad. One day, somehow, someone 'picked me out'.
> On that occasion there was a woman standing behind me,
> her lips blue with cold, who, of course, had never in
> her life heard my name. Jolted out of the torpor
> characteristic of all of us, she said into my ear
> (everyone whispered there) — 'Could one ever describe
> this?' And I answered — 'I can.' It was then that
> something like a smile slid across what had previously
> been just a face.
>
> [The 1st of April in the year 1957. Leningrad]
> [from *Requiem* by Anna Ahmatova, translated by SS]

Years before he published his translation, Soldatow referred to *Requiem* to illustrate a principled person's response to the world:

> You can't sit still in a corner and just look when the world around you demands an answer, or a commitment.
>
> Commitment has become a very strange word. It has been grossly devalued, broken, sent to the graveyard, like many words these days. Some of them have managed to cling on, barely alive, on the outskirts. Like Truth, sent to end its days breaking stones in the Gulag with Idealism, coughing its lungs out. And Morality, planning revenge and egging Poetry on, quoting the words of a peasant woman to the Russian poet Ahmatova, 'You are a Poet. You must remember this and one day write it down.' [SS 1990 'Introduction']

burnt the scribbled drafts in the ashtray

This series of poems by Anna Ahmatova 'represents a sublime example of the poetry of witness, and it demonstrates how art can transform ugly, painful and ephemeral existence into real and voiced experience that the whole world will want to commemorate,' said Australian composer Moya Henderson, who had long wanted to set *Requiem* to music; she first presented her tribute at the Sydney Opera House in 2010.

She said that Ahmatova intended the suffering of the women of Leningrad to stand for the suffering of humankind.

> Stalin's purge was directed most specifically against men, the most likely challengers to the power of the dictator. However, certain women — those as significant as Ahmatova was to her people — also posed a threat to the regime. For this reason, the poems of the Requiem could never be kept as written documents. Ahmatova and her friend, Lydia Chukovskaya (a novelist) learnt the poems by heart, then burnt the scribbled drafts in the ashtray. [Moya Henderson]

it may seem that the problem is in the Russian language itself

In his archives, Soldatow kept many photocopied pages from various texts: translations of and writings about Ahmatova.

He wrote notes on translating from Russian.

In Moscow in 1991 he had with him translations into English by Elaine Feinstein and Amanda Haight but like other Russian speakers was dissatisfied by them. Soldatow would have known what Joseph Brodsky said, that Russian poetry had not been lucky with its translations into English:

> It has been so unlucky that it may seem that the problem is in the Russian language itself — a synthetic, too flexible language which cannot be reproduced adequately in analytic English with its 'iron word-order'. Successful translations are rare. [Brodsky]

Brodsky is reviewing a selection of poems credited to two authors, working in what he calls the tandem method: one knows Russian, the other knows poetry. In this case, the result did not please him.

Sasha, though, knew both Russian and poetry. And he knew music.

the trembling fear inside a hollow laugh

Australian composer and festival director Jonathan Mills met Sasha in the early 80s through his friend from university days, Hannah Fink, who introduced him to the 'privileged, bohemian world' of her parents Margaret and Leon, where he inevitably came across Sasha. Lovely, gently charismatic, and often drunk, Mills recalls. They'd see each other at parties, meet the same people.

Years later, Mills accepted a commission to write an orchestral piece, as part of the commemorations for the Centenary of Australian Federation. The South Australian commission was to acknowledge the return by the Australian Army of the parade grounds in Adelaide behind the Festival Centre to the people of South Australia. Mills wanted to commemorate Lionel Matthews, a fearless South Australian army officer who won two Military Crosses in the process of the fall of Singapore and who was tortured to death in the Kuching prison in North Borneo in 1944. Matthews had been moved from the horrific prison of war work camp Sandakan. Of the 2500 remaining Australian and British troops in Sandakan, six survived.

Mills' father, a heart surgeon of distinction, had himself been tortured as a prisoner of war at Sandakan, and while he could not talk of that he told Jonathan of a kind of secret society, the recognition between people who had had experience of torture, a hyper-sensitivity to physical violence. There is not much that can be said to someone who has been suffering from the trauma of torture other than through poetry; the only response is a heightened state of empathy, his father told him. Familiar with Russian poetry, he introduced Jonathan to Ahmatova's *Requiem*, which he chose as one of the three texts for his new piece *Sandakan Threnody*.

But although DM Thomas and other literary luminaries had written translations, they tended to be flowery; none of them seemed quite right. 'Talk to Sasha,' advised Hannah Fink. Sasha sent Mills 'a torrent of emails.' They met, and Sasha gave Mills his own translation. 'And it was a revelation,' Mills tells me, and reads aloud some of the lines from *Requiem*'s Epilogue:

> I've learnt how faces fall,
> How terror can escape from lowered eyes,
> How suffering can etch cruel pages
> Of cuneiform-like marks upon the cheeks.
> I know how dark or ash-blond strands of hair
> Can suddenly turn white. I've learned to recognise
> The fading smiles upon submissive lips,
> The trembling fear inside a hollow laugh.[...] [Mills interview]

To Mills, this was the clearest expression of the stoicism that that generation took to the grave with them.

> I wanted to understand the Russian really well. Sasha brought me the Cyrillic script, and the transliteration into our alphabet, spoke it, then took me syllable by syllable through the poetry. I saw a very different Sasha, I

saw a person absolutely in command of a world, a very complete world. Much more than a world of ideas, a world that he brought with him from childhood, and a world that evolved with him from childhood in Australia. [...] Sasha's pain is in those few lines. [...] He was very moved by the context in which his wonderful translation of Ahmatova was to be performed: as a homage to, as an elegy to those who perished in prison camps in remote jungles, and I suspect he felt it was entirely appropriate for him to be present in this sort of context, there was something personally appropriate. [Mills interview]

I came to realise how extraordinary his translation was in comparison to [those of] some pretty exceptional literary figures of immense distinction. It's so much more musical, it's so much more sparse, and austere, but rich at the same time. [Mills interview]

Mills read Sasha's translation of the *Requiem* to a group of the surviving prisoners of war from Sandakan and their families at one of their reunions. They were all in tears, he says. As a consequence of their experience, they had built a carapace, they were habitually so very guarded, just as people would have been in the Russia of Ahmatova's time.

The only thing they had no defence against was kindness and beauty. They said to me, we don't need to be eulogised, we need someone to write something beautiful as a memorial. [Mills interview]

Sandakan Threnody was performed by the Adelaide Symphony Orchestra on the parade grounds on 21 October 2001. Sasha did not attend, but he did attend the performance at the Concert Hall of the Sydney Opera House, on 28 April 2004.

And as for the source of Sasha's familiarity with the pain and silence given expression in the *Requiem*?

I think his way of conveying [that] was the complete command of the poetic, linguistic and translational dimension in which his work resonates. It was a very well-tended garden. To which we were treated. And it was a very ordered garden in complete contrast to the disorder of most parts of his life. [Mills interview]

streets ahead of any translation I have come across

Probably heartened by his experience with Jonathan Mills, in 2002 Soldatow set out his credentials, and some requests, in an email:

> I am fluent in both Russian and English. I have translated AA's *Requiem* and am current working on *Poem Without a Hero* as a one woman play. I know there are many versions of this poem but it reads to me as a possible theatre piece. I am interested in ALL versions of the published work and any MSS. Most translations I have read are way off the mark, as with 'Requiem'. You first of all need to recognise her classical Russian, her allusions, her knowledge of Old Slavonic and then try the musicality of her language into a comprehensible English. I am not impressed by Proffer/Humensky's Ann Arbor edition, nor by Haight's (just as I am not impressed by Nabokov's 'Onegin' though the annotations are invaluable). I want access to originals — there is a publication in German of *Requiem* which contains material never published in Russian. Is there someone who can provide me with a checklist of available material on *Poem Without a Hero*? Any hints? In turn I can send you a copy of my *Requiem*, no strings attached. I don't want to sound arrogant but it is streets ahead of any translation I have come across. A part of it was set to music and performed in Adelaide last year. [SS email to 'Edward Bonver' 17.2.2002]

The part set to music was for composer Jonathan Mills. Soldatow concludes:

> *Poem Without a Hero* is dead set for performance (very demanding for actor) but excluding the forward and dedications.
> Keep in touch if you are interested or have any ideas. I'll send this again (I have) to yr e [...] Cheers [SS email to 'Edward Bonver' 17.2.2002]

It was sent to an email address that no longer exists and I could not find the intended recipient. I could not find if they were related to or the same as the Yevgeny Bonver whose translation is placed next to Soldatow's on a web page with details of Ahmatova's life and work. [Bonver]

Soldatow's translation of *Requiem* is quite different from the one by Bonver. The reader might contemplate how mysterious it is, the way languages can never be exactly translated, how variously languages might work; this is evident whenever different translations, especially of poetic works, are read side by side.

And maybe especially so when Russian, or another unrelated or only distantly related language that works quite differently, is translated to English.

no k in Russian it is AHMATOVA

Soldatow continued to make notes on translations from Russian. His notes are scholarly, knowledgable. He knows what he's talking about. He might have been a great translator of more Ahmatova, of more of the great Russian writers.

He arrived at a curious insistence; in 2004 he wrote

> ...there is no k in /Russian it is AHMATOVA [SS paper dated 21.12.2004, printed 15.5.2005]

What about Mayakovsky, though? The K in that? Apparently Sasha meant there is no K in Ahmatova's name; though the name is usually spelled Akhmatova, Soldatow came to insist it should be spelled without the k and began to spell it that way.

This was puzzling, to this non-Russian speaker, until explained thus by a long-time student and reader in Russian:

> [...] I notice now that it's the 'k' in the 'kh' pair Sasha took objection to, preferring to use just an 'h'. It's the transliteration of the Russian letter X, which is pronounced like the Scottish 'ch' in 'loch' and is almost universally transliterated as 'kh'. (It's almost always Chekhov, not Chehov.) There you go. I don't suppose it matters much whether you use an 'h' or a 'kh'. In 'Mayakovsky' it's a different sound: 'k'. [Robert Dessaix email 24.12.2019]

Soldatow was correct, his step-sister Olga Krasser told me. Still, I can't find other instances of the poet's name spelled without the K.

an inconsolable shadow looks for me

As things seem to get only worse in our world — any year of this century, at least — you might turn to Ahmatova's poem to express some of our shared desolation and search for hope or consolation.

Scott Horton, on his blog at *Harper's Magazine*, posted part of Soldatow's translation in 2007 — a year after Soldatow died. Horton is a lecturer at Columbia University, a human rights lawyer, and a contributing editor at *Harper's Magazine*; he had been counsel to Russian Human Rights activists Andrei Sakharov and Elena Bonner, who among other things was Anna Ahmatova's doctor at one point.

On the web page, because of a change of font for the site, the original Russian now is corrupted, but the translation, or part of it, is intact.

> If someone someday in this country
> Decides to raise a memorial to me,
> I give my consent to this festivity
> But only on this condition — do not build it
> By the sea where I was born,
> I have severed my last ties with the sea;
> Nor in the Tsar's Park by the hallowed stump
> Where an inconsolable shadow looks for me;
> Build it here where I stood for three hundred hours
> And no one slid open the bolt.
> November 14, 2007 [Horton]

Horton, who says he has a 'reasonable passive knowledge of Russian', replied to my enquiry affirming his choice of Soldatow's translation was well considered:

> I have long been an admirer of Anna Ahmatova and her poetry and of this poem in particular. I decided to post it and following my usual practice searched through existing translations trying to identify the best. I picked Sasha Soldatow's for its fidelity to the original and lyrical qualities. [Scott Horton email 1.10.2020]

the fallacy of my faith

In an interview in 2009, Christos Tsiolkas is asked about the works of fiction, poetry or art that shaped him. He named Anna Ahmatova's poem *Requiem* as an example of a piece that taught him something about the world's bitter realities: it made him confront the fallacy, he says, of his faith in Bolshevism. [quoted in Crikey blog 2009] Soldatow had introduced Tsiolkas to *Requiem*.

Requiem leaves us with the certain knowledge that faith in any ideology — political, religious — however idealistic its original intentions, might have to contend with the degenerate uses it might be employed for. (Perhaps with an inevitable atrophy.)

livre d'artiste

In late 2017 Nicholas Pounder, who says the work is too important to languish at the back of a mass-market paperback, decided to produce a limited edition publication of *Requiem*, with the original Russian poem and Soldatow's translation. It is presented as a beautifully designed creation with linocuts by G.W. Bot, the kind of object usually called *livre d'artiste*, Pounder told me; the kind of production that could not be hurried; hand-made, it would be produced on fine papers in a boxed edition, not exceeding ten copies.

From the late 1980s to the early 90s, Sasha had presented Pounder with a series of his watercolour self-portraits. They remain on Pounder's apartment wall. He can always be relied on to express appreciation for Soldatow's work, his 'diverse achievements'. As he created the *Requiem*'s very limited edition he hoped it would be held in public collections, and indicate Soldatow's seriousness about the poetic record.

> He was sometimes other than frivolous. To make something so special might seem contradictory, but for me it is carving a cross so to speak. [Pounder email 1.11.2019]

I ask Pounder why it might seem contradictory. He explained something about its aesthetic, and that it was Sasha who'd taught him so much about artisanal printing:

> In short because it is more Catherine the Great and Hermitage than Kropotkin — more St Petersburg than Leningrad. A New Left /post New Left artist book sensibility/aesthetic would have been more Ed Ruscha in Sasha's living antagonism. For myself, dogged by the internecine battles between the 'democratic multiple' and the 'livre d'artiste'. The designer collectible (livre d'artiste) would have been anathema to Sasha — the champion of appropriation. But then he was my earliest tutor in pre-press: he taught me the simple short cuts to imposition and printing from paper plates…and my second earliest memories are the scent of rubber solution and the flash of a scalpel. Light box and square were his dexterous dominating guide.
>
> In 1995 I saw in Portland, Oregon (USA) among the remains of the Russian diaspora, samizdat printing of Ahmatova bound into the frail cloth of folk headscarves. I thought of Sasha. [Pounder email 4.11.2019]

hypnotic intensity, chaotic structure

In 2020 the production was complete: the poem, the translation, the linocuts by Bot, and an introduction by Sasha Grishin which helps the reader appreciate the particular achievement of this translation:

> In 1993 the Russian-Australian intellectual, Sasha Soldatow, produced this new translation of the poem into English that captures more faithfully than its predecessors the hypnotic intensity of Ahmatova's verse with its lack of a unifying or consistent metre, the chaotic structure of rhyming patterns and its mixture of styles and literary conventions. Akhmatova seamlessly blends the language of the Gospels, folklore, Russian Orthodox Church ritual, and elegiac, odic and lyrical conventions with stark, chilling prose. [Grishin]

The boxed, limited edition copies were bought at once by the National Library of Australia, the State Library of NSW and the State Library of Victoria, as well as private individuals. These acquisitions fulfil Pounder's hope that it would be held in public collections.

One cannot doubt that were there an afterlife, Sasha Soldatow, fourteen years after his death, would be alert to this splendid production, its sincere tribute to the lastingness of his most careful work.

39
'I See'

the end (from interviews, emails, diaries, poems)

My challenge is to discover the joy of old age, but I suspect I'll have to invent it for myself [SS 1996 *Jump Cuts* 222]

Meredith Burgmann He'd lost the joie de vivre a bit and was drinking too much. I remember seeing him in hospital a few times. Repeated surgeries is what I seem to remember. I remember feeling sad when I saw him. I've had too many friends drink themselves to death. There's nothing much you can do.

John Fink Before he died, he was at Mum's still quite a lot, cooking, and I remember he was shaking a lot, he'd be picking these herbs and he'd be like [mimes shaking] and I'd look at him and I'd be, is it that you're just so used to it you can't see it.

Pam Brown It had happened already. His mind had been diminished greatly by his drug and alcohol use. He'd had to have the pin taken out of his hip, from the fall in Moscow, he'd had it in too long. Jane and I went to see him in hospital. We found him really boring, complaining about the menu; he was like the wingey-est of patients; nothing witty about anything he was doing… We said, he's not the Sasha we know. Then he used to ring me up at work occasionally, I was working at the library, and he'd go on and on and on about what was wrong with the drug and alcohol counsellor. Then he'd ring Jane and tell her the same thing…It was bizarre, it was a sad sad thing. I was open to him but I couldn't do those conversations. It was just terrible, he was so repetitive and nothing going on.

And one day he rang and said, I'm staying with Bruce and Guy now, and he said, there was a place called Dov on the corner, would you come and have a coffee, I said okay, I hadn't seen him for a couple of years, I thought okay, I thought good, maybe something will happen, maybe we'll re-constitute our friendship. Then about two hours before we were going to meet he rang and said he was going to a party, so he wasn't coming to meet me as that was more important, and I went okay that's fine Sash, and put the phone down, and I thought, I didn't want to meet him anyway.

Gill Leahy I felt I failed him in the final years; it was a thing everybody couldn't handle, watching him kill himself.

Jack Ellis When I talk to people about it, it would appear the hepatitis infection he got when he was living with Maggie, was actually what killed him, his liver was damaged by the hepatitis and rather than do what one should do which is take care of it he punished it further. It was swollen, he had a funny torso, that side of his belly would stick out, as far as I know it came from that Hep A infection, and his liver was sclerotic from that.

Meredith Rogers He rang me up so I brought him home here for dinner. It wasn't a happy encounter. The pub...Percy's... [was] not really anywhere anyone stayed, it was weird to be having a room there. And there was something slipping about the way he was dressed you know he was always so well...it was beginning to slip...I always felt as if I failed him. Because he was so generous.

Joanna Savill I hadn't seen him for a really long time. And I saw Margaret Fink [in 2006] and I said to her, have you seen Sash, how is he, and she said, he's not great but I do see him. She'd kept up with him because Margaret is amazing and keeps things going. She said, as it happens I'm going to have lunch with him at Otto, Margaret has a tab at all the Fink group restaurants, and was having her regular table at Otto on a Friday; she said why don't you come along and surprise him. I said I'd love to do that. I joined them and he was delighted. We had a lovely time but I was shocked at how shaky he was. I offered to drive him home to his apartment in Redfern. We went upstairs and spent the afternoon together, we talked about plants and gardening, he gave me a cutting of something in a pot, and we had a lovely time but I was shocked at how fragile he was. Physically fragile, shaky; mentally he was okay I thought.

[His apartment] in a Housing Commission block was fine, a bit shabby, a bit neglected, there wasn't a great sense of housekeeping, he had a lot of his things but he'd already given away a lot when he'd moved and stuff had gone to the Mitchell Library. No, he wasn't the same Sash but I wasn't the same, we had all grown up and done different things. But we had such a lovely time and I was so happy about it. Bruce used to pop in and see him, he was really amazing and he looked after him a lot in that period. And then of course one day I got a call from Bruce saying, Sash is in hospital, he's in a coma, do you want to come and see him, and I said, absolutely.

Sasha Soldatow The closer [the surgery] comes, the more daunting tho in a funny way I'm looking forward to it all — it's a bit like booking for OS trip and you want to go instantly.

Margot Nash I went to see him in hospital, I saw him two days before he died, I hadn't seen him for a while, I found it too hard, he'd deteriorated so much and was drinking so much. So I went in. I knew Christos was sitting with him in the daytime and I didn't know if anyone would be with him at night so I went in one evening and he was alone. And they say the hearing is the last to go, I don't think he could see me, I said, Sasha it's Margot, and he went [makes sounds]. He smelt terrible, he had that rotting liver smell, he looked terrible, he couldn't talk, but he knew I was there, I just sat there and told him what I was doing, and he knew I was there and he died the next day or the day after.

Joanna Savill He was not conscious; I still remember he was breathing very heavily, he had liver failure and looked dreadful. I sat with him and I said, I feel bad I haven't seen you for so long, and I have so many great memories…and you did so much for me when I came back to live in Australia and I thought this god-forsaken bloody country what am I doing here, and you made it seem so much more interesting, and I told him all those things very sad [crying] and he died a day or two later.

But I was happy I got to spend that time with him. Who knows if he heard any of it. He was such a special person, and in so many lives, and he was a mad crazy bugger and he used to irritate people and confront people and antagonise people and call them out on their pathetic behaviour but he had a great spirit and great talent and he had a way of looking at things from a different point of view, he was great at rallying people and getting people together.

Natasha Soldatow The last time I saw Sash was the night that he died. Bruce rang me out of the blue and said, Sasha's really sick, and he said he's in the hospital and he's not doing well, and within 24 hours I was in Sydney. Bruce […] said you can come and stay. We went to the hospital to see Sasha and that night he passed away.

Olga Krasser I spoke to Sasha for the last time [on the phone] when he already was not able to talk, but Bruce was sitting by his bedside and Bruce said he can hear. He was dying, and Bruce said, he can still hear and I'm sure he'd love to hear from you, I told him how much I love him, I told him we will renew our friendship when the time comes, and I talked and I cried, and Bruce thinks that he heard it all.

Valek Sadovchikoff I saw Sasha in the hospital when he was dying, and he was already in a coma. I spoke to him for a long time, and I could swear he was present.

Virginia Bell I visited Sasha in hospital when he was dying. Bruce and Christos were with him; his skin was yellow and he was comatose. The three of us chatted for some time. Whenever he stirred either Bruce or Christos leapt to comfort him. It struck me that while he may have alienated many of his friends, Sash had succeeded in inspiring real love in these two very kind men.

Pam Brown He wasn't in my life then, we were living in that little flat in Rose Bay, and one day Bruce rang and said, Sasha's in hospital and he's dying, would you come and see him. And I hadn't had anything to do with him and my immediate reaction was, oh no I don't want to do that, it was really strange, but that's what I said, but about an hour later I said, what was I doing. I did love this man a lot and we were very close friends so I rang back and said yes, what ward, and came up. And that day Christos was there, he had come and was sleeping on the floor. He'd come in to see Sasha and was so sweet, Christos is a loving person, there he was looking after Sasha. Someone brought some music in, some classical music that Sasha loved, I think Margaret organised that.

He was unconscious, but I think he knew we were there, he looked terrible, I won't go into that, he was all yellow as his liver had failed, he looked like a skinny little bird. And then I ran into Anne Summers in the street and I said you know Sasha's in there and he's dying. And she went to see him. There were so many people, lots of people came to see him dying, which was great. And I went again and I sang Mr Block, there was no one else in the room, because we used to sing that. [Sings softly] *Oh Mr Block you were born by mistake.* Do you know that song? [Sings] *Oh Mr Block you were born by mistake. You take the cake you make me ache. Take a rock around your block and go jump in the lake. And do it for freedom's sake!* You know, like solidarity sake or something. Mr Block was a boss and it was Joe Hill worker song. So I sang it to Sasha in bed thinking he'll hear me, he'll join in. So I'm glad I did go and say goodbye. But it was a very sad death I think. He just collapsed.

Jack Ellis Sasha had borrowed a lot of art books from the library, I picked them up from his place, I brought them [to the hospital], and he said, I wanted tincture, and I worked out he meant picture, so I showed him pictures, so the last thing he saw were landscapes from Cezanne, and he went into a coma, and they kept him in a coma and then he dreamt into death.

Ken Bolton

         An email from Pam
says Sasha has died
        — who might have quoted the line
    "All I want is boundless love"

            His *attitude*

might have quoted that—

[...]

I am glad to be alive
       — as Sasha was.

         "Heaps!"
I hear him say

       & see him momentarily
shoulders hunched together, leaning forward
holding a glass, at about eye height,
          a toast
to heaps of life, to boundlessness &
         boundless love—
& fun
    but really, mostly, boundless love

would you call his haircuts, usually, 'gamin'? His skin was
olive, his features fine, his lips were full. He was beautiful,
& alert.
    My friend. Gone.

[From "Boundless (Sasha)"]

Invitation

'Writer, painter, translator, musician, anarchist, cook, entertainer, drinker, rabble rouser, sometime-bohemian, collector of old tickets, explorer, encourager, friend to many."

Friends and relatives of SASHA are invited to attend his burial, Saturday next (September 9, 2006) to be held at Rookwood General Cemetery, commencing at 11 a.m.

Please meet at Rookwood General Cemetery Office, Hawthorne Avenue, Rookwood, at 10.44 a.m.'

Gillian Leahy There was a funeral at Rookwood. We meant to have it graveside but it rained so much the hole fell in so it was not possible so we were moved to a chapel. I sang, it was packed, there were people outside as well. Bruce gave a great talk.

Bruce Pulsford I was strangely enchanted if also troubled by his disrespect for conventional things, his wicked humour, his great success at surrounding himself with friends who adored him. I liked that he was Russian, that he said he knew a lot about painting and literature and music. I liked that he collected old tickets, could go on and on about mushrooms and artichokes, loved to cook and drink. I was intrigued that he saw and experienced beauty intensely and personally in the sometimes most obscure of things — an old door with peeling paint — as well as in a great works of art. I don't think I realised it at the time but Sasha seems to invite me — as he did all of his friends — to experience these things just as intensely and immediately. We just need to open ourselves to them. Perhaps Sasha — he'd hate this too — was in fact all along a good Buddhist — he really did inhabit the moment of whatever he was doing ... [talk at funeral]

Tim Herbert Rookwood for SS funeral. Torrential rain and grave collapse seems very Russian or Sasha mischievous sprite, inner babooshka let loose. ... I wanted to add something about the music selected for Rookwood service, in particular Jessye Norman singing one of Strauss's Four Last Songs, when I know Sasha preferred Elisabeth Schwarzkopf version. 'These are songs, not arias,' he explained to me. He was still ticking us off at Rockwood I guess...[diary and email]

Olga Krasser I went to his funeral, I couldn't say anything, any time I wanted to stand up and say something about Sasha, I couldn't talk.

Judith Brett I remember him saying when we were in our early 20s he said he didn't expect to live beyond 30. So he didn't set up any life for himself beyond 30. It's like he didn't imagine a more adult self, he was like the grasshopper.

I saw the open coffin because Russians do have open coffins.

Susan Varga I went early [to the funeral] to see him in his coffin which most people didn't want to do. I found [the open coffin] quite odd — I thought, has he asked for this. I thought he probably has...is he being flamboyant to the end, wants us to see him. I thought, I'll go if that's what you want Sasha. It was very moving.

YOU ARE ALL INVITED TO A WAKE FOR SASHA FOLLOWING THIS SERVICE AT:
THE QUARRYMANS HOTEL
CORNER PYRMONT BRIDGE ROAD AND HARRIS STREET PYRMONT.

Susan Varga I won this photograph at the auction [held at the wake]. I paid $400 for it, as I knew it was to help pay for the funeral expenses.

Michael Hurley The Melbourne memorial for Sasha was held late one wintry Sunday afternoon. It was organised by Helen Barnes and Jan McKemmish in a bar in a building that later became Grub café in Moor Street, Fitzroy. It too is now no more. About thirty or so attended, including Dorothy Porter, Julia Zemiro, Kirsty Machon, Peter Ronge and Leigh Raymond. Jan, Bruce [Sims], maybe George Papaellinas, Kirsty and I all spoke. Others may have too. Leigh thinks Jan spoke gratefully and admiringly of Sasha's editing skills, and the shaping of text. I liked Sasha's writing. He has a substantial entry in my book, *A Guide to Gay and Lesbian Writing in Australia.* Bruce and George had written an obituary for Sasha published in *The Australian.* I checked my memory of the mood of the event with Helen, Bruce, Leigh and Kirsty. They confirmed my sense of it as a sad, subdued and sombre occasion. The lights were low. Composer Elizabeth Drake played the piano.

Elizabeth Drake It was the Revolutionary Étude Opus 10 # 12 by Chopin. Sasha had given me the lp of Maurizio Pollini playing the complete Chopin Études. He also gave me the *Four Last Songs of Richard Strauss* sung by Jessie Norman. Hence the Revolutionary Study at the wake and *Four Last Songs # 3* at the grave.

Gig Ryan Sasha was always brilliant to talk to about Russian poetry — & scathing of most translations. He was full of joie-de-vivre and to see him was to be tossed into a world of gleeful — thoughtful — sedition of every kind.

Dorothy Porter I remember a very glamorous, magical, legendary figure — who was also a man of extraordinary sweetness + generosity to a young, callow timid poet. He also wrote a terrific translation of Ahmatova's *Requiem* which I treasure.

Sasha Soldatow TO GIVE then to my friends any remaining items of my personal property which they want, any dispute to be resolved solely by my Executors and Trustees whose decision will be final. *Last Will and Testament*

PLEASE COME TO SASHA'S PARTY — TOMBOLA.
WHY?
TO REMEMBER SASHA AND JOIN IN ON HIS TOMBOLA.
WHERE?
GILL LEAHY'S
WHEN?
SUNDAY 27 MAY 2007
WHAT'S A TOMBOLA?
IT'S A KIND OF LUCKY DIP: TAKE A TICKET, RECEIVE AN ITEM FROM AMONG SASHA'S STUFF.

Margot Nash I got this book of Yevtushenko poems, this beautiful book of Yevtushenko with his [Sasha's] name and it's full of things. 'The tension between the requirements of the State, him being a State writer' — this is [Sasha] referring to Yevtushenko — 'and the needs of creativity if such a thing can be said of him'...Here's a ticket...it's got MTA written on it... wait there's more, little notes...a newspaper cutting about Yevtushenko. So he's kept all these little things inside [this book]. 'Cold War survivor takes a novel approach' [newspaper clipping, 1991]...Here's another little note: 'I have a sneaking feeling Yev. had a foreign as well as a Soviet market in mind when he wrote this little novella...' But of course [Sasha has] highlighted, he's written [notes] in pen not even in pencil. So that's my first little treasure. The other treasure from the tombola, this, it's like a little grinding stone, and I keep the rings I'm wearing at the moment on it.

Meredith Rogers He gave me when I was staying in Bruce's flat, I kind of didn't want him to give them to me it was kind of a farewell, it was a set of little coloured liqueur glasses, beautiful; they're on a shelf in another room.

Sasha Soldatow The Sasha Prize is to be awarded annually to the author of a work of fiction, regardless of category and including books, pamphlets posters, translations, film scripts, photographs, fanzines or any other form of original production in any language, which has been published in Australia in the then-previous 12–18 months, and which has not received the recognition which it deserves… The winner of the prize is to be decided solely by my Literary Executors and Trustees whose decision will be final and not subject to any form of appeal or review. *Last Will and Testament*

Gill Leahy Bruce and I haven't been able to do much about it, There is $1300 in the account and that's all. It was hoped from a sale of his good paintings, ephemera etc there'd be enough money to fund an unpublished writer. Which is a difficult thing in itself, how do you find an unpublished writer? How do you advertise? So that's one part of the will we have not been able to execute yet. The prize would be like one percent of, it would be like $50, hardly worth it. And we used the money we raised on the headstone, I haven't seen it, there's something written on it.

George Papaellinas His service to others as sounding board, editor and moral compass was his major achievement. As well as offering concrete and steady support, he could be infuriatingly contradictory and difficult too sometimes. That's why most of his friends stuck by him, I imagine. […] 'Don't just be ordinary, be extraordinary,' he demanded of those around him. Always! 'And always demand honesty from people! The truth is everything…'

Sasha Soldatow **I DIRECT** that my body not be cremated but instead buried with a simple marker containing my name, dates of birth and death and the words "I SEE". I do not wish to be buried with or next to other members of my family. *LAST WILL AND TESTAMENT dated 23. 4. 97*

Pam Brown

*

    already
  passing Rookwood Cemetery
I crane to see   —   the train's too fast   —
      hello Sasha
his patched-up bones are there
    in the independent section,
  in 'good company' said Bruce,
      'close to a Pacific Islander'
but he's here, on the train, with me,
      every time it passes Rookwood
and we're disagreeing   (*what are you*
  trying to SAY, Pam?)   and, ridiculous but true,
we are   more often
  weeping, laughing, weeping
      because   IT'S ALL TOO HARD

it was

*

Natasha Soldatow He and I would laugh and talk and people around us would be like what are you two on about, we'd be laughing, we had this great communication always, I could go six or seven years without seeing him then see him and it would be like I'd seen him every day in that time, there was always for me that sense of family, that we belonged together, and that was so nice. I never ever had a bad word said to me from Sash, never a cross word, never a frown nothing, he was always so happy to see us, he always put us children before any adult in a room.

Olga Krasser I asked him, who was the love of your life. Bruce. That's what Sasha said, he was sad when he said it, no other man for me, Bruce was the love of my life.

Nicholas Pounder I've been taking trains and planes and buses and looking at young people now and they are now embodying what Sasha was and predicted: queerdom, defiance, don't give a fuck attitude.

Bruce Sims In spite of dwelling on Sasha's peculiarities, I shouldn't omit saying I miss him frequently for his unique and challenging perspective on things. I often think: What would Sasha say about that?

Margot Nash He was so fun and so kind and I think he really taught me, he did make me a better writer, the attention to detail, and punctuation, the sentence, the right word.

One of the other connections I had with Sasha — food and cooking. Up there you can see the Romertopf cooking pots, I've got two, they're unfired, you soak them in water before cooking. It was always the story, that Margaret Fink used a whole bottle of Moet et Chandon in one of these to cook a chook [laughs]. He'd use wine, so I have cooked chooks often in my Romertopf pot, not in Moet et Chandon, in white wine, a slow cook, it's a delicious way of cooking, so that's one of Sasha's legacies.[email 20 August 2018]

Jack Ellis Hi Inez, I went to visit Sasha today. I've attached a photo. Jack [email 20,8.2018]

Acknowledgments

My thanks to the following people for agreeing to be interviewed for this book and for reading and approving their quotations. In several cases they read beyond their own contribution, for which more thanks.

Geoff Adlide December 2019 phone
John Allen October 2019
Dennis Altman April 2019
Vivien Altman December 2019
Monica Attard May 2018
Wendy Bacon January 2018, November 2019
John Basten December 2018
Virginia Bell September 2018
Ric Benson phone July 2020
Richard Brennan July 2020
Judith Brett April 2019
Pam Brown April 2018
Meredith Burgmann November 2018
Andy Carruthers May 2020 phone
Jenny Coopes September 2018
Stephen Corbett September 2019
Jan Cornall February 2020
Joy Damousie April 2019
Elizabeth Drake February 2020
Laurie Duggan April 2019
Ben Fink phone 2020
Hannah Fink email July 2019
Jack Ellis August 2018
John Fink May 2019
Margaret Fink March 2018
Denis Gallagher August 2018
Bill Harding August 2019
Tim Herbert + Denis Gallagher August 2018
Sue Howe December 2018
Fiona Inglis June 2018
Jason Johnston email March 2019
Rosemary Johnston April 2019
Olga Krasser December 2019 phone
Gillian Leahy April 2018, February 2020
Amanda Lohrey May 2019 email

David Marr August 2018
Megan McMurchy October 2018
Ian Millis May 2018
Jonathan Mills January 2022
Ray Misson April 2019
Anne Mitchell April 2019
Bruce Moore December 2018
Margot Nash August 2018
Jane Palfreyman September 2018
John Paramor June 2018
Nicholas Pounder June 2019
Bruce Pulsford August 2018
Inge Riebe May–June 2018
Benjamin Riley March 2018
Nigel Roberts January 2020 email
Meredith Rogers phone September 2021
Valek Sadovchikoff April 2019
Joanna Savill July 2018
Samantha Sinnayah phone July 2021
Natasha Soldatow April 2019
Amanda Stewart December 2018
Larry Strange September 2019
Oliver Strewe December 2018
Tony Taylor September 2018
Lyn + John Tranter September 2018
Christos Tsiolkas May 2018
Susan Varga December 2018
John Walker July 2020 email
Nadia Wheatley and Ken Searle December 2018
Gerard Windsor April 2019
Sue Woolfe April 2019

It was also good to talk to: Gil Appleton; Chris Bettle; Ken Bolton; Martin Fabinyi; Andre Frankowitz; Helen Grace; Gaby Mason; Humphrey McQueen; Tony Taylor; Tom Thompson.

I hate to think I've left anyone off these acknowledgments who should be on it, please be in touch if I have.

Thanks to those who agree to be quoted from personal correspondence or published works.

This biography came about through a suggestion from Gina Ward. I hardly knew I'd taken it up when I'd gone too far in research not to actually write it. Thanks are due to Gina for that and some reading of early draft chapters.

My immense thanks to my editor Bruce Sims, who read draft chapters from an early stage, has been understanding and encouraging all along, undertook to edit the book before any certain publishing was in place, and patiently saw it through all the drafts, so many drafts. His invaluable labour was gifted to this project. As Sasha said of him, he's worth a million a week. Thanks to Joanna Savill for offering to do the final proofreading and providing many useful comments. And to Chris Edwards for the design of the cover and book and more useful suggestions.

Wendy Bacon and Chris Nash were helpful from an early stage, discussing drafts and locating archival material. Thanks also to Pam Brown, Nicholas Pounder, Margaret Fink for invaluable materials and discussions.

My thanks to Baden Offord, Christopher McFarlane and John Ryan who invited me to stay in their house on Bundjalung country during 2019 where I was able to do substantial work and find much peace.

Most of the work on this book was done on unceded Gadigal land.

Thanks to Susan Varga for sponsoring research trips to Melbourne and Canberra. Chris Nash gave me the recorder I used for interviews. Thanks to Julie Brumlik for little luxuries.

Thanks to librarians Bruce Carter and Stephanie Volkens and other librarians at the Mitchell Library in Sydney, where Sasha Soldatow's archives are held; and to librarians at the National Library in Canberra.

The publication of this biography was funded by donors at a crowdfunding campaign; my thanks to all of them. Thanks to Nicholas Pounder for the artistic publication of a poem, and to Valek Sadovchikoff for printing a poster, as thank-you gifts to donors.

With deepest gratitude for the sustaining friendships that saw me through this work: from my heart thanks and love to everyone who shared coffees drinks meals walks viewings correspondences and confidences.

Finally thanks to the Australian people for the age pension that enabled my survival and ability to write during this time.

References

1. All by Sasha Soldatow (called SS in text references)

197-? 'My life and hard times as an artist and poet in Sydney, the city of sin, where there is hardly sufficient compassion to enable a true creator to survive in the manner to which they expect to be accustomed. How I worshiped an ideal that led me to fall on unfashionable times' 1 sheet ([2] p.) ; 34 cm.. [Nd]

1973 'and they all lived together in a little crooked house' Foundation Day *Tharunka* 2 August pp.20, 21

1973 'Muscles Make a Man. It's All in Our Head' *Tharunka*, September

1973 'The Victoria Street Experiment' *Contemporary Art Society Broadsheet* September pp.3-8

1973 *It'll Never Get Better if You Picket* [pamphlet]

1973 'Fragments of a Communique' *Contemporary Art Society of Australia Broadsheet* September pp.17-18

1973 'Out of the Closet Into the Clique' *The Living Daylights* 16 October

1973 'The Carnal Curiosity of the Pre-Teen' *The Living Daylights* 13 November

1973 'Psychiatric Liberation' *Camp Ink* Volume 3 number 6

1974 'Dancing with Developers' *The Living Daylights* 9 April

1974 'Bankstown Interview' *Scrounge* Number 13, 19 April pp.13-15

1975 'Epilogue' short story in *Gay Liberation Press* issue no. 7, pp.41-45

1975 'Withdrawal' *Patterns* no 5 March pamphlet

1976 'Getting Professional' *Nation Review* 22 October

1977 'Justice is Just Arse' *Nation Review* 10 February

1977 'OLD NEGRO, HE HOES, PICKS COTTON, AND IS FULL OF GOOD HUMOUR SAYS WHO? Thoughts about the National Gallery of Victoria's exhibition of photographs, titled 'Farm Security Administration' pamphlet dated December 1977 — also published in *Arts Melbourne: A Journal of Australian and 20th Century Art* in 1978

1977 *The Adventures of Rock-and-Roll Sally*, privately published edition of 20 copies

1978 *'Attention! Campaign man with money to spare'*, SS with Larry Strange, paper distributed at the 4th National Homosexual Conference, Sydney, August 1978

1978 'Snaps from a Gay Album' *Anarchist Honi Soit* September

1978 Cameron Allen Love Sheet (pamphlet) July

1978 Not Guilty. Not Insane. The Sandra Wilson Campaign

1979 'An example of social relations under capitalism' unpublished, dated 11 January

1979 'A Fist Full of Lice' *Campaign* February

1979 'Breaking the Silence' *Film News* September

1980 'I'm a metasexual' *Magazine* Vol. 1 no 1, p.5

1980 'Revolution or Reformism' *Gay Information* May/June 1980:6 p.18
1980 'White Noise' and 'Work in Progress' *Ganymede. A journal of gay poetics.* 3/4 1980 [Later in 'Tim' in PDNO]
1980 interview and extracts from The Only Sensible News in *Magazine* Vol 1 no 1
1980 *Politics of the Olympics* Cassell Australia
1982 'Losers Keepers' with Larry Strange *Australian Society* 3 December
1982/3 'Politics and Common Sense' *Gay Information* Summer 1982/83: p.58
1983 'Intimacy' in Bradstock, Dunne, Sargent, Wakeling [eds] *Edge City On Two Different Plans: a collection of lesbian and gay writing from Australia*, Sydney Gay Writers Collective
1983 'What is this gay community shit?' *Honi Soit* 11 April [check]
1983 What Is This Gay Community Shit? (pamphlet) 1983
1984 'KAL Flight 007 In Soviet Sights' *New Journalist*
1987 'A web of intrigue' review of *Remember the Tarantella* by Finola Moorhead Australian 26-27 December
1987 'New Gay Writing. SS interviewed by Gary Dunne', *Outrage* No 55 p.40
1987 'Pleasure' *Australian Literary Quarterly* 3 October
1987 'Practicing Dying' in Denis Gallagher [ed] *Love and Death: An Anthology of Poetry and Prose* pp.26-28
1987 'Where the poor are powerful' *SMH Summer Agenda* Tuesday 29 December p,13 [2/3 of broadsheet page, w photos; about Bondi beach: 'in the first of a series on Australia's coastal cultures, Sasha Soldatow strips away the glitz of Bondi'
1987 *Poofs, Lezzos and the State* (with others), pamphlet
1987 *Private — Do Not Open* Penguin Books
1987 in *Rewording* Poets Union conference papers
1987 'The politics of the sentence' *Outrage*
1988 'Green light or red light' review by SS of *A Green Light* by Ray Mooney, *ABR* July
1988 'Hey, Mind Your Language' *Vogue Australia*, September
1988 Excerpt from 'the Gloves of Mr Menzies' to be published by Picador in July 1989. In *Cargo*
1988 Hooton, Henry Arthur (Harry) (1908-1961) *Australian Dictionary of Biography* Volume 14 1996; online 2006
1988 SS 'The melodrama of adolescence' review of *The Onion Man* Max Dann *ABR* September
1989 'Percy Grainger's Theory of Music' *Cargo* 7: This issue featuring writing from gay male perspectives November BlackWattle Press p.19
1989 'Victory' from *The Gloves of Mr Menzies Meanjin* March (Vol. 48, No. 1)
1990 'Introduction' Pamela Brown *Selected Poems* 1971-1990
1990 'Lost voices' by SS in *FMG* Dec/Feb 24 [about Vladimir Vysotsky who died of alcoholism]

1990 *Harry Hooton: Poet of the 21st Century* [edited, and Introduction]
1990 *The Adventures of Rock-n-Roll Sally* BlackWattle Press
1990 "A Touch of Mortality' in Yahp, Daly, Falconer [eds] *My Look's Caress: a collection of modern romances* 92-94
1991 'Memento Mori' 1991 in Gary Dunne [ed] *Travelling on love in a time of uncertainty: contemporary Gay Fiction* BlackWattle Press p.34
1991 'Prologue from The Gloves of Mr Menzies' *Antipodes* Vol. 5. No. 1, May
1992 'Gay writing: the good, the bad and the very funny' review of *Angel Tails* by Tim Herbert, *The Male Cross-Dresser Support Group* by Tama Janowitz and *Love, Zena Beth* by Diane Salvatore *Sydney Morning Herald* (*SMH*), 19 September
1992 'Party fun' *Outrage* no 115 December
1992 'Wit and pace but it's all surface' review of *Maybe the Moon* by Armistead Maupin *SMH* 28 November
1993 'tony, maybe' by SS November *Outrage* [memoir of primary school days]
1993 'Where are the phrases of yesteryear?' review of Michael Heyward *The Ern Malley Affair* UQP 1993 in *Arena*
1993 10 December 1993 'Say no to sauerkraut' Wild Card in *Sydney Star Observer*
1993 'Beyond the valley of the club bunnies' Wild Card 12 November
1993 'A river finds its level' *Burn* June 1993 pp.37-39
1993 'The Archeology of Mr Soldatow' interview with Kirsty Machon *Sydney Star Observer* 2 September
1993 *Mayakovsky in Bondi* BlackWattle Press
1994 'Love Piss' Gary Donne [ed] *Fruit: a new anthology of Contemporary Australian Gay Writing* BlackWattle Press
1994 'the big sweat — famous excuses' [humour piece] *sydney star observer mardi gras festival* 94. 19 February
1994 Boobs 'n' bums Wild Card, *Sydney Star Observer* 1 July
1994 'Sickiatrists and other fakts' Wild Card, *Sydney Star Observer* 11 March
1994 'Prizes galore, but hurry' Wild Card, *Sydney Star Observer* 14 January
1994 'Ho Ho Hmm: The Only Sensible Awards' for this year' Wild Card, *Sydney Star Observer* 15 December
1994 'Very depressing news' Wild Card, *Sydney Star Observer* 17 November
1994 'Big smiling cultural pigs' Wild Card, *Sydney Star Observer* 20 October
1994 'D flat & more frou-frou' Wild Card, *Sydney Star Observer* 20 September
1994 'March of the petty pen pushers' Wild Card, *Sydney Star Observer* 25 August
1994 'More gay community shit' Wild Card, *Sydney Star Observer* 29 July
1994 'Stories of the state' Wild Card, *Sydney Star Observer* 3 June
1994 'Suicide or self-deliverance?' Wild Card, *Sydney Star Observer* 6 May
1995 'But is it queer?' review of Steve McLeod and Gerry North [eds] *Divertika ABR* April p.26
1995 'The Secret of Death' *RePublica:* issue 2 The new land lies before us. George Papaellinas (ed.). Angus & Robertson 151-153

1996 *Jump Cuts: an Autobiography* (with Christos Tsiolkas) Vintage
1996 'Where are the Phrases of Yesteryear?' review of Michael Heyward *The Ern Malley Affair UTS Review* Vol 2 no 1
1996 'A Writing Life' review of *Sumner Locke Elliott: Writing Life* by Sharon Clark ABR August 12-13
1996 'Kaddish' *Republica* 4 82
1996 'None shall sleep' *Island* no 69 Summer
1996 'Self Portrait' *Meanjin* 1 — 1996 'Australian Queer' issue (edited by Chris Berry & Annamarie Jagose) pp.100-103
1996 'Undertow with Sasha Soldatow' *Campaign* August (Review of Treasures from the exhibition at AGNSW)
1996 'Undertow with SS' *Campaign* September (on Olympics and drugs)
1996 'Undertow with SS' *Campaign* October (on Naples, Pompeii)
1996 'Undertow with SS' *Campaign* December (on change and essence)
1996 'When the revolution comes' review of *Men Talk: Fourteen Australian men talk about their lives, loves and feelings after two decades of feminism* by Jan Bowen [ed] ABR June
1996 [as Dramaturge] the lower depths by maxim gorky adapted by patrick guerrera & sasha soldatow performed by students of Level Crossing. Wharf 2 13-16 November
1996 'Hooton, Henry Arthur (Harry) (1908-1961)' *Australian Dictionary of Biography* Vol 14 1996; published online in 2006 https://adb.anu.edu.au/biography/hooton-henry-arthur-harry-10539
1997 'Undertow with SS' *Campaign* January (on jealousy)
1997 'Undertow with SS' *Campaign* October (on Vietnam)
2000 'Away with the pixies' *SMH Spectrum* 23 December p.7 review of *The Night Listener* by Armistead Maupin
2001 'Australian Mahagonny' ABR April 2001 pp.26,27 two books on Broome: Anne Coombs & Susan Varga *Broometime*; John Bailey *The White Divers of Broome*
2002 'Friendship is a book open to interpretation' *Sunday Age* 3 March (review of Embers by Sandor Marai)
nd 'Seven Songs' [unpublished poem] [2002 or 2003]

2. By others

Addiction Center https://www.addictioncenter.com/benzodiazepines/valium/withdrawal-detox/

Allen, John 2019 'Cabaret Conspiracy' in *Golden Mile Gallery* book ebook

Altman, Dennis 1983 'Foreword' *Edge City On Two Different Plans* Bradstock et al

Ang, Sen; Gay Hawkins; Lamia Dabboussy 2008 *The SBS Story: The Challenge of Cultural Diversity* UNSW

Arneil, Chris nd 'Gay Waves Lives On' *National Film and Sound Archive of Australia* https://www.nfsa.gov.au/latest/gaywaves-classic-lgbti-radio-keeps-making-waves

Arrow, Michelle 2019 *The Seventies: the personal the political and the making of modern Australia* NewSouth

Attard, Monica 1997 *Russia: Which Way Paradise?* Doubleday

australasian small press review No 1. 1975 Editors Tom and Wendy Whitton Published by: Second Back Row Press Printed by Tomato Press

australasian small press review No. 2 1975 Editors Tom and Wendy Whitton. Published by: Second Back Row Press Printed by Tomato Press

australasian small press review No. 3 1976 Editors Tom and Wendy Whitton. Published by: Second Back Row Press Printed by Tomato Press

australasian small press review No. 4 1976 Editors Tom and Wendy Whitton. Published by: Second Back Row Press cover Printed by Tomato Press

australasian small press review No. 5 1977 Editors Tom and Wendy Whitton. Published by: Second Back Row Press printed by Fastprint

australasian small press review No. 6 [June 1978 inside not on cover] (edited by tom thompson. Published by Tom and Wendy Whitton, June 1978 [looks different now]

australasian small press review No. 7 & 8 [nd] (edited by tom thompson [sic] and published by Second Back Row Press, January 1979.)

Bacon, Wendy 2011 'Being Free By Acting Free' *Overland* Autumn https://overland.org.au/previous-issues/issue-202/essay-wendy-bacon/

Bacon, Wendy 2020 'Newspapers, free speech and activism in Sydney since 1969' 14 February https://www.wendybacon.com/2020/newspapers-free-speech-and-activism-in-sydney-since-1969

Bacon, Wendy 2021 'Green Bans Turn Fifty' *City Hub* 22 June https://cityhubsydney.com.au/2021/06/green-bans-turn-fifty/

Baranay, Inez 1987 interview with Sasha Soldatow. *Ariel Book News* August

Baranay, Inez 2006 'Really Talking: remembering Sasha Soldatow' *Perilous Adventure* Issue 10 April http://perilousadventures.net/1004/baranay.html Also in Local Time: a memoir 2015

Baranay, Inez 2011 'The Idea of Europe' *Antipodes* December 154–157 http://www.inezbaranay.com/wp-content/uploads/2011/09/Antipodes-Idea-of-Europe.pdf [Also in *Local Time: a memoir* 2015]

Barcan, Alan 2011 'The arrival of the New Left at Sydney University, 1967–1972' *History of Education Review* 14 October https://www.emerald.com/insight/content/doi/10.1108/08198691111177235/full/html [requires permission]

Barnes, Julian 2020 Diary. *London Review of Books* https://www.lrb.co.uk/the-paper/v09/n20/julian-barnes/diary

Barney, S 1996 Review of *Jump Cuts Rolling Stone* September

Barrowclough, Nikki 2004 'This bohemian life' *Good Weekend* 6 March

Bateman, Philippa [nd] 'FLASHBACK: When Australia Led the Way' *good pitch australia* https://goodpitch2australia.com.au/1206-2/

Beggs, Zanny 2019 *The Beehive* (film about Juanita Nielsen https://zannybegg.com/the-beehive/)

Bennie, Angela 2004 'Anything Goes' *Sydney Morning Herald* 4 November https://www.smh.com.au/entertainment/art-and-design/anything-goes-20041105-gdk1tc.html

Billson, Anne 2019 'Say what? Why film translators are in a war of words over subtitles' https://www.theguardian.com/film/2019/apr/25/say-what-why-film-translators-are-in-a-war-of-words-over-subtitles

Black Wattle Mission Statement: https://www.austlit.edu.au/austlit/page/A58835

Blazey, Peter 1996 'From Breathless to a scream' *The Australian* 3–4 August 1996

Bongiorno, Frank 2014 'Reconsidering the end of the homosexual' *The Australian* 22 February https://www.theaustralian.com.au/arts/review/reconsidering-the-end-of-the-homosexual/news-story/08fd89f2008cb760338ea341bf26b3df?sv=33dc72329d4a7ea339ce0c36d6dc0738

Bolton, Ken 2010 'Boundless Love' from *A Whistled Bit of Bop*, Vagabond Press

Bonver, Yevgeny 'Akhmatova' *World Literature* http://www.all-art.org/world_literature/akhmatova1.htm

Bradstock, Dunne, Sargent, Wakeling [eds] 1983 *Edge City On Two Different Plans: a collection of lesbian and gay writing from Australia* Sydney Gay Writers Collective

Brennan, Richard 1975 'Mr Tough Guy was a Gay Deceiver' *Nation Review* May–June [reprint, no pagination]

Brodsky, Joseph 1973 'Translating Akhmatova' translated by Carl R. Proffer *New York Review of Books* 9 August https://www.nybooks.com/articles/1973/08/09/translating-akhmatova/

Brown, Pam see also Wakeling, Corey and Pam Brown 2012

Brown, Pam *Little Episodes* https://www.poetrylibrary.edu.au/poets/brown-pam/little-episodes-0212101

Brown, Pam 1997 Letter *Australian Book Review* June 1997 page 4

Brown, Pam 2006 Vale Sasha Soldatow, *the deletions* http://thedeletions.blogspot.com/2006/09/vale-sasha-soldatow.html

Brown, Pam 2006 'In Hanoi' http://thedeletions.blogspot.com/2006/09/sasha-some-further-notes.html

Brown, Pam 2008 'Train train' from *True Thoughts*, Salt Publishing
Burgmann, Meredith & Verity Burgmann 2017 [1998] *Green Bans Red Union: the saving of a city* NewSouth
Burgmann, Meredith & Verity Burgmann 2011 'Green bans movement' *Dictionary of Sydney* https://dictionaryofsydney.org/entry/green_bans_movement
Calder, William 2017 An excerpt from 'Pink Ink: The Golden Era for Gay and Lesbian Magazines' *Archer* http://archermagazine.com.au/2017/01/queer-media-history-excerpt-pink-ink-golden-era-gay-lesbian-magazines/
Calder, William Francis 2015, 2016 'Abstract.' *Gay Print Media's Golden Era: Australian Magazines and Newspapers 1970–2000* (PhD, online) 'Pink Ink: The Golden Era for Gay and Lesbian Magazines' by Cambridge Scholars Publishing. (2016)
Cargo 6 1989 This issue featuring writing from lesbian perspectives. Jill Taylor [ed] May BlackWattle Press
Cargo 7 1989 This issue featuring writing from gay male perspectives November BlackWattle Press [includes 'Percy Grainger's Theory of Music' by SS p.19]
Cargo 10 1991 This issue featuring writing from lesbian perspectives Jill Taylor & Roberta Snow [eds] February BlackWattle Press
Cargo 11 1991 writing from gay perspectives BlackWattle Press June
Cargo 13 1992 [lesbian perspectives] BlackWattle Press June
Carruthers, A.J. 2017 'Lives of the experimental poets' *Jacket* https://jacket2.org/commentary/lives-experimental-poets-1to3
Chapman, Michael 1996 'Tempting taste of poofter prose' in Books [section] *Sydney Star Observer* 25 July p.20
Clews, Simon 1996 'Soldatow, Tsiolkas and Godard' review of *Jump Cuts*, *Australian Book Review*, August
Connell, Robert 1988 Review of *PDNO* in *The Book Magazine*, Vol. 1 no 3 December 1987/January 1988
Coombs, Anne 1996 *Sex and Anarchy: the life and death of the Sydney Push* Viking
Cosic, Miriam 2016 'How an editor brings the writer's work squalling into the world' *Financial Review* https://www.afr.com/afr-magazine/anna-funder-christos-tsiolkas-tim-flannery-on-the-editorwriter-relationship-20160112-gm49x0
Dalziel, Robyn 1988 Review of *PDNO The Age Monthly Review* March
D'Cruz, Carolyn and Mark Pendleton 2014 *After Homosexual: The Legacies of Gay Liberation* UWA Press
Debord, Guy 1969 *Society of the Spectacle* various editions
Decent, Campion 1993 'What is this community bullshit?' *Sydney Star Observer* 11 June
della 'Gay Power The Real Facts' *Tharunka* Vol 16, No. 14, 22 July p.7
Denholm, Michael 1979 *Small Press Publishing in Australia: the early 1970s* [1970's on cover] Second Back Row Press. Sydney.
Denholm, Michael 1992 *Small Press Publishing in Australia: the late 1970s to the mid to late 1980s* Volume II. Footprint. Footscray Victoria

Dunne, Gary 1987 'The politics of the sentence: New Gay Writing. Sasha Soldatow interviewed by Gary Dunne.' *Outrage*. No 55 p.40

Dunne, Gary 1990 *As If Overnight* BlackWattle Press and https://epdf.pub/as-if-overnight.html [also in] 2021 *Darlinghurst Boys* [includes *As If Overnight, Shadows on the Dance Floor*, and *Tottering Towards Darlinghurst*]

Dunne, Gary [ed] 1991 *Travelling on love in a time of uncertainty: contemporary Gay Fiction* BlackWattle Press includes 'Memento Mori' by SS

Dunne, Gary [ed] 1994 *Fruit: a new anthology of Contemporary Australian Gay Writing*. BlackWattle Press includes 'Love Piss' by SS

Durbin, Kate 2021 'Moving Houses: A Conversation with Zenobia Frost' *LA Review of Books* https://lareviewofbooks.org/article/moving-houses-a-conversation-with-zenobia-frost/?fbclid=IwAR2428dP5VNtR33-FY1d_4Lfv2p-6k7WaGgxNPIPSB3NhYFomR-G_D1117c]

English, David 1987 Review of *PDNO Times on Sunday* 13 September

Falkiner, Heather 1987 Review of *PDNO The Australian* 10 October

Feinstein, Eileen 2013 'Book of a lifetime' *Independent* 24 October 2013 https://www.independent.co.uk/arts-entertainment/books/reviews/book-of-a-lifetime-hope-against-hope-by-nadezhda-mandelstam-8901975.html

Fiske, Pat 1985 restored 2017 *Rocking the Foundations* (documentary film)

Gallagher, Denis 1987 [ed] *Love and Death: An Anthology of Poetry and Prose*, Print's Realm Rozelle

Gessen, Masha 2020 'What Lessons Does the AIDS Crisis Offer for the Coronavirus Pandemic?' *New Yorker* 8 April https://www.newyorker.com/news/our-columnists/what-lessons-does-the-aids-crisis-offer-for-the-coronavirus-pandemic?

Grace, Helen 1997 Sasha (50th birthday party) [video] https://vimeo.com/415829024

Grishin, Sasha 2020 'Introduction' to Akhamtova's *Requiem* translated by Sasha Soldatow, limited edition livre d'artist Polar Bear Press

Hawker, Philippa 1996 'Paperbacks' [column] *The Age* 14 September

Henderson, Moya 2010 in 'Moya Henderson talks about her Anna Akhmatova's Requiem' Australian Music Centre https://www.australianmusiccentre.com.au/article/moya-henderson-talks-about-her-em-anna-akhmatova-s-requiem-em

Herbert, Tim 1992 *Angel Tails* BlackWattle Press

Hindsight 2012 'Women Behind Bars' [radio program] Radio National https://www.abc.net.au/radionational/programs/archived/hindsight/women-behind-bars/3932334

Holmes, Richard 1985 *Footsteps: adventures of a Romantic biographer* HarperCollins

Horton, Scott 2007 *blog* https://harpers.org/blog/2007/11/from-akhmatovas-requiem/November 14, 2007

Hurley, Michael 1996 *A Guide to Gay and Lesbian Writing in Australia* Allen&Unwin
Hurley, Michael 2010 'Gay and Lesbian Writing and Publishing in Australia, 1961–2001' Australian Literary Studies · May
Johnson, Fenton 2018 'The Future of Queer: A manifesto' *Harpers* https://harpers.org/archive/2018/01/the-future-of-queer/
Johnston, Craig 1999 *A Sydney gaze; the making of gay liberation* Wild & Woolley
Johnston, Robert 1993 'Appointment with a publisher' *Campaign* November 1993
Kakmi, Dmetri 1996 '.' A radical book' review of *Jump Cuts. The Age* 6 September p.3
Kenny, Robert 1978 [nd probably 1978] "AND NOW LET US DISCUSS WHAT IS WRONG WITH OLD WRITING" [caps in original] *australasian small press review* 7 & 8 pp.7–12
Kiley, Dean 1993 'Mayakovsky in Bondi' *Burn* September 1993 [interview with SS]
Knox, Malcolm 2010 'The Interview: Colm Toibin' *Sydney Morning Herald* 15 May
Kochai, Jamil Jan 2019 "This week in fiction" *New Yorker* 30 December https://www.newyorker.com/books/this-week-in-fiction/jamil-jan-kochai-01-06-20
Leahy, Terry 1996 'SEX AND THE AGE OF CONSENT: The Ethical Issues' *Social Analysis: The International Journal of Anthropology* No. 39 (April), pp.27–55
Lorange, Astrid 2011 'Problems are flowers and fade' *Jacket* 2011 https://jacket2.org/?q=commentary/problems-are-flowers-and-fade
Lucas 1983 'Festival averse to verse' *Sydney Morning Herald* 24 January
Lucas, Robin 1987 Review of *PDNO Sydney Morning Herald* 5 September
Machon, Kirsty 1993 'The Archeology of Mr Soldatow' *Sydney Star Observer* 22 September
Marr, David 'A spirit gone to another place' (obituary) https://www.smh.com.au/national/a-spirit-gone-to-another-place-20060909-gdocqr.html
Martin, Sylvia 2020 *Sky Swimming: reflections on auto/biography, people and place* UWA Publishing
McAsey, Jennifer 1990 'Dogged writer takes fight over latest rejection slip to court' *The Age* Thursday 1 March
McCulloch, Helen 1996 'Friends' Review of *Jump Cuts Screaming Hyena* no 7 Spring pp.28–29
McQueen, Humphrey 2020 'Jack Mundey' http://www.surplusvalue.org.au/McQueen/BLF/Jack%20Mundey%20Tribute.pdf) (2010[20]),
Michaels, Eric 1990 *Unbecoming: An Aids Diary* Empress Publishing
Miller, Damien 1996 'Hard Copy' review of *Jump Cuts Campaign* October
Milliss, Ian 2014 'Art as a Verb' *Milliss* https://milliss.com/art-as-a-verb/
Milliss, Ian 2019 Art Into Journalism *Extra Extra* November 2019 http://www.extra-extra.press/2019/11/12/art-into-journalism/
Mohr, Rick 2017 'Tharunka to Thor THE SOCIAL AND POLITICAL CONTEXT' 13 April https://107.org.au/event/tharunka-thor-journalism-politics-art-1970-1973/
New Matilda 2011 'The Green Bans That Saved Sydney' https://newmatilda.com/2011/07/19/green-bans-saved-sydney/

NSW Law Reports 1973 https://nswlr.com.au/view/1973-1-NSWLR-87

O'Brien, Angela 1994 'A history of Drama in Teacher Education' *The University of Melbourne* https://must.unimelb.edu.au/article/a-history-of-drama-in-teacher-education-at-melbourne/

Papaellinas, George and Bruce Sims 2006 'Creative soul never far from revolution' (obituary) *The Australian*, 15 Sep http://www.theaustralian.news.com.au/wireless/story/0,8262,8-20412498,00.html

Pateras, Anthony with James Rushford 2020 *Jump Cuts* adaptation https://www.anthonypateras.com/discography-2001-2020/jump-cuts-2020

Pink Ink 1991 An anthology of australian lesbian and gay writers Wicked Women Publications

Pinkham, Sophie 2017 'When were you thinking of shooting yourself' *London Review of Books* Vol. 39 No. 4 16 February https://www.lrb.co.uk/the-paper/v39/n04/sophie-pinkham/when-were-you-thinking-of-shooting-yourself

Pledger, David 2018 *Daily Review* 9 August https://dailyreview.com.au/pick-me-as-next-australia-council-ceo-and-heres-why/76987/

Pounder, Nicholas [nd] *Nicholas Pounder Rare Books New Series Catalogue 4* https://ilab.org/sites/default/files/catalogs/files/1038_

Rawlins, Adrian 1991 'Not poetry, Railery: Review' *Overland* 122 pp.81–83.

Reasonable Grounds 2011 'Ray Denning and lessons unlearnt in our justice system' Thursday, 25 August http://reasonablegrounds.blogspot.com/2011/08/ray-denning-and-lessons-unlearnt-in-our.html

Reed, Lou 1972, 1990 'Murder Mystery' first published in *Paris Review* Issue 53 1972. Quoted in Sasha Soldatow 'Inverse Reverse and Perverse Lou Reed in concert' *Rock-n-Roll Sally* (1990).

Richardson, Owen 1996 'Cappuccino chat: light, fluffy and not much substance' review of *Jump Cuts Sunday Age* 20 October

Robbins, Susan 1993 'High Art & Rude Bits' *Sydney Star Observer* 15 October

Roberts, Mark 2012 'The long haul ...' *Rochford Street Review* https://rochfordstreetreview.com/2012/01/27/the-long-haul-pat-woolley-responds-to-michael-wildings-a-publishing-memoir/

Roberts, Nigel 2020 'Sasha' in *Portraits/Self Portraits*. NSW, Tamarama: Polar Bear Press

Robinson, Peter 2014 'Noted works: after Homosexual' *The conversation* 24 July https://theconversation.com/noted-works-after-homosexual-29336

Robinson, Shirleene 2011 'HIV/AIDS and Gay Community Print News Media in 1980s Australia' Chapter 6 in *Out Here: Gay and Lesbian Perspectives VI* edited by Yorick Smaal and Graham Willett Monash UP

Rogers, Meredith 2008 '*Arts Melbourne* and the End of the Seventies: the ideology of the collective versus collective ideologies' in *When You Think About Art, a history of the George Paton Gallery* (1971–2008)

Roszak, Theodor 1969 *The Making of a Counter-Culture* Doubleday

Sharkey, Michael 1993 'Dirty details just a decoy' *The Australian* 23 December
Sharkey, Michael 2012 *The Poetic Eye: Occasional Writings 1982–2012*
Shulman, Alix Kates 1991'Dances with Feminists' *The Emma Goldman Papers* https://www.lib.berkeley.edu/goldman/Features/danceswithfeminists.html
Slackbastard blog 2008 http://slackbastard.anarchobase.com/?p=1071 4 March
Solnit, Rebecca 2020 *Recollections of My Nonexistence*
Sullivan, Jane 2010 'The Battle for *Meanjin*' *SMH* https://www.smh.com.au/entertainment/books/the-battle-for-meanjin-20101127-18b4f.html
Swanson, Elizabeth 1987 'Foreword' *The Australian* 10 October 1987
Swearing in Ceremony of John Basten QC Supreme Court: Lawlink NSW http://classic.austlii.edu.au/au/journals/NSWJSchol/2005/5.pdf
Symons, A.J.A 1934 *The Quest for Corvo: an experiment in biography* Macmillan
Tin Alley Players https://must.unimelb.edu.au/1971/07/31/no-common-theme-the-dumb-waiter-snow-angel-oflaherty-29071971-2/
Tranter, John http://johntranter.net/archives/4216
Tsiolkas, Christos 2009 'Discomfort is sometimes what is most precious to me about great art' *Crikey* https://blogs.crikey.com.au/literaryminded/2009/01/29/discomfort-is-sometimes-what-is-most-precious-to-me-about-great-art-christos-tsiolkas-on-the-slap/
Wakeling, Corey and Pam Brown 2012 Pam Brown's Sydney: Poetry in the 70s: In Conversation with Corey Wakeling *Cordite Poetry Review* No theme 10 1 May 2012 http://cordite.org.au/interviews/wakeling-brown/
Wallace, Christine 1987 *Germaine Greer: Untamed Shrew* Pan Macmillan https://books.google.com.au/books?isbn=174334189X
Wallace, Chris 2020 'Palace letters' reveal the palace's fingerprints on the dismissal of the Whitlam government' *The Conversation* July 14 2020 https://theconversation.com/palace-letters-reveal-the-palaces-fingerprints-on-the-dismissal-of-the-whitlam-government-142476
Whitton, Wendy 1975 'small press in action: Tomato Press' *australasian small press review no.2* p.20
Wilding, Michael 1980 'Small Presses and Little Magazines in the 1970s' *Australian Literary Studies* vol. 9 no. 4
Wilson, Melanie Suzanne 2015 'David Marr: A man of conviction' https://atthefestival.wordpress.com/2015/05/20/david-marr-a-man-of-conviction/
Wolf-Tasker, Alla 2006 *Lake House — A Culinary Journey in Country Australia* Hardie Grant
Wotherspoon, Garry 1991 *City of the Plain: history of a gay sub-culture* Hale & Iremonger
Young, Mark 2000 'A Season in Hell' *Big Smoke: New Zealand Poems, 1960–1975* http://www.nzepc.auckland.ac.nz/authors/young/hell.asp

Index of Names

Adlide, Geoff 404, 405, 460
Allan, Micky 182, 187,
Allen, Cameron 201
Allen, John 225, 226, 227
Altman, Dennis 33, 36, 41, 166, 168, 169, 170, 238, 240, 24427,
Altman, Vivien 70, 206,
Anderson, John 27,
Armfield, Neil 334, 343,
Arms, Jane 59, 201, 259-262, 264,
Armstrong, Gillian 144
Astley, Thea 174
Attard, Monica 326-7, 329, 332-34, 340-43, 345, 348-49, 351-356, 371,
Bacon, Wendy 18, 20-25, 27, 30, 32, 35, 95- 98, 97 [photo], 102-1108, 110 111, 114, 118, 151, 317
Barlow, Annette 366
Barnes, Julian 312
Barrowclough, Nikki 143
Bashford, Kerry 344
Basten, John 308-312
Batache, Eddy 16-166, 168
Bell, Virginia 117-118, 120-121, 124,
Bensley, Pete 117, 124
Benson, Ric 55-56
Blazey, Peter 244, 245 [photo], 278, 393, 394,
Bolton, Ken 50, 182, 183, 223, 480
Boucher, Ken 62
Brennan, Teresa 111,
Brennan, Richard 31, 32,
Brett, Judith 54-55, 59, 64, 65, 71, 164, 197, 481,
Bridge, Loma 127
Brown, Pam 50, 84, 122, 127-128, 128 [photo], 150-151, 173, 177-179, 179 [photo], 182-183, 186187, 202, 216, 220-223, 230-232, 234, 241-242, 291-293, 316, 322, 327-328, 340, 343, 414, 415, 425, 429, 476, 479
Burgmann, Meredith 95, 98-100, 105, 374-376, 378, 407, 476
Burgmann, Verity 95
Burns, Joanne 225, 232, 245,
Cargher, John 221
Carruthers, Andy 298
Carter, Bruce 40

Chesler, Phyllis 138
Chin, Lee Lin 247
Christie, Mary 187
Coombs, Anne 30-31, 34,317,
Coopes, Jenny 31-32, 46, 104, 111,118, 123-124, 126,190,206, 212,220,
Corbett, Stephen 159, 206, 208-210
Cork, Gail 301-302, 444, 445-447
Cornall, Jan 225
Crayford, Peter 159
Dambelli, Giuliano 13, 146
Damousie, Joy 449-450
Daniel, Helen 413
Davidson, Jim 181
Davis, Judy 144
de Maria, William 112
Debord, Guy 35
del Favaro, Dennis 111
Denning, Ray 122-123, 127, 216, 292
Desmond Jones, Rae 232
Dessaix, Robert 246, 393, 472
Deveson, Anne 115
Dignam, Arthur 146
Drake, Elizabeth 221-225, 221 [photo], 482
Duggan, Laurie 183-184, 188, 224-225
Dunne, Gary 236, 237, 243-246, 244 [photo], 258, 262, 317,
Dunstan, Don 159
Dunstan, Graeme 22
Ellis, Jack 419-423, 426, 453-458, 460, 463-464, 477, 486
Emu 405, 408
Evatt, Clive 159
Fabinyi, Martin 177
Falkiner, Suzanne 302
Fargher, Matthew 343-344
Fell, Liz 22,30, 33, 34,36,104, 111,118, 440, 464
Fink, Ben 148-149
Fink, Hannah 146
Fink, John 13, 146-148, 461, 476
Fink, Margaret 13, 28-30, 33,39,116,143-144, 150,153-154, 163-164, 171, 191, 199, 217,
    223,255, 263, 269, 277, 292-295, 298, 317, 319, 321, 325, 328-330, 339, 414, 422,
    433-434, 439, 452, 477. 486
Fiske, Pat 104
Forbes, John 182, 188
Fowler, John 244

Fowler, Mick 104
Friend, Donald 274-275
Gallagher, Denis 41, 111 [photo], 136, 178, 239, 240, 243, 279, 317m 487
Goldman, Emma 38, 114, 412, 413
Grace, Helen 421
Grainger, Percy 223-225, 242
Green, Dorothy 289
Greer, Germaine 23, 28, 33, 288
Grenville, Kate 249, 302
Harding, Bill 149, 170-171, 175
Hare, Denise 317
Hassert, Reinhardt 164-168
Herbert, Tim 41, 136, 243, 246, 278, 317, 481
Hilder, Brett 130
Hodgson, Val 20, 22
Hooton, Harry 14, 28, 122, 143144, 150, 164, 272, 279, 286-298, 304, 308, 319, 327, 448-450, 460,
Horton, Scott 472-473
Howe, Sue 30, 81, 11-118, 126, 152, 155, 206, 220, 222, 314-317, 320, 322-323, 362,
Hurley, Michael 239, 482
Inglis, Fiona 277, 368-369, 392
Jackson, Linda 159
Johns, Brian 258-259, 262
Johnson, Rosemary 56, 59
Johnston, Jason 251, 257
Johnston, Martin 249, 256, 257, 317
Jones, Jill. 241
Kee, Jenny 159
King, Arthur 95, 96-98
Kingston, Peter 159
Kinsella, John 298-299
Knobel, Paul 244
Kostakidis, Mary 247
Krasser, Olga [nee Sadovchikoff] 77, 78-79, 81-83, 472, 478, 481, 485
L'Amour, Fifi 225
Leahy, Gill 22, 25, 30, 33-34, 111, 151, 268, 303, 317, 422, 477, 481, 483, 484
Leahy, Terry 408
Lee, Jenny 361
Lester, Paul 177
Lo Schiavo, Fabian 231
Lohrey, Amanda 368, 400
Lorange, Astrid 296-297
Loukakis, Angelo 369

Lurie, Caroline 364-365, 359
Lyssiotis, Peter 55
Mackinolty, Chips 229
MacLean, Steve 146
Macleod, Mark 173-175, 265, 425
Manne, Robert 55
Marr, David 29, 211, 213, 215, 217, 246, 266, 268, 306, 319, 333, 336-337, 36-365, 368, 399, 418
McCutcheon, Sandy 409, 462
McGregor, Robbie 163, 207
McGregror, Peter 231
McKemmish, Jan. 302, 365, 366, 482
McKinnon, Laurin 241-242, 244, 244 [photo], 303, 317, 361, 383, 384
McMurchy, Megan 153, 277,
McNeill, Ian 243
McQueen, Humphrey 283, 272, 289, 451
Meier, Rebecca 111, 220
Menzies, Robert, PM 94, 361
Milliss, Ian 94-97, 101, 103-105, 119, 121, 172
Mills, Jonathan 468-470
Misson, Ray 59-61, 169
Mitchell, Anne 56-61, 169
Mobbs, Barbara 362-363
Modjeska, Drusilla 264,
Mohr, Rick 31-31, 107
Molnar, George 23, 104,
Moore, Bruce 62-63
Moorhouse, Frank 25, 180, 181, 231, 233
Morrisey, Dave 111
Morrison, Brian 111
Moshinsky, Elijah 55
Mundey, Jack 98
Munster, George. 22
Murray, Les [football commentator] 247
Nash, Chris 24, 317, 379
Nash, Margot 303, 382, 478, 483, 486
Neill, Sam 144
Nielsen, Juanita 96
Owens, Joe 98
Papaellinas, George 300, 305, 356, 376, 379, 463, 482, 484
Paramor, John 146, 171, 175-176, 197
Pateras, Anthony 391
PiO 180, 295

Pitt, Marie 290
Pitts, Graham 111
Porter, Dorothy 385, 482, 483
Pounder, Nicholas 15, 153, 154, 156, 162, 186, 289, 456, 485
Pringle, Bob 98, 100
Pritchard, Jeune 199, 212, 220
Prothero, Barry 117, 118
Pulsford, Bruce. 128[photo], 270[photo], 176, 268-286, 305, 308, 317, 347, 348, 355-356, 361, 378, 400, 421-424, 426, 431, 438, 443-444, 447, 461, 465, 381
Rawlins, Adrian 296, 298
Reed, Bill 62
Reed, Lou 139, 140, 227-228
Rees, Alan 20
Rendell, Craig 272, 347, 363
Riebe, Inge 427-429, 434,
Riley, Benjamin 39, 44-45, 52-53,
Roberts, Nigel 184-186
Rogers, Meredith 62, 162, 198, 477, 484
Rorem, Ned 171-172
Roux, Suzi 142
Rush, Geoffrey 343
Ryan, Gig 483
Sadovchikoff Soldatow Samsonova, Lily [mother] 55, 64-65, 72, 77-84, 88, 90-92, 192-193, 318-319, 439, 440, 451-452
Sadovchikoff, Olga see Krasser, Olga
Sadovchikoff, Valek 77-84, 86-87, 452, 479
Sadovchikoff, Valentin Valentinavich 10, 77, 78, 84, 91, 439
Samson, Maria Adamovna 71 [photo], 72, 80-81, 91
Saville, Joanna 13-16, 146, 164, 252, 254-256, 274m 279, 477, 478
Sclavenitis, Tassio 243
Searle, Ken 188, 259
Shapcott, Tom 234, 302, 307-308
Sharkey, Michael 232-233, 377
Sharp, Chris 111, 190
Sims, Bruce 64, 151-152, 258-259, 262-263, 364, 439
Sinnayah, Samantha 162
Sisters of Perpetutual Indulgence 231
Smilde, Roelof 32, 104, 212
Soldatow, Lily see Sadovchikoff Soldatow Samsonova, Lily
Soldatow, Michael 64, 77 80-81, 86-89, 91, 451, 452
Soldatow, Natasha 79-80, 86-90, 451
Soldatow, Olga 72, 79, 91, 92
Soldatow, Sophie 72, 91

Staples, Jimmy 23
Stewart, Amanda 122, 223, 225, 229–230, 234, 279, 291, 296
Strange, Larry 47, 126, 153, 182, 189–208, 212, 213, 227, 269
Stretch, Brendon 177
Stretton, Andrea 362
Strewe, Oliver 415–418
Summers, Anne 36, 104, 113, 152, 479
Taylor, Andrew 187, 188
Theeman, Frank 97, 104
Thompson, Tom 23–233, 295, 363–364, 414
Thoms, Albie 159
Throsby, Maryse 227
Tidswell, Craig 187
Toibin, Colm 401
Tranter, John 181, 183, 249, 256,
Tranter, Kirsten 278–279291
Tranter, Lyn 249, 264, 277, 366
Try, Mark 244
Tsiolkas, Christos 169, 203, 237, 246, 263, 285, 369, 379–396, 397–403, 406, 409, 412, 421, 425, 451, 458
Turner, Richard 243
Varga, Susan 29. 30, 71, 95, 99, 105, 110, 151, 317, 382, 440, 449, 482
Vinson, Tony 120
Walker, John 272, 363
Ward, Gina 39
Wark, McKenzie 396
Waters, Darcy 19, 30, 31, 36, 95, 104, 151, 317, 434
Whaley, George 62
Wheatley, Nadia 249–252, 255–257
White, Peter 25
Wilding, Michael 180, 185
Willbanks, Raymond 362
Wills, Sue 33
Windsor, Gerard 249, 253–254
Wolf-Tasker, Alla 85
Woolf, Sue 249, 253
Woolley, Pat 109, 177, 185
Wotherspoon, Gary 41, 42, 47,133
Yang, William 146, 243, 246
Yates, Priscilla 175–176
Zemiro, Jane 127

www.ingramcontent.com/pod-product-compliance
Lightning Source LLC
Chambersburg PA
CBHW030250010526
44107CB00053B/1646